THE TRIUMPH
OF TRUTH

A LIFE OF MARTIN LUTHER

Jean Henri Merle d'Aubigné

Translated by Henry White

Edited by Mark Sidwell

journeyforth®

Greenville, South Carolina

Library of Congress Cataloging-in-Publication Data

Merle d'Aubigné, J. H. (Jean Henri), 1794-1872.
   The triumph of truth: a life of Martin Luther / Jean Henri Merle d'Aubigné; translated
by Henry White; edited by Mark Sidwell.
      p. cm.
   Includes bibliographical references and index.
   Summary: Examines the life of the German monk who led the Protestant Reformation
in Europe from its beginning in 1517 until his death in 1546.
   ISBN 0-89084-876-9
   1. Luther, Martin, 1483-1546. [1. Luther, Martin, 1483-1546. 2. Reformers.]
I. Sidwell, Mark, 1958-   . II. Title.
BR325.M4391996
284.1'092—dc20
[B]   95-48441
                                                                                          CIP
                                                                                           AC

NOTE: The fact that materials produced by other publishers are referred to in this volume
does not constitute an endorsement by Bob Jones University Press of the content or
theological position of materials produced by such publishers. The position of Bob Jones
University Press, and the University itself, is well known. Any references and ancillary
materials are listed as an aid to the reader and in an attempt to maintain the accepted
academic standards of the publishing industry.

The Triumph of Truth:
A Life of Martin Luther
Jean Henri Merle d'Aubigné

Cover illustration: *Martin Luther Discovering Justification by Faith*
   by Edward Matthew Ward,
   Bob Jones University Collection of Sacred Art
Cover designer: Brian Johnson
Project editor: Doug Rumminger

© 1996 by BJU Press
Greenville, South Carolina 29614
JourneyForth Books is a division of BJU Press

Printed in the United States of America

ISBN 978-0-89084-876-0

15   14   13   12   11   10   9   8   7   6   5   4   3

Contents

	Introduction	vii
1	Luther's Early Life and Training	1
2	University Days	9
3	In the Augustinian Monastery	15
4	Staupitz	21
5	The University of Wittenberg	29
6	Luther at Rome	33
7	Doctor of the Holy Scriptures	41
8	"Learn to Know Christ and Him Crucified"	49
9	Luther Before the Nobility	57
10	Indulgences	63
11	"Nets to Catch Silver"	73
12	The Ninety-five Theses	79
13	Reaction to the Theses	89
14	Tetzel's Attack	97
15	Rome Responds	105
16	Luther's "Paradoxes"	115
17	Luther and Leo X	123
18	The Pope Takes Action	129
19	Melancthon	137
20	Journey to Augsburg	145
21	Before Cardinal Cajetan	155
22	Return from Augsburg	167
23	A New Envoy from Rome	177
24	Eck Challenges Luther	191
25	The Leipzig Disputation (Part 1)	201

26	The Leipzig Disputation (Part 2)	211
27	The Aftermath of Leipzig	219
28	Charles V and the Nobility	227
29	The Appeal to the German Nobility	237
30	"Arise, O Lord"—The Papal Bull	245
31	*The Babylonian Captivity of the Church*	251
32	"It Is Christ Who Has Begun These Things"	261
33	Luther Responds to the Bull	269
34	Political Maneuvering	275
35	The Diet of Worms Convenes	283
36	Conflict and Controversy at Worms	291
37	Luther Summoned to Worms	301
38	Luther Journeys to Worms	309
39	"Here I Stand"	317
40	Attempts at Compromise	329
41	Captured	339
42	"Captive with and Against My Will"	347
43	On Marriage and Monasticism	353
44	Making God Speak German	357
45	The Zwickau Prophets	363
46	Luther Returns	371
47	Luther and Henry VIII	381
48	The Peasants' War (Part 1)	391
49	The Peasants' War (Part 2)	403
50	Luther's Marriage	409
51	Triumph in Death	415
	Editor's Afterword	419
	Index of Persons	423

*"And though this world, with devils filled,
Should threaten to undo us,
We will not fear, for God hath willed
His truth to triumph through us."*

*—from "A Mighty Fortress Is Our God"
by Martin Luther
Translated by Frederick H. Hedge*

Jean Henri Merle d'Aubigné (1794-1872)

Introduction
by Mark Sidwell

The subject of this book is famous. Most Christians have at least heard of Martin Luther. Many may even be generally familiar with his life story. For those who are not, the following pages will give a fuller introduction to the great reformer and his work. The author of this work, however, is probably less well known, certainly less well known than during his lifetime.

Jean Henri Merle d'Aubigné was born in 1794 in Geneva. His name represents the joining of two illustrious French families who had fled religious persecution in their native country. Probably the most famous of his ancestors was Theodore Agrippa d'Aubigné (1550-1630), French soldier, poet, and historian—a man "who fought with the pen and the sword" in the words of Jules Bonnet. D'Aubigné had formerly been a councilor to King Henry IV of France, the king who abandoned the Huguenot (French Protestant) faith to become a Catholic in order to take the French throne. In 1620, after the death of Henry IV, d'Aubigné left France for the haven of Geneva. Another ancestor of the historian, Jean-Louis Merle of Nîmes, fled France when King Louis XIV revoked the Edict of Nantes in 1685, thus taking away the Protestants' freedom of worship.

After these two families were finally joined in marriage, the historian's uncle and then his father joined the two names as well. He was born "Jean Henri Merle d'Aubigné," not simply "Jean Henri Merle." (This fact has often confused English readers, who sometimes refer to him simply as "d'Aubigné"; he is correctly referred to as "Merle d'Aubigné" or simply "Merle.") Thus even the author's name represented a heritage of courageous faith against oppression.

Merle's family experienced tragedy when he was only five years old. He grew up during the era of the Napoleonic wars, and his home city of Geneva was soon annexed to Napoleon's French empire. Merle's father, Aimé-Robert Merle d'Aubigné, was a prosperous businessman who served the Napoleonic cause. In 1799 he disappeared while on a mission for Napoleon's government, probably the victim of enemy troops. Merle's mother was left to rear Jean Henri and his two brothers by herself.

Young Merle developed an interest in the ministry as a young man, although his family had originally planned for him to enter business, as his father had done. At the age of seventeen, Merle wrote in his journal, "If I enter commerce, I will be able to become rich and to give myself up to all pleasures; but perhaps I will abandon myself too much to the love of money, to evil pleasures, and then I will be lost for eternity. If on the other hand I embrace the holy ministry, I will be poor, and I will have a difficult life; but I will be obliged to seek God, to live in conformity to His will, and so my soul will be saved." Since study for the ministry exempted Merle from French military service, his mother supported his desire. Merle entered the Genevan Academy in 1813.

Geneva had been one of the great centers of the Reformation in the sixteenth century. It was the city of John Calvin, the giant of the Reformation second only to Martin Luther in importance. After he lived in Geneva for a time, Scottish reformer John Knox called the city under Calvin "the most perfect school of Christ that ever was in the earth since the days of the Apostles. In other places, I confess Christ to be truly preached; but manners and religion so sincerely reformed, I have not yet seen in any other place." From Geneva the recovered gospel of salvation through Christ alone spread across Europe.

By Merle's day, however, Geneva was no longer a center of Christian truth. Most of the ministers of the state church were Unitarians. They denied Christ's deity, the inspiration and authority of the Scriptures, and the natural sinfulness of man. Students for the ministry rarely studied Bible in the Genevan Academy. A classmate of Merle said, "During the four years I attended the theological teachers of Geneva, I did not, as part of my studies, read one single chapter of the Word of God, except a few Psalms and chapters, exclusively with a view to learning Hebrew, and . . . I did not receive one single lesson of exegesis of the Old and New Testaments."

Not all of the ministers in Geneva were liberal. Some, particularly in the rural areas outside the city limits, clung to the biblical faith of Calvin and the other reformers. Merle was much impressed with the testimony and preaching of orthodox Genevan minister J.S.I. Cellérier, although Merle was not converted under his preaching. But just as God brought John Calvin from France to reform the city in the 1500s, so in the 1800s God brought to Geneva His instruments to carry revival to the city. And as Calvin's work in Geneva spread abroad, so the new revival eventually touched all of Europe.

The awakening in Geneva was actually one part—in many ways one of the earliest expressions—of a revival that touched Protestants in Switzerland, France, the Netherlands, and Germany. Known as the *réveil* (French for "awakening"), this revival saw the Holy Spirit draw earnest seekers after truth to Christ. Merle, however, was at first cold toward this movement.

When the revival broke out, one Genevan wrote a pamphlet that defended the deity of Christ and criticized the pastors of the state church of Geneva for their unbelief. Merle's fellow theological students chose him as their leader and spokesman to read publicly a letter protesting the pamphlet. Merle and all but two of his fellow students signed the protest.

But Merle's attitude changed under the ministry of a remarkable Scotsman named Robert Haldane (1764-1842). An independently wealthy businessman, Haldane devoted his time and money to furthering the cause of Christ wherever he found opportunity. On a visit to Geneva, Haldane was dismayed with how little even the theological students knew of the gospel. He decided to remedy that situation by renting rooms in Geneva and holding Bible studies with the students from the school of theology.

Some twenty or thirty students came to hear Haldane—over the objections of their Unitarian teachers. Although his French was not at all fluent, Haldane, with the help of the students who knew English, spoke on the Book of Romans. One of the attendees at these sessions said of Haldane, "He knew the Scriptures like a Christian who has had for his Teacher the same Holy Spirit by whom they were dictated." Another said, "He never wasted his time in arguing against our so-called reasonings, but at once pointed with his finger to the Bible, adding the simple words, '*Look here—how readest thou?* There it stands written with the finger of God.'"

Merle d'Aubigné was among those students who listened with keen attention to the Scottish evangelist. Having been taught by his Unitarian teachers that man was naturally good, Merle had difficulty accepting the doctrine of the natural depravity of man's heart. After some study and discussion, Merle told Haldane, "Now I see that doctrine in the Bible."

"Yes," replied Haldane, "but do you see it in your heart?"

Merle said later, "That was but a simple question, but it came home to my conscience. It was the sword of the Spirit; and from that time I saw that my heart was corrupted, and knew from the Word of God that I can be saved by grace alone."

Merle was converted and noted later that "after having remained in the cheerless principles of Unitarianism until nearly the conclusion of my studies at the academy of Geneva, I had been seized by the Word of God." Years later, looking at the apartments where he and the others heard Haldane, Merle said, "There is the cradle of the Second Reformation of Geneva."

Merle finished his studies and was ordained in the state church in 1817. There was tension, however, between the leadership of the church and the supporters of the *réveil*. This unrest and the confusion it caused motivated Merle to go to Germany for further study.

The year 1817 was the three hundredth anniversary of the Reformation, three hundred years since Martin Luther had nailed his Ninety-five Theses to the door of the church of Wittenberg. The celebration fired the young Genevan's imagination. He stopped at Eisenach, the site of both Luther's birth and death. He visited Wartburg Castle on October 31, 1817, the actual anniversary of the nailing of the theses. There Merle viewed the castle where Luther had been kept a half-unwilling prisoner for his own protection. He saw the rooms in which Luther had done much of his translation work for the German Bible. His thoughts dwelt on the Reformation.

Later, on November 23, he wrote in his journal, "I want to compose a history of the Reformation. I want this history to be scholarly and to present facts not yet known; I want it to be profound and to unravel the causes and the effects of this great movement; I want it to be interesting and to make the authors of the transformation known by their letters, their writings, their words." Merle desired his history to be "truly Christian and suited to stimulate the religious spirit."

Merle went to the University of Berlin in 1817 to study. Among his teachers was August Neander, perhaps the leading church historian of the age. The young Genevan appreciated Neander's stress on the spiritual in history. Also Neander used biography to focus on outstanding individuals who represented the movements and forces that shaped the course of history. This emphasis appealed to Merle. He saw God's work in the individual as the basis of God's work in society, and Merle would later use Luther to typify the whole Reformation. Student and teacher enjoyed a certain theological sympathy, although Merle was more orthodox. "It was not possible to speak with Neander of inspiration, nor of irresistible grace, nor of eternal damnation," wrote Merle's daughter, "but one could agree wonderfully with him on church history."

After his study, Merle became pastor of a French-speaking church in Hamburg, Germany, in 1818. He won the hearts of his congregation with his evangelical, compassionate preaching. But he offended the leadership of the church, who preferred less "emotion" in their services. Merle then went to Brussels, today part of Belgium but at that time under Dutch control. From 1823 to 1831 he pastored a French-speaking church there. Merle preached with great eloquence and power, and the king and queen of Netherlands were sometimes among his hearers. His work in Belgium ended, however, when the Belgians successfully revolted from Dutch control in 1830 and achieved their independence.

In 1831 Merle d'Aubigné returned to Geneva. There he joined the Société évangélique de Genève, originally a protest group standing for orthodoxy within Geneva's state church. The dominantly Unitarian leadership of the church opposed Merle and the other leaders of the Société and suspended them. Eventually, in 1849, the Société formed its own independent free church.

Perhaps the most important effort of the Société évangélique de Genève was to found a theological school to train men for the ministry—apart from the spiritually deadening atmosphere of the Genevan Academy. Thus, in 1831 Jean Henri Merle d'Aubigné became the new school's first president and its professor of church history. From then until his death in 1872, Merle taught—and touched—a stream of students who passed through his classroom. His commanding presence and stringent academic requirements led his students to nickname him "Jupiter," after the chief god of Roman mythology.

Merle taught, lectured, and traveled. He went all over Europe speaking at international conferences and promoting Christian causes. (When he visited London in 1862, Pastor C. H. Spurgeon of the Metropolitan Tabernacle shortened his sermon to allow Merle to briefly address the congregation.) During the bloody Austro-Italian War (1859), Merle called for Christians to minister to the wounded in time of war. "It is especially in times of war that Christians must show themselves children of peace," he wrote. The Société évangélique formed a committee to organize help for those suffering the ravages of war. Merle was a member of that committee, along with Jean Henri Dunant, who from this pioneer effort went on to become one of the founders of the International Red Cross.

But most of all, J. H. Merle d'Aubigné wrote.

Merle had published a few articles and sermons while he was a pastor, but with the new position in Geneva he launched into his dream of writing a history of the Reformation. He published the first volume in 1835. Sales in French were poor. Then the history was translated into English, and sales soared. (Merle said that the first three volumes sold only 4,000 copies in French but between 150,000 and 200,000 in English.) The enormous popularity of the English edition encouraged the historian to press forward with his project. In fact, as Merle continued to issue new volumes, he eventually published some volumes in English before issuing them in French.

Merle d'Aubigné wrote two sets: *The History of the Reformation in the Sixteenth Century* (5 volumes, 1835-53) and *The History of the Reformation in Europe in the Time of Calvin* (8 volumes, 1863-78; the last three volumes edited and published by his son-in-law after Merle's death). The first set outsold the second by far, but both were surprisingly popular for a multivolume work of history. Merle also wrote a few other works, such as a defense of Oliver Cromwell, but it was his history of the Reformation that made him famous.

The appeal of Merle's work is the result of several factors. His style is flowing—and dramatic. This sense of drama is evident throughout and is heightened by the author's extensive use of original quotations from the persons he describes. Merle was not simply seeking dramatic effect in these quotations; he hoped to guarantee the greatest possible accuracy. He wrote, "The work of the historian is neither a work of the imagination like that of the poet, nor a mere conversation about times gone by, as some writers of our day appear to imagine. History is a faithful description of past events; and when the historian can relate them by making use of the language of those who took part in them, he is more certain of describing them just as they were."

Merle wrote during the growth of a movement in historical writing that sought to go back to the sources, to write "history as it really happened." Increasingly, European archives were opening and providing a wealth of materials for study, and Merle faithfully used those materials in his writing. Today we understand how difficult it is to achieve true objectivity in historical writing. The original sources an author quotes may themselves be in error, and a writer reveals his own views in the quotations he selects and how he arranges them. Nonetheless, Merle d'Aubigné relied much more heavily on the writings of the reformers and their opponents than he did on the contemporary writings of other historians. This quality gives his work a freshness and immediacy not always found in historical writing.

But for the Christian, Merle's appeal undoubtedly lies also in his personal faith and how that faith shaped his philosophy of history. He placed first and foremost God's providential control not only of the events of the Reformation but also of all history. In his preface to the first volume Merle wrote, "These volumes . . . lay down in the chief and foremost place this simple and pregnant principle: GOD IN HISTORY." He said later in that preface, "In history God should be acknowledged and proclaimed. The history of the world should be set forth as the annals of the government of the sovereign King."

In keeping with his stress on faith, Merle always wanted to include the "inner" aspect of history, not just trace the outward actions of his subjects. What Luther *did* was important, but to the Genevan historian, what Luther *thought* was also important—probably more so. "In my opinion," Merle wrote, "the very essence of the Reformation is its doctrines and its inward life." Merle believed that one cannot really understand the Reformation apart from faith and Scripture.

More than that, Merle believed that God accomplished the Reformation through Scripture. Merle wrote, "The only true reformation is that which emanates from the Word of God. The Holy Scriptures, by bearing witness to the incarnation, death, and resurrection of the Son of God, create in man by the Holy Ghost a faith which justifies him. That faith which produces in him a new life, unites him to Christ. . . . From the regeneration of individuals naturally results the regeneration of the church."

Readers of Merle's work should keep in mind his emphasis on the Reformation as a positive expression of God's will and Word. Critics often accuse him of being anti-Catholic. There is no question that he soundly criticizes much within Roman Catholicism, but he does so because he finds that system at odds with Scripture. Merle's goal was not primarily to attack the pope or the Roman Catholic church but to record what he saw as the triumph of God's truth in the Reformation. When the pope and church opposed that truth, Merle did not spare them. Merle must have heartily agreed with Luther when he quoted the reformer's words to Cardinal Cajetan: "My greatest joy will be to witness the triumph of what is according to God's Word."

Why does Merle's work still endure? The liveliness of his style, his extensive and remarkable use of original quotations, and the rich biographical color of his work make it enjoyable to read. More than that, Merle's evangelical fervor, his commitment to biblical truth, and his fundamental sympathy with the spirit of the Reformation strike a responsive chord in the heart of the Christian.

Merle found common cause between himself and the Protestant Reformation. It is not surprising that he called the *réveil* the "Second Reformation of Geneva." The Reformation—whatever its profound social, political, and economic effects—was fundamentally a spiritual awakening, a revival of religion. Merle wrote about a phenomenon he had personally experienced. Likewise, when he wrote of Martin Luther, the monk who rose from the depths of self-loathing and misery in sin to calm assurance and courage in the righteousness of Christ, Merle described the travail and triumph in his own soul. Without pressing the point too far, Jean Henri Merle d'Aubigné may have been writing not only history but also something of his autobiography when he traced the history of the Reformation.

Sources

Biéler, Blanche. *Un Fils du Refuge: Jean-Henri Merle d'Aubigné.* Geneva: Editions Labor, 1934.

Bonnet, Jules. *Notice sur la vie et les écrits de M. Merle d'Aubigné.* Paris: Grassart, 1874.

de Goltz, H. *Genève religieuse au dix-neuvième siècle.* Translated from the German by C. Malan-Sillem. Geneva: Henri Georg, 1862.

Good, James I. *History of the Swiss Reformed Church Since the Reformation.* Philadelphia: Publication and Sunday School Board of the Reformed Church in the United States, 1913.

Haldane, Alexander. *The Lives of Robert and James Haldane.* 1852. Reprint, Edinburgh: Banner of Truth Trust, 1990. See pp. 413-62.

Houghton, S. M. Introduction to *The Reformation in England,* by J. H. Merle d'Aubigné. Edinburgh: Banner of Truth Trust, 1962.

Merle d'Aubigné, J. H. *D'Aubigné and His Writings.* Edited by Robert Baird. New York: Baker and Scribner, 1846.

Roney, John. "Jean Henri Merle d'Aubigné" In *Historians of the Christian Tradition,* edited by Michael Banman and Martin I. Klauber. Nashville: Broadman and Holman, 1995, pp. 167-89.

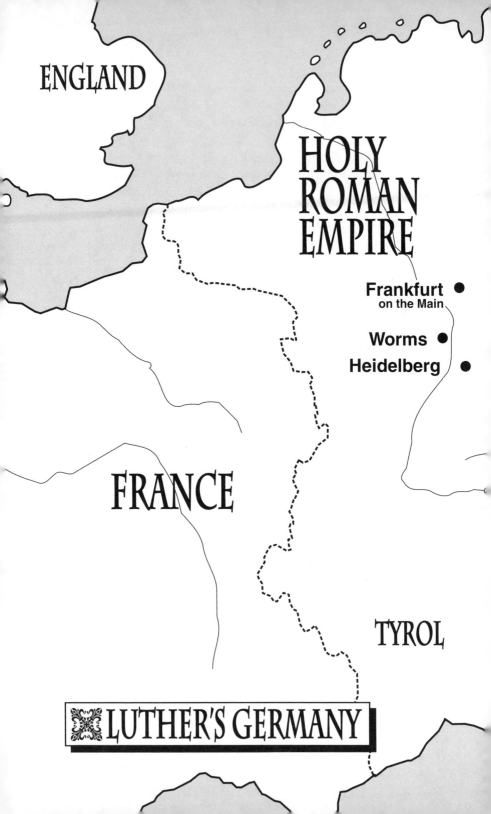

ENGLAND

HOLY
ROMAN
EMPIRE

Frankfurt ●
on the Main

Worms ●

Heidelberg ●

FRANCE

TYROL

LUTHER'S GERMANY

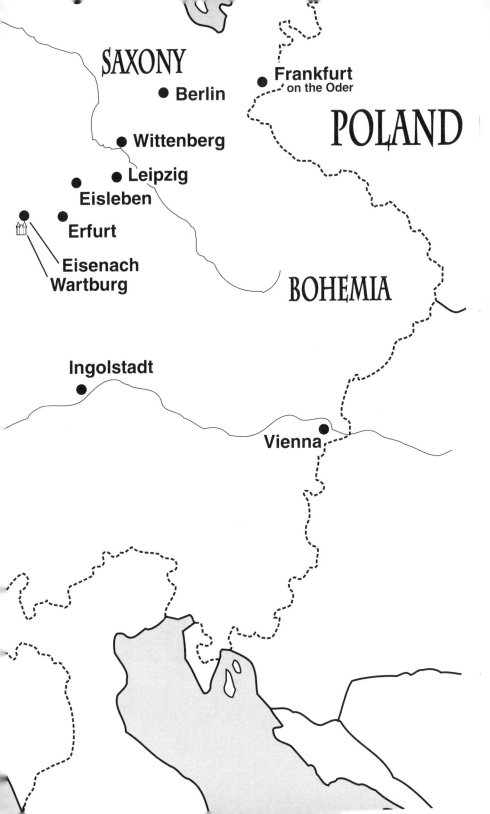

A portrait of Martin Luther dated 1529, after a painting by Lucas Cranach (1472-1553) (German Information Center)

Chapter 1
Luther's Early Life and Training

In the village of Mora, near the Thuringian forests, had dwelt, doubtless for centuries, an ancient and numerous family of the name of Luther. As was customary with the Thuringian peasants, the eldest son always inherited the dwelling and the paternal fields, while the other children departed elsewhere in quest of a livelihood. One of these, by name John Luther, married Margaret Lindemann, the daughter of an inhabitant of Neustadt, in the see of Würzburg. The married pair quitted the plains of Eisenach and went to settle in the little town of Eisleben, in Saxony, to earn their bread by the sweat of their brows.

John Luther was an upright man, diligent in business, frank, and carrying the firmness of his character even to obstinacy. With a more cultivated mind than that of most men of his class, he used to read much. Books were then rare, but John omitted no opportunity of procuring them. They formed his relaxation in the intervals of repose snatched from his severe and constant labors. Margaret possessed all the virtues that can adorn a good and pious woman. Her modesty, her fear of God, and her prayerful spirit were particularly remarked. She was looked upon by the matrons of the neighborhood as a model whom they should strive to imitate.

It is not precisely known how long the married pair had been living at Eisleben when the future reformer was born on St. Martin's Eve, November 10, 1483. The first thought of his pious parents was to dedicate to God, according to the faith they professed, the child that He had given them. On the morrow, which happened to be Tuesday, the father carried his son to St. Peter's Church, and there he received the rite of infant baptism, and was called Martin in commemoration of the day.

The child was not six months old when his parents quitted Eisleben to repair to Mansfeldt, which is only five leagues distant. The mines of that neighborhood were then very celebrated. John

Luther, who was a hard-working man, feeling that perhaps he would be called upon to bring up a numerous family, hoped to gain a better livelihood for himself and his children in that town. It was here that the understanding and strength of young Luther received their first development; here his activity began to display itself, and here his character was declared in his words and in his actions. The plains of Mansfeldt, the banks of the Wipper were the theater of his first sports with the children of the neighborhood.

The first period of their abode at Mansfeldt was full of difficulty to the worthy John and his wife. At first they lived in great poverty. "My parents," said the reformer, "were very poor. My father was a poor woodcutter, and my mother has often carried wood upon her back, that she might procure the means of bringing up her children. They endured the severest labor for our sakes." The example of the parents whom he revered and the habits they inspired in him early accustomed Luther to labor and frugality. How many times, doubtless, he accompanied his mother to the wood, there to gather up his little bundle of twigs!

There are promises of blessing on the labor of the righteous, and John Luther experienced their realization. Having attained somewhat easier circumstances, he established two smelting furnaces at Mansfeldt. Beside these furnaces little Martin grew in strength, and with the produce of this labor his father afterwards provided for his studies. "It was from a miner's family," said the good Mathesius, "that the spiritual *founder* of Christendom was to go forth: an image of what God would do in purifying the sons of Levi through him, and refining them like gold in His furnaces." Respected by all for his integrity, for his spotless life, and good sense, John Luther was made councilor of Mansfeldt, capital of the earldom of that name.

John took advantage of his new position to court the society which he preferred. He had a great esteem for learned men and often invited to his table the clergy and schoolmasters of the place. His house offered a picture of those social meetings of his fellow citizens, which did honor to Germany at the commencement of the sixteenth century. It was a mirror in which were reflected the numerous images that followed one another on the agitated scene of the times. The child profited by them. No doubt the sight of these men, to whom so much respect was shown in his father's house, excited more than once in little Martin's heart the ambitious desire of becoming himself one day a schoolmaster or a learned man.

As soon as he was old enough to receive instruction, his parents endeavored to impart to him the knowledge of God, to train him up in His fear, and to mold him to Christian virtues. They exerted all their care in this earliest domestic education. The father would often kneel at the child's bedside and fervently pray aloud, begging the Lord that his son might remember His name and one day contribute to the propagation of the truth. The parent's prayer was most graciously listened to.

His parents' piety, their activity and austere virtue, gave the boy a happy impulse and formed in him an attentive and serious disposition. The system of education which then prevailed made use of chastisement and fear as the principle incentives to study. Martin's impetuous character gave frequent occasion for punishment and reprimand. "My parents," said Luther in afterlife, "treated me harshly, so that I became very timid. My mother one day chastised me so severely about a nut, that the blood came. They seriously thought that they were doing right; but they could not distinguish character, which, however, is very necessary in order to know when or where or how chastisement should be inflicted. It is necessary to punish, but the apple should be placed beside the rod."

At school the poor child met with treatment no less severe. His master flogged him fifteen times successively in one morning. "We must," said Luther, when relating this circumstance, "we must whip children, but we must at the same time love them." With such an education Luther learned early to despise the charms of a merely sensual life. "What is to become great should begin small," justly observes one of his oldest biographers, "and if children are brought up too delicately and with too much kindness from their youth, they are injured for life."

Martin learned something at school. He was taught his catechism, the Ten Commandments, the Apostles' Creed, the Lord's Prayer, some hymns, some forms of prayer, and Latin; he learned all that could be taught in the Latin school of Mansfeldt. But the child's thoughts do not appear to have been there directed to God. The only religious sentiment that could then be discovered in him was fear. Every time he heard Jesus Christ spoken of, he turned pale with affright, for the Savior had only been represented to him as an offended judge.

John Luther wished to make his son a scholar. The day that was everywhere beginning to dawn had penetrated even into the house of the Mansfeldt miner, and there it awakened ambitious thoughts. The remarkable disposition, the persevering application of his son, made John conceive the liveliest expectations. Accordingly, in 1497, when Martin had attained the age of fourteen years, his father resolved to part with him and send him to the Franciscan school at Magdeburg. His mother was forced to consent, and Martin prepared to quit the paternal roof.

Magdeburg was like a new world to Martin. In the midst of numerous privations, for he scarcely had enough to live upon, he inquired; he listened.

This was a rude apprenticeship for Luther. Thrown upon the world at the age of fourteen, without friends or protectors, he trembled in the presence of his masters, and in the hours of recreation he painfully begged his bread in company with children poorer than himself. "I used to beg with my companions for a little food," said he, "that we might have the means of providing for our wants. One day, at the time the church celebrates the festival of Christ's nativity, we were wandering together through the neighboring villages, going from house to house and singing in four parts the usual carols on the infant Jesus, born at Bethlehem.

"We stopped before a peasant's house that stood by itself at the extremity of the village. The farmer, hearing us sing our Christmas hymns, came out with some food which he intended to give us. He called out in a high voice and with a harsh tone, 'Boys, where are you?' Frightened at these words, we ran off as fast as our legs would carry us. We had no reason to be alarmed, for the farmer offered us assistance with great kindness; but our hearts no doubt were rendered timorous by the menaces and tyranny with which the teachers were then accustomed to rule over their pupils, so that a sudden panic had seized us. At last, however, as the farmer continued calling after us, we stopped, forgot our fears, ran back to him, and received from his hands the food intended for us."

A year had scarcely passed away, when John and Margaret, hearing what difficulty their son found in supporting himself at Magdeburg, sent him to Eisenach, where there was a celebrated school, and in which town they had many relatives. They had other children, and although their means had increased, they could not maintain their son in a place where he was unknown. The furnaces and the industry of John Luther did little more than provide for the support of his family. He hoped that when Martin arrived at Eisenach he would more easily find the means of subsistence, but he was not more fortunate in this town. His relations who dwelt there took no care of him, or perhaps, being very poor themselves, they could not give him any assistance.

When the young scholar was pinched by hunger, he was compelled, as at Magdeburg, to join with his schoolfellows in singing from door to door to obtain a morsel of bread. Often, instead of food, the poor and modest Martin received nothing but harsh words. Then, overwhelmed with sorrow, he shed many tears in secret, and thought with anxiety of the future.

One day in particular, he had already been repulsed from three houses and was preparing to return fasting to his lodgings when, having reached the square of St. George, he stopped motionless, plunged in melancholy reflections, before the house of a worthy citizen. Must he for want of bread renounce his studies and return to labor with his father in the mines of Mansfeldt? Suddenly a door opened—a woman appeared on the threshold, Ursula, the wife of Conrad Cotta and a daughter of the burgomaster of Ilefeld. The Eisenach chronicles style her "the pious Shunamite," in remembrance of her who so earnestly constrained the prophet Elisha to stay and eat bread with her. The Christian Shunamite had already more than once noticed the youthful Martin in the assemblies of the faithful; she had been affected by the sweetness of his voice and by his devotion. She had heard the harsh words that had been addressed to the scholar, and seeing him stand thus sadly before her door, she came to his aid, beckoned him to enter, and gave him food to appease his hunger.

Conrad approved of his wife's benevolence. He even found so much pleasure in the boy's society that a few days after, he took him to live entirely with him. Henceforward Luther's studies were secured; he was not obliged to return to the mines of Mansfeldt and bury the talents that God had entrusted to him. At a time when he knew not what would become of him, God opened the heart and the house of a Christian family.

Luther passed in Cotta's house a very different kind of life from that which he had hitherto known. His existence glided away calmly, exempt from want and care: his mind became more serene, his character more cheerful, and his heart more open. All his faculties awoke at the mild rays of charity, and he began to exult with life, joy, and happiness. His prayers were more fervent, his thirst for knowledge greater, and his progress in study more rapid.

To literature and science he added the charms of the fine arts, for they also were advancing in Germany. The men whom God destines to act upon their contemporaries are themselves at first influenced and carried away by all the tendencies of the age in which they live. Luther learned to play on the flute and on the lute. With this latter instrument he used often to accompany his fine alto voice, and thus cheered his heart in the hours of sadness. He took delight in testifying by his melody his lively gratitude toward his adoptive mother, who was passionately fond of music. He himself loved the art even to old age and composed the words and airs of some of the finest hymns that Germany possesses. Many have even passed into our language.

These were happy times for young Luther; he could never think of them without emotion. It was in remembrance of this Christian woman who had fed him when all the world repulsed him, that he gave utterance to this beautiful thought: "There is nothing sweeter on earth than the heart of a woman in which piety dwells."

Luther was never ashamed of these days in which, oppressed by hunger, he used in sadness to beg the bread necessary for his studies and his livelihood. Far from that, he used to reflect with gratitude on the extreme poverty of his youth. He looked upon it as one of the means that God had employed to make him what he afterwards became, and he accordingly thanked Him for it. The poor children who were obliged to follow the same kind of life touched his heart. "Do not despise," said he, "the boys who go singing through the streets, begging a little bread for the love of God; I also have done the same. It is true that somewhat later my father supported me with much love and kindness at the University of Erfurt, maintaining me by the sweat of his brow; yet I have been a poor beggar. And now, by means of my pen, I have risen so high that I would not change lots with the Grand Turk himself. Nay more, should all the riches of the earth be heaped one upon the other, I would not take them in exchange for what I possess. And yet I should not be where I am if I had not gone to school—if I had not learned to write."

The strength of his understanding, the liveliness of his imagination, the excellence of his memory, soon carried him beyond all his schoolfellows. He made rapid progress, especially in Latin, in eloquence, and in poetry. He wrote speeches and composed verses. As he was cheerful, obliging, and had what is called "a good heart," he was beloved by his masters and by his schoolfellows.

Among the professors he attached himself particularly to John Trebonius, a learned man, of an agreeable address, and who had all that regard for youth which is so well calculated to encourage them. Martin had noticed that whenever Trebonius entered the schoolroom, he raised his cap to salute the pupils—a great condescension in those pedantic times. This had delighted the young man. He saw that he was something. The respect of the master had elevated the scholar in his own estimation. The colleagues of Trebonius, who did not adopt the same custom, having one day expressed their astonishment at his extreme condescension, he replied, and his answer did not the less strike the youthful Luther, "There are among these boys men of whom God will one day make burgomasters, chancellors, doctors, and magistrates. Although you do not yet see them with the badges of their dignity, it is right that you should treat them with respect." Doubtless the young scholar listened with pleasure to these words and perhaps imagined himself already with the doctor's cap upon his head.

Chapter 2
University Days

Luther had now reached his eighteenth year. He had tasted the sweets of literature; he burned with a desire of knowledge; he sighed for a university education and wished to repair to one of those fountains of learning where he could slake his thirst for letters. His father required him to study the law. Full of hope in the talents of his son, he already pictured him discharging the most honorable functions among his fellow citizens, gaining the favor of princes, and shining on the theater of the world. It was determined that the young man should go to Erfurt.

Luther arrived at this university in 1501. The new disciple applied himself to study the philosophy of the Middle Ages in the works of Occam, Scotus, Bonaventure, and Thomas Aquinas. He began to study the masterpieces of antiquity, the writings of Cicero, Virgil, and other classic authors. He was not content, like the majority of students, with learning their productions by heart: he endeavored to fathom their thoughts, to imbibe the spirit which animated them, to appropriate their wisdom to himself, to comprehend the object of their writings, and to enrich his mind with their pregnant sentences and brilliant images. He often addressed questions to his professors, and soon outstripped all his fellow students. Luther was blessed with a retentive memory and a strong imagination, and all that he read or heard remained constantly present to his mind; it was as if he had seen it himself.

But even at this period, the young man of eighteen did not study merely to cultivate his intellect: he had those serious thoughts, that heart directed heavenward, which God gives to those of whom He resolves to make His most zealous ministers. Luther was sensible of his entire dependence upon God—simple and powerful conviction, which is at once the cause of deep humility and of great actions. Every morning he began the day with prayer; he then went to church and afterward applied to his studies, losing not a moment in the whole course of the day. "To pray well," he was in the habit of saying, "is the better half of study."

The young student passed in the university library all the time he could snatch from his academic pursuits. Books were as yet rare, and it was a great privilege for him to profit by the treasures brought together in this vast collection. One day—he had then been two years at Erfurt, and was twenty years old—he opened many books in the library one after another, to learn their writers' names. One volume that he came to attracted his attention; it was a Bible, a rare book, unknown in those times.

His interest was greatly excited; he was filled with astonishment at finding other matters than those fragments of the Gospels and Epistles that the church selected to be read to the people during public worship every Sunday throughout the year. Until this day he had imagined that they composed the whole Word of God. And now he saw so many pages, so many chapters, so many books of which he had no idea. With eagerness and with indescribable emotion he turned over these leaves from God.

He returned home with a full heart. "O that God would give me such a book for myself," thought he. He soon returned to the library to pore over his treasure. He read it again and again, and then, in his astonishment and joy, he returned to read it once more. The first glimmerings of a new truth were then beginning to dawn upon his mind. In that Bible the Reformation lay hid.

It was in the same year that Luther took his first academic degree, that of bachelor. The excessive labor to which he had devoted himself in order to pass his examination occasioned a dangerous illness. Death seemed approaching him; serious reflections occupied his mind. Many friends came to visit him on his bed of sickness. Among their number was a venerable and aged priest, who had watched with interest the student of Mansfeldt in his labors and in his academic career. Luther could not conceal the thoughts that occupied his mind.

"Soon," said he, "I shall be called away from this world."

But the old man kindly replied, "My dear bachelor, take courage; you will not die of this illness. Our God will yet make of you a man who, in turn, shall console many. For God layeth His cross upon those whom He loveth, and they who bear it patiently acquire much wisdom."

These words struck the young invalid. The old man had poured sweet consolation into his heart, had revived his spirits. "This was the first prediction that the worthy doctor heard," says Mathesius, Luther's friend, who records the fact, "and he often used to call it to mind."

When Luther recovered, there was a great change in him. The Bible, his illness, the words of the aged priest, seem to have made a new appeal to him; but as yet there was nothing decided in his mind. Another circumstance awakened serious thoughts within him. It was the festival of Easter, probably in the year 1503. Luther was going to pass a short time with his family, and wore a sword according to the custom of the age. He struck against it with his foot, and the blade fell out, cutting one of the principal arteries. Luther, whose only companion had run off in haste to seek for assistance, finding himself alone, and seeing the blood flowing copiously without being able to check it, lay down on his back and put his finger on the wound; but the blood escaped in despite of his exertions, and Luther, feeling the approach of death, cried out, "O Mary, help me!"

At last a surgeon arrived from Erfurt, who bound up the cut. The wound opened in the night, and Luther fainted, again calling loudly upon the Virgin. "At that time," said he in afteryears, "I should have died relying upon Mary." Ere long he abandoned that superstition and invoked a more powerful Savior.

He continued his studies. In 1505 he was admitted Master of Arts and Doctor of Philosophy. The ceremony was conducted, as usual, with great pomp. A procession by torchlight came to pay honor to Luther. The festival was magnificent. It was a general rejoicing. Luther, encouraged perhaps by these honors, felt disposed to apply himself entirely to the law, in conformity with his father's wishes.

But the will of God was different. While Luther was occupied with various studies, and beginning to teach the physics and ethics of Aristotle with other branches of philosophy, his heart ceased not from crying to him that religion was the one thing needful, and that above all things he should secure his salvation. He knew the displeasure that God manifests against sin; he called to mind the penalties that His Word denounces against the sinner; and he asked himself, with apprehension, whether he was sure of possessing the divine favor. His conscience answered, No. His character was prompt and decided: he resolved to do all that might insure him a firm hope of immortality.

It was in the summer of the year 1505 that Luther, whom the ordinary university vacations left at liberty, resolved to go to Mansfeldt to revisit the dear scenes of his childhood and to embrace his parents. Perhaps also he wished to open his heart to his father, to sound on him the plan that he was forming in his mind, and obtain his permission to engage in another profession. He foresaw all the difficulties that awaited him. The idle life of the majority of priests was displeasing to the active miner of Mansfeldt. Besides, the ecclesiastics were but little esteemed in the world; for the most part their revenues were scanty; and the father, who had made great sacrifices to maintain his son at the university, and who now saw him teaching publicly in a celebrated school, although only in his twentieth year, was not likely to renounce the proud hopes he had cherished.

We are ignorant of what passed during Luther's stay at Mansfeldt. Perhaps the decided wish of his father made him fear to open his heart to him. He again quitted his father's house to take his seat on the benches of the academy. He was already within a short distance of Erfurt, when he was overtaken by a violent storm, such as often occurs in these mountains. The lightning flashed, the bolt fell at his feet. Luther threw himself upon his knees. His hour, perhaps, had come. Death, the judgment, and eternity summoned him with all their terrors, and he heard a voice that he could no longer resist.

"Encompassed with the anguish and terror of death," as he said himself, he made a vow, if the Lord delivered him from this danger, to abandon the world and devote himself entirely to God. After rising from the ground, having still present to him that death which must one day overtake him, he examined himself seriously and asked what he ought to do. The thoughts that once agitated him now returned with greater force. He had endeavored to fulfill all his duties, but what was the state of his soul? Could he appear before the tribunal of a terrible God with an impure heart? He must become holy. He had now as great a thirst for holiness as he had formerly for knowledge. But where could he find it, or how could he attain it? To what school of holiness should he direct his steps? He would enter a cloister: the monastic life would save him. Oftentimes had he heard speak of its power to transform the heart, to sanctify the sinner, to make man perfect. He would enter a monastic order. He would there become holy: thus would he secure eternal life.

Such was the event that changed the calling, the whole destiny of Luther.

Luther reentered Erfurt. He communicated his intention to no one. But one evening he invited his university friends to a cheerful, but frugal, supper. Music once more enlivened their social meeting. It was Luther's farewell to the world. Henceforth, instead of these amiable companions of his pleasures and his studies, he would have monks; instead of this gay and witty conversation, the silence of the cloister; and for these merry songs, the solemn strains of the quiet chapel. God called him, and he must sacrifice everything.

The repast excited his friends: Luther himself was the soul of the party. But at the very moment that they were giving way without restraint to their gaiety, the young man could no longer control the serious thoughts that filled his mind. He spoke; he made known his intention to his astonished friends. They endeavored to shake it, but in vain. And that very night, Luther, fearful perhaps of their importunate solicitations, quit his lodgings. He left behind him all his clothes and books; he had no Bible as yet.

He repaired alone, in the darkness of night, to the convent of the hermits of St. Augustine. He asked admittance. The gate opened and closed again. Behold him separated forever from his parents, from the companions of his studies, and from the world. It was August 17, 1505; Luther was then twenty-one years and nine months old.

Chapter 3
In the Augustinian Monastery

Luther was with God at last. His soul was in safety. He was now about to find that holiness which he so much desired. The monks were astonished at the sight of the youthful doctor and extolled his courage and his contempt of the world. Luther had also hastened to communicate to his parents the great change that had taken place in his life. His father was amazed. He trembled for his son. His weakness, his youth, the violence of his passions, all led John Luther to fear that when the first moment of enthusiasm was over, the idle habits of the cloister would make the young man fall either into despair or into some great sin. He knew that this kind of life had already been the destruction of many. Besides, the councilor-miner of Mansfeldt had formed very different plans for his son. He had hoped that he would contract a rich and honorable marriage. And now all his ambitious projects were overthrown in one night by this imprudent step.

John wrote a very angry letter to his son, in which he spoke to him in a contemptuous tone, as Luther informs us, while he had addressed him always in a friendly manner after he had taken his Master of Arts degree. He withdrew all his favor and declared him disinherited from his paternal affection. In vain did his father's friends, and doubtless his wife, endeavor to soften him; in vain did they say, "If you would offer a sacrifice to God, let it be what you hold best and dearest, even your son, your Isaac." The inexorable councilor of Mansfeldt would listen to nothing.

Not long after, however, the plague appeared and deprived John Luther of two of his sons. About this time someone came and told the bereaved father, "The monk of Erfurt is dead also." His friends seized the opportunity of reconciling the father to the young novice. "If it should be a false alarm," said they to him, "at least sanctify your affliction by cordially consenting to your son's becoming a monk."

"Well, so be it," replied John Luther, with a heart bruised, yet still half rebellious, "and God grant he may prosper."

Some time after this, when Luther, who had been reconciled to his father, related to him the event that had induced him to enter a monastic order—"God grant," replied the worthy miner, "that you may not have taken for a sign from heaven what was merely a delusion of the Devil."

When Martin Luther entered the convent, he changed his name and assumed that of Augustine. The monks had received him with joy. It was no slight gratification to their vanity to see one of the most esteemed doctors of the age abandon the university for a house belonging to their order. Nevertheless, they treated him harshly, and imposed on him the meanest occupations. They imagined, besides, by this means to prevent him from devoting himself so much to his studies, from which the convent could reap no advantage. The former Master of Arts had to perform the offices of porter, to open and shut the gates, to wind up the clock, to sweep the church, and to clean out the cells.

Then, when the poor monk, who was at once doorkeeper, sexton, and menial servant of the cloister, had finished his work, "Away with your wallet through the town!" cried the friars; and laden with his bread bag, he wandered through all the streets of Erfurt, begging from house to house, obliged perhaps to present himself at the doors of those who had once been his friends or his inferiors. On his return, he had either to shut himself up in a low and narrow cell, whence he could see nothing but a small garden a few feet square, or recommence his humble tasks.

But he put up with all. Naturally disposed to devote himself entirely to whatever he undertook, he had become a monk with all his soul. Besides, how could he have thought of sparing his body, or have had any regard for what might please the flesh? It was not thus that he could acquire the humility, the sanctity which he had come to seek within the walls of the cloister.

The poor monk, oppressed with toil, hastened to employ in study all the moments that he could steal from these mean occupations. He voluntarily withdrew from the society of the brethren to give himself up to his beloved pursuits; but they soon found it out and, surrounding him with murmurs, tore him from his books, exclaiming, "Come, come; it is not by studying, but by begging bread, corn, eggs, fish, meat, and money, that a monk renders himself useful to the cloister!" Luther submitted: he laid aside his books and took up his bag again.

This severe apprenticeship did not, however, last so long as Luther might have feared. The prior of the convent, at the intercession of the university to which Luther belonged, freed him from the humiliating duties that had been laid upon him. The youthful monk then returned to his studies with new zeal. The works of the Fathers of the church, especially of St. Augustine, attracted his attention. The exposition of the psalms by this illustrious doctor and his book *On the Letter and the Spirit* were his favorite study. Nothing struck him more than the sentiments of this father on the corruption of man's will and on divine grace. He felt by his own experience the reality of that corruption and the necessity for that grace. The words of St. Augustine corresponded with the sentiments of his heart. If he could have belonged to any other school than that of Jesus Christ, it would undoubtedly have been to that of Augustine of Hippo.

To this course of reading he added other exercises. He was heard in the public discussions unravelling the most complicated trains of reasoning and extricating himself from a labyrinth whence none but he could have found an outlet. All his auditors were filled with astonishment. But he had not entered the cloister to acquire the reputation of a great genius: it was to seek food for his piety. He therefore regarded these labors as mere digressions.

He loved above all things to draw wisdom from the pure source of the Word of God. He found in the convent a Bible fastened by a chain, and to this chained Bible he was continually returning. He had but little understanding of the Word, yet was it his most pleasing study. It sometimes happened that he passed a whole day meditating upon a single passage. At other times he learned fragments of the prophets by heart. He especially desired to acquire from the writings of the prophets and the apostles a perfect knowledge of God's will, to grow up in greater fear of His name, and to nourish his faith by the sure testimony of the Word.

The young monk studied with such industry and zeal that it often happened that he did not repeat the daily prayers for three or four weeks together. But he soon grew alarmed at the thought that he had transgressed the rules of his order. He then shut himself up to repair his negligence and began to repeat conscientiously all the prayers he had omitted, without a thought of either eating or drinking. Once even, for seven weeks together, he scarcely closed his eyes in sleep.

Burning with desire to attain that holiness in quest of which he had entered the cloister, Luther gave way to all the rigor of an ascetic life. He endeavored to crucify the flesh by fastings, mortifications, and watchings. Shut up in his cell, as in a prison, he struggled unceasingly against the deceitful thoughts and the evil inclinations of his heart. A little bread and a small herring were often his only food.

At the period of which we are speaking, nothing was too great a sacrifice that might enable him to become a saint, to acquire heaven. Never did the Roman church possess a more pious monk. Never did cloister witness more severe or indefatigable exertions to purchase eternal happiness. When Luther had become a reformer and had declared that heaven was not to be obtained by such means as these, he knew very well what he was saying. "I was indeed a pious monk," wrote he to Duke George of Saxony, "and followed the rules of my order more strictly than I can express. If ever monk could obtain heaven by his monkish works, I should certainly have been entitled to it. Of this all the friars who have known me can testify. If it had continued much longer, I should have carried my mortifications even to death, by means of my watchings, prayers, reading, and other labors."

Luther did not find in the tranquility of the cloister and in monkish perfection that peace of mind which he had looked for there. He wished to have the assurance of his salvation: this was the great want of his soul. Without it, there was no repose for him. But the fears that had agitated him in the world pursued him to his cell. Nay, they were increased. The faintest cry of his heart reechoed loud beneath the silent arches of the cloister. God had led him thither, that he might learn to know himself, and to despair of his own strength and virtue. His conscience, enlightened by the divine Word, told him what it was to be holy; but he was filled with terror at finding neither in his heart nor in his life that image of holiness which he had contemplated with admiration in the Word of God. A sad discovery, and one that is made by every sincere man. No righteousness within, no righteousness without; all was omission, sin, impurity. The more ardent the character of Luther, the stronger was that secret and constant resistance which man's nature opposes to good; and it plunged him into despair.

The monks and divines of the day encouraged him to satisfy the divine righteousness by meritorious works. But what works, thought he, can come from a heart like mine? How can I stand before the holiness of my Judge with works polluted in their very source? "I saw that I was a great sinner in the eyes of God," said he, "and I did not think it possible for me to propitiate Him by my own merits."

A tender conscience inclined Luther to regard the slightest fault as a great sin. He had hardly discovered it, before he endeavored to expiate it by the severest mortifications. "I tortured myself almost to death," said he, "in order to procure peace with God for my troubled heart and agitated conscience; but surrounded with thick darkness, I found peace nowhere."

The practices of monastic holiness, which had lulled so many consciences to sleep, and to which Luther himself had had recourse in his distress, soon appeared to him the unavailing remedies of an empirical and deceptive religion. "While I was yet a monk, I no sooner felt assailed by any temptation, than I cried out, I am lost! Immediately I had recourse to a thousand methods to stifle the cries of my conscience. I went every day to confession, but that was of no use to me. Then bowed down by sorrow, I tortured myself by the multitude of my thoughts. Look, exclaimed I, thou art still envious, impatient, passionate. It profiteth thee nothing, O wretched man, to have entered this sacred order."

Luther passed his life in a continual struggle. The young monk crept like a shadow through the long galleries of the cloister that reechoed with his sorrowful moanings. His body wasted away; his strength began to fail him; it sometimes happened that he remained like one dead.

On one occasion, overwhelmed with sorrow, he shut himself up in his cell, and for several days and nights allowed no one to approach him. One of his friends, Lucas Edemberger, feeling anxious about the unhappy monk and having a presentiment of the condition in which he was, took with him some boys who were in the habit of singing in the choirs and knocked at the door of the cell. No one opened; no one answered.

The good Edemberger, still more alarmed, broke open the door. Luther lay upon the floor insensible, and giving no signs of life. His friend strove in vain to recall him to his senses: he was still motionless. Then the choristers began to sing a sweet hymn. Their clear voices acted like a charm on the poor monk, to whom music was ever one of his greatest pleasures: gradually he recovered his strength, his consciousness, and life. But if music could restore his serenity for a few moments, he required another and a stronger remedy to heal him thoroughly: he needed that mild and subtle sound of the gospel which is the voice of God Himself (I Kings 19:12). He knew it well. And therefore his troubles and his terrors led him to study with fresh zeal the writings of the prophets and of the apostles.

Chapter 4
Staupitz

Luther was not the first monk who had undergone such trials. The gloomy walls of the cloisters often concealed the most abominable vices that would have made every upright mind shudder had they been revealed; but often also they hid Christian virtues that expanded there in silence, and which, had they been exposed to the eyes of the world, would have excited universal admiration. The possessors of these virtues, living only with themselves and with God, attracted no attention, and were often unknown to the modest convent in which they were enclosed: their lives were known only to God.

Yet if one of these men was called to some high station, he there displayed virtues whose salutary influence was long and widely felt. The candle was set on a candlestick, and it illumined the whole house. Many were awakened by this light. Thus from generation to generation were these pious souls propagated; they were seen shining like isolated torches at the very times when the cloisters were often little other than impure receptacles of the deepest darkness.

A young man had been thus distinguished in one of the German convents. His name was John Staupitz. From his tenderest youth he had had a taste for knowledge and a love of virtue. He felt the need of retirement to devote himself to letters. He soon discovered that philosophy and the study of nature could not do much toward eternal salvation. He therefore began to learn divinity, but especially endeavored to unite practice with knowledge. "For," says one of his biographers, "it is in vain that we assume the name of divine, if we do not confirm that noble title by our lives."

The study of the Bible and of the Augustinian theology, the knowledge of himself, the battles that he, like Luther, had had to fight against the deceits and lusts of his heart, led him to the Redeemer. He found peace to his soul in faith in Christ. The doctrine of election by grace had taken strong hold of his mind. The integrity of his life, the extent of his knowledge, the eloquence of his speech, not less than a striking exterior and dignified manners, recommended him to his contemporaries. Frederick the Wise, elector of Saxony, made him his friend, employed him in various embassies, and founded the University of Wittenberg under his direction. This disciple of St. Paul and St. Augustine was the first dean of the theological faculty of that school whence the light was one day to issue to illumine the schools and churches of so many nations. He was present at the Lateran Council as proxy of the archbishop of Salzburg, became provincial of his order in Thuringia and Saxony, and afterwards became vicar-general of the Augustinians for all Germany.

Staupitz was grieved at the corruption of morals and the errors of doctrine that were devastating the church. His writings on the love of God, on Christian faith, and on conformity with the death of Christ, and the testimony of Luther, confirm this. But he considered the former evil of more importance than the latter. Besides the mildness and indecision of his character, his desire not to go beyond the sphere of action he thought assigned to him, made him fitter to be a restorer of a convent than the reformer of the church. He would have wished to raise none but distinguished men to important offices; but not finding them, he submitted to employ others. "We must plough," said he, "with such horses as we can find; and with oxen, if there are no horses."

We have witnessed the anguish and the internal struggles to which Luther was a prey in the convent of Erfurt. At this period a visitation of the vicar-general was announced. In fact Staupitz came to make his usual inspection. This friend of Frederick, the founder of the University of Wittenberg and chief of the Augustinians, exhibited much kindness to those monks who were under his authority. Luther soon attracted his attention. Staupitz, whose discernment had been exercised by long experience, easily discovered what was passing in his mind and distinguished the youthful monk above all who surrounded him. He had had to struggle like Luther, and therefore he could understand him. Above all, he could point out to him the road to peace which he himself had found.

Luther's heart found an echo in that of Staupitz. The vicar-general understood him, and the monk felt a confidence toward him that he had as yet experienced for none. Up to this time no one had understood Luther. One day, when at table in the refectory, the young monk, dejected and silent, scarcely touched his food. Staupitz, who looked earnestly at him, said at last, "Why are you so sad, brother Martin?"

"Ah," replied he, with a deep sigh, "I do not know what will become of me."

"These temptations," resumed Staupitz, "are more necessary to you than eating and drinking."

These two men did not stop there; and ere long, in the silence of the cloister, took place that intimate intercourse which powerfully contributed to lead forth the future reformer from his state of darkness.

"It is in vain," said Luther despondingly to Staupitz, "that I make promises to God: sin is ever the strongest."

John Staupitz, Luther's superior in the Augustinian monastic order and his spiritual guide and friend

"O my friend," replied the vicar-general, looking back on his own experience, "more than a thousand times have I sworn to our holy God to live piously, and I have never kept my vows. Now I swear no longer, for I know I cannot keep my solemn promises. If God will not be merciful toward me for the love of Christ, and grant me a happy departure when I must quit this world, I shall never, with the aid of all my vows and all my good works, stand before Him. I must perish."

The young monk was terrified at the thought of divine justice. He laid open all his fears to the vicar-general. He was alarmed at the unspeakable holiness of God and His sovereign majesty. "Who may abide the day of his coming? and who shall stand when he appeareth?" (Mal. 3:2).

Staupitz resumed: "Why," said he, "do you torment yourself with all these speculations and these high thoughts? Look at the wounds of Jesus Christ, to the blood that He has shed for you: it is there that the grace of God will appear to you. Instead of torturing yourself on account of your sins, throw yourself into the Redeemer's arms. Trust in Him, in the righteousness of His life, in the atonement of His death. Do not shrink back; God is not angry with you; it is you who are angry with God. Listen to the Son of God. He became man to give you the assurance of divine favor. He says to you, 'You are my sheep; you hear my voice; no man shall pluck you out of my hand.'"

But Luther did not find in himself the repentance which he thought necessary for salvation: he replied, and it is the usual answer of distressed and timid minds, "How can I dare believe in the favor of God, so long as there is no real conversion in me? I must be changed before He will accept me."

His venerable guide showed him that there can be no real conversion, so long as man fears God as a severe judge. "What will you say then," asked Luther, "to so many consciences to which a thousand insupportable tasks are prescribed in order that they may gain heaven?"

Then he heard this reply of the vicar-general: "There is no real repentance except that which begins with the love of God and of righteousness. What others imagine to be the end and accomplishment of repentance is on the contrary only its beginning. In order that you may be filled with the love of what is good, you must first be filled with love for God. If you desire to be converted, do not be curious about all these mortifications and all these tortures. Love Him who first loved you."

These words indeed penetrated to the bottom of the young monk's heart, like a sharp arrow of a strong man. In order to repent, we must love God. Guided by this new light, he began to compare the Scriptures. He looked out all the passages that treat of repentance and conversion.

"Hitherto," exclaims he, "although I carefully dissembled the state of my soul before God and endeavored to express toward Him a love which was a mere constraint and a fiction, there was no expression in Scripture so bitter to me as that of *repentance*. But now there is none so sweet, or more acceptable. O how delightful are all God's precepts when we read them, not only in books, but also in our Savior's precious wounds!"

Although Luther had been consoled by Staupitz's words, he nevertheless fell sometimes into despondency. Sin was again felt in his timid conscience, and then all his previous despair banished the joy of salvation. "O my sin, my sin, my sin!" cried the young monk one day in the presence of the vicar-general, with a tone of profound anguish.

"Well, would you only be a sinner in appearance," replied the latter, "and have also a Savior only in appearance? Then know that Jesus Christ is the Savior even of those who are great, real sinners and deserving of utter condemnation."

The vicar-general showed Luther the paternal designs of Providence in permitting these temptations and these various struggles that his soul was to undergo. By such trials God prepares for Himself the souls that He destines for some important work. We must prove the vessel before we launch it into the wide sea. If there is an education necessary for every man, there is a particular one for those who are destined to act upon their generation. This is what Staupitz represented to the monk of Erfurt. "It is not in vain," said he to him, "that God exercises you in so many conflicts: you will see that He will employ you, as His servant, for great purposes."

Staupitz went further: he gave him many valuable directions for his studies, exhorting him, henceforward, to derive all his theology from the Bible and to put away the systems of the schools. "Let the study of the Scriptures," said he, "be your favorite occupation."

Never was good advice better followed out. What particularly delighted Luther was the present Staupitz made him of a Bible. He studied the Scriptures, and especially the epistles of St. Paul, with ever-increasing zeal. To these he added the works of St. Augustine alone. All that he read was imprinted deeply in his mind. His struggles had prepared his heart to understand the Word. The soil had been plowed deep; the incorruptible seed sank into it with power. When Staupitz quitted Erfurt, a new dawn had risen upon Luther.

But the work was not yet finished. The vicar-general had prepared the way: God reserved its accomplishment for a humbler instrument. The conscience of the young Augustinian had not yet found repose. His body gave way at last under the conflict and the tension of his soul. He was attacked by an illness that brought him to the brink of the grave. This was the second year of his abode in the convent. All his distresses and all his fears were aroused at the approach of death. His own impurity and the holiness of God again disturbed his mind.

One day, as he lay overwhelmed with despair, an aged monk entered his cell and addressed a few words of comfort to him. Luther opened his heart to him and made known the fears by which he was tormented. The venerable old man was incapable of following up that soul in all its doubts, as Staupitz had done; but he knew his creed and had found in it much consolation to his heart. He therefore applied the same remedy to his young brother. Leading him back to that Apostles' Creed which Luther had learned in early childhood at the school of Mansfeldt, the aged monk repeated this article with kind good nature: "I believe in the forgiveness of sins." These simple words, which the pious brother pronounced with sincerity in this decisive moment, diffused great consolation in Luther's heart. "I believe," he repeated to himself ere long on his bed of sickness, "I believe in the forgiveness of sins."

"Ah," said the monk, "you must believe not only in the forgiveness of David's and of Peter's sins, for this even the devils believe. It is God's command that we believe our own sins are forgiven us. Hear what St. Bernard says in his discourse on the Annunciation: 'The testimony of the Holy Ghost in thy heart is this: Thy sins are forgiven thee.'"

From this moment light sprung up in the heart of the young monk of Erfurt. The word of grace had been pronounced: he had believed in it. He disclaimed all merit of salvation and resigned himself confidingly to the grace of God in Jesus Christ. He did not at first perceive the consequences of the principle he had just admitted; he was still sincere in his attachment to the church, and yet he had no further need of her; for he had received salvation immediately from God Himself, and henceforth Roman Catholicism was virtually destroyed in him. Luther's mental health restored that of his body, and he soon rose from his bed of sickness. He had received a new life in a twofold sense.

Luther had been two years in the cloister and was to be ordained priest. He had received much, and saw with delight the prospect afforded by the sacerdotal office of freely distributing what he had freely received. He wished to take advantage of the ceremony that was about to take place to become thoroughly reconciled with his father. He invited him to be present, and even requested him to fix the day. John Luther, who was not yet entirely pacified with regard to his son, nevertheless accepted the invitation and named Sunday, May 2, 1507.

At last the day arrived. The miner of Mansfeldt did not fail to be present at his son's ordination. He gave him indeed no unequivocal mark of his affection and of his generosity by presenting him on this occasion with twenty florins.

The ceremony took place. Hieronymus, bishop of Brandenburg, officiated. At the moment of conferring on Luther the power of celebrating mass, he placed the chalice in his hands and uttered these solemn words: *Accipe potestatem sacrificandi pro vivis et mortuis.* ("Receive the power of sacrificing for the quick and the dead.") Luther at that time listened calmly to these words, which conferred on him the power of doing the work of the Son of God; but he shuddered at them in afteryears. "If the earth did not then open and swallow us both up," said he, "it was owing to the great patience and long-suffering of the Lord."

The father afterwards dined at the convent with his son, the young priest's friends, and the monks. The conversation fell on Martin's entrance into the monastery. The brothers loudly extolled it as a most meritorious work, upon which the inflexible John, turning to his son, asked him, "Have you not read in Scripture, that you should obey your father and mother?" These words struck Luther; they presented in quite a new aspect the action that had brought him into the bosom of the convent, and they long reechoed in his heart.

Luther was not destined to remain hidden in an obscure convent. The time was come for his removal to a wider stage. Staupitz, with whom he always remained in close communication, saw clearly that the young monk's disposition was too active to be confined within so narrow a circle. He spoke of him to the Elector Frederick of Saxony; and this enlightened prince invited Luther in 1508, probably about the end of the year, to become professor at the University of Wittenberg. Luther had been three years in the cloister at Erfurt.

Chapter 5
The University of Wittenberg

In the year 1502, Frederick the Elector founded a new university at Wittenberg. He declared in the charter confirming the privileges of this school that he and his people would look to it as to an oracle. At that time he had little thought in how remarkable a manner this language would be verified. The university declared that it selected St. Augustine for its patron, a choice that was very significant. This new institution, which possessed great liberty and which was considered as a court of final appeal in all cases of difficulty, was admirably fitted to become the cradle of the Reformation, and it powerfully contributed to the development of Luther and of Luther's work.

On his arrival at Wittenberg, he repaired to the Augustinian convent, where a cell was allotted to him; for though a professor, he did not cease to be a monk. He had been called to teach physics and dialectics. In assigning him this duty, regard had probably been paid to the philosophical studies he had pursued at Erfurt and to the degree of Master of Arts which he had taken. Thus Luther, who hungered and thirsted after the Word of God, was compelled to devote himself almost exclusively to the study of the Aristotelian scholastic philosophy. "By God's grace, I am well," wrote he to Braun, "except that I have to study philosophy with all might. From the first moment of my arrival at Wittenberg, I was earnestly desirous of exchanging it for that of theology; but," added he, lest it should be supposed he meant the theology of the day, "it is of a theology which seeks the kernel in the nut, the wheat in the husk, the marrow in the bones, that I am speaking. Be that as it may, God is God; man is almost always mistaken in his judgments, but this is our God. He will lead us with goodness forever and ever." The studies that Luther was then obliged to pursue were of great service to him in enabling him in afteryears to combat the errors of the schoolmen.

But he could not stop there. The desire of his heart was about to be accomplished. That same power which some years before had driven Luther from the bar into a monastic life was now impelling him from philosophy toward the Bible. He zealously applied himself to the acquisition of the ancient languages, and particularly of Greek and Hebrew, in order to draw knowledge and learning from the very springs whence they gushed forth. He was all his life indefatigable in labor. A few months after his arrival at the university, he solicited the degree of Bachelor of Divinity. He obtained it at the end of March 1509 with the particular summons to devote himself to biblical theology.

Every day, at one in the afternoon, Luther was called to lecture on the Bible: a precious hour both for the professor and his pupils, and one which led them deeper and deeper into the divine meaning of those revelations so long lost to the people and to the schools.

He began his course by explaining the Psalms, and thence passed to the epistle to the Romans. It was more particularly while meditating on this portion of Scripture that the light of truth penetrated his heart. In the retirement of his quiet cell, he used to consecrate whole hours to the study of the divine Word, this epistle of St. Paul lying open before him. On one occasion, having reached the seventeenth verse of the first chapter, he read this passage from the prophet Habakkuk: "The just shall live by faith." This precept struck him. There is then for the just a life different from that of other men, and this life is the gift of faith. This promise, which he received into his heart as if God Himself had placed it there, unveiled to him the mystery of the Christian life and increased this life in him. Years after, in the midst of his numerous occupations, he imagined he still heard these words: "The just shall live by faith."

Luther's lectures thus prepared had little similarity to what had been heard till then. It was not an eloquent rhetorician or a pedantic schoolman that spoke, but a Christian who had felt the power of revealed truths, who drew them forth from the Bible, poured them out from the treasures of his heart, and presented them all full of life to his astonished hearers. It was not the teaching of a man, but of God.

This entirely new method of expounding the truth made a great noise; the news of it spread far and wide and attracted to the newly established university a crowd of youthful foreign students. Even many professors attended Luther's lectures; and among others Mellerstadt, first rector of the university. "This monk," said he, "will put all the doctors to shame; he will bring in a new doctrine and reform the whole church; for he builds upon the Word of Christ, and no one in the world can either resist or overthrow that Word."

Staupitz, who was the instrument of God to develop all the gifts and treasures hidden in Luther, requested him to preach in the church of the Augustinians. The young professor shrunk from this proposal. He desired to confine himself to his academical duties; he trembled at the thought of increasing them by those of the ministry. In vain did Staupitz solicit him: "No, no," replied he, " it is no slight thing to speak before men in the place of God." Staupitz persisted; but the ingenious Luther, says one of his biographers, found fifteen arguments, pretexts, and evasions to defend himself against this invitation.

At length, the chief of the Augustinians persevering in his attack, Luther said, "Ah, doctor, by doing this you deprive me of life. I shall not be able to hold out three months."

"Well, so be it, in God's name," replied the vicar-general, "for our Lord God has also need on high of devoted and skillful men." Luther was forced to yield.

In the middle of the square at Wittenberg stood an ancient chapel, thirty feet long and twenty wide, whose walls, propped up on all sides, were falling into ruin. An old pulpit, made of planks and three feet high, received the preacher. It was in this wretched place that the preaching of the Reformation began. "This building," adds Myconius, one of Luther's contemporaries, who records these circumstances, "may well be compared to the stable in which Christ was born." It was in this wretched enclosure that God willed, so to speak, that His well-beloved Son should be born a second time. Among those thousands of cathedrals and parish churches with which the world is filled, there was not one at that time which God chose for the glorious preaching of eternal life.

Luther preached: everything was striking in the new minister. His expressive countenance, his noble air, his clear and sonorous voice, captivated all his hearers. Before his time, the majority of preachers had sought rather what might amuse their congregations than what would convert them. The great seriousness that pervaded all Luther's sermons, and the joy with which the knowledge of the gospel had filled his heart, imparted to his eloquence an authority, a warmth, and an unction that his predecessors had not possessed.

Soon the little chapel could not hold the hearers who crowded to it. The council of Wittenberg then nominated Luther their chaplain and invited him to preach in the city church. The impression he there produced was greater still. The energy of his genius, the eloquence of his style, and the excellency of the doctrines that he proclaimed equally astonished his hearers. His reputation extended far and wide, and Frederick the Wise himself came once to Wittenberg to hear him.

This was the beginning of a new life for Luther. The slothfulness of the cloister had been succeeded by great activity. Freedom, labor, the earnest and constant action to which he could now devote himself at Wittenberg, succeeded in reestablishing harmony and peace within him. Now he was in his place, and the work of God was soon to display its majestic progress.

Chapter 6
Luther at Rome

Luther was teaching both in the academical hall and in the church when he was interrupted in his labors. In 1510, or according to others in 1511 or 1512, he was sent to Rome. Seven convents of his order were at variance on certain points with the vicar-general. The acuteness of Luther's mind, his powerful language, and his talents for discussion were the cause of his selection as agent for these seven monasteries before the pope.

He set out and crossed the Alps. But he had scarcely descended into the plains of the rich and voluptuous Italy before he found at every step subjects of astonishment and scandal. The poor German monk was entertained in a wealthy convent of the Benedictines on the banks of the Po, in Lombardy. The splendor of the apartments, the richness of their dress, and the delicacy of their food confounded Luther. Marble, silk, luxury in all its forms—what a novel sight for the humble brother of the poor convent of Wittenberg! He was astonished and was silent; but when Friday came, what was his surprise at seeing the Benedictine table groaning under a load of meat. Upon this he resolved to speak. "The church and the pope," said he, "forbid such things."

The Benedictines were irritated at this reprimand by the unpolished German. But Luther having persisted, and perhaps threatened to make their irregularities known, some thought the simplest course would be to get rid of their importunate guest. The porter of the convent forewarned him of the danger he incurred by a longer stay. He accordingly quitted this epicurean monastery and reached Bologna, where he fell dangerously ill. Some have attributed this to the effects of poison; but it is more reasonable to suppose that the change of diet affected the frugal monk of Wittenberg, whose usual food was bread and herrings.

He again relapsed into the sorrow and dejection so natural to him. To die thus, far from Germany, under this burning sky, and in a foreign land—what a sad fate. The sense of his sinfulness troubled him; the prospect of God's judgment filled him with dread. But at the very moment that these terrors had reached their highest pitch, the words of St. Paul that had already struck him at Wittenberg, "The just shall live by faith," recurred forcibly to his memory and enlightened his soul like a ray from heaven. Thus restored and comforted, he soon regained his health and resumed his journey toward Rome.

At length, after a toilsome journey under a burning Italian sun, at the beginning of summer, he drew near the seven-hilled city. His heart was moved within him: his eyes sought after the queen of the world and of the church. As soon as he discovered the eternal city in the distance, the city of St. Peter and St. Paul, the metropolis of Catholicism, he fell on his knees, exclaiming, "Holy Rome, I salute thee!"

Luther was in Rome: the Wittenberg professor stood in the midst of the eloquent ruins of consular and imperial Rome, of the Rome of so many martyrs and confessors of Jesus Christ. Here had lived all those great men at whose history his heart had so often beat with emotion. He beheld their statues, the ruins of the monuments that bore witness to their glory. But all that glory, all that power had fled; his feet trampled on their dust. At each step he called to mind the sad presentiments of Scipio shedding tears as he looked upon the ruins, the burning palaces, and tottering walls of Carthage, and exclaimed, "Thus will it one day be with Rome!" "And in truth," said Luther, "the Rome of the Scipios and Caesars has become a corpse. There are such heaps of rubbish that the foundations of the houses are now where once stood the roofs."

But with these profane ashes are mingled other and holier ones: he recalled them to mind. The burial place of the martyrs was not far from that of the generals of Rome and of her conquerors. Christian Rome with its sufferings had more power over the heart of the Saxon monk than pagan Rome with all its glory. Here that letter arrived in which Paul wrote, "The just shall live by faith." Luther was not far from Appii Forum and the three Taverns. Here was the house of Narcissus; there the palace of Caesar, where the Lord delivered the apostle from the jaws of the lion (II Tim. 4:17).

But Rome at this time presented a very different aspect. The warlike Julius II filled the papal chair. Luther often related a trait in the character of this pope. When the news reached him that his army had been defeated by the French before Ravenna, he was repeating his daily prayers. He flung away the book, exclaiming with a terrible oath, "And Thou too art become a Frenchman. . . . Is it thus Thou dost protect Thy church?" Then turning in the direction of the country to whose arms he thought to have recourse, he added, "Saint Switzer, pray for us." Ignorance, levity, and dissolute manners, a profane spirit, a contempt for all that is sacred, a scandalous traffic in divine things—such was the spectacle afforded by this unhappy city. Yet the pious monk remained for some time longer in his delusions.

Fervent and meek, he visited all the churches and chapels; he believed in all the falsehoods that were told him; he devoutly performed all the holy practices that were required there, happy in being able to execute so many good works from which his fellow-countrymen were debarred. "Oh, how I regret," said the pious German to himself, "that my father and mother are still alive. What pleasure I should have in delivering them from the fire of purgatory by my masses, my prayers, and by so many other admirable works!" He had found the light, but the darkness was far from being entirely expelled from his understanding. His heart was converted; his mind was not yet enlightened: he had faith and love, but he wanted knowledge. It was no trifling matter to emerge from that thick night which had covered the earth for so many centuries.

Luther several times repeated mass at Rome. He officiated with all the unction and dignity that such an action appeared to him to require. But what affliction seized the heart of the Saxon monk at witnessing the sad and profane mechanicalness of the Roman priests as they celebrated the sacrament of the altar. These, on their part, laughed at his simplicity. One day when he was officiating, he found that the priests at an adjoining altar had already repeated seven masses before he had finished one. "Quick, quick," cried one of them, "send our Lady back her Son," making an impious allusion to the transubstantiation of the bread into the body and blood of Jesus Christ. At another time Luther had only just reached the gospel, when the priest at his side had already terminated the mass. "*Passa, passa!*" cried the latter to him, "make haste; have done with it at once!"

His astonishment was still greater when he found in the dignitaries of the papacy what he had already observed in the inferior clergy. It was the fashion at the papal court to attack Christianity, and you could not pass for a well-bred man unless you entertained some erroneous or heretical opinion on the doctrines of the church. They had endeavored to convince Erasmus, by means of certain extracts from Pliny, that there was no difference between the souls of men and of beasts; and some of the pope's youthful courtiers maintained that the orthodox faith was the result of the crafty devices of a few saints.

Luther's quality of envoy from the German Augustinians procured him invitations to numerous meetings of distinguished ecclesiastics. One day, in particular, he was at table with several prelates, who displayed openly before him their buffoonery and impious conversation and did not scruple to utter in his presence a thousand mockeries, thinking no doubt that he was of the same mind as themselves. Among other things, they related before the monk, laughing and priding themselves upon it, how, when they were repeating mass at the altar, instead of the sacramental words that were to transform the bread and wine into the flesh and blood of our Savior, they pronounced over the elements this derisive expression: *Panis es, et panis manebis; vinum es et vinum manebis.* ("Bread thou art, and bread thou shalt remain; wine thou art, and wine thou shalt remain.") Then, continued they, we elevate the host, and all the people bow down and worship it.

Luther could hardly believe his ears. His disposition, although full of animation and even gaiety in the society of friends, was remarkably serious whenever sacred matters were concerned. The mockeries of Rome were a stumbling block to him. "I was," said he, "a thoughtful and pious young monk. Such language grieved me bitterly. If 'tis thus they speak at Rome, freely and publicly at the dinner table, thought I to myself, what would it be if their actions corresponded to their words; and if all, pope, cardinals, and courtiers, thus repeat the mass! And how they must have deceived me who have heard them read devoutly so great a number."

Luther often mixed with the monks and citizens of Rome. If some few extolled the pope and his party, the majority gave a free course to their complaints and to their sarcasms. What stories had they not to tell about the reigning pope, or Alexander VI, or about so many others! One day his Roman friends related how Caesar Borgia, Alexander's oldest son, having fled from Rome, was taken in Spain. As they were going to try him, he called for mercy and asked for a confessor to visit him in his prison. A monk was sent to him, whom he slew, put on his hood, and escaped. "I heard that at Rome; and it is a positive fact," says Luther.

The disorders without the churches were not less shocking to him. "The police of Rome is very strict and severe," said he. "The judge or captain patrols the city every night on horseback with three hundred followers; he arrests every one that is found in the streets: if they meet an armed man, he is hung or thrown into the Tiber. And yet the city is filled with disorder and murder; while in those places where the Word of God is preached uprightly and in purity, peace and order prevail, without calling for the severity of the law." "No one can imagine what sins and infamous actions are committed in Rome," said he at another time; "they must be seen and heard to be believed. Thus, they are in the habit of saying, If there is a hell, Rome is built over it: it is an abyss whence issues every kind of sin."

This spectacle made a deep impression even then upon Luther's mind; it was increased ere long. "The nearer we approach Rome, the greater number of bad Christians we meet with," said he, many years after. Machiavelli, one of the most profound geniuses of Italy, but also one of unenviable notoriety, who was living at Florence when Luther passed through that city on his way to Rome, has made the same remark: "The strongest symptoms," said he, "of the approaching ruin of Christianity"—by which he means Roman Catholicism—"is, that the nearer people approach the capital of Christendom, the less Christian spirit is found in them. The scandalous examples and the crimes of the court of Rome are the cause why Italy has lost every principle of piety and all religious feeling. We Italians are indebted principally to the church and priests for having become impious and immoral." Luther, somewhat later, was sensible of the very great importance of this journey. "If they would give me one hundred thousand florins," said he, "I would not have missed seeing Rome."

This visit was also very advantageous to him in regard to learning. Luther took advantage of his residence in Italy to penetrate deeper into the meaning of the Holy Scriptures. He took lessons in Hebrew from a celebrated rabbi named Elias Levita. It was at Rome that he partly acquired that knowledge of the Divine Word, under the attacks of which Rome was destined to fall.

But this journey was most important to Luther in another respect. We have seen how he at first gave himself up to all the vain observances which the church enjoined for the expiation of sin. One day, among others, wishing to obtain an indulgence promised by the pope to all who should ascend on their knees what is called Pilate's Staircase, the poor Saxon monk was humbly creeping up those steps, which he was told had been miraculously transported from Jerusalem to Rome. But while he was performing this meritorious act, he thought he heard a voice of thunder crying from the bottom of his heart, as at Wittenberg and Bologna, "The just shall live by faith." These words, that twice before had struck him like the voice of an angel from God, resounded unceasingly and powerfully within him. He rose in amazement from the steps up which he was dragging his body: he shuddered at himself; he was ashamed of seeing to what a depth superstition had plunged him. He flew far from the scene of his folly.

This powerful text had a mysterious influence on the life of Luther. We should here listen to what Luther himself says on the matter. "Although I was a holy and blameless monk, my conscience was nevertheless full of trouble and anguish. I could not endure those words, 'The righteousness of God.' I had no love for that holy and just God who punishes sinners. I was filled with secret anger against Him: I hated Him, because, not content with frightening by the law and the miseries of life us wretched sinners, already ruined by original sin, He still further increased our tortures by the gospel.

"But when, by the Spirit of God, I understood these words, when I learned how the justification of the sinner proceeds from the free mercy of our Lord through faith, then I felt born again like a new man; I entered through the open doors into the very paradise of God. Henceforward, also, I saw the beloved and Holy Scriptures with other eyes. I perused the Bible; I brought together a great number of passages that taught me the nature of God's work. And as previously I had detested with all my heart these words, 'The righteousness of God,' I began from that hour to value them and to love them as the sweetest and most consoling words in the Bible. In very truth, this language of St. Paul was to me the true gate of paradise."

It was thus Luther found what had been overlooked, at least to a certain degree, by all doctors and reformers, even by the most illustrious of them. It was in Rome that God gave this clear view of the fundamental doctrine of Christianity. He had gone to the city of the pontiffs for the solution of certain difficulties concerning a monastic order; he brought away from it in his heart the reformation of the church.

Chapter 7
Doctor of the Holy Scriptures

Luther quitted Rome and returned to Wittenberg: his heart was full of sorrow and indignation. Turning his eyes with disgust from the pontifical city, he directed them with hope to the Holy Scriptures—to that new life which the Word of God seemed then to promise to the world. This Word increased in his heart by all that the church lost. He separated from the one to cling to the other. The whole of the Reformation was in that one movement. It set God in the place of the priest.

Staupitz and the elector did not lose sight of the monk whom they had called to the University of Wittenberg. It appears as if the vicar-general had a presentiment of the work that was to be done in the world, and that, finding it too difficult for himself, he wished to urge Luther toward it. There is nothing more remarkable, nothing perhaps more mysterious than this person, who is seen everywhere urging forward Luther in the path where God calls him, and then going to end his days sadly in a cloister. The preaching of the young professor had made a deep impression on the prince; he had admired the strength of his understanding, the forcibleness of his eloquence, and the excellency of the matters that he expounded. The elector and his friend, desirous of advancing a man of such great promise, resolved that he should take the high degree of Doctor of Divinity.

Staupitz repaired to the convent and took Luther into the garden, where, alone with him under a tree that Luther in afteryears delighted to point out to his disciples, the venerable father said to him, "My friend, you must now become doctor of the Holy Scriptures."

Luther shrunk at the very thought: this eminent honor startled him. "Seek a more worthy person," replied he. "As for me, I cannot consent to it."

The vicar-general persisted: "Our Lord God has much to do in the church: He has need at this time of young and vigorous doctors."

"But I am weak and sickly," replied Luther. "I have not long to live. Look out for some strong man."

"The Lord has work in heaven as well as on earth," replied the vicar-general; "dead or alive, He has need of you in His council."

"It is the Holy Ghost alone that can make a Doctor of Divinity," then urged the monk, still more alarmed.

"Do what your convent requires," said Staupitz, "and what I, your vicar-general, command; for you have promised to obey us."

"But my poverty," resumed the brother—"I have no means of defraying the expenses incidental to such a promotion."

"Do not be uneasy about that," replied his friend; "the prince has done you the favor to take all the charges upon himself." Pressed on every side, Luther thought it his duty to give way.

Andrew Bodenstein of the city of Carlstadt was at that time dean of the theological faculty, and it is by the name of Carlstadt that this doctor is generally known. He was also called "the A. B. C." Melancthon first gave him this designation on account of the three initials of his name. Carlstadt was of a serious and gloomy character, perhaps inclined to jealousy, and of a restless temper, but full of desire for knowledge, and of great capacity. He frequented several universities to augment his stores of learning, and studied theology at Rome. On his return from Italy, he settled at Wittenberg and became Doctor of Divinity. "At this time," he said afterwards, "I had not yet read the Holy Scriptures." This remark gives us a very correct idea of what theology then was.

Carlstadt, besides his functions of professor, was canon and archdeacon. Such was the man who in afteryears was destined to create a schism in the Reformation. At this time he saw in Luther only an inferior, but the Augustinian ere long became an object of jealousy to him. "I will not be less great than Luther," said he one day. Very far from anticipating at that period the great destinies of the young professor, Carlstadt conferred on his future rival the highest dignity of the university.

On October 18, 1512, Luther was received licentiate in divinity and took the following oath: "I swear to defend the evangelical truth with all my might." On the day following, Carlstadt solemnly conferred on him, in the presence of a numerous assembly, the insignia of Doctor of Divinity. He was made a biblical doctor and not a doctor of sentences; and was thus called to devote himself to the study of the Bible and not to that of human traditions. He then pledged himself by an oath to his well-beloved and holy Scriptures. He promised to preach them faithfully, to teach them with purity, to study them all his life, and to defend them, both in disputation and in writing, against all false teachers, so far as God should give him ability.

This solemn oath was Luther's call to the Reformation. By imposing on his conscience the holy obligation of searching freely and boldly proclaiming the Christian truth, this oath raised the new doctor above the narrow limits to which his monastic vow would perhaps have confined him. Called by the university, by his sovereign, in the name of the imperial majesty and of the see of Rome itself, and bound before God by the most solemn oath, he became from that hour the most intrepid herald of the Word of Life. On that memorable day Luther was armed champion of the Bible.

We may accordingly look upon this oath, sworn to the Holy Scriptures, as one of the causes of the revival of the church. The sole and infallible authority of the Word of God was the primary and fundamental principle of the Reformation. Every reform in detail that was afterwards carried out in the doctrine, morals, or government of the church, and in its worship, was but a consequence of this first principle. Ere long the courageous voices of all the reformers proclaimed this mighty principle, at the sound of which Rome shall crumble into dust: "Christians receive no other doctrines than those founded on the express words of Jesus Christ, of the apostles, and of the prophets. No man, no assembly of doctors, has a right to prescribe new ones."

Luther's position was changed. The summons that he had received became to the reformer as one of those extraordinary calls which the Lord addressed to the prophets under the old covenant and to the apostles under the new. The solemn engagement that he made produced so deep an impression upon his soul that the recollection of this oath was sufficient, in afteryears, to console him in the midst of the greatest dangers and of the fiercest conflicts. "I have gone forward in the Lord's name," said he in a critical moment, "and I have placed myself in His hands. His will be done. Who prayed Him to make me a doctor? . . . If it was He who created me such, let Him support me; or else, if He repent of what He has done, let Him deprive me of my office. This tribulation therefore alarms me not. I seek one thing only, which is to preserve the favor of God in all that He has called me to do with Him." At another time he said, "He who undertakes anything without a divine call seeks his own glory. But I, Doctor Martin Luther, was forced to become a doctor. Popery desired to stop me in the performance of my duty; but you see what has happened to it, and worse still will befall it. They cannot defend themselves against me. I am determined, in God's name, to tread upon the lions, to trample dragons and serpents under foot. This will begin during my life, and will be accomplished after my death."

From the period of his oath, Luther no longer sought the truth for himself alone: he sought it also for the church. This was the third epoch of his development. His entrance into the cloister had turned his thoughts toward God; the knowledge of the remission of sins, and of the righteousness of faith, had emancipated his soul; his doctor's oath gave him that baptism of fire by which he became a reformer of the church.

His ideas were soon directed in a general manner toward the Reformation. In an address he declared that the corruption of the world originated in the priests' teaching so many fables and traditions, instead of preaching the pure Word of God. The Word of Life, in his view, alone had the power of effecting the spiritual regeneration of man. Thus then already he made the salvation of the world depend upon the reestablishment of sound doctrine, and not upon a mere reformation of manners. Yet Luther was not entirely consistent with himself; he still entertained contradictory opinions, but a spirit of power beamed from all his writings; he courageously broke the bonds with which the systems of the schools had fettered the thoughts of men; he everywhere passed beyond the limits within which previous ages had so closely confined him and opened up new paths. God was with him.

The first adversaries that he attacked were those famous schoolmen, whom he had himself so much studied and who then reigned supreme in all the academies. He accused them of Pelagianism; and forcibly inveighing against Aristotle, the father of the schools, and against Thomas Aquinas, he undertook to hurl them both from the throne whence they governed: the one philosophy and the other theology.

"Aristotle, Porphyry, the sententiary divines"—the schoolmen—he wrote to Lange, "are useless studies in our days. I desire nothing more earnestly than to unveil to the world that comedian who has deceived the church by assuming a Greek mask and to show his deformity to all." In every public discussion he was heard repeating, "The writings of the apostles and prophets are surer and more sublime than all the sophisms and all the divinity of the schools." Such language was new, but men gradually became used to it. About a year after, he was able to write with exultation, "God is at work. Our theology and St. Augustine advance admirably, and prevail in our university. Aristotle is declining; he is tottering toward his eternal ruin that is near at hand. The lectures on *The Sentences* produce nothing but weariness. No one can hope for hearers, unless he professes the biblical theology."

There was at that time at the elector's court a person remarkable for his wisdom and his candor: this was George Spalatin. He was born at Spalatus or Spalt in the bishopric of Eichstadt and had been originally curate of the village of Hogenkirch, near the Thuringian forests. He was afterwards chosen by Frederick the Wise to be his secretary, chaplain, and tutor to his nephew John Frederick, who was one day to wear the electoral crown.

Spalatin was a simple-hearted man in the midst of the court: he appeared timid in the presence of great events, circumspect and prudent, like his master, before the ardent Luther, with whom he corresponded daily. Like Staupitz, he was better suited for peaceful times. Spalatin was not a man to effect great undertakings, but he faithfully and noiselessly performed the task imposed upon him. He was at first one of the principal aids of his master in collecting those relics of saints, of which Frederick was so long a great admirer. But he, as well as the prince, turned by degrees toward the truth. The faith, which then reappeared in the church, did not lay such violent hold upon him as upon Luther: it guided him by slower methods. He became Luther's friend at court; the minister through whom passed all matters between the reformer and the princes; the mediator between the church and the state.

All Luther's hearers listened with admiration as he spoke, whether from the professor's chair or from the pulpit, of that faith in Jesus Christ. His teaching diffused great light. Men were astonished that they had not earlier acknowledged truths that appeared so evident in his mouth. "The desire of self-justification," said he, "is the cause of all the distresses of the heart. But he who receives Jesus Christ as a Savior, enjoys peace; and not only peace, but purity of heart. All sanctification of the heart is a fruit of faith. For faith is a divine work in us, which changes us and gives us a new birth, emanating from God Himself. It kills the old Adam in us; and by the Holy Ghost which is communicated to us, it gives us a new heart and makes us new men. It is not by empty speculations," he again exclaimed, "but by this practical method, that we can obtain a saving knowledge of Jesus Christ."

It was at this time that Luther preached those discourses on the ten commandments that have come down to us under the title of "Popular Declamations." They contain errors no doubt; Luther became enlightened only by degrees. "The path of the just is as the shining light, that shineth more and more unto the perfect day" (Prov. 4:18). But what truth, simplicity, and eloquence are found in these discourses. How well can we understand the effect that the new preacher must have produced upon his audience and upon his age. We will quote but one passage taken from the beginning.

Luther ascended the pulpit of Wittenberg, and read these words: "Thou shalt have no other gods before me" (Exod. 20:3). Then turning to the people who crowded the sanctuary, he said, "All the sons of Adam are idolaters and have sinned against this first commandment."

Doubtless this strange assertion startled his hearers. He proceeded to justify it: "There are two kinds of idolatry: one external, the other internal.

"The external, in which man bows down to wood and stone, to beasts, and to the heavenly host.

"The internal, in which man, fearful of punishment, or seeking his own pleasure, does not worship the creature, but loves him in his heart, and trusts in him.

"What kind of religion is this? You do not bend the knee before riches and honors, but you offer them your heart, the noblest portion of yourselves. . . . Alas, you worship God in body, but the creature in spirit.

"This idolatry prevails in every man until he is healed by the free gift of the faith that is in Christ Jesus.

"And how shall this cure be accomplished?

"Listen. Faith in Christ takes away from you all trust in your own wisdom, righteousness, and strength; it teaches you that if Christ had not died for you, and had not thus saved you, neither you nor any other creature would have been able to do it. Then you learn to despise all those things that are unavailing to you.

"Nothing now remains to you but Jesus Christ, Christ alone, Christ all-sufficient for your soul. Hoping for nothing from any creature, you have only Christ, from whom you hope for everything, and whom you love above everything.

"Now Christ is the one sole and true God. When you have Him for your God, you have no other gods."

But it was particularly in his lecture room, before an enlightened and youthful audience, hungering for the truth, that he displayed all the treasures of God's Word. "He explained Scripture in such a manner," says his illustrious friend Melancthon, "that, in the judgment of all pious and well-informed men, it was as if a new morn had risen upon the doctrine, after a long night of darkness. He showed the difference that existed between the law and the gospel. He refuted the then-prevalent error of the churches and of the schools that men by their works merit the remission of sins and become righteous before God by an outward discipline. He thus led men's hearts back to the Son of God. Like John the Baptist, he pointed to the Lamb of God that has taken away the sins of the world; he explained how sin is freely pardoned on account of the Son of God, and that man receives this blessing through faith.

"He made no change in the ceremonies. On the contrary, the established discipline had not in his order a more faithful observer and defender. But he endeavored more and more to make all understand these grand and essential doctrines of conversion, of the remission of sins, of faith, and of the true consolation that is to be found in the cross. Pious minds were struck and penetrated by the sweetness of this doctrine; the learned received it with joy. One might have said that Christ, the apostles, and the prophets were now issuing from the obscurity of some impure dungeon."

The firmness with which Luther relied on the Holy Scriptures imparted great authority to his teaching. But other circumstances added still more to his strength. In him every action of his life corresponded with his words. It was known that these discourses did not proceed merely from his lips: they had their source in his heart and were practiced in all his works. And when, somewhat later, the Reformation burst forth, many influential men, who saw with regret these divisions in the church, won over beforehand by the holiness of the reformer's life and by the beauty of his genius, not only did not oppose him, but further still, embraced that doctrine to which he gave testimony by his works. The more men loved Christian virtues, the more they inclined to the reformer. All honest divines were in his favor. This is what was said by those who knew him, and particularly by the wisest man of his age, Melancthon, and by Erasmus, the illustrious opponent of Luther. Envy and prejudice have dared to speak of his disorderly life. Wittenberg was changed by this preaching of faith, and that city became the focus of a light that was soon to illumine all Germany and to shine on all the church.

Chapter 8

"Learn to Know Christ and Him Crucified"

Luther took advantage of every opportunity that occurred, as professor, preacher, or monk, and also of his extensive correspondence, to communicate his treasure to others. One of his former brethren in the convent of Erfurt, the monk George Spenlein, was then residing in the convent of Memmingen, perhaps after having spent a short time at Wittenberg.

"I should be very glad to know," wrote he to friar George, "what is the state of your soul. Is it not tired of its own righteousness? Does it not breathe freely at last, and does it not confide in the righteousness of Christ? In our days, pride seduces many, and especially those who labor with all their might to become righteous. Not understanding the righteousness of God that is given to us freely in Christ Jesus, they wish to stand before Him on their own merits. But that cannot be. When you were living with me, you were in that error, and so was I. I am yet struggling unceasingly against it, and I have not yet entirely triumphed over it.

"Oh, my dear brother, learn to know Christ and Him crucified. Learn to sing unto Him a new song, to despair of yourself, and to say to Him, 'Thou, Lord Jesus Christ, art my righteousness, and I am Thy sin. Thou hast taken what was mine and hast given me what was Thine. What Thou wast not, Thou didst become, in order that I might become what I was not.' Beware, my dear George, of pretending to such purity as no longer to confess yourself a sinner; for Christ dwells only with sinners. He came down from heaven, where He was living among the righteous, in order to live also among sinners. Meditate carefully upon this love of Christ, and you will taste all its unspeakable consolation. If our labors and afflictions could give peace to the conscience, why should Christ have died? You will not find peace, save in Him, by despairing of yourself and of your works and in learning with what love He opens His arms to you, taking all your sins upon Himself and giving thee all His righteousness."

Spenlein was not the only man whom he sought to instruct in this fundamental doctrine. The little truth that he found in this respect in the writings of Erasmus made him uneasy. It was of great importance to enlighten a man whose authority was so great and whose genius was so admirable. But how was he to do it? His court friend, Spalatin, the elector's chaplain, was much respected by Erasmus: it was to him that Luther applied. "What displeases me in Erasmus, who is a man of such extensive learning, is, my dear Spalatin," wrote Luther, "that by the righteousness of works and of the law, of which the apostle speaks, he understands the fulfilling of the ceremonial law. The righteousness of the law consists not only in ceremonies, but in all the works of the Decalogue. Even if these works should be accomplished without faith in Christ, they may, it is true, produce a Fabricius, a Regulus, and other men perfectly upright in the eyes of the world; but they then deserve as little to be styled *righteousness* as the fruit of the medlar to be called a fig. For we do not become righteous, as Aristotle maintains, by performing righteous works; but when we are become righteous, then we perform such works. The man must first be changed, and afterwards the works. Abel was first accepted by God, and then his sacrifice." Luther continues: "Fulfill, I beseech you, the duty of a friend and of a Christian by communicating these matters to Erasmus."

"I am reading Erasmus," says Luther on another occasion, "but he daily loses his credit with me. I like to see him rebuke with so much firmness and learning the grovelling ignorance of the priests and monks, but I fear that he does not render great service to the doctrine of Jesus Christ. What is of man is dearer to him than what is of God. We are living in dangerous times. A man is not a good and judicious Christian because he understands Greek and Hebrew. Jerome, who knew five languages, is inferior to Augustine, who understood but one; although Erasmus thinks the contrary. I very carefully conceal my opinions concerning Erasmus, through fear of giving advantage to his adversaries. Perhaps the Lord will give him understanding in His time."

The helplessness of man and the omnipotence of God were the two truths that Luther desired to reestablish. That truly is a great

Erasmus of Rotterdam, an engraving by Albrecht Dürer. A brilliant scholar and pointed critic of corruption within the Roman Catholic church, Erasmus also helped lay the basis for the Reformation by publishing the New Testament in its original Greek. A proverb of the times was "Luther hatched the egg that Erasmus laid." But when it became apparent that Luther's actions would split the church, Erasmus turned against the German reformer.

reformation which vindicates on earth the glory of heaven and which pleads before man the rights of the Almighty God. No one knew better than Luther the intimate and indissoluble bond that unites the gratuitous salvation of God with the free works of man. No one showed more plainly than he that it is only by receiving all from Christ that man can impart much to his brethren. He always represented these two actions, that of God and that of man, in the same picture. And thus it is that, after explaining to the friar Spenlein what is meant by saving righteousness, he adds, "If thou firmly believest those things, as is thy duty—for cursed is he who does not believe them—receive thy brethren who are still ignorant and in error, as Jesus Christ has received thee. Bear with them patiently. Make their sins thine own; and if thou hast any good thing, impart it to them. 'Receive ye one another,' says the apostle, 'as Christ also received us, to the glory of God' (Rom. 15:7).

"It is a deplorable righteousness that cannot bear with others because it finds them wicked, and which thinks only of seeking the solitude of the desert, instead of doing them good by long-suffering, prayer, and example. If thou art the lily and the rose of Christ, know that thy dwelling place is among thorns. Only take care lest, by thy impatience, by thy rash judgments, and thy secret pride, thou dost thyself become a thorn. Christ reigns in the midst of His enemies. If He had desired to live only among the good, and to die for those only who loved Him, for whom, I pray, would He have died, and among whom would He have lived?"

It is affecting to see how Luther practiced these charitable precepts. An Augustinian monk of Erfurt, George Leiffer, was exposed to many trials. Luther became informed of this, and within a week after writing the preceding letter to Spenlein, he came to him with words of comfort. "I learn that you are agitated by many tempests and that your soul is tossed to and fro by the waves. The cross of Christ is divided among all the world, and each man has his share. You should not therefore reject that which has fallen to you. Receive it rather as a holy relic, not in a vessel of silver or of gold, but in what is far better, in a heart of gold, in a heart full of meekness. If the wood of the cross has been so sanctified by the body and blood of Christ that we consider it as the most venerable relic, how much more should the wrongs, persecutions, sufferings, and hatred of men be holy relics unto us, since they have not only been touched by Christ's flesh, but have been embraced, kissed, and blessed by His infinite charity."

The hour drew nigh in which the Reformation was to burst forth. God hastened to prepare the instrument that He had determined to employ. The elector, having built a new church at Wittenberg, to which he gave the name of All Saints, sent Staupitz in the Low Countries to collect relics for the ornament of the new edifice. The vicar-general commissioned Luther to replace him during his absence, and in particular to make a visitation of the forty monasteries of Misnia and Thuringia.

Luther repaired first to Grimma, and thence to Dresden. Everywhere he endeavored to establish the truths that he had discovered, and to enlighten the members of his order. "Do not bind yourselves to Aristotle or to any other teacher of a deceitful philosophy," said he to the monks, "but read the Word of God with diligence. Do not look for salvation in your own strength or in your good works, but in the merits of Christ and in God's grace."

An Augustinian monk of Dresden had fled from his convent and was at Mentz, where the prior of the Augustinians had received him. Luther wrote to the latter, begging him to send back the stray sheep, and added these words so full of charity and truth: "I know that offenses must needs come. It is no marvel that man falls, but it is so that he rises again and stands upright. Peter fell that he might know he was but a man. Even in our days the cedars of Lebanon are seen to fall. The very angels—a thing that exceeds all imagination—have fallen in heaven, and Adam in paradise. Why then should we be surprised if a reed is shaken by the whirlwind, or if a smoking taper is extinguished?"

From Dresden Luther proceeded to Erfurt and reappeared to discharge the functions of vicar-general in that very convent where, eleven years before, he had wound up the clock, opened the gates, and swept out the church. He nominated to the priorship of the convent his friend John Lange, a learned and pious, but severe, man: he exhorted him to affability and patience. "Put on," wrote he to him shortly after, "a spirit of meekness toward the prior of Nuremberg; this is but proper, seeing that he has assumed a spirit of bitterness and harshness. Bitterness is not expelled by bitterness, that is to say, the Devil by the Devil; but sweetness dispels bitterness, that is to say, the finger of God casts out the evil spirit." We must perhaps regret that Luther did not on various occasions remember this excellent advice.

At Neustadt on the Orla there was nothing but disunion. Dissensions and quarrels reigned in the convent, and all the monks were at war with their prior. They assailed Luther with their complaints. The prior, Michael Dressel, laid all his troubles before the doctor. "Peace, peace," said he. "You seek peace," replied Luther, "but it is the peace of the world, and not the peace of Christ that you seek. Do you not know that our God has set His peace in the midst of war? He whom no one disturbs has not peace. But he who, troubled by all men and by the things of this life, bears all with tranquility and joy, he possesses the true peace. You say with Israel, Peace, peace; and there is no peace. Say rather with Christ, The cross, the cross; and there will be no cross. For the cross ceases to be a cross as soon as we can say with love, O blessed cross, there is no wood like thine!" On his return to Wittenberg, Luther, desiring to put an end to these dissensions, permitted the monks to elect another prior.

Luther returned to Wittenberg after an absence of six weeks. He was afflicted at all that he had seen, but the journey gave him a better knowledge of the church and of the world, increased his confidence in his intercourse with society, and afforded him many opportunities of founding schools, of pressing this fundamental truth, that "Holy Scripture alone shows us the way to heaven," and of exhorting the brethren to live together in holiness, chastity, and peace.

There is no doubt that much good seed was sown in the different Augustinian convents during this journey of the reformer. The monastic orders, which had long been the support of Rome, did perhaps more for the Reformation than against it. This is true in particular of the Augustinians. Almost all the pious men of liberal and elevated mind who were living in the cloisters turned toward the gospel. A new and generous blood ere long circulated through these orders, which were, so to speak, the arteries of the German church. As yet nothing was known in the world of the new ideas of the Wittenberg Augustinian, while they were already the chief topic of conversation in the chapters and monasteries. Many a cloister thus became a nursery of reformers. As soon as the great struggle took place, pious and able men issued from their obscurity, and abandoned the seclusion of a monastic life for the active career of ministers of God's Word. At the period of this inspection of 1516, Luther awakened many drowsy souls by his words. Hence this year has been named "the morning star of the gospel day."

Luther resumed his usual occupation. He was at this period overwhelmed with labor: it was not enough that he was professor, preacher, and confessor; he was burdened still further by many temporal occupations having reference to his order and his convent. "I have need almost continually," writes he, "of two secretaries; for I do nothing else all the day long but write letters. I am preacher to the convent, I read the prayers at table, I am pastor and parish minister, director of studies, the prior's vicar—that is to say, prior eleven times over—inspector of the fish-ponds at Litzkau, counsel to the inns of Herzberg at Torgau, lecturer on St. Paul, and commentator on the Psalms. I have rarely time to repeat the daily prayers and to sing a hymn; without speaking of my struggles with flesh and blood, with the Devil and the world. Learn from this what an idle man I am."

About this time the plague broke out in Wittenberg. A great number of the students and teachers quitted the city. Luther remained. "I am not certain," wrote he to his friend at Erfurt, "if the plague will let me finish the Epistle to the Galatians. Its attacks are sudden and violent: it is making great ravages among the young in particular. You advise me to fly. Whither shall I fly? I hope that the world will not come to an end if brother Martin dies. If the pestilence spreads, I shall disperse the brothers in every direction; but as for me, my place is here; duty does not permit me to desert my post, until He who has called me shall summon me away. Not that I have no fear of death, for I am not Paul, I am only his commentator; but I hope the Lord will deliver me from fear."

Chapter 9
Luther Before the Nobility

Luther displayed the same courage before the mighty of this world that he had shown amidst the most formidable evils. The elector was much pleased with Staupitz, the vicar-general, who had made a rich harvest of relics in the Low Countries. Luther gives an account of them to Spalatin; and this affair of the relics, occurring at the very moment when the Reformation is about to begin, is a singular circumstance. Most certainly the reformers had little idea to what point they were tending. A bishopric appeared to the elector the only recompense worthy the services of the vicar-general.

Luther, to whom Spalatin wrote on the subject, strongly disapproved of such an idea. "There are many things which please your prince," replied he, "and which, nevertheless, are displeasing to God. I do not deny that he is skillful in the matters of this world, but in what concerns God and the salvation of souls, I account him, as well as his councilor Pfeffinger, sevenfold blind. I do not say this behind their backs, like a slanderer; do not conceal it from them, for I am ready myself and on all occasions to tell it them both to their faces. Why would you," continues he, "surround this man [Staupitz] with all the whirlwinds and tempests of episcopal cares?"

The elector was not offended with Luther's frankness. "The prince," wrote Spalatin, "often speaks of you, and in honorable terms." Frederick sent the monk some very fine cloth for a gown. "It would be too fine," said Luther, "if it were not a prince's gift. I am not worthy that any man should think of me, much less a prince, and so great a prince as he. Those are my best friends who think the worst of me. Thank our prince for his kindness to me; but I cannot allow myself to be praised either by you or by any man; for all praise of man is vain, and only that which comes from God is true."

The excellent chaplain was unwilling to confine himself to his court functions. He wished to make himself useful to the people; but like many individuals in every age, he desired to do it without offense and without irritation, by conciliating the general favor. "Point out," wrote he to Luther, "some work that I may translate into our mother tongue; one that shall give general satisfaction, and at the same time be useful."

"Agreeable and useful!" replied Luther. "Such a question is beyond my ability. The better things are, the less they please. What is more salutary than Jesus Christ? And yet He is to the majority a savor of death. You will tell me that you wish to be useful only to those who love what is good. In that case make them hear the voice of Jesus Christ: you will be useful and agreeable, depend upon it, to a very small number only; for the sheep are rare in this region of wolves."

It was in the course of the year 1517 that Luther entered into communication with Duke George of Saxony. The house of Saxony had at that time two chiefs. Two princes, Ernest and Albert, carried off in their youth from the castle of Altenburg by Kunz of Kaufungen, had, by the treaty of Leipzig, become the founders of two houses. The Elector Frederick, son of Ernest, was, at the period we are describing, the head of the Ernestine branch; and his cousin Duke George, of the Albertine. Dresden and Leipzig were both situated in the states of this duke, whose residence was in the former of these cities. His mother, Sidonia, was daughter of George Podiebrad, king of Bohemia. The long struggle that Bohemia had maintained with Rome, since the time of John Huss, had not been without influence on the prince of Saxony. He had often manifested a desire for a reformation. "He has imbibed it with his mother's milk," said the priests; "he is by birth an enemy of the clergy." He annoyed the bishops, abbots, canons, and monks in many ways; and his cousin the Elector Frederick was compelled more than once to interfere in their behalf.

It seemed that Duke George would be one of the warmest partisans of a reformation. The devout Frederick, on the other hand, who had in former years worn the spurs of Godfrey in the holy sepulcher, and girding himself with the long and heavy sword of the conqueror of Jerusalem, had made oath to fight for the church, like that ancient and valiant knight, appeared destined to be the most ardent champion of Rome. But in all that concerns the gospel, the anticipations of human wisdom are frequently disappointed. The reverse of what we might have supposed took place. The duke would have been delighted to humiliate the church and the clergy, to humble the bishops, whose princely retinue far surpassed his own; but it was another thing to receive into his heart the evangelical doctrine that would humble it, to acknowledge himself a guilty sinner, incapable of being saved, except by grace alone. He would willingly have reformed others, but he cared not to reform himself. He would perhaps have set his hand to the task of compelling the bishop of Mentz to be contented with a single bishopric and to keep no more than fourteen horses in his stables, as he said more than once; but when he saw another than himself step forward as a reformer, when he beheld a simple monk undertake this work, and the Reformation gaining numerous partisans among the people, the haughty grandson of the Hussite king became the most violent adversary of the reform to which he had before shown himself favorable.

In the month of July 1517, Duke George requested Staupitz to send him an eloquent and learned preacher. Luther was recommended to him as a man of extensive learning and irreproachable conduct. The prince invited him to preach at Dresden in the castle chapel, on the feast of St. James the elder.

The day arrived. The duke and his court repaired to the chapel to hear the Wittenberg preacher. Luther joyfully seized this opportunity of testifying to the truth before such an assemblage. He selected his text from the gospel of the day: "Then came to him the mother of Zebedee's children with her sons," etc. (Matt. 20:20-23). He preached on the unreasonable desires and prayers of men, and then spoke emphatically on the assurance of salvation. He established it on this foundation, that those who receive the Word of God with faith are the true disciples of Jesus Christ, elected to eternal life. He next treated of gratuitous election and showed that this doctrine, if presented in union with the work of Christ, has great power to dispel the terrors of conscience, so that men, instead of flying far from the righteous God at the sight of their own unworthiness, are gently led to seek their refuge in Him. In conclusion, he related an allegory of three virgins, from which he deduced edifying instructions.

The Word of truth made a deep impression on his hearers. Two of them in particular seemed to pay very great attention to the sermon of the Wittenberg monk. The first was a lady of respectable appearance, who was seated on the court benches, and on whose features a profound emotion might be traced. It was Madame de la Sale, first lady to the duchess. The other was a licentiate in canon law, Jerome Emser, councilor and secretary to the duke. Emser possessed great talents and extensive information. A courtier and skillful politician, he would have desired to be on good terms with the two contending parties—to pass at Rome for a defender of the papacy and at the same time shine in Germany among the learned men of the age. But under this pliant mind was concealed a violent character. It was in the palace chapel at Dresden that Luther and Emser first met; they were afterwards to break more than one lance together.

The dinner hour arrived for the inhabitants of the palace, and in a short time the ducal family and the persons attached to the court were assembled at table. The conversation naturally fell on the preacher of the morning. "How were you pleased with the sermon?" said the duke to Madame de la Sale.

"If I could hear but one more like it," replied she, "I should die in peace."

"And I," replied George angrily, "would rather give a large sum not to have heard it; for such discourses are only calculated to make people sin with assurance."

The master having thus made known his opinion, the courtiers gave way uncontrolled to their dissatisfaction. Each one had his censure ready. Some maintained that in his allegory of the three virgins, Luther had in view three ladies of the court; on which there arose interminable babbling. They rallied the three ladies whom the monk of Wittenberg had thus, they said, publicly pointed out. He is an ignorant fellow, said some; he is a proud monk, said others. Each one made his comment on the sermon and put what he pleased in the preacher's mouth. The truth had fallen in the midst of a court that was little prepared to receive it. Everyone mangled it after his own fashion. But while the Word of God was thus an occasion of stumbling to many, it was for the first lady a stone of uprising. Falling sick a month after, she confidently embraced the grace of the Savior and died with joy.

As for the duke, it was not perhaps in vain that he heard this testimony to the truth. Whatever may have been his opposition to the Reformation during his life, we know that at his death he declared that he had no hope save in the merits of Jesus Christ.

Luther returned zealously to work. He was preparing six or seven young theologians who were shortly to undergo an examination for a license to teach. Free will was the great subject treated of. There had been, from the very commencement of Christianity, a struggle more or less keen between the two doctrines of man's liberty and his enslavement. Some schoolmen had taught, like Pelagius and other doctors, that man possessed of himself the liberty or the power of loving God and of performing good works. Luther denied this liberty, not to deprive man of it, but in order that he might obtain it. The struggle in this great question is not therefore, as is generally said, between liberty and slavery: it is between a liberty proceeding from man, and one that comes from God.

Those who style themselves the partisans of liberty say to man, "Thou hast the power of performing good works; thou hast no need of greater liberty." The others, who are called the partisans of servitude, say, on the contrary, "True liberty is what thou needest, and God offers it thee in His gospel." On the one side, they speak of liberty, to perpetuate slavery; on the other, they speak of slavery, to give liberty. Such was the contest in the times of St. Paul, of St. Augustine, and of Luther. Those who say, "Change nothing," are the champions of slavery; the others who say, "Let your fetters fall off," are the champions of liberty.

But we should deceive ourselves were we to sum up all the Reformation in that particular question. It is one of the numerous doctrines maintained by the Wittenberg doctor, and that is all. It would be indulging in a strange delusion to pretend that the Reformation was a fatalism, an opposition to liberty. It was a noble emancipation of the human mind. Snapping the numerous bonds with which the hierarchy had bound men's minds—restoring the ideas of liberty, of right, of free examination—it set free its own age, ourselves, and the remotest posterity. Let it not be said that the Reformation delivered man from every human despotism, but made him a slave by proclaiming the sovereignty of grace. It desired, no doubt, to lead back the human will, to confound it with and render it entirely subject to the divine will. But what kind of philosophy is that which does not know that an entire conformity with the will of God is the sole, supreme, and perfect liberty and that man will be really free, only when sovereign righteousness and eternal truth alone have dominion over him?

Luther protested not only against the pretended goodness of man's will but still more against the pretended light of his understanding in respect to divine things. In truth, scholasticism had exalted man's reason as well as his will. This theology, as some of its doctors have represented it, was at bottom nothing but a kind of rationalism. In the theses that were the signal of the Reformation, Luther censured the church and the popular superstitions which had added indulgences, purgatory, and so many other abuses to the gospel. But before that, he assailed the schools and rationalism, which had taken away from that very gospel the doctrine of the sovereignty of God, of His revelation, and of His grace. The Reformation attacked rationalism before it turned against superstition. It proclaimed the rights of God before it cut off the excrescences of man. It was positive before it became negative. This has not been sufficiently observed; and yet if we do not notice it, we cannot justly appreciate that religious revolution and its true nature.

But it was not on this field that the battle was to be fought. So long as Luther was content to revive forgotten doctrines, men were silent; but when he pointed out abuses that injured all the world, everybody listened.

And yet Luther had no idea of becoming a reformer. "Considering my ignorance," said he, "I deserve only to be hidden in some corner, without being known to any one under the sun." But a mighty hand drew him from this corner in which he would have desired to remain unknown to the world. A circumstance independent of Luther's will threw him into the field of battle, and the war began. It is this providential circumstance which the course of events now calls upon us to relate.

Chapter 10
Indulgences

A great agitation prevailed at that time among the German people. The church had opened a vast market upon earth. From the crowds of purchasers and the shouts and jokes of the sellers, it might have been called a fair, but a fair conducted by monks. The merchandise that they were extolling, and which they offered at a reduced price, was, said they, the salvation of souls.

These dealers traversed the country in a handsome carriage, accompanied by three horsemen, living in great state, and spending freely. One might have thought it some archbishop on a progress through his diocese, with his retinue and officers, and not a common chapman or a begging monk. When the procession approached a town, a deputy waited on the magistrate and said, "The grace of God and of the holy father is at your gates." Instantly everything was in motion in the place. The clergy, the priests and nuns, the council, the schoolmasters and their pupils, the trades with their banners, men and women, young and old, went out to meet these merchants, bearing lighted tapers in their hands, and advancing to the sound of music and of all the bells, "so that they could not have received God Himself with greater honor," says a historian.

The salutations being exchanged, the procession moved toward the church. The pontiff's bull of grace was carried in front on a velvet cushion, or on cloth of gold. The chief of the indulgence merchants came next, holding a large red wooden cross in his hand. All the procession thus moved along amid singing, prayers, and the smoke of incense. The sound of the organ and loud music welcomed the merchant-monk and his attendants into the temple. The cross that he had carried was placed in front of the altar; on it was suspended the coat of arms of the pope, and so long as it remained there, the clergy of the place, the penitentiaries, and the undercommissaries with white wands, came daily, after vespers, or before the salutation, to render it homage. This great affair excited a lively sensation in the quiet cities of Germany.

One person in particular attracted the attention of the spectators at these sales. It was he who carried the red cross, and who played the chief part. He was robed in the Dominican dress and moved with an air of arrogance. His voice was sonorous and seemed in its full strength, although he had already attained his sixty-third year. This man, the son of a Leipzig goldsmith named Diez, was known as John Diezel, or Tetzel. He had studied in his native city, had taken the degree of bachelor in 1487, and two years after had entered the Dominican order. Numerous honors had been heaped upon his head. Bachelor of Divinity, prior of the Dominicans, apostolic commissary, inquisitor—he had, from the year 1502, uninterruptedly filled the office of dealer in indulgences. The skill that he had acquired as subordinate had soon procured him the nomination as chief commissary. He received eighty florins a month; all his expenses were paid; a carriage and three horses were at his disposal; but his subsidiary profits, as may be easily imagined, far exceeded his stipend. In 1507 he gained at Freiburg two thousand florins in two days. It would have been difficult to find in all the convents of Germany a man better qualified than Tetzel for the business with which he was charged. To him all means were good that filled his chest. Raising his voice and displaying the eloquence of a mountebank, he offered his indulgences to all comers, and knew better than any tradesman how to extol his wares.

The pope who then sat in St. Peter's chair was Leo X of the illustrious family of the Medici. He was clever, sincere, full of gentleness and meekness. His manners were affable, his liberality unbounded, his morals superior to those of his court.

To this amiable character he united many of the qualities of a great prince. He was a friend of the arts and sciences. In his presence were represented the first Italian comedies, and there were few of his time that he had not seen performed. He was passionately fond of music; every day his palace reechoed with the sound of instruments, and he was frequently heard humming the airs that had been executed before him. He loved magnificence, he spared no expense in festivals, sports, theaters, presents, or rewards.

No court surpassed in splendor and in luxury that of the sovereign pontiff. But to religious feelings Leo was quite a stranger. "He possessed such charming manners," said Sarpi, "that he would have been a perfect man, if he had had some knowledge of religion and greater inclination to piety, about which he never troubled himself."

Leo required large sums of money. He had to provide for his great expenses, find means for his extensive liberality, fill the purse of gold which he flung daily among the people, keep up the licentious shows of the Vatican, satisfy the numerous calls of his relatives and of his courtiers, who were addicted to pleasures, endow his sister who had married Prince Cibo, natural son of Pope Innocent VIII, and defray the cost of his taste for literature, the arts, and luxury. His cousin, Cardinal Pucci, who was as skillful in the science of amassing as Leo in that of squandering money, advised him to have recourse to indulgences. The pope therefore published a bull, announcing a general indulgence, the produce of which should be applied, said he, to the building of St. Peter's, that monument of sacerdotal magnificence. In a letter given at Rome, under the seal of the Fisherman, in November 1517, Leo required of his commissary of indulgences 147 gold ducats, to purchase a manuscript of the thirty-third book of Livy. Of all the uses to which he applied the money of the Germans, this was undoubtedly the best. Yet it was a strange thing to deliver souls from purgatory to procure the means of purchasing a manuscript of the history of the Roman wars.

There was at that time in Germany a youthful prince who in many respects was the very image of Leo X: this was Albert, younger brother of the Elector Joachim of Brandenburg. This young man, at the age of twenty-four years, had been created archbishop and elector of Mentz and of Magdeburg; two years later he was made cardinal. Albert had neither the virtues nor the vices that are often met with in the superior dignitaries of the church. Young, frivolous, and worldly, but not without generous sentiments, he saw clearly many of the abuses of Roman Catholicism and cared little for the fanatical monks who surrounded him. His equity inclined him to acknowledge, in part at least, the justice of the demands of the friends of the gospel. At the bottom of his heart he was not violently opposed to Luther. Capito, one of the most distinguished reformers, was long his chaplain, his counsellor, and his intimate confidant. "He did not despise the gospel," said Capito; "on the contrary, he highly esteemed it and for a long time prevented the monks from attacking Luther." But he would have desired the latter not to compromise him, and that, while pointing out doctrinal errors and the vices of the inferior clergy, he should beware of exposing the failings of bishops and of princes. Above all, he feared to see his name mixed up in the matter.

Albert's profane and frivolous disposition, much more than the susceptibilities and fears of his self-love, was destined to alienate him from the Reformation. Affable, witty, handsome, sumptuous, extravagant, delighting in the luxuries of the table, in costly equipages, in magnificent buildings, in licentious pleasures, and in the society of literary men, this young archbishop-elector was in Germany what Leo X was in Rome. His court was one of the most magnificent in the empire. He was ready to sacrifice to pleasure and to greatness all the presentiments of truth that might have stolen into his heart. Nevertheless, even to the last, he evinced a certain resistance and better convictions; more than once he gave proofs of his moderation and of his equity.

Albert, like Leo, had need of money. Some rich merchants of Augsburg, named Fugger, had made him advances. He was called upon to pay his debts. Besides, although he had monopolized two archbishoprics and one bishopric, he had not the means of paying for his *pallium.* This ornament, made of white wool, besprinkled with black crosses, and blessed by the pope, who sent it to the archbishops as an emblem of their dignity, cost them 26,000, or according to some accounts, 30,000 florins. Albert very naturally formed the project of resorting to the same means as the pontiff to obtain money. He solicited the general farming of indulgences, or "of the sins of the Germans," as they said at Rome.

Sometimes the popes themselves worked them; at other times they farmed them, as some governments still farm gambling houses. Albert proposed sharing the profits of this business with Leo. The pope, in accepting the terms, exacted immediate payment of the price of the pallium. Albert, who was reckoning on the indulgences to meet this demand, again applied to the Fuggers, who thinking it a safe speculation, made the required advance on certain conditions, and were named treasurers of this undertaking. They were the royal bankers of this epoch; they were afterwards made counts for the services they had rendered.

The pope and the archbishop having thus divided beforehand the spoils of the good souls of Germany, it was next a question who should be commissioned to realize the investment. It was at first offered to the Franciscans, and their superior was associated with Albert. But these monks wished to have no share in it, for it was already in bad odor among all good people. The Augustinians, who were more enlightened than the other religious orders, cared still less about it. The Franciscans, however, feared to displease the pope, who had just sent a cardinal's hat to their general Forli, a hat that had cost this poor mendicant order 30,000 florins. The superior judged it more prudent not to refuse openly; but he made all kinds of objections to Albert. They could never come to an understanding; and accordingly the elector joyfully accepted the proposition to take the whole matter to himself.

The Dominicans, on their part, coveted a share in the general enterprise about to be set on foot. Tetzel, who had already acquired great reputation in this trade, hastened to Mentz, and offered his services to the elector. They called to mind the ability he had shown in publishing the indulgences for the knights of the Teutonic order of Prussia and Livonia: his proposals were accepted, and thus the whole traffic passed into the hands of his order.

Let us listen to one of the harangues Tetzel delivered after the elevation of the cross.

"Indulgences," said he, "are the most precious and the most noble of God's gifts.

"This cross"—pointing to the red cross—"has as much efficacy as the very cross of Jesus Christ.

"Come, and I will give you letters, all properly sealed, by which even the sins that you intend to commit may be pardoned.

"I would not change my privileges for those of St. Peter in heaven; for I have saved more souls by my indulgences than the apostle by his sermons.

"There is no sin so great that an indulgence cannot remit; and even if any one—which is doubtless impossible—had offered violence to the blessed Virgin Mary, mother of God, let him pay—only let him pay well, and all will be forgiven him.

"Reflect then, that for every mortal sin you must, after contrition and confession, do penance for seven years, either in this life or in purgatory: now, how many mortal sins are there not committed in a day, how many in a week, how many in a month, how many in a year, how many in a whole life! Alas, these sins are almost infinite, and they entail an infinite penalty in the fires of purgatory. And now, by means of these letters of indulgence, you can once in your life, in every case except four, which are reserved for the apostolic see, and afterwards in the article of death, obtain a plenary remission of all your penalties and all your sins."

Tetzel even entered into financial calculation. "Do you not know," said he, "that if any one desires to visit Rome, or any country where travelers incur danger, he sends his money to the bank, and for every hundred florins that he wishes to have, he gives five or six or ten more, that by means of the letters of this bank he may be safely repaid his money at Rome or elsewhere. And you, for a quarter of a florin, will not receive these letters of indulgence, by means of which you may introduce into paradise, not a vile metal, but a divine and immortal soul, without its running any risk.

"But more than this," said he, "indulgences avail not only for the living, but for the dead.

"For that, not even repentance is necessary.

"Priest, noble, merchant, wife, youth, maiden, do you not hear your parents and your other friends who are dead, and who cry from the bottom of the abyss, We are suffering horrible torments; a trifling alms would deliver us; you can give it, and you will not!

"At the very instant," continued Tetzel, "that the money rattles at the bottom of the chest, the soul escapes from purgatory and flies liberated to heaven.

"O stupid and brutish people, who do not understand the grace so richly offered! Now heaven is everywhere opened. Do you refuse to enter now? When, then, will you enter? Now you can ransom so many souls. Stiffnecked and thoughtless man, with twelve groats you can deliver your father from purgatory, and you are ungrateful enough not to save him. I shall be justified in the day of judgment; but you, you will be punished so much the more severely for having neglected so great salvation. I declare to you, though you should have but a single coat, you ought to strip it off and sell it, in order to obtain this grace. The Lord our God no longer reigns. He has resigned all power to the pope."

Then seeking to make use of other arms besides, he added, "Do you know why our most holy Lord distributes so rich a grace? It is to restore the ruined church of St. Peter and St. Paul, so that it may not have its equal in the world. This church contains the bodies of the holy apostles Peter and Paul, and those of a multitude of martyrs. These saintly bodies, through the present state of the building, are now, alas, beaten upon, inundated, polluted, dishonored, reduced to rottenness by the rain and the hail. Alas, shall these sacred ashes remain longer in the mire and in degradation?"

(This description failed not to produce an impression on many, who burned with a desire to come to the aid of poor Leo X, who had not the means of sheltering the bodies of St. Peter and St. Paul from the weather.)

Then addressing the docile souls and making an impious application of Scripture, he exclaimed, "Blessed are the eyes which see the things that ye see: for I tell you, that many prophets and kings have desired to see those things which ye see, and have not seen them; and to hear those things which ye hear, and have not heard them!" And in conclusion, pointing to the strongbox in which the

Facsimile of an indulgence issued by Pope Leo X and sold by Tetzel. In Catholic teaching, all Christians (except saints, who go directly to heaven) must spend a certain amount of time suffering in purgatory to pay for sins that were not purged in life. The church, however, can grant to a sinner an indulgence that trims time from the stay in purgatory in return for performing some good work. One way to earn an indulgence is to give a cash gift. This practice soon degenerated into "selling" indulgences.

money was received, he generally finished his pathetic discourse by three appeals to his auditory: "Bring, bring, bring!" "He used to shout these words with such a horrible bellowing," wrote Luther, "that one would have said it was a mad bull rushing on the people and goring them with his horns." When his speech was ended, he left the pulpit, ran toward the money-box, and in sight of all the people flung into it a piece of money, taking care that it should rattle loudly.

The speech being concluded, the indulgence was considered as "having established its throne in the place with due solemnity." Confessionals decorated with the pope's arms were ranged about: the undercommissaries and the confessors whom they selected were considered the representatives of the apostolic penitentiaries of Rome at the time of a great jubilee; and on each of their confessionals were posted in large characters their names, surnames, and titles.

Then thronged the crowd around the confessors. Each came with a piece of money in his hand. Men, women, and children, the poor, and even those who lived on alms, all found money. The penitentiaries, after having explained anew to each individual privately the greatness of the indulgence, addressed this question to the penitents: "How much money can you conscientiously spare to obtain so complete a remission?"

Four precious graces were promised to those who should aid in building the basilica of St. Peter. "The first grace that we announce to you," said the commissaries, in accordance with the letter of their instructions, "is the full pardon of every sin." Next followed three other graces: first, the right of choosing a confessor, who, whenever the hour of death appeared at hand, should give absolution from all sin, and even from the greatest crimes reserved for the apostolic see; secondly, a participation in all the blessings, works, and merits of the Catholic church, prayers, fasts, alms, and pilgrimages; thirdly, redemption of the souls that are in purgatory.

To obtain the first of these graces, it was requisite to have contrition of heart and confession of mouth, or at least an intention of confessing. But as for the three others, they might be obtained without contrition, without confession, simply by paying. Christopher Columbus, extolling the value of gold, had said ere this with great seriousness, "Whoever possesses it can introduce souls into paradise." Such was the doctrine taught by the archbishop of Mentz and by the papal commissaries. Greater blessings could not be offered at a lower rate.

The confession over, and that was soon done, the faithful hastened to the vendor. One alone was charged with the sale. His stall was near the cross. He cast inquiring looks on those who approached him. He examined their manner, their gait, their dress, and he required a sum proportionate to the appearance of the individual who presented himself. Kings, queens, princes, archbishops, bishops, were, according to the scale, to pay twenty-five ducats for an ordinary indulgence. Abbots, counts, and barons, ten. The other nobles, the rectors, and all those who possessed an income of five hundred florins, paid six. Those who had two hundred florins a year paid one; and others, only a half. Moreover, if this tariff could not be carried out to the letter, full powers were given the apostolical commissioner; and all was to be arranged according to the data of "sound reason" and the generosity of the donor. For particular sins, Tetzel had a particular tax. For polygamy it was six ducats; for sacrilege and perjury, nine ducats; for murder, eight ducats; for witchcraft, two ducats.

The apostolical commissaries sometimes met with difficulties in their trade. It frequently happened, both in towns and villages, that the men were opposed to this traffic, and forbade their wives to give anything to these merchants. What could their pious spouses do? "Have you not your dowry or other property at your own disposal?" asked the vendors. "In that case you can dispose of it for so holy a work, against the will of your husbands."

We give one of these letters of absolution. It is worthwhile learning the contents of these diplomas which led to the reformation of the church.

> May our Lord Jesus Christ have pity on thee, N. N., and absolve thee by the merits of His most holy passion. And I, in virtue of the apostolical power that has been confided to me, absolve thee from all ecclesiastical censures, judgments, and penalties which thou mayest have incurred; moreover, from all excesses, sins, and crimes that thou mayest have committed, however great and enormous they may be, and from whatsoever cause, were they even reserved for our most holy father the pope and for the apostolic see. I blot out all the stains of inability and

all marks of infamy that thou mayest have drawn upon thyself on this occasion. I remit the penalties that thou shouldst have endured in purgatory. I restore thee anew to participation in the sacraments of the church. I incorporate thee afresh in the communion of saints, and reestablish thee in the purity and innocence which thou hadst at thy baptism. So that in the hour of death, the gate by which sinners enter the place of torments and punishment shall be closed against thee, and, on the contrary, the gate leading to the paradise of joy shall be open. And if thou shouldst not die for long years, this grace will remain unalterable until thy last hour shall arrive.

In the name of the Father, Son, and Holy Ghost, Amen.

Friar John Tetzel, commissary, has signed this with his own hand.

All the believers were required to confess in the place where the red cross was set up. None were excepted but the sick and aged, and pregnant women. If, however, there chanced to be in the neighborhood some noble in his castle, some great personage in his palace, there was also an exemption for him, as he would not like to be mixed up with this crowd, and his money was well worth the pains of fetching from his mansion. There was no vein in the gold mine that they did not find the means of working.

Then came what was the end and aim of the whole business: the reckoning of the money. For greater security, the chest had three keys: one was in Tetzel's keeping; the second in that of a treasurer delegated by the house of Fugger of Augsburg, to whom this vast enterprise had been consigned; the third was confided to the civil authority. When the time was come, the money-boxes were opened before a public notary, and the contents were duly counted and registered. Must not Christ arise and drive out these profane money-changers from the sanctuary?

When the mission was over, the dealers relaxed from their toils. The instructions of the commissary-general forbade them, it is true, to frequent taverns and places of bad repute, but they cared little for this prohibition. Sin could have but few terrors for those who made so easy a traffic in it. "The collectors led a disorderly life," says a Catholic historian, "they squandered in taverns, gambling-houses, and places of ill-fame, all that the people had saved from their necessities." It has even been asserted that when they were in the taverns they would often stake the salvation of souls on a throw of the dice.

Chapter 11
"Nets to Catch Silver"

But now let us turn to the scenes which this sale of the pardon of sins at that time gave rise to in Germany. At Magdeburg, Tetzel refused to absolve a rich lady, unless, as he declared to her, she would pay one hundred florins in advance. She requested the advice of her usual confessor, who was a Franciscan. "God grants the remission of sins gratuitously," replied the monk; "He does not sell it." He begged her, however, not to communicate to Tetzel the counsel she had received from him. But this merchant having notwithstanding heard a report of this opinion so contrary to his interests, exclaimed, "Such a counsellor deserves to be banished or to be burned."

Tetzel rarely found men enlightened enough, and still more rarely men who were bold enough, to resist him. In general he easily managed the superstitious crowd. He had set up the red cross of the indulgences at Zwickau, and the worthy parishioners had hastened to drop into his strong-box the money that would deliver them. He was about to leave with a well-stored purse, when, on the eve of his departure, the chaplains and their acolytes asked him for a farewell supper. The request was just. But how contrive it? The money was already counted and sealed up. On the morrow he caused the great bell to be tolled.

The crowd rushed into the church; each one imagined something extraordinary had happened, seeing that the business was over. "I had resolved," said he, "to depart this morning, but last night I was awakened by groans. I listened attentively; they came from the cemetery. Alas, it was some poor soul. I myself will be the first to give, and he that does not follow my example will merit condemnation." What heart would not have replied to this appeal? Who knows, besides, what soul it is thus crying from the cemetery? The offerings were abundant, and Tetzel entertained the chaplains and their acolytes with a joyous repast, the expense of which was defrayed by the offerings given in behalf of the soul of Zwickau.

The indulgence merchants had visited Hagenau in 1517. The wife of a shoemaker, taking advantage of the authorization given in the commissary-general's instructions, had procured a letter of indulgence contrary to her husband's will and had paid a gold florin. She died shortly after. As the husband had not caused a mass to be said for the repose of her soul, the priest charged him with contempt of religion, and the magistrate of Hagenau summoned him to appear in court. The shoemaker put his wife's indulgence in his pocket, and went to answer the accusation.

"Is your wife dead?" asked the magistrate.

"Yes," replied he.

"What have you done for her?"

"I have buried her body and commended her soul to God."

"But have you had a mass said for the repose of her soul?"

"I have not: it was of no use; she entered heaven at the moment of her death."

"How do you know that?"

"Here is the proof." As he said these words, he drew the indulgence from his pocket, and the magistrate, in presence of the priest, read in so many words that, at the moment of her death, the woman who had received it would not go into purgatory but would at once enter into heaven. "If the reverend gentleman maintains that a mass is still necessary," added the widower, "my wife has been deceived by our most holy father the pope; if she has not been, it is the priest who deceives me." There was no reply to this, and the shoemaker was acquitted.

One on whom Tetzel made the deepest impression was doubtless Myconius, afterwards celebrated as a reformer and historian of the Reformation. He had received a Christian education. "My son," his father, a pious Franconian, would often say to him, "pray frequently; for all things are given to us gratuitously from God alone. The blood of Christ," added he, "is the only ransom for the sins of the whole world. O my son, though three men only should be saved by Christ's blood, believe, and believe with assurance, that thou art one of those three men. It is an insult to the Savior's blood to doubt that He can save." And then, cautioning his son against the traffic that was now beginning to be established in Germany,

"Roman indulgences," said he again, "are nets to catch silver and which serve to deceive the simple-minded. Remission of sins and eternal life are not to be purchased with money."

At the age of thirteen, Myconius was sent to the school at Annaberg to finish his studies. Tetzel arrived in this city shortly after and remained there two years. The people flocked in crowds to hear his sermons. "There is no other means of obtaining eternal life," cried Tetzel in a voice of thunder, "than the satisfaction of works. But this satisfaction is impossible for man. He can therefore only purchase it from the Roman pontiff."

When Tetzel was about to quit Annaberg, his sermons became more earnest. "Soon," cried he in threatening accents, "I shall take down the cross, shut the gates of heaven, and extinguish the brightness of the sun of grace that beams before your eyes." And then assuming a tender tone of exhortation, "Now is the accepted time; behold, now is the day of salvation." Again raising his voice, Tetzel, who was addressing the inhabitants of a country whose wealth consisted in its mines, shouted out, "Bring your money, citizens of Annaberg; contribute bounteously in favor of indulgences, and your mines and your mountains shall be filled with pure silver." Finally, at Whitsuntide, he declared that he would distribute his letters to the poor gratuitously and for the love of God.

The youthful Myconius was one of Tetzel's hearers. He felt an ardent desire to take advantage of this offer. "I am a poor sinner," said he to the commissaries in Latin, "and I have need of a gratuitous pardon."

"Those alone," replied the merchants, "can have part in Christ's merits who lend a helping hand to the church, that is to say, who give money."

"What is the meaning, then," asked Myconius, "of those promises of a free gift posted on the gates and walls of the churches?"

"Give at least a groat," said Tetzel's people, after having vainly interceded with their master in favor of the young man.

"I cannot."

"Only six deniers."

"I am not worth so many."

The Dominicans began to fear that he came on purpose to entrap them. "Listen," said they, "we will make you a present of the six deniers."

The young man replied indignantly, "I will have no bought indulgences. If I desired to buy them, I should only have to sell one of my school books. I desire a gratuitous pardon, and for the love of God alone. You will render an account to God for having allowed a soul to be lost for six deniers."

"Who sent you to entrap us?" exclaimed the vendors.

"Nothing but the desire of receiving God's pardon could have made me appear before such great gentlemen," replied the young man as he withdrew.

"I was very sad at being thus sent away unpitied. But I felt, however, a Comforter within me who said that there was a God in heaven who pardons repentant souls without money and without price, for the love of His Son Jesus Christ. As I took leave of these folks, the Holy Spirit touched my heart. I burst into tears, and prayed to the Lord with anguish: 'O God,' cried I, 'since these men have refused to remit my sins, because I wanted money to pay them, do Thou, Lord, have pity on me and pardon them of Thy pure grace.' I repaired to my chamber, I prayed to my crucifix which was lying on my desk; I put it on a chair, and fell down before it. I cannot describe to you what I experienced. I begged God to be a father to me, and to do with me whatever He pleased. I felt my nature changed, converted, transformed. What had delighted me before, now became an object of disgust. To live with God and to please Him was my earnest, my sole desire."

A Saxon nobleman, who had heard Tetzel at Leipzig, was much displeased by his falsehoods. Approaching the monk, he asked him if he had the power of pardoning sins that men have an intention of committing. "Most assuredly," replied Tetzel, "I have received full powers from his holiness for that purpose."

"Well, then," answered the knight, "I am desirous of taking a slight revenge on one of my enemies, without endangering his life. I will give you ten crowns if you will give me a letter of indulgence that shall fully justify me."

Tetzel made some objections; they came, however, to an arrangement by the aid of thirty crowns. The monk quitted Leipzig shortly after. The nobleman and his attendants lay in wait for him in a wood between Jütterbock and Treblin; they fell upon him, gave him a slight beating, and took away the well-stored indulgence chest the inquisitor was carrying with him. Tetzel made a violent outcry and carried his complaint before the courts. But the noble-man showed the letter which Tetzel had signed himself, and which exempted him beforehand from every penalty. Duke George, whom this action had at first exceedingly exasperated, no sooner read the document than he ordered the accused to be acquitted.

This traffic everywhere occupied men's thoughts and was every-where talked of. It was the topic of conversation in castles, in academies, and in the burghers' houses, as well as in taverns, inns, and all places of public resort. The scoffers found ample food for raillery. Complaints and sarcasms might everywhere be heard on the love of money that devoured the clergy. They did not stop there. They attacked the power of the keys and the authority of the sovereign pontiff.

Stories were told of the gross and immoral conduct of the traffickers in indulgences. To pay their bills to the carriers who transported them and their merchandise, the innkeepers with whom they lodged, or whoever had done them any service, they gave a letter of indulgence for four souls, for five, or for any number according to circumstances. Thus, these certificates of salvation circulated in the inns and markets like banknotes or other paper money. "Pay, pay," said the people, "that is the head, belly, tail, and all the contents of their sermons."

A miner of Schneeberg met a seller of indulgences. "Must we credit," asked he, "what you have so often told us of the power of indulgences and of the papal authority and believe that we can, by throwing a penny into the chest, ransom a soul from purgatory?" The merchant affirmed it was so. "Ah," resumed the miner, "what a merciless man, then, the pope must be, since for want of a wretched penny he leaves a poor soul crying in the flames so long. If he has no ready money, let him store up some hundred thousand crowns, and deliver all these souls at once. We poor people would very readily repay him both interest and capital."

The Germans were wearied with this scandalous traffic that was carried on in the midst of them. They could no longer endure the impositions of these master cheats of Rome, as Luther called them. No bishop, no theologian, however, dared oppose their quackery and their frauds. All monks were in suspense. Men asked one another if God would not raise up some mighty man for the work that was to be done, but nowhere did he appear.

Chapter 12
The Ninety-five Theses

Luther, as far as we are acquainted, heard of Tetzel for the first time at Grimma in 1516, just as he was commencing his visitation of the churches. It was reported to Staupitz, who was still with Luther, that there was a seller of indulgences at Würzen named Tetzel, who was making a great noise. Some of his extravagant expressions were quoted, and Luther exclaimed with indignation, "If God permit, I will make a hole in his drum."

Tetzel was returning from Berlin, where he had met with the most friendly reception from the Elector Joachim, the farmer-general's brother, when he took his station at Jüterbock. Staupitz, availing himself of the confidence the Elector Frederick placed in him, had often called his attention to the abuses of the indulgences and the scandalous lives of the vendors. The princes of Saxony, indignant at this disgraceful traffic, had forbidden the merchant to enter their provinces. He was therefore compelled to remain in the territories of his patron the archbishop of Magdeburg, but he approached Saxony as near as he could. Jüterbock was only four miles from Wittenberg. "This great purse-thresher," said Luther, "began to thresh bravely throughout the country so that the money began to leap and fall tinkling into the box." The people flocked in crowds from Wittenberg to the indulgence market of Jüterbock.

Luther was one day seated in the confessional at Wittenberg. Many of the townspeople came successively and confessed themselves guilty of great excesses. Adultery, licentiousness, usury, ill-gotten gains—such were the crimes acknowledged to the minister of the Word by those souls of which he would one day have to give an account. He reprimanded, corrected, and instructed. But what was his astonishment when these individuals replied that they would not abandon their sins. Greatly shocked, the pious monk declared that since they would not promise to change their lives, he could not absolve them. The unhappy creatures then appealed to their letters of indulgence; they showed them and maintained their efficacy. But Luther replied that he had nothing to do with these papers and added, "Except ye repent, ye shall all likewise perish." They cried out and protested, but the doctor was immovable. They must cease to do evil and learn to do well, or else there was no absolution. "Have a care," added he, "how you listen to the clamors of these indulgence merchants: you have better things to do than buy these licenses which they sell at so vile a price."

The inhabitants of Wittenberg, in great alarm, hastily returned to Tetzel: they told him that an Augustinian monk had treated his letters with contempt. The Dominican at this intelligence bellowed with anger. He stormed from the pulpit, employing insults and curses; and to strike the people with greater terror, he had a fire lighted several times in the marketplace, declaring that he had received an order from the pope to burn all heretics who presumed to oppose his most holy indulgences.

Such is the fact that was, not the cause, but the first occasion of the Reformation. A pastor, seeing the sheep of his fold in a course in which they must perish, sought to withdraw them from it. Luther, who was impelled equally by obedience to the Word of God and charity toward men ascended the pulpit.

"No one can prove by Scripture that the righteousness of God requires a penalty or satisfaction from the sinner," said the faithful minister of the Word to the people of Wittenberg. "The only duty it imposes is a true repentance, a sincere conversion, a resolution to bear the cross of Christ, and to perform good works. It is a great error to pretend of one's self to make satisfaction for our sins to God's righteousness; God pardons them gratuitously by His inestimable grace."

Next attacking the pretenses under which indulgences were published, he continued, "They would do much better to contribute for love of God to the building of St. Peter's than to buy indulgences with this intention. But, say you, shall we then never purchase any? I have already told you, and I repeat it: my advice is that no one should buy them. Leave them for drowsy Christians, but you should walk apart and for yourselves. We must turn the faithful aside from indulgences and exhort them to the works which they neglect."

Finally, glancing at his adversaries, Luther concluded in these words: "And should any cry out that I am a heretic, for the truth I preach is very prejudicial to their strongbox, I care but little for their clamors. They are gloomy and sick brains, men who have never tasted the Bible, never read the Christian doctrine, never comprehended their own doctors, and who lie rotting in the rags and tatters of their own vain opinions. May God grant both them and us a sound understanding. Amen." After these words the doctor quitted the pulpit, leaving his hearers in great emotion at such daring language.

Luther's words produced little effect. Tetzel continued his traffic and his impious discourses without disturbing himself. Would Luther resign himself to these crying abuses, and would he keep silence? As pastor, he had earnestly exhorted those who had recourse to his services; as preacher, he had uttered a warning voice from the pulpit. It still remained for him to speak as a theologian; he had yet to address not merely a few souls in the confessional, not merely the assembly of the faithful at Wittenberg, but all those who were, like himself, teachers of the Word of God.

It was not the church he thought of attacking; it was not the pope he was bringing to the bar: on the contrary, it was his respect for the pope that would not allow him to be silent longer on the monstrous claims by which the pontiff was discredited. He must take the pope's part against those impudent men who dare mingle his venerable name with their scandalous traffic. Far from thinking of a revolution which should overthrow the primacy of Rome, Luther believed he had the pope and Catholicism for his allies against these barefaced monks.

The Festival of All Saints was a very important day for Wittenberg and, above all, for the church the elector had built there and which he had filled with relics. On that day the priests used to bring out these relics, ornamented with gold, silver, and precious stones, and exhibit them before the people, who were astonished and dazzled at such magnificence. Whoever visited the church on that festival and made confession obtained a rich indulgence. Accordingly, on this great anniversary, pilgrims came to Wittenberg in crowds.

On October 31, 1517, at noon on the day preceding the festival, Luther walked boldly toward the church, to which a superstitious crowd of pilgrims was repairing, and posted upon the door ninety-five theses, or propositions, against the doctrine of indulgences.

Neither the elector, nor Staupitz, nor Spalatin, nor any even of his most intimate friends had been made acquainted with his intentions.

Luther therein declared, in a kind of preface, that he had written these theses with the express desire of setting the truth in the full light of day. He declared himself ready to defend them on the morrow, in the university, against all opponents. Great was the attention they excited: they were read and passed from mouth to mouth. Ere long the pilgrims, the university, and the whole city were in commotion.

We give some of these propositions, written with the pen of the monk and posted on the door of the church of Wittenberg:

1. When our Lord and Master Jesus Christ says *repent,* He means that the whole life of believers upon earth should be a constant and perpetual repentance.
4. Repentance and sorrow—that is, true penance—endure as long as a man is displeased with himself—that is, until he passes from this life into eternity.
6. The pope cannot remit any condemnation, but only declare and confirm the remission of God, except in the cases that appertain to himself. If he does otherwise, the condemnation remains entirely the same.
8. The laws of ecclesiastical penance ought to be imposed solely on the living, and have no regard to the dead.
21. The commissaries of indulgences are in error when they say that by the papal indulgence a man is delivered from every punishment and is saved.
27. They preach mere human follies who maintain that as soon as the money rattles in the strongbox, the soul flies out of purgatory.
28. This is certain, that as soon as the money tinkles, avarice and love of gain arrive, increase, and multiply. But the support and prayers of the church depend solely on God's will and good pleasure.
32. Those who fancy themselves sure of salvation by indulgences will go to perdition along with those who teach them so.
36. Every Christian who truly repents of his sins enjoys an entire remission both of the penalty and of the guilt, without any need of indulgences.
37. Every true Christian, whether dead or alive, participates in all the blessings of Christ or of the church by God's gift, and without a letter of indulgence.

42. We should teach Christians that the pope has no thought or desire of comparing in any respect the act of buying indulgences with any work of mercy.

43. We should teach Christians that he who gives to the poor or lends to the needy does better than he who purchases an indulgence.

45. We should teach Christians that whoever sees his neighbor in want, and yet buys an indulgence, does not buy the pope's indulgence, but incurs God's anger.

46. We should teach Christians that if they have no superfluity, they are bound to keep for their own households the means of procuring necessaries, and ought not to squander their money in indulgences.

47. We should teach Christians that the purchase of an indulgence is a matter of free choice and not of commandment.

48. We should teach Christians that the pope, having more need of prayers offered up in faith than of money, desires prayer more than money when he dispenses indulgences.

50. We should teach Christians that if the pope knew of the extortions of the preachers of indulgences, he would rather the mother church of St. Peter were burned and reduced to ashes than see it built up with the skin, the flesh, and the bones of his flock.

51. We should teach Christians that the pope—as it is his duty—would distribute his own money to the poor whom the indulgence sellers are now stripping of their last farthing, even were he compelled to sell the mother church of St. Peter.

52. To hope to be saved by indulgences is a lying and an empty hope, although even the commissary of indulgences, nay, farther, the pope himself, should pledge their souls to guarantee it.

53. They are the enemies of the pope and of Jesus Christ who, by reason of the preaching of indulgences, forbid the preaching of the Word of God.

62. The true and precious treasure of the church is the holy gospel of the glory and grace of God.

71. Cursed be he who speaks against the indulgence of the pope.

72. But blessed be he who speaks against the foolish and impudent language of the preachers of indulgences.

76. The indulgence of the pope cannot take away the smallest daily sin, as far as regards the guilt or the offense.

79. It is blasphemy to say that the cross adorned with the arms
of the pope is as effectual as the cross of Christ.

81. This shameless preaching, these impudent commendations
of indulgences, make it difficult for the learned to defend
the dignity and honor of the pope against the calumnies of
the preachers and the subtle and crafty questions of the
common people.

86. Why, say they, does not the pope, who is richer than the
richest Croesus, build the mother church of St. Peter with
his own money rather than with that of poor Christians?

94. We should exhort Christians to diligence in following
Christ, their head, through crosses, death, and hell.

95. For it is far better to enter into the kingdom of heaven
through much tribulation than to acquire a carnal security
by the consolations of a false peace.

Such was the commencement of the work. The germs of the
Reformation were contained in these propositions of Luther. The
abuses of indulgences were attacked therein, and this is their most
striking feature; but beneath these attacks was a principle which,
although attracting the attention of the multitude in a less degree,
was one day to overthrow the edifice of Roman Catholicism. The
evangelical doctrine of a free and gratuitous remission of sins was
there for the first time publicly professed. Luther himself acknowledged afterwards that, in proclaiming justification by faith, he had
laid the axe at the root of the tree. "It is doctrine we attack in the
adherents of the papacy," said he. "Huss and Wycliffe only attacked
their lives; but in attacking their doctrine, we take the goose by the
neck. Everything depends on the Word, which the pope has taken
from us and falsified. I have vanquished the pope, because my
doctrine is of God, and his is of the Devil."

But if Luther's theses were strong by the strength of the truth
they proclaimed, they were not the less so by the faith of their
champion. He had boldly drawn the sword of the Word: he had done
so in reliance on the power of truth. He had felt that by leaning on
God's promises, he could afford to risk something, to use the
language of the world. "Let him who desires to begin a good work,"
said he when speaking of this daring attack, "undertake it with
confidence in the goodness of his cause, and not, which God forbid,
expecting the support and consolation of the world. Moreover, let
him have no fear of man or of the world; for these words will never

lie: It is good to trust in the Lord, and assuredly he that trusteth in the Lord shall not be confounded. But let him that will not or who cannot risk something with confidence in God, take heed how he undertakes anything." Luther, after having posted his theses on the gate of All Saints' church, retired, no doubt, to his tranquil cell, full of the peace and joy that spring from an action done in the Lord's name and for the sake of eternal truth.

Whatever be the boldness that prevails in these propositions, they still bespeak the monk who refused to admit a single doubt on the authority of the see of Rome. But while attacking the doctrine of indulgences, Luther had unwittingly touched on certain errors whose discovery could not be agreeable to the pope, seeing that sooner or later they would call his supremacy in question. Luther was not so far-sighted; but he was sensible of the extreme boldness of the step he had just taken, and consequently thought it his duty to soften down their audacity as far as he could in conformity with the truth. He therefore set forth these theses as doubtful propositions on which he solicited the information of the learned; and appended to them, conformably with the established usage, a solemn declaration that he did not mean to affirm or say anything contrary to the Holy Scriptures, the Fathers of the church, and the rights and decretals of the Roman see.

Frequently, in afteryears, as he contemplated the immense and unexpected consequence of this courageous attack, Luther was astonished at himself and could not understand how he had ventured to make it. An invisible and mightier hand than his held the clue and led the herald of truth along a path that was still hidden from him and from the difficulties of which he would perhaps have shrunk, if he had foreseen them, and if he had advanced alone and of his own accord. "I entered into this controversy," said he, "without any definite plan, without knowledge or inclination; I was taken quite unawares, and I call God, the searcher of hearts, to witness."

Luther had become acquainted with the source of these abuses. Someone brought him a little book adorned with the arms of Albert, archbishop of Mentz and Magdeburg, which contained the regulations to be followed in the sale of indulgences. It was this young prelate, then, this graceful prince, who had prescribed, or at least sanctioned all this quackery. In him Luther saw only a superior whom he should fear and respect. Not wishing to beat the air at hazard, but rather to address those who are charged with the government of the church, Luther sent him a letter abounding at once in frankness and humility. It was on the very day he posted up the theses that the doctor wrote to Albert. Luther at the same time forwarded his theses to the archbishop and added a postscript inviting him to read them, in order to convince himself on how slight a foundation the doctrine of indulgences was based.

Thus Luther's whole desire was for the sentinels of the church to awaken and resolve to put an end to the evils that were laying it waste. All his prayers, all his entreaties were unavailing. The youthful Albert, engrossed by pleasures and ambitious designs, made no reply to so solemn an appeal. The bishop of Brandenburg, a learned and pious man to whom he sent his theses, replied that he was attacking the power of the church; that he would bring upon himself much trouble and vexation; that the thing was above his strength; and he earnestly advised him to keep quiet. The princes of the church stopped their ears against the voice of God, which was manifested with such energy and tenderness through the mouth of Luther. They would not understand the signs of the times; they were struck with that blindness which has caused the ruin of so many powers and dignities. "They both thought," said Luther afterwards, "that the pope would be too strong for a poor mendicant friar like me."

Although the bishops failed him, God did not. The Head of the church, who sitteth in the heavens, and to whom all power is given upon earth, had Himself prepared the soil and deposited the seed in the hands of His minister; He gave wings to the seeds of truth, and He scattered it in an instant throughout the length and breadth of His church.

No one appeared next day at the university to attack Luther's propositions. The Tetzel traffic was too much decried and too shameful for any one but himself or his followers to dare take up the glove. But these theses were destined to be heard elsewhere than under the arched roof of an academic hall. Scarcely had they been nailed to the church door of Wittenberg than the feeble sounds of the hammer were followed throughout all Germany by a mighty blow that reached even the foundations of haughty Rome, threatening with sudden ruin the walls, the gates, and the pillars of Catholicism, stunning and terrifying her champions, and at the same time awakening thousands from the sleep of error.

These theses spread with the rapidity of lightning. A month had not elapsed before they were at Rome. "In a fortnight," says a contemporary historian, "they were in every part of Germany, and in four weeks they had traversed nearly the whole of Christendom, as if the very angels had been their messengers and had placed them before the eyes of all men. No one can believe the noise they made." Somewhat later they were translated into Dutch and Spanish, and a traveler sold them in Jerusalem. "Everyone," said Luther, "complained of the indulgences; and as all the bishops and doctors had kept silence, and nobody was willing to bell the cat, poor Luther became a famous doctor, because, as they said, there came one at last who ventured to do it. But I did not like this glory, and the tune was nearly too high for my voice."

Many of the pilgrims, who had thronged to Wittenberg from every quarter for the Feast of All Saints, carried back with them, instead of indulgences, the famous theses of the Augustinian monk. By this means they contributed to their circulation. Every one read them, meditated and commented on them. Men conversed about them in all the convents and in all the universities. The pious monks who had entered the cloisters to save their souls, all upright and honorable men, were delighted at this simple and striking confession of the truth, and heartily desired that Luther would continue the work he had begun.

At length one man had found courage to undertake the perilous struggle. This was a reparation accorded to Christendom: the public conscience was satisfied. Piety saw in these theses a blow aimed at every superstition; the new theology hailed in it the defeat of the scholastic dogmas; princes and magistrates considered them as a barrier raised against the invasions of the ecclesiastical power; and the nation rejoiced at seeing so positive a *veto* opposed by this monk to the cupidity of the Roman chancery.

"I observe," remarked Erasmus, one of the principal rivals of the reformer, "that the greater their evangelical piety and the purer their morals, the less are men opposed to Luther. His life is praised even by those who cannot endure his faith. The world was weary of a doctrine so full of puerile fables and human ordinances, and thirsted for that living, pure, and hidden water which springs from the veins of the evangelists and apostles. Luther's genius was fitted to accomplish these things, and his zeal would naturally catch fire at so glorious an enterprise."

Chapter 13
Reaction to the Theses

We must follow these propositions into whatever place they penetrated, into the studies of the learned, the cells of the monks, and the halls of princes, to form an idea of the various, but prodigious, effects they produced in Germany.

The cautious Erasmus was in the Low Countries when these propositions reached him. He internally rejoiced at witnessing his secret wishes for the rectifying of abuses expressed with so much courage: he approved of the author, exhorting him only to greater moderation and prudence. Nevertheless, when someone reproached Luther's violence in his presence, "God," said he, "has given me a physician who cuts deep into the flesh, because the malady would otherwise be incurable." And when a little later the elector of Saxony asked his opinion on Luther's business, he replied with a smile, "I am not at all surprised that it has made so much noise, for he has committed two unpardonable crimes: he has attacked the pope's tiara and the monks' bellies."

Doctor Flek, prior of the monastery of Steinlausitz, had long discontinued reading the Mass, but without telling anyone the real cause. One day he found Luther's theses posted up in the refectory: he went up to them, began to read, and had only perused a few, when, unable to contain his joy, he exclaimed, "Ah, ah, he whom we have so long expected is come at last, and he will show you monks a trick or two!" Then looking into the future, says Mathesius, and playing on the meaning of the *Wittenberg* ("mountain of wisdom"), "All the world," said he, "will go and seek wisdom on the mountain, and will find it." He wrote to the doctor to continue the glorious struggle with boldness.

The Emperor Maximilian, predecessor of Charles V, read and admired the theses of the monk of Wittenberg; he perceived his ability and foresaw that this obscure Augustinian might one day become a powerful ally for Germany in her struggle against Rome.

He accordingly said to the elector of Saxony through his envoy, "Take great care of the monk Luther, for the time may come when we shall have need of him." And shortly after, being in diet with Pfeffinger, the elector's privy councilor, he said to him, "Well, what is your Augustinian doing? In truth his propositions are not contemptible. He will play the monks a pretty game."

At Rome, even in the Vatican, these theses were not so badly received as might have been imagined. Leo X judged rather as a patron of letters than as pope. The amusement they gave him made him forget the severe truths they contained; and as Sylvester Prierio, the master of the sacred palace, who had the charge of examining the books, requested him to treat Luther as a heretic, he replied, "Brother Martin Luther is a very fine genius, and all that is said against him is mere monkish jealousy."

There were few men on whom Luther's theses produced a deeper impression than Myconius, the scholar of Annaberg whom Tetzel had so mercilessly repulsed. Myconius had entered a convent. On the very night of his arrival he dreamed he saw immense fields of wheat all glistening with ripe ears. "Cut," said the voice of his guide; and when he alleged his want of skill, his conductor showed him a reaper working with inconceivable activity. "Follow him, and do as he does," said the guide. Myconius, as eager after holiness as Luther had been, devoted himself while in the monastery to all the vigils, fasts, mortifications, and practices invented by men. But at last he despaired of ever attaining his object by his own exertions. He neglected his studies and employed himself in manual labors only. At one time he would bind books; at another, work at the turner's lathe, or any laborious occupation. This outward activity was unable to quiet his troubled conscience. God had spoken to him, and he could no longer fall back into his previous lethargy. This state of anguish endured several years.

At length the year 1517 arrived; Luther's theses were published; they were circulated through Christendom and penetrated also into the monastery where the scholar of Annaberg was concealed. He hid himself in a corner of the cloister with another monk, John Voigt, that he might read them at his ease. Here were the selfsame truths he had heard from his father: his eyes were opened; he felt a voice within him responding to that which was then reechoing through Germany, and great consolation filled his heart. "I see plainly," said he, "that Martin Luther is the reaper I saw in my dream, and who taught me to gather the ears." He began immediately to profess the doctrine that Luther had proclaimed.

The monks grew alarmed as they heard him; they argued with him and declared against Luther and against his convent. "This convent," replied Myconius, "is like our Lord's sepulcher: they wish to prevent Christ's resurrection, but they will fail." At last his superiors, finding they could not convince him, interdicted him for a year and a half from all intercourse with the world, permitting him neither to write nor receive letters, and threatening him with imprisonment for life. But the hour of his deliverance was at hand. Being afterwards nominated pastor of Zwickau, he was the first who declared against the papacy in the churches of Thuringia. "Then," said he, "was I enabled to labor with my venerable father Luther in the gospel-harvest."

Some of the reformer's contemporaries, however, foresaw the serious consequences to which these daring propositions might lead, and the numerous obstacles they would encounter. They expressed their fears aloud and rejoiced with trembling. "I am much afraid," wrote the excellent canon of Augsburg, Bernard Adelmann, to his friend Pirckheimer, "that the worthy man must give way at last before the avarice and power of the partisans of indulgences. His representations have produced so little effect that the bishop of Augsburg, our primate and metropolitan, has just ordered, in the pope's name, fresh indulgences for St. Peter's at Rome. Let him haste to secure the aid of princes; let him beware of tempting God; for he must be void of common sense if he overlooks the imminent peril he incurs."

Not only did a great number of Luther's friends entertain fears as to this proceeding, but many even expressed their disapprobation. The bishop of Brandenburg, grieved at seeing so violent a quarrel break out in his diocese, would have desired to stifle it. He resolved to effect this by mildness. "In your theses on indulgences," said he to Luther, through the abbot of Lenin, "I see nothing opposed to the catholic truth; I myself condemn these indiscreet proclamations; but for the love of peace, and for regard to your bishop, discontinue writing upon this subject." Luther was confounded at being addressed with such humility by so great a dignitary. Led away by the first impulse of his heart, he replied with emotion, "I consent: I would rather obey than perform miracles, if that were possible."

The Elector Frederick beheld with regret the commencement of a combat that was justifiable no doubt, but the results of which could not be foreseen. No prince was more desirous of maintaining the public peace than Frederick. Yet what an immense conflagration might not be kindled by this spark. What violent discord, what rending of nations, might not this monkish quarrel produce. The elector gave Luther frequent intimations of the uneasiness he felt.

Even in his own order, and in his own convent at Wittenberg, Luther met with disapprobation. The prior and subprior were terrified at the outcry made by Tetzel and his companions. They repaired trembling and alarmed to brother Martin's cell and said, "Pray do not bring disgrace upon our order. The other orders, and especially the Dominicans, are already overjoyed to think that they will not be alone in their shame." Luther was moved at these words; but he soon recovered and replied, "Dear fathers, if this work be not of God, it will come to naught; but if it be, let it go forward." The prior and subprior made no answer. "The work is still going forward," added Luther, after recounting his anecdote, "and, God willing, it will go on better and better unto the end. Amen."

Luther had many other attacks to endure. At Erfurt, he was blamed for the violent and haughty manner in which he condemned the opinions of others. He was also accused of precipitation and levity. "They require moderation in me," answered Luther, "and they trample it underfoot in the judgment they pass on me. . . . We can always see the mote in our brother's eye, and we overlook the beam in our own. . . . Truth will not gain more by my moderation than it will lose by my rashness."

"I desire to know," continues he, addressing Lange, "what errors you and your theologians have found in my theses? Who does not know that a man rarely puts forth any new idea without having some appearance of pride, and without being accused of exciting quarrels? If humility herself should undertake something new, her opponents would accuse her of pride. Why were Christ and all the martyrs put to death? Because they seemed to be proud condemners of the wisdom of the time, and because they advanced novelties, without having first humbly taken counsel of the oracles of the ancient opinions.

"Do not let the wise of our days expect from me humility, or rather, hypocrisy enough to ask their advice before publishing what duty compels me to say. Whatever I do will be done, not by the prudence of men, but by the counsel of God. If the work be of God, who shall stop it? If it be not, who can forward it? Not my will, nor theirs, nor ours; but Thy will, O holy Father, which art in heaven."

The reproaches and accusations which were showered upon Luther from every quarter could not fail, however, to produce some impression on his mind. He had been deceived in his hopes. He had expected to see the heads of the church and the most distinguished scholars in the nation publicly unite with him; but the case was far otherwise. He felt himself alone in the church, alone against Rome, alone at the foot of that ancient and formidable building whose foundations penetrated to the center of the earth, whose walls soared to the clouds, and against which he had aimed so daring a blow. He was troubled and dispirited. Doubts, which he fancied he had overcome, returned to his mind with fresh force.

No one can paint better than himself the combat in his own soul: "I began this business," said he, "with great fear and trembling. Who was I then, I, a poor, wretched, contemptible friar, more like a corpse than a man—who was I to oppose the majesty of the pope, before whom not only the kings of the earth and the whole world trembled, but even, if I may so speak, heaven and hell were constrained to obey the signal of his eyes?

"No one can know what my heart suffered during these first two years, and into what despondency, I may say into what despair, I was sunk. . . . There were, it is true, many pious Christians who were pleased with my propositions and valued them highly; but I could not acknowledge them and consider them as the instruments of the Holy Ghost; I looked only to the pope, to the cardinals, bishops, theologians, lawyers, monks, and priests. It was from them I expected to witness the influence of the Spirit. However, after gaining the victory over all their arguments by Scripture, I at last surmounted through Christ's grace, but with great anguish, toil, and pain, the only argument that still checked me, namely, that I should 'listen to the church'; for, from the bottom of my heart, I reverenced the pope's church as the true church; and I did so . . . with . . . sincerity and veneration."

The reproaches, the timidity, and the silence of his friends had discouraged Luther; the attacks of his enemies produced a contrary effect: this is a case of frequent occurrence. The adversaries of the truth, who hope by their violence to do their own work, are doing that of God Himself. Tetzel took up the gauntlet, but with a feeble hand. Luther's sermon, which had been for the people what the theses had been for the learned, was the object of his first reply. He refuted this discourse point by point, after his own fashion; he then announced that he was preparing to meet his adversary more fully in certain theses which he would maintain at the University of Frankfurt on the Oder. "Then," said he, replying to the conclusion of Luther's sermon, "each man will be able to judge who is the heresiarch, heretic, schismatic—who is mistaken, rash, and slanderous. Then it will be clear to the eyes of all who it is that has a dull brain, that has never felt the Bible, never read the Christian doctrines, never understood his own doctors. In support of the propositions I advance, I am ready to suffer all things—prisons, scourging, drowning, and the stake."

Luther replied without naming Tetzel; Tetzel had not named him. But there was no one in Germany who could not write at the head of their publications the names they thought proper to conceal. Tetzel, in order to set a higher value upon his indulgences, endeavored to confound the repentance required by God with the penance imposed by the church. Luther sought to clear up this point.

"To save words," said he, in his picturesque language, "I throw to the winds—which, besides, have more leisure than I—his other remarks, which are mere artificial flowers and dry leaves, and will content myself with examining the foundations of his edifice of burs.

"The penance imposed by the holy father cannot be that required by Christ, for what the holy father imposes he can dispense with; and if these two penances were one and the same thing, it would follow that the pope takes away what Christ imposes, and destroys the commandment of God. Well, if he likes it, let him abuse me," continues Luther, after quoting other erroneous interpretations by Tetzel, "let him call me heretic, schismatic, slanderer, and whatever he pleases: I shall not be his enemy for that, and I shall pray for him as for a friend. But I cannot suffer him to treat the Holy Scriptures, our consolation (Rom. 15:4), as a sow treats a sack of oats."

When Luther came to Tetzel's invectives, he answered them in this manner: "When I hear these invectives, I fancy it is a donkey braying at me. I am delighted with them, and I should be very sorry were such people to call me a good Christian."

"Finally," added he, challenging his adversary to battle, "although it is not usual to burn heretics for such matters, here am I at Wittenberg, I, Doctor Martin Luther. Is there any inquisitor who is determined to chew iron and to blow up rocks? I beg to inform him that he has a safe-conduct to come hither, open gates, bed and board secured to him, and all by the gracious cares of our worthy prince Duke Frederick, elector of Saxony, who will never protect heresy."

We see that Luther was not wanting in courage. He relied upon the Word of God, and it is a rock that never fails us in the storm. But God in His faithfulness afforded him other assistance. The burst of joy by which the multitude welcomed Luther's theses had been soon followed by a gloomy silence. The learned had timidly retreated before the calumnies and abuse of Tetzel and the Dominicans. The bishops, who had previously exclaimed against the abuse of indulgences, seeing them attacked at last, had not failed, by a contradiction that is by no means rare, to discover that the attack was unseasonable. The greater portion of the reformer's friends were alarmed. Many had fled away. But when the first terror was over, a contrary movement took place in their minds. The monk of Wittenberg, who for some time had been almost alone in the midst of the church, soon gathered around him again a numerous body of friends and admirers.

There was one who, although timid, yet remained faithful during this crisis, and whose friendship was his consolation and support. This was Spalatin. Luther had not sent his propositions either to the prince or to any of his court. It would appear that the chaplain expressed some astonishment to his friend in consequence. "I was unwilling," replied Luther, "that my theses should reach our most illustrious prince, or any of his court, before they had been received by those who think themselves especially designated in them, for fear they should believe I had published them by the prince's order, or to conciliate his favor, and from opposition to the bishop of Mentz. I understand there are many persons who dream such things. But now I can safely swear, that my theses were published without the knowledge of Duke Frederick."

If Spalatin consoled his friend and supported him by his influence, Luther, on his part, endeavored to answer the questions put to him by the unassuming chaplain. Among others, the latter asked one that has been often proposed in our days: "What is the best method of studying Scripture?"

"As yet, most excellent Spalatin," Luther replied, "you have only asked me things that were in my power. But to direct you in the study of the Holy Scriptures is beyond my ability. If, however, you absolutely wish to know my method, I will not conceal it from you.

"It is very certain that we cannot attain to the understanding of Scripture either by study or by the intellect. Your first duty is to begin by prayer. Entreat the Lord to grant you, of His great mercy, the true understanding of His Word. There is no other interpreter of the Word of God than the author of this Word, as He Himself has said: 'They shall be taught of God.' Hope for nothing from your own labors, from your own understanding: trust solely in God and in the influence of His Spirit. Believe this on the word of a man who has had experience."

Luther found further consolation in the friendship of respectable laymen. Christopher Scheurl, the excellent secretary of the imperial city of Nuremberg, gave him the most affecting marks of his regard. Luther, who had done little to circulate his theses, had not sent them to Scheurl any more than to the elector and his court. The secretary of Nuremberg expressed his astonishment at this. "My design," answered Luther, "was not to give my theses such publicity. I only desired to confer on their contents with some of those who remain with us or near us. If they had been condemned, I would have destroyed them. If they had been approved of, I purposed publishing them. But they have now been printed over and over again, and circulated so far beyond all my hopes, that I repent of my offspring; not because I fear the truth should be made known to the people, 'twas this alone I sought; but that is not the way to instruct them. They contain questions that are still doubtful to me, and if I had thought my theses would have created such a sensation, there are some things I should have omitted, and others I should have asserted with greater confidence." In afteryears Luther thought differently. "You will find in my earlier writings," said he many years after, "that I very humbly conceded many things to the pope, and even important things, that now I regard and detest as abominable and blasphemous."

Chapter 14
Tetzel's Attack

Men's minds had recovered a little from their first alarm. Luther himself felt inclined to declare that his theses had not the scope attributed to them. New events might turn aside the general attention, and this blow aimed at the Roman doctrine be lost in air like so many others. But the partisans of Rome prevented the affair from ending thus. They fanned the flame instead of quenching it.

Tetzel and the Dominicans replied with insolence to the attack that had been made on them. Burning with the desire of crushing the impudent monk who had dared to trouble their commerce and of conciliating the favor of the Roman pontiff, they uttered a cry of rage; they maintained that to attack the indulgence ordained by the pope was to attack the pope himself, and they summoned to their aid all the monks and divines of their school. Tetzel indeed felt that an adversary like Luther was too much for him alone. Greatly disconcerted at the doctor's attack and exasperated to the highest degree, he quitted the vicinity of Wittenberg and repaired to Frankfurt on the Oder, where he arrived in the month of November 1517.

The university of this city, like that of Wittenberg, was of recent date; but it had been founded by the opposite party. Conrad Wimpina, an eloquent man, the ancient rival of Pollich of Mellerstadt, and one of the most distinguished theologians of the age, was a professor there. Wimpina cast an envious glance on the doctor and university of Wittenberg. Their reputation galled him. Tetzel requested him to answer Luther's theses, and Wimpina wrote two lists of antitheses, the object of the first being to defend the doctrine of indulgences, and the second the authority of the pope.

On January 20, 1518, took place that disputation prepared so long beforehand, announced with so much pomp, and on which Tetzel founded such great hopes. On every side he had beaten up for recruits. Monks had been sent from all the cloisters in the neighborhood, and they met to the number of about three hundred.

Tetzel read his theses. They even contained this declaration, that "whoever says that the soul does not escape out of purgatory as soon as the money tinkles in the chest is in error."

But above all, he put forward propositions according to which the pope seemed actually seated as God in the temple of God, according to the apostle's expression. It was convenient for this shameless trafficker to take shelter, with all his disorders and scandals, under the mantle of the pope. He declared himself ready to maintain the following propositions before the numerous assembly by which he was surrounded:

3. We should teach Christians that the pope, by the greatness of his power, is above the whole universal church, and superior to the councils, and that we should implicitly obey his decrees.

4. We should teach Christians that the pope alone has the right of deciding in all matters of Christian faith; that he alone and no one besides him has power to interpret the meaning of Scripture according to his own views, and to approve or condemn all the words or writings of other men.

5. We should teach Christians that the judgment of the pope cannot err in matters concerning the Christian faith, or which are necessary to the salvation of the human race.

6. We should teach Christians that, in matters of faith, we should rely and repose more on the pope's sentiments, as made known by his decisions, than on the opinions of all the learned, which are derived merely from Scripture.

8. We should teach Christians that those who injure the honor or dignity of the pope are guilty of high treason and deserve to be accursed.

17. We should teach Christians that there are many things which the church regards as indisputable articles of universal truth, although they are not to be found in the canon of the Bible or in the writings of the ancient doctors.

44. We should teach Christians to regard as obstinate heretics all who declare by their words, acts, or writings that they will not retract their heretical propositions, even should excommunication after excommunication fall upon them like hail or rain.

48. We should teach Christians that those who protect the errors of heretics, and who by their authority prevent them from being brought before the judge who has a right to hear them,

are excommunicated; that if in the space of a year they do not change their conduct, they will be declared infamous and cruelly punished with divers chastisements, according to the law, and for a warning to other men.

50. We should teach Christians that those who scribble so many books and waste so much paper, who dispute and preach publicly and wickedly about oral confession, the satisfaction of works, the rich and great indulgences of the bishop of Rome, and his power; that the persons who take part with those who preach or write such things, who are pleased with their writings, and circulate them among the people and over the world; that those who speak in private of these things in a contemptuous and shameless manner—should expect to incur the penalties before mentioned, and to precipitate themselves, and others with them, into eternal condemnation of the judgment day, and into merited disgrace even in this world. For 'if so much as a beast touch the mountain, it shall be stoned.'"

We see that Tetzel did not attack Luther only. He probably had the elector of Saxony in view in his forty-eighth thesis. To threaten every contradictor with cruel punishments was the argument of an inquisitor, to which there were no means of replying. The three hundred monks whom Tetzel had collected stared and listened with admiration to what he had said. The theologians of the university were too fearful of being ranked with the abettors of heresy, or else were too strongly attached to Wimpina's principles, openly to attack the astonishing theses that had just been read.

All this affair, about which there had been so much noise, seemed then destined to be a mere sham fight; but among the crowd of students present at the disputation was a youth about twenty years of age named John Knipstrow. He had read Luther's theses and had found them conformable to the doctrines of Scripture. Indignant at beholding the truth publicly trodden underfoot without anyone appearing in its defense, this young man raised his voice, to the great astonishment of all the assembly, and attacked the presumptuous Tetzel.

The poor Dominican, who had not reckoned on any oppositions, was quite confused. After a few exertions, he deserted the field of battle and gave way to Wimpina. The latter resisted more vigorously; but Knipstrow pressed him so closely that, to finish a struggle so unbecoming in his eyes, the president, Wimpina himself, declared the disputation over and immediately proceeded to confer the degree of doctor upon Tetzel in recompense of this glorious combat. In order to get rid of the young orator, Wimpina had him sent to the convent of Pyritz in Pomerania, with an order that he should be strictly watched.

Tetzel, wishing to retrieve the check he had experienced, had recourse to the final argument of Rome and of the inquisitors: to fire. He caused a pulpit and a scaffold to be erected in one of the public walks in the environs of Frankfurt. Thither he repaired in solemn procession, with his insignia of inquisitor of the faith. He gave vent to all his violence from the pulpit. He hurled thunderbolts and exclaimed with his stentorian voice that the heretic Luther deserved to suffer death at the stake. Next, placing the doctor's propositions and sermon on the scaffold, he burned them. He knew better how to do this than to maintain theses. At this time he met with no gainsayers: his victory was complete. The impudent Dominican reentered Frankfurt in triumph.

These theses of Tetzel's form an important epoch in the Reformation. They changed the ground of dispute; they transported it from the indulgence markets to the halls of the Vatican and diverted it from Tetzel to the pope. In the place of that despicable broker whom Luther had so firmly grasped, they substituted the sacred person of the head of the church. Luther was filled with astonishment. It is probable that he would ere long have taken this step himself, but his enemies spared him the trouble. It was henceforward no question of a discredited traffic, but of Rome itself; and the blow by which a daring hand had tried to demolish Tetzel's shop, shook the very foundations of the pontifical throne.

Tetzel's theses served as a rallying cry to the troops of Rome. An uproar against Luther broke out among the monks. Luther's name resounded everywhere from the pulpits of the Dominicans, who addressed themselves to the passions of the people. They called the bold doctor a madman, a seducer, and a demoniac. His doctrine was cried down as the most horrible heresy. "Only wait a fortnight, or a month at most," said they, "and this notorious heretic will be burned." If it had depended solely on the Dominicans, the fate of John Huss would soon have been that of the Saxon doctor also; but God was watching over him. His life was destined to

A Roman Catholic cartoon attacking Luther shows the Devil playing Luther as a set of bagpipes. The bagpipes were probably intended to imply that Luther simply "droned on" in his teaching.

accomplish what the ashes of the Bohemian reformer had begun; for each does the work of God, one by his death, the other by his life.

Many began already to exclaim that the whole University of Wittenberg was deeply tainted with heresy, and pronounced it infamous. "Let us drive out that villain and all his partisans," continued they. In many places these cries succeeded in exciting the passions of the multitude. The public attention was directed against those who shared Luther's opinions; and wherever the monks were the strongest, the friends of the gospel experienced the effects of their hatred. It was thus, with regard to the Reformation, that our Savior's prophecy began to be accomplished: "Men will revile you, and persecute you, and say all manner of evil against you falsely, for my sake." In every age this is the recompense bestowed by the world on the decided friends of the gospel.

When Luther was informed of Tetzel's theses, and of the general attack of which they were the signal, his courage immediately took fire. He felt the necessity of opposing such adversaries face to face, and his intrepid soul had no difficulty in coming to such a decision. But at the same time their weakness revealed to him his own strength, and inspired him with the consciousness of what he really was. "I have more difficulty to refrain from despising my adversaries," wrote he about this time to Spalatin, "and from sinning in this way against Jesus Christ, than I should have in conquering them. They are so ignorant of human and divine things that it is disgraceful to have to fight against them. And yet it is this very ignorance which gives them their inconceivable arrogance and their brazen face."

But the strongest encouragement to his heart, in the midst of this general hostility, was the intimate conviction that his cause was that of truth. "Do not be surprised," wrote he to Spalatin at the beginning of 1518, "that I am so grossly insulted. I listen to their abuse with joy. If they did not curse me, we could not be so firmly assured that the cause I have undertaken is that of God Himself. Christ has been set up for a sign to be spoken against." Said he on another occasion, "I know that from the very beginning of the world the Word of God has been of such a nature that whoever desired to publish it to the world has been compelled, like the apostles, to abandon all things, and to expect death. If it were not so, it would not be the Word of Jesus Christ."

One thing, however, sometimes agitated Luther: the thought of the dissensions his courageous opposition might produce. He knew that a single word might set the world on fire. At times his imagination beheld prince arrayed against prince, and perhaps people against people. His patriotic heart was saddened; his Christian charity, alarmed. He would have desired peace; and yet he must speak, for such was the Lord's will. "I tremble," said he, "I shudder at the idea that I may be an occasion of discord between such mighty princes."

Tetzel, after his *auto-da-fé* at Frankfurt, had hastened to send his theses into Saxony. They will serve as an antidote, thought he, against Luther's. A man from Halle, commissioned by the inquisitor to circulate his theses, arrived at Wittenberg. The students of the university, still indignant that Tetzel should have burned their master's propositions, had scarcely heard of his arrival before they sought him out, surrounded him, mobbed and frightened him. "How can you dare bring such things here?" said they. Some of them bought part of the copies he had with him, others seized the remainder. They thus became masters of his whole stock, amounting to eight hundred copies; and then, unknown to the elector, the senate, the rector, Luther, and all the professors, they posted the following words on the university boards: "Whoever desires to be present at the burning and funeral of Tetzel's theses, must come to the market place at two o'clock."

Crowds assembled at the appointed hour, and the Dominican's propositions were consigned to the flames in the midst of noisy acclamations. One copy escaped the conflagration, which Luther sent afterwards to his friend Lange of Erfurt. The news of this academic execution soon spread through all Germany and made a great noise. Luther was deeply pained at it. "I am surprised," wrote he to his old master, Jodocus, at Erfurt, "you should have believed I allowed Tetzel's theses to be burned. Do you think I have so taken leave of my senses? But what could I do? When I am concerned, everybody believes whatever they like concerning me. . . . I shall work so long as God gives me strength, and with His help I shall fear nothing." "What will come of it," said he to Lange, "I know not, except that the peril in which I am involved becomes greater on this very account."

The theses of Tetzel and of Wimpina, although little esteemed, produced a certain effect. They aggravated the dispute; they widened the rent in the mantle of the church; they brought questions of the highest interest into the controversy. The chiefs of the church began, accordingly, to take a nearer view of the matter and to declare strongly against the reformer. "Truly, I do not know on whom Luther relies," said the bishop of Brandenburg, "since he thus ventures to attack the power of the bishops." Perceiving that this new conjuncture called for new measures, the bishop came himself to Wittenberg. But he found Luther animated with that interior joy which springs from a good conscience and determined to give battle. The bishop saw that the Augustinian monk obeyed a power superior to his own and returned in anger to Brandenburg. One day during the winter of 1518, as he was seated before the fire, he said, turning to those who surrounded him, "I will not lay my head down in peace, until I have thrown Martin into the fire, like this brand"; and he flung the billet into the flames.

The revolution of the sixteenth century was not destined to be accomplished by the heads of the church, any more than that of the first century had been by the Sanhedrin and by the synagogue. The chiefs of the clergy in the sixteenth century were opposed to Luther, to the Reformation, and to its ministers; as they had been to Jesus Christ, to the gospel, to His apostles, and, as too frequently happens in every age, to the truth. "The bishops," said Luther, speaking of the visit the prelate of Brandenburg had paid him, "begin to perceive that they ought to have done what I am doing, and they are ashamed of it. They call me proud and arrogant: I will not deny that I am so; but they are not the people to know either what God is, or what we are."

Chapter 15
Rome Responds

A more formidable resistance than that made by Tetzel was already opposed to Luther. Rome had answered. A reply had gone forth from the walls of the sacred palace. It was not Leo X who had condescended to speak of theology: " 'Tis a mere monkish squabble," he said one day; "the best way is not to meddle with it." And at another time he observed, "It is a drunken German that has written these theses; when the fumes have passed off, he will talk very differently." A Roman Dominican, Sylvester Mazzolini of Prierio, master of the sacred palace, filled the office of censor, and it was in this capacity that he first became acquainted with the theses of the Saxon monk.

A Catholic censor and Luther's theses—what a contrast! Freedom of speech, freedom of inquiry, freedom of belief come into collision in the city of Rome with that power which claims to hold in its hands the monopoly of intelligence and to open and shut at pleasure the mouth of Christendom. The struggle of Christian liberty, which engenders children of God, with pontifical despotism, which produces slaves of Rome, is typified, as it were, in the first days of the Reformation in the encounter of Luther and Prierio.

The Roman censor, prior-general of the Dominicans, empowered to decide on what Christendom should profess or conceal and on what it ought to know or be ignorant of, hastened to reply. He published a writing, which he dedicated to Leo X. In it he spoke contemptuously of the German monk and declared with assurance that "he should like to know whether this Martin had an iron nose or a brazen head, which cannot be broken." And then, under the form of a dialogue, he attacked Luther's theses, employing by turns ridicule, insult, and menaces.

This combat between the Augustinian of Wittenberg and the Dominican of Rome was waged on the very question that is the principle of the Reformation, namely, "What is the sole infallible authority for Christians?" Here is the system of the church, as set forth by its most independent organs:

The letter of the written word is dead without the spirit of interpretation, which alone reveals its hidden meaning. Now, this spirit is not given to every Christian, but to the church—that is, to the priests. It is great presumption to say that He who promised the church to be with her always, even to the end of the world, could have abandoned her to the power of error. It will be said, perhaps, that the doctrine and the constitution of the church are no longer such as we find them in the sacred oracles. Undoubtedly, but this change is only in appearance; it extends only to the form and not to the substance. We may go further: this change is progression. The vivifying power of the divine Spirit has given a reality to what in Scripture was merely an idea; it has filled up the outline of the Word; it has put a finishing touch to its rude sketches; it has completed the work of which the Bible only gave the first rough draft. We must therefore understand the sense of the Holy Scriptures as settled by the church, under the guidance of the Holy Spirit.

From this point the Catholic doctors diverge. General councils, said some, are the representatives of the church. The pope, said others, is the depository of the spirit of interpretation, and no one has a right to understand the Scriptures otherwise than as decreed by the Roman pontiff. This was the opinion of Prierio.

Such was the doctrine opposed by the master of the sacred palace to the infant Reformation. He put forward propositions on the power of the church and of the pope, at which the most shameless flatterers of the church of Rome would have blushed. Here is one of the principles he advanced at the head of his writing: "Whoever relies not on the teaching of the Roman church, and of the Roman pontiff, as the infallible rule of faith, from which the Holy Scriptures themselves derive their strength and their authority, is a heretic."

Then, in a dialogue in which Luther and Prierio were the speakers, the latter sought to refute the doctor's propositions. The opinions of the Saxon monk were altogether strange to a Roman censor; and accordingly, Prierio showed that he understood neither the emotions of his heart nor the springs of his conduct. He measured the doctor of the truth by the petty standard of the servants of Rome. "My dear Luther," said he, "if you were to receive from our lord the pope a good bishopric and a plenary indulgence for repairing your church, you would sing in a softer strain, and you would extol the indulgences you are now disparaging." The Italian, so proud of his elegant manners, occasionally assumed the most scurrilous tone: "If it is the nature of dogs to bite," said he to Luther, "I fear you had a dog for your father." The Dominican at last wondered at his own condescension in speaking to the rebellious monk and ended by showing his adversary the cruel teeth of an inquisitor. "The Roman church," said he, "the apex of whose spiritual and temporal power is in the pope, may constrain by the secular arm those who, having once received the faith, afterwards go astray. It is not bound to employ reason to combat and vanquish rebels."

These words, traced by the pen of a dignitary of the Roman court, were very significant. Still, they did not frighten Luther. The Bible had molded the reformer and begun the Reformation. Luther needed not the testimony of the church in order to believe. His faith had come from the Bible itself, from within and not from without. He was so intimately convinced that the evangelical doctrine was immovably founded on the Word of God that in his eyes all external authority was useless. This experiment made by Luther opened a new futurity to the church. The living source that had welled forth for the monk of Wittenberg was to become a river to slake the thirst of nations.

In order that we may comprehend the Word, the Spirit of God must give understanding, said the church; and it was right so far. But its error had been in considering the Holy Spirit as a monopoly accorded to a certain class and supposing that it could be confined exclusively within assemblies or colleges, in a city or in a conclave. "The wind bloweth where it listeth," had said the Son of God, speaking of God's Spirit; in another place, "They shall *all* be taught of God." The corruption of the church, the ambition of the pontiffs, the passions of the councils, the quarrels of the clergy, the pomp of the prelates, had banished that Holy Ghost. The church, degraded by its love of power and of riches, dishonored in the eyes of the people by the venal use it made of the doctrine of life—the church, which sold salvation to replenish the treasuries drained by its haughtiness and debauchery, had forfeited all respect, and sensible men no longer attached any value to her testimony. Despising so debased an authority, they joyfully turned toward the divine Word and to its infallible authority as toward the only refuge remaining to them in such a general disorder.

The age, therefore, was prepared. The bold movement by which Luther changed the resting-place of the sublimest hopes of the human heart and with a hand of power transported them from the walls of the Vatican to the rock of the Word of God was saluted with enthusiasm. This is the work that the reformer had in view in his reply to Prierio.

He passes over the principles which the Dominican had set forth in the beginning of his work: "But," said he, "following your example, I will also lay down certain fundamental principles.

"The first is this expression of St. Paul: 'Though we, or an angel from heaven, preach any other gospel unto you than that which we have preached unto you, let him be accursed.'

"The second is this passage from St. Augustine to St. Jerome: 'I have learned to render to the canonical books alone the honor of believing most firmly that none of them has erred; as for the others, I do not believe in what they teach, simply because it is they who teach them.' "

Here we see Luther laying down with a firm hand the essential principles of the Reformation: the Word of God, the whole Word of God, nothing but the Word of God. "If you clearly understand these points," continues he, "you will also understand that your dialogue is wholly overturned by them, for you have only brought forward the expressions and opinions of St. Thomas." Then, attacking his adversary's axioms, he frankly declares that he believes popes and councils can err. He complains of the flatteries of the Roman courtiers, who ascribe both temporal and spiritual power to the pope. He declares that the church exists virtually in Christ alone and representatively in the councils.

Nevertheless, Luther speaks of Leo with respect. "I know," said he, "that we may compare him to Daniel in Babylon; his innocence has often endangered his life." He concludes by a few words in reply to Prierio's threats: "Finally, you say that the pope is at once pontiff and emperor, and that he is mighty to compel obedience by the secular arm. Do you thirst for blood? I protest that you will not frighten me . . . by . . . the threatening noise of your words. If I am put to death, Christ lives, Christ my Lord and the Lord of all, blessed forevermore. Amen."

Prierio published an answer and then a third book, *On the Irrefragable Truth of the Church and of the Roman Pontiff,* in which, relying upon the ecclesiastical law, he asserted that although the pope should make the whole world go with him to hell, he could neither be condemned nor deposed. The pope was at last obliged to impose silence on Prierio.

A new adversary ere long entered the lists; he also was a Dominican. James Hochstraten, inquisitor at Cologne, shuddered at Luther's boldness. It was necessary for monkish darkness and fanaticism to come into contact with him who was destined to give them a mortal blow. Monasticism had sprung up as the primitive truth began to disappear. Since then, monks and errors had grown up side by side. The man had now appeared who was to accelerate their ruin, but these robust champions could not abandon the field of battle without a struggle. It lasted all the reformer's life, but in Hochstraten this combat is singularly personified: Hochstraten and Luther, the free and courageous Christian with the impetuous slave of monkish superstitions. Hochstraten lost his temper, grew furious, and called loudly for the heretic's death. It was by the stake he wished to secure the triumph of Rome. "It is high treason against the church," exclaimed he, "to allow so horrible a heretic to live one hour longer. Let the scaffold be instantly erected for him!" This murderous advice was, alas, but too effectually carried out in many countries; the voices of numerous martyrs, as in the primitive times of the church, gave testimony to the truth, even in the midst of flames. But in vain were the sword and the stake invoked against Luther. The Angel of the Lord kept watch continually around him and preserved him.

Luther answered Hochstraten in few words, but with great energy: "Go," said he in conclusion, "go, thou raving murderer, who criest for the blood of thy brethren; it is my earnest desire that thou forbear to call me Christian and faithful, and that thou continue, on the contrary, to decry me as a heretic. Understandest thou these things, bloodthirsty man, enemy of the truth? And if thy mad rage should hurry thee to undertake anything against me, take care to act with circumspection and to choose thy time well. God knows what is my purpose, if He grant me life. My hope and my expectation, God willing, will not deceive me." Hochstraten was silent.

A more painful attack awaited the reformer. A distinguished professor, by name John Meyer, was then teaching at the University of Ingolstadt in Bavaria. He was born at Eck, and was commonly styled Doctor Eck. He was a friend of Luther, who esteemed his talents and his information. He was full of intelligence, had read much, and possessed an excellent memory. He united learning with eloquence. His gestures and his voice expressed the vivacity of his genius. Eck, as regards talent, was in the south of Germany what Luther was in the north. They were the two most remarkable theologians of that epoch, although having very different tendencies. Ingolstadt was almost the rival of Wittenberg. The reputation of these two doctors attracted from every quarter to the universities where they taught a crowd of students eager to listen to their teaching. Their personal qualities, not less than their learning, endeared them to their disciples. The character of Dr. Eck has been attacked, but one trait of his life will show that his heart was not closed against generous impulses.

Among the students whom his reputation had attracted to Ingolstadt was a young man named Urban Regius, born on the shores of an Alpine lake. On his arrival at Ingolstadt, Urban followed the philosophical courses and gained the professor's favor. Compelled to provide for his own wants, he was obliged to undertake the charge of some young noblemen. He had not only to watch over their conduct and their studies but even to provide with his own money the books and clothing that they stood in need of. These youths dressed with elegance and were fond of good living. Regius, in his embarrassed condition, entreated the parents to withdraw their sons. "Take courage," was their reply. His debts increased; his creditors became pressing: he knew not what to do.

The emperor was at that time collecting an army against the Turks. Recruiting parties arrived at Ingolstadt, and in his despair Urban enlisted. Dressed in his military uniform, he appeared in the ranks at their final review previous to leaving the town. At that moment, Dr. Eck came into the square with several of his colleagues. To his great surprise he recognized his pupil among the recruits. "Urban Regius," said he, fixing on him a piercing glance.

"Here," replied the young soldier.

"Pray, what is the cause of this change?"

The young man told his story. "I will take the matter upon myself," replied Eck, who then took away his halberd and bought him off. The parents, threatened by the doctor with their prince's displeasure, sent the money necessary to pay their children's expenses. Urban Regius was saved and became somewhat later one of the bulwarks of the Reformation.

Doctor Eck, the celebrated professor of Ingolstadt, the deliverer of Urban Regius, and Luther's friend, had received the famous theses. Eck was not a man to defend the abuse of indulgences, but he was a doctor of the schools and not of the Bible: well versed in the scholastic writings, but not in the Word of God. If Prierio had represented Rome, if Hochstraten had represented the monks, Eck represented the schoolmen. The schools, which for five centuries past had domineered over Christendom, far from giving way at the first blow of the reformer, rose up haughtily to crush the man who dared pour out upon them the floods of his contempt. Eck and Luther, the school and the Word, had more than one struggle; but it was now that the combat began.

Eck could not but find errors in many of Luther's positions. Nothing leads us to doubt the sincerity of his convictions. He as enthusiastically maintained the scholastic opinions as Luther did the declarations of the Word of God. We may even suppose that he felt no little pain when he found himself obliged to oppose his old friend; it would seem, however, from the manner of his attack, that passion and jealousy had some share in his motives.

He gave the name of "Obelisks" to his remarks against Luther's theses. A copy fell into the hands of Link, a friend of Luther and preacher at Nuremberg. The latter hastened to send it to the reformer. Eck was a far more formidable adversary than Tetzel, Prierio, or Hochstraten: the more his work surpassed theirs in learning and in subtlety, the more dangerous it was. He assumed a tone of compassion toward his "feeble adversary," being well aware that pity inflicts more harm than anger. He insinuated that Luther's propositions circulated the Bohemian poison, that they savored of Bohemia; and by these malicious allusions, he drew upon Luther the unpopularity and hatred attached in Germany to the name of John Huss and to the schismatics of his country.

The malice that pervaded this treatise exasperated Luther, but the thought that this blow came from an old friend grieved him still more. Luther poured out the deep sorrow of his heart in a letter to Egranus, pastor at Zwickau. "In the 'Obelisks' I am styled a venomous man, a Bohemian, a heretic, a seditious, insolent, rash person. I pass by the milder insults, such as drowsy-headed, stupid, ignorant, contemner of the sovereign pontiff, etc. This book is brimful of the blackest outrages. Yet he who penned them is a distinguished man with a spirit full of learning and a learning full of spirit; and what causes me the deepest vexation, he is a man who was united to me by a great and recently contracted friendship: it is John Eck, Doctor of Divinity, chancellor of Ingolstadt, a man celebrated and illustrious by his writings. If I did not know Satan's thoughts, I should be astonished at the fury which has led this man to break off so sweet and so new a friendship, and that too without warning me, without writing to me, without saying a single word."

But if Luther's heart was wounded, his courage was not cast down. On the contrary, he rose up invigorated for the contest. "Rejoice, my brother," said he to Egranus, whom a violent enemy had likewise attacked, "rejoice, and do not let these flying leaves affright thee. The more my adversaries give way to their fury, the farther I advance. I leave the things that are behind me, in order that they may bay at them, and I pursue what lies before me, that they may bay at them in their turn."

Eck was sensible how disgraceful his conduct had been and endeavored to vindicate himself in a letter to Carlstadt. In it he styled Luther "their common friend" and cast all the blame on the bishop of Eichstadt, at whose solicitation he pretended to have written his work. He said that it had not been his intention to publish the "Obelisks"; that he would have felt more regard for the bonds of friendship that united him to Luther; and demanded, in conclusion, that Luther, instead of disputing publicly with him, should turn his weapons against the Frankfurt divines.

All these fine phrases did not persuade Luther, who was yet inclined to remain silent. "I will swallow patiently," said he, "this sop, worthy of Cerberus." But his friends differed from him: they solicited, they even constrained him to answer. He therefore replied to the "Obelisks" by his "Asterisks," opposing—as he said, playing on the words—to the rust and livid hue of the Ingolstadt doctor's "Obelisks," the light and dazzling brightness of the stars of heaven. In this work he treated his adversary with less severity than he had shown his previous antagonists, but his indignation pierced through his words.

He showed that in these chaotic "Obelisks" there was nothing from the Holy Scriptures, nothing from the Fathers of the church, nothing from the ecclesiastical canons; that they were filled with scholastic glosses, opinions, mere opinions and empty dreams; in a word, the very things that Luther had attacked. The "Asterisks" are full of life and animation. The author is indignant at the errors of his friend's book, but he pities the man. He professes anew the fundamental principle which he laid down in his answer to Prierio: "The supreme pontiff is a man and may be led into error, but God is truth and cannot err." Further on he says to the scholastic doctor, "It would be great impudence assuredly for any one to teach in the philosophy of Aristotle what he cannot prove by the authority of that ancient author. You grant it. It is, *a fortiori,* the most impudent of all impudence to affirm in the church and among Christians what Christ Himself has not taught. Now, where is it found in the Bible that the treasure of Christ's merits is in the hands of the pope?"

He adds further, "As for the malicious reproach of Bohemian heresy, I bear this calumny with patience through love of Christ. I live in a celebrated university, in a well-famed city, in a respectable bishopric, in a powerful duchy, where all are orthodox, and where, undoubtedly, so wicked a heretic would not be tolerated."

Luther did not publish the "Asterisks"; he communicated them solely to his friends. They were not given to the public till long after.

This rupture between the two doctors of Ingolstadt and Wittenberg made a great sensation in Germany. They had many friends in common. Scheurl especially, who appears to have been the man by whom the two doctors had been connected, was alarmed. He was one of those who desired to see a thorough reform in the German church by means of its most distinguished organs. But if, at the very outset, the most eminent theologians of the day should fall to blows— if, while Luther came forward with novelties, Eck became the representative of antiquity, what disruption might not be feared? Would not numerous partisans rally round each of these two chiefs, and would not two hostile camps be formed in the bosom of the empire?

Scheurl endeavored therefore to reconcile Eck and Luther. The latter declared his willingness to forget everything; that he loved the genius, that he admired the learning of Dr. Eck, and that what his old friend had done had caused him more pain than anger. "I am ready," said he to Scheurl, "for peace and for war, but I prefer peace. Apply yourself to the task; grieve with us that the Devil has thrown among us this beginning of discord, and afterwards rejoice that Christ in His mercy has crushed it." About the same time he wrote Eck a letter full of affection, but Eck made no reply. He did not even send him any message. It was no longer a season for reconciliation. The contest daily grew warmer. Eck's pride and implacable spirit soon broke entirely the last ties of that friendship which every day grew weaker.

Such were the struggles that the champion of the Word of God had to sustain at the very entrance of his career.

Chapter 16
Luther's "Paradoxes"

Luther, not content with announcing the gospel truth in the place of his residence, both to the students of the academy and to the people, was desirous of scattering elsewhere the seed of sound doctrine. In the spring of 1518, a general chapter of the Augustinian order was to be held at Heidelberg. Luther was summoned to it as one of the most distinguished men of the order. Immediately after the festival of Easter, he set out calmly on foot on April 13, 1518.

He took with him a guide named Urban, who carried his little baggage, and who was to accompany him as far as Würzburg. At Weissenfels, the pastor, whom he did not know, immediately recognized him as the Wittenberg doctor and gave him a hearty welcome. At Erfurt, two other brothers of the Augustinian order joined him. At Judenbach, they fell in with the elector's privy councilor, Degenhard Pfeffinger, who entertained them at the inn where they had found him. "I had the pleasure," wrote Luther to Spalatin, "of making this rich lord a few groats poorer; you know how I like on every opportunity to levy contributions on the rich for the benefit of the poor, especially if the rich are my friends." He reached Coburg overwhelmed with fatigue. "All goes well, by God's grace," wrote he, "except that I acknowledge having sinned in undertaking this journey on foot. But for that sin I have no need, I think, of the remission of indulgences; for my contrition is perfect, and the satisfaction plenary. I am overcome with fatigue, and all the conveyances are full. Is not this enough, and more than enough, of penance, contrition, and satisfaction?"

The reformer of Germany, unable to find room in the public conveyances, and no one being willing to give up his place, was compelled, notwithstanding his weariness, to leave Coburg the next morning humbly on foot. He reached Würzburg the second Sunday after Easter, toward evening. Here he sent back his guide.

At Würzburg, Luther had met his two friends, the vicar-general Staupitz and Lange, the prior of Erfurt, who had offered him a place in their carriage. They thus traveled together for three days, conversing with one another. On April 21, they arrived at Heidelberg. Luther lodged at the Augustinian convent.

The elector of Saxony had given him a letter for the Count Palatine Wolfgang, duke of Bavaria. Luther repaired to his magnificent castle, the situation of which excites, even to this day, the admiration of strangers. The monk from the plains of Saxony had a heart to admire the situation of Heidelberg, where the two beautiful valleys of the Rhine and the Neckar unite. He delivered his letter to James Simler, steward of the household. The latter on reading it observed, "In truth, you have here a valuable letter of credit." The count palatine received Luther with much kindness and frequently invited him to his table, together with Lange and Staupitz. So friendly a reception was a source of great comfort to Luther. "We were very happy and amused one another with agreeable and pleasant conversation," said he, "eating and drinking, examining all the beauties of the palatine palace, admiring the ornaments, arms, cuirasses—in fine, everything remarkable contained in this celebrated and truly regal castle."

But Luther had another task to perform. Having arrived at a university which exercised great influence over the west and south of Germany, he was there to strike a blow that should shake the churches of these countries. He began, therefore, to write some theses which he purposed maintaining in a public disputation. Such discussions were not unusual; but Luther felt that this one, to be useful, should lay forcible hold upon men's minds. His disposition, besides, naturally led him to present truth under a paradoxical form. The professors of the university would not permit the discussion to take place in their large theater, and Luther was obliged to take a hall in the Augustinian convent. April 26 was the day appointed for the disputation.

Luther's reputation attracted a large audience: professors, students, courtiers, citizens, came in crowds. The following are some of the doctor's "Paradoxes"; for so he designated his theses.

1. The law of God is a salutary doctrine of life. Nevertheless, it cannot aid man in attaining to righteousness; on the contrary, it impedes him.

3. Man's works, however fair and good they may be, are, however, to all appearance, nothing but deadly sins.

4. God's works, however unsightly and bad they may appear, have, however, an everlasting merit.

9. To say that works done out of Christ are truly dead but not deadly is a dangerous forgetfulness of the fear of God.

13. Since the fall of man, freewill is but an idle word; and if man does all he can, he still sins mortally.

18. It is certain that man must altogether despair of himself in order to be made capable of receiving Christ's grace.

22. The wisdom which endeavors to learn the invisible perfections of God in His works puffs up, hardens, and blinds a man.

23. The law calls forth God's anger, kills, curses, accuses, judges, and condemns whatsoever is not in Christ.

24. Yet this wisdom is not evil, and the law is not to be rejected; but the man who studies not the knowledge of God under the cross turns to evil whatever is good.

25. That man is not justified who performs many works, but he who without works has much faith in Christ.

26. The law says, Do this; and what it commands is never done. Grace says, Believe in Him; and immediately all things are done.

28. The love of God finds nothing in man, but creates in him what He loves. The love of man proceeds from His well-beloved.

Five doctors of divinity attacked these theses. They had read them with all the astonishment that novelty excites. Such theology appeared very extravagant; and yet they discussed these points, according to Luther's own testimony, with a courtesy that inspired him with much esteem for them, but at the same time with earnestness and discernment. Luther, on his side, displayed wonderful mildness in his replies, unrivalled patience in listening to the objections of his adversaries, and all the quickness of St. Paul in solving the difficulties opposed to him. His replies were short, but full of the Word of God, and excited the admiration of his hearers. "He is in all respects like Erasmus," said many, "but surpasses him in one thing: he openly professes what Erasmus is content merely to insinuate."

The disputation was drawing to an end. Luther's adversaries had retired with honor from the field; the youngest of them, Doctor George Niger, alone continued the struggle with the powerful champion. Alarmed at the daring propositions of the monk and not knowing what further arguments to have recourse to, he exclaimed, with an accent of fear, "If our peasants heard such things, they would stone you to death!" At these words the whole auditory burst into a loud laugh.

Never had an assembly listened with so much attention to a theological discussion. The first words of the reformer had aroused their minds. Questions which shortly before would have been treated with indifference were now full of interest. On the countenances of many of the hearers a looker-on might have seen reflected the new ideas which the bold assertions of the Saxon doctor had awakened in their minds.

Three young men in particular were deeply moved. One of them, Martin Bucer by name, was a Dominican, twenty-seven years of age, who, notwithstanding the prejudices of his order, appeared unwilling to lose one of the doctor's words. He was born in a small town of Alsace and had entered a convent at sixteen. He soon displayed such capacity that the most enlightened monks entertained the highest expectations of him. "He will one day be the ornament of our order," said they. His superiors had sent him to Heidelberg to study philosophy, theology, Greek, and Hebrew. At that period Erasmus published several of his works, which Bucer read with avidity.

Soon appeared the earliest writings of Luther. The Alsatian student hastened to compare the reformer's doctrines with the Holy Scriptures. Some misgivings as to the truth of the pope's religion arose in his mind. It was thus that the light was diffused in those days.

The elector-palatine took particular notice of the young man. His strong and sonorous voice, his graceful manners and eloquent language, the freedom with which he attacked the vices of the day, made him a distinguished preacher. He was appointed chaplain to the court and was fulfilling his functions when Luther's journey to Heidelberg was announced. No one repaired with greater eagerness to the hall of the Augustinian convent. He took with him paper, pens, and ink, intending to take down what the doctor said. But while his hand was swiftly tracing Luther's words, the finger of God, in more indelible characters, wrote on his heart the great truths he heard. The first gleams of the doctrine of grace were diffused through his soul during this memorable hour. The Dominican was gained over to Christ.

Not far from Bucer stood John Brentz or Brentius, then nineteen years of age. He was the son of a magistrate in a city of Swabia, and at thirteen had been entered as student at Heidelberg. None manifested greater application. He rose at midnight and began to study. This habit became so confirmed that during his whole life he could not sleep after that hour. In later years he consecrated these tranquil moments to meditation on the Scriptures. Brentz was one of the first to perceive the new light then dawning on Germany. He welcomed it with a heart abounding in love. He eagerly perused Luther's works. But what was his delight when he could hear the writer himself at Heidelberg! One of the doctor's propositions more especially startled the youthful scholar; it was this: "That man is not justified before God who performs many works; but he who without works has much faith in Jesus Christ."

A pious woman of Heilbronn on the Neckar, wife of a senator of that town, named Snepf, had imitated Hannah's example and consecrated her first-born son to the Lord with a fervent desire to see him devote himself to the study of theology. This young man, who was born in 1495, made rapid progress in learning; but either from taste, or from ambition, or in compliance with his father's wishes, he applied to the study of jurisprudence. The pious mother was grieved to behold her child, her Ehrhard, pursuing another career than that to which she had consecrated him. She admonished him, entreated him, prayed him continually to remember the vow she had made on the day of his birth. Overcome at last by his mother's perseverance, Ehrhard Snepf gave way. Ere long he felt such a taste for his new studies that nothing in the world could have diverted him from them.

He was very intimate with Bucer and Brentz, and they were friends until death; "for," says one of their biographers, "friendships based on the love of letters and of virtue never fail." He was present with his two friends at the Heidelberg discussion. The paradoxes and courage of the Wittenberg doctor gave him a new impulse. Rejecting the vain opinion of human merits, he embraced the doctrine of the free justification of the sinner.

The next day Bucer went to Luther. "I had a familiar and private conversation with him," said Bucer, "a most exquisite repast, not of dainties, but of truths that were set before me. To whatever objection I made, the doctor had a reply and explained everything with the greatest clearness. Oh, would to God that I had time to write more!" Luther himself was touched with Bucer's sentiments. "He is the only brother of his order," wrote he to Spalatin, "who is sincere; he is a young man of great promise. He received me with simplicity and conversed with me very earnestly. He is worthy of our confidence and love."

Brentz, Snepf, and many others, excited by the new truths that began to dawn upon their minds, also visited Luther; they talked and conferred with him; they begged for explanations on what they did not understand. The reformer replied, strengthening his arguments by the Word of God. Each sentence imparted fresh light to their minds. A new world was opening before them.

After Luther's departure, these noble-minded men began to teach at Heidelberg. They felt it their duty to continue what the man of God had begun and not allow the flame to expire which he had lighted up. The students will speak when the teachers are silent. Brentz, although still so young, explained the Gospel of St. Matthew, at first in his own room, and afterwards, when the chamber became too small, in the theater of philosophy. The theologians, envious at the crowd of hearers this young man drew around him, became irritated. Brentz then took orders and transferred his lectures to the college of the Canons of the Holy Ghost. Thus the fire already kindled up in Saxony now glowed in Heidelberg. The centers of light increased in number. This period has been denominated the seed-time of the Palatinate.

But it was not the Palatinate alone that reaped the fruits of the Heidelberg disputation. These courageous friends of the truth soon became shining lights in the church. They all attained to exalted stations and took part in many of the debates which the Reformation occasioned. Strasburg and, a little later, England were indebted to Bucer for a purer knowledge of the truth. Snepf first declared it at Marburg, then at Stuttgart, Tübingen, and Jena. Brentz, after having taught at Heidelberg, continued his labors for a long period at Tübingen and at Halle in Swabia.

This disputation carried forward Luther himself. He increased daily in the knowledge of the truth. "I belong to those," said he, "who improve by writing and by teaching others, and not to those who from nothing become on a sudden great and learned doctors."

He was overjoyed at seeing with what avidity the students of the schools received the dawning truth, and this consoled him when he found the old doctors so deep-rooted in their opinions. "I have the glorious hope," said he, "that as Christ, when rejected by the Jews, turned to the Gentiles, we shall now also behold the new theology, that has been rejected by these gray-beards with their empty and fantastical notions, welcomed by the rising generation."

The chapter being ended, Luther thought of returning to Wittenberg. The count palatine gave him a letter for the elector, dated May 1, in which he said that "Luther had shown so much skill in the disputation, as greatly to contribute to the renown of the University of Wittenberg." He was not allowed to return on foot. The Nuremberg Augustinians conducted him as far as Würzburg, whence he proceeded to Erfurt with the friars from that city.

Luther quitted Erfurt in the carriage belonging to the convent, which took him to Eisleben. From thence, the Augustinians of the place, proud of a doctor who had shed such glory on their order and on their city, his native place, conveyed him to Wittenberg with their own horses and at their own expense. Everyone desired to bestow some mark of affection and esteem on this extraordinary man whose fame was constantly increasing.

He arrived on the Saturday after Ascension Day. The journey had done him good, and his friends thought him improved in appearance and stronger than before his departure. They were delighted at all he had to tell them. Luther rested some time after the fatigues of his journey and his dispute at Heidelberg, but this rest was only a preparation for severer toils.

Chapter 17
Luther and Leo X

Truth at last had raised her head in the midst of Christendom. Victorious over the inferior ministers of the papacy, she was now to enter upon a struggle with its chief in person. We are about to contemplate Luther contending with Rome.

It was after his return from Heidelberg that he took this bold step. His early theses on the indulgences had been misunderstood. He determined to explain their meaning with greater clearness. From the clamors that a blind hatred extorted from his enemies, he had learned how important it was to win over the most enlightened part of the nation to the truth: he therefore resolved to appeal to its judgment by setting forth the basis on which his new convictions were founded. It was requisite at once to challenge the decision of Rome: he did not hesitate to send his explanations thither. While he presented them with one hand to the enlightened and impartial readers of his nation, with the other he laid them before the throne of the sovereign pontiff.

These explanations of his theses, which he styled *Resolutions,* were written in a very moderate tone. Luther endeavored to soften down the passages that had occasioned the greatest irritation, and thus gave proof of genuine humility. But at the same time he showed himself to be unshaken in his convictions, and courageously defended all the propositions which truth obliged him to maintain. He repeated once more that every truly penitent Christian possesses remission of sins without papal indulgences; that the pope, like the meanest priest, can do no more than simply declare what God has already pardoned, that the treasury of the merits of the saints, administered by the pope, was a pure chimera, and that the Holy Scriptures were the sole rule of faith.

"I care not for what pleases or displeases the pope. He is a man like other men. There have been many popes who loved not only errors and vices, but still more extraordinary things. I listen to the pope as pope; that is to say, when he speaks in the canons according to the canons, or when he decrees some article in conjunction with a council, but not when he speaks after his own ideas. Were I to do otherwise, ought I not to say with those who know not Christ, that the horrible massacres of Christians by which Julian II was stained were the good deeds of a gentle shepherd toward Christ's flock?"

"I cannot help wondering," continues Luther, "at the simplicity of those who have asserted that the two swords of the gospel represent, one the spiritual, the other the secular power. Yes, the pope wields a sword of iron; it is thus he exhibits himself to Christendom, not as a tender father, but as a formidable tyrant. Alas, an angry God has given us the sword we longed for and taken away that which we despised. In no part of the world have there been more terrible wars than among Christians. Why did not that acute mind which discovered this fine commentary interpret in the same subtle manner the history of the two keys entrusted to St. Peter, and lay it down as a doctrine of the church that one key serves to open the treasures of heaven, the other, the treasures of the earth?"

"It is impossible," says Luther in another place, "for a man to be a Christian without having Christ; and if he has Christ, he possesses at the same time all that belongs to Christ. What gives peace to our consciences is this: by faith our sins are no longer ours, but Christ's, on whom God has laid them all; and on the other hand, all Christ's righteousness belongs to us, to whom God has given it. Christ lays His hand on us, and we are healed. He casts His mantle over us, and we are sheltered; for He is the glorious Savior, blessed forevermore."

While Luther attacked the papacy, he spoke honorably of Leo X. "The times in which we live are so evil," said he, "that even the most exalted individuals have no power to help the church. We have at present a very good pope in Leo X. His sincerity, his learning inspire us with joy. But what can be done by this one man, amiable and gracious as he is? He was worthy of being pope in better days. In our age we deserve none but such men as Julius II and Alexander VI."

He then comes to the point: "I will say what I mean boldly and briefly: the church needs a reformation. And this cannot be the work either of a single man, as the pope, or of many men, as the cardinals and councils; but it must be that of the whole world, or rather, it is a work that belongs to God alone. As for the time in which such a reformation should begin, He alone knows who has created all time. The dike is broken, and it is no longer in our power to restrain the impetuous and overwhelming billows."

This is a sample of the declarations and ideas which Luther addressed to his enlightened fellow countrymen.

Luther was still filled with respect for the head of the church. He supposed Leo to be a just man and a sincere lover of the truth. He resolved, therefore, to write to him. A week after, on Trinity Sunday, May 30, 1518, he penned a letter, of which we give a few specimens.

"To the most blessed Father Leo X, sovereign bishop, Martin Luther, an Augustinian friar, wishes eternal salvation.

"I am informed, most holy father, that wicked reports are in circulation about me, and that my name is in bad odor with your holiness. I am called a heretic, apostate, traitor, and a thousand other insulting names. What I see fills me with surprise; what I learn fills me with alarm. But the only foundation of my tranquility remains, a pure and peaceful conscience. Deign to listen to me, most holy father, to me who am but a child and unlearned."

After relating the origin of the whole matter, Luther thus continues: "In all the taverns nothing was heard but complaints against the avarice of the priests and attacks against the power of the keys and of the sovereign bishop. Of this the whole of Germany is a witness. When I was informed of these things, my zeal was aroused for the glory of Christ, as it appeared to me; or, if another explanation be sought, my young and warm blood was inflamed.

"I forewarned several princes of the church; but some laughed at me, and others turned a deaf ear. The terror of your name seemed to restrain everyone. I then published my disputation.

"And behold, most holy father, the conflagration that is reported to have set the whole world on fire.

"Now what shall I do? I cannot retract, and I see that this publication draws down upon me an inconceivable hatred from every side. I have no wish to appear before the world; for I have no learning, no genius, and am far too little for such great matters; above all, in this illustrious age, in which Cicero himself, were he living, would be compelled to hide himself in some dark corner.

"But in order to quiet my adversaries and to reply to the solicitations of many friends, I here publish my thoughts. I publish them, holy father, that I may be in greater safety under the shadow of your wings. All those who desire it will thus understand with what simplicity of heart I have called upon the ecclesiastical authority to instruct me, and what respect I have shown to the owner of the keys. If I had not behaved with propriety, it would have been impossible for the most serene Lord Frederick, duke and elector of Saxony, who shines among the friends of the apostolic and Christian truth, to have ever endured in his University of Wittenberg a man so dangerous as I am asserted to be.

"For this reason, most holy father, I fall at the feet of your holiness and submit myself to you, with all that I have and with all that I am. Destroy my cause or espouse it; declare me right or wrong; take away my life or restore it, as you please. I shall acknowledge your voice as the voice of Jesus Christ, who presides and speaks through you. If I have merited death, I shall not refuse to die; the earth is the Lord's, and all that is therein. May He be praised through all eternity. Amen. May He uphold you forever. Amen."

While he was thus looking with confidence toward Rome, Rome already entertained thoughts of vengeance against him. As early as April 3, Cardinal Raphael of Rovera had written to the Elector Frederick, in the pope's name, intimating that his orthodoxy was suspected and cautioning him against protecting Luther. "Cardinal Raphael," said the latter, "would have had great pleasure in seeing me burned by Frederick." Thus was Rome beginning to sharpen her weapons against Luther. It was through his protector's mind that she resolved to aim the first blow. If she succeeded in destroying that shelter under which the monk of Wittenberg was reposing, he would become an easy prey to her.

The German princes were very tenacious of their reputation for orthodoxy. The slightest suspicion of heresy filled them with alarm. The court of Rome had skillfully taken advantage of this disposition. Frederick, moreover, had always been attached to the religion of his forefathers, and hence Raphael's letter made a deep impression on his mind. But it was a rule with the elector never to act precipitately. He knew that truth was not always on the side of the strongest. The disputes between the empire and Rome had taught him to mistrust the interested views of that court. He had found out that to be a Christian prince, it was not necessary to be the pope's slave.

Pope Leo X and Two Cardinals by Raphael (Scala Institute)

"He was not one of those profane persons," said Melancthon, "who order all changes to be arrested at their very commencement. Frederick submitted himself to God. He carefully perused the writings that appeared, and did not allow that to be destroyed which he believed to be true." It was not from want of power; for, besides being sovereign in his own states, he enjoyed in the empire a respect very little inferior to that which was paid to the emperor himself.

Luther no longer stood alone; and although his faith required no other support than that of God, a phalanx which defended him against his enemies had grown up around him. The German people had heard the voice of the reformer. From his sermons and writings issued those flashes of light which aroused and illumined his contemporaries. The energy of his faith poured forth in torrents of fire on their frozen hearts. The life that God had placed in this extraordinary mind communicated itself to the dead body of the church. Christendom, motionless for so many centuries, became animated with religious enthusiasm. The people's attachment to Roman Catholic superstitions diminished day by day; there were always fewer hands that offered money to purchase forgiveness; and at the same time Luther's reputation continued to increase. The people turned toward him and saluted him with love and respect as the intrepid defender of truth and liberty. Undoubtedly all men did not see the depth of the doctrines he proclaimed. For the greater number it was sufficient to know that he stood up against the pope, and that the dominion of the priests and monks was shaken by the might of his word.

But for a great number also, Luther's coming was something more than this. The Word of God, which he so skillfully wielded, pierced their hearts like a two-edged sword. In many bosoms was kindled an earnest desire of obtaining the assurance of pardon and eternal life. Since the primitive ages, the church had never witnessed such hungering and thirsting after righteousness. If the eloquence of Peter the Hermit and of St. Bernard had inspired the people of the Middle Ages to assume a perishable cross, the eloquence of Luther prevailed on those of his day to take up the real cross, the truth which saves. Thus the simple Word of truth had raised a powerful army for Luther.

Chapter 18
The Pope Takes Action

This army was very necessary, for the nobles began to be alarmed, and the empire and the church were already uniting their power to get rid of this troublesome monk. If a strong and courageous prince had then filled the imperial throne, he might have taken advantage of this religious agitation, and in reliance upon the Word of God and upon the nation, have given a fresh impulse to the ancient opposition against the papacy. But Maximilian was too old, and he had determined, besides, on making every sacrifice in order to attain the great object of his life, the aggrandizement of his house, and consequently the elevation of his grandson.

The emperor was at that time holding an imperial diet at Augsburg. Six electors had gone thither in person at his summons. All the Germanic states were there represented. The kings of France, Hungary, and Poland had sent their ambassadors. These princes and envoys displayed great magnificence. The Turkish war was one of the causes for which the diet had been assembled. The legate of Leo X earnestly urged the meeting on this point. The states, learning wisdom from the bad use that had formerly been made of their contributions, and wisely counseled by the Elector Frederick, were satisfied with declaring they would reflect on the matter, and at the same time produced fresh complaints against Rome. A Latin discourse, published during the diet, boldly pointed out the real danger to the German princes. "You desire to put the Turk to flight," said the author. "This is well, but I am very much afraid that you are mistaken in the person. You should look for him in Italy, and not in Asia."

Another affair of no less importance was to occupy the diet. Maximilian desired to have his grandson Charles, already king of Spain and Naples, proclaimed king of the Romans, and his successor in the imperial dignity. The pope knew his own interests too well to desire to see the imperial throne filled by a prince whose power in Italy might be dangerous to himself. The emperor imagined he had already won over most of the electors and the states, but he met with a vigorous resistance from Frederick. All solicitations proved unavailing; in vain did the ministers and the best friends of the elector unite their entreaties to those of the emperor; he was immovable, and showed on this occasion, as it has been remarked, that he had firmness of mind not to swerve from a resolution which he had once acknowledged to be just. The emperor's design failed.

Henceforth Maximilian sought to gain the goodwill of the pope in order to render him favorable to his plans; and to give more striking proof of his attachment, he wrote to him as follows, on August 5: "Most holy father, we have learned these few days since that a friar of the Augustinian order, named Martin Luther, has presumed to maintain certain propositions on the traffic of indulgences; a matter that displeases us the more because this friar has found many protectors, among whom are persons of exalted station. If your holiness, and the very reverend fathers of the church—that is, the cardinals—do not soon exert your authority to put an end to these scandals, these pernicious teachers will not only seduce the simple people, but they will involve great princes in their destruction. We will take care that whatever your holiness may decree in this matter for the glory of God Almighty shall be enforced throughout the whole empire."

This letter must have been written immediately after some warm discussion between Maximilian and Frederick. On the same day, the elector wrote to Raphael of Rovera. He had learned, no doubt, that the emperor was writing to the Roman pontiff, and to parry the blow, he put himself in communication with Rome.

"I shall never have any other desire," says he, "than to show my submission to the universal church.

"Accordingly, I have never defended either the writings or the sermons of Doctor Martin Luther. I learn, besides, that he has always offered to appear, under a safe-conduct, before impartial, learned, and Christian judges, in order to defend his doctrine, and to submit, in case he should be convicted of error by the Scriptures themselves."

Leo X, who up to this time had let the business follow its natural course, aroused by the clamors of the theologians and monks,

ᐊMAXIMILIANVSᐊ

Emperor Maximilian I, ruler of the Holy Roman Empire

nominated an ecclesiastical commission at Rome empowered to try Luther, and in which Sylvester Prierio, the reformer's great enemy, was at once accuser and judge. The case was soon prepared, and the court summoned Luther to appear before it in person within sixty days.

Luther was tranquilly awaiting at Wittenberg the good effects that he imagined his submissive letter to the pope would produce, when on August 7, only two days after the letters of Maximilian and of Frederick were sent off, he received the summons of the Roman tribunal. "At the very moment I was expecting a blessing," said he, "I saw the thunderbolt fall upon me. I was the lamb that troubled the water the wolf was drinking. Tetzel escaped, and I was to permit myself to be devoured."

This summons caused general alarm in Wittenberg; for whatever course Luther might take, he could not escape danger. If he went to Rome, he would there become the victim of his enemies. If he refused to appear, he would be condemned for contumacy, as was usual, without the power of escaping; for it was known that the legate had received orders to do everything he could to exasperate the emperor and the German princes against the doctor. His friends were filled with consternation. Luther himself saw that no one could save him but the elector; yet he would rather die than compromise his prince. At last his friends agreed on an expedient that would not endanger Frederick. Let him refuse Luther a safe-conduct, and then the reformer would have a legitimate excuse for not appearing at Rome.

On August 8, Luther wrote to Spalatin, begging him to employ his influence with the elector to have his cause heard in Germany. "See what snares they are laying for me," wrote he also to Staupitz, "and how I am surrounded with thorns. But Christ lives and reigns, the same yesterday, today, and forever. My conscience assures me that I have been teaching the truth, although it appears still more odious because I teach it. The church is the womb of Rebecca. The children must struggle together, even to the risk of the mother's life. As for the rest, pray the Lord that I feel not too much joy in this trial. May God not lay this sin to their charge."

Luther's friends did not confine themselves to consultations and complaints. Spalatin wrote, on the part of the elector, to Renner the emperor's secretary, "Doctor Martin Luther willingly consents to be judged by all the universities of Germany, except Leipzig, Erfurt, and Frankfurt on the Oder, which have shown themselves partial. It is impossible for him to appear at Rome in person."

The University of Wittenberg wrote a letter of intercession to the pope: "The weakness of his frame," they said, speaking of Luther, "and the dangers of the journey render it difficult and even impossible for him to obey the order of your holiness. His distress and his prayers incline us to sympathize with him. We therefore entreat you, most holy father, as obedient children, to look upon him as a man who has never been tainted with doctrines opposed to the tenets of the Roman church."

The university, in its solicitude, wrote the same day to Charles of Miltitz, a Saxon gentleman and the pope's chamberlain, in high estimation with Leo X. In this letter they gave Luther a more decided testimony than they had ventured to insert in the first. "The reverend father Martin Luther, an Augustinian," it ran, "is the noblest and most distinguished member of our university. For many years we have seen and known his talents, his learning, his profound acquaintance with the arts and literature, his irreproachable morals, and his truly Christian behavior."

While men were anxiously looking for the result of this affair, it was terminated more easily than might have been expected. The legate Cajetan, mortified at his ill success in the commission he had received to excite a general war against the Turks, wished to exalt and give luster to his embassy in Germany by some other brilliant act. He thought that if he could extinguish heresy he should return to Rome with honor. He therefore entreated the pope to entrust this business to him. Leo for his part was highly pleased with Frederick for his strong opposition to the election of the youthful Charles. He felt that he might yet stand in need of his support. Without further reference to the summons, he commissioned the legate, by a brief dated August 23, to investigate the affair in Germany. The pope would lose nothing by this course of proceeding; and even if Luther could not be prevailed on to retract, the noise and scandal that his presence at Rome must have occasioned would be avoided.

"We charge you," said Leo, "to summon personally before you, to prosecute and constrain without any delay, and as soon as you shall have received this paper from us, the said Luther, who has already been declared a heretic by our dear brother Jerome, bishop of Ascoli."

The pope then proceeded to utter the severest threats against Luther: "Invoke for this purpose the arm and aid of our very dear son in Christ, Maximilian, and of the other princes of Germany, and of all the communities, universities, and potentates, ecclesiastic or secular. And if you get possession of his person, keep him in safe custody, that he may be brought before us.

"If he return to his duty, and beg forgiveness for so great a misdeed, of his own accord and without solicitation, we give you power to receive him into the unity of our holy mother the church.

"If he persist in his obstinacy, and you cannot secure his person, we authorize you to proscribe him in every part of Germany; to banish, curse, and excommunicate all those who are attached to him; and to order all Christians to flee from their presence.

"And in order that this contagious disease may be the more effectually eradicated, you will excommunicate all prelates, religious orders, universities, communities, counts, dukes, and potentates, the Emperor Maximilian always excepted, who shall not aid in seizing the aforesaid Martin Luther and his adherents, and send them to you under good and safe guard. And if, which God forbid, the said princes, communities, universities, and potentates, or any belonging to them, shall in any manner offer an asylum to the said Martin and his adherents, give him privately or publicly, by themselves or by others, succor and counsel, we lay under interdict all these princes, communities, universities, and potentates, with their cities, towns, countries, and villages, as well as the cities, towns, countries, and villages in which the said Martin may take refuge, so long as he shall remain there, and three days after he shall have quitted them.

"As for the laymen, if they do not immediately obey your orders without delay or opposition, we declare them infamous, the most worthy emperor always excepted, incapable of performing any lawful act, deprived of Christian burial, and stripped of all the fiefs they may hold either from the apostolic see, or from any lord whatsoever."

When Luther became acquainted with this brief, he thus expressed his indignation: "This is the most remarkable part of the affair: the brief was issued on August 23; I was summoned on August 7, so that between the brief and the summons sixteen days elapsed. Now make the calculation, and you will find that my Lord Jerome, bishop of Ascoli, proceeded against me, pronounced judgment, condemned me, and declared me a heretic, before the summons reached me, or at the most within sixteen days after it had been forwarded to me. Now where are the sixty days accorded me in the summons? They began on August 7; they should end on October 7. Is this the style and fashion of the Roman court, which on the same day summons, exhorts, accuses, judges, condemns, and declares a man guilty who is so far from Rome, and who knows nothing of all these things? What reply can they make to this? No doubt they forgot to clear their brains with hellebore before having recourse to such trickery."

But while Rome secretly deposited her thunders in the hands of her legate, she sought by sweet and flattering words to detach from Luther's cause the prince whose power she dreaded most. On the same day, August 23, 1518, the pope wrote to the elector of Saxony. He had recourse to the wiles of that ancient policy which we have already noticed and endeavored to flatter the prince's vanity.

"Dear son," wrote the pontiff, "when we think of your noble and worthy family; of you who are its ornament and head; when we call to mind how you and your ancestors have always desired to uphold the Christian faith, and the honor and dignity of the holy see, we cannot believe that a man who abandons the faith can rely upon your highness' favor, and daringly give the rein to his wickedness. Yet it is reported to us from every quarter that a certain friar, Martin Luther, hermit of the order of St. Augustine, has forgotten, like a child of the evil one and despiser of God, his habit and his order, which consist in humility and obedience, and that he boasts of fearing neither the authority nor the punishment of any man, being assured of your favor and protection.

"But as we know that he is deceived, we have thought fit to write to your highness and to exhort you in the Lord to watch over the honor of your name, as a Christian prince, the ornament, glory, and sweet savor of your noble family; to defend yourself from these calumnies; and to guard yourself not only from so serious a crime as that imputed to you, but still further, even from the suspicion that the rash presumption of this friar tends to bring upon you."

Leo X at the same time informed the elector that he had commissioned the cardinal of St. Sixtus to investigate the matter and requested him to deliver Luther into the legate's hands, "for fear," added he, still returning to his first argument, "the pious people of our own or of future times should one day lament and say, 'The most pernicious heresy with which the church of God has been afflicted sprung up under the favor and support of that high and worthy family.'"

Thus had Rome taken her measures. With one hand she scattered the intoxicating incense of flattery; in the other, she held concealed her terrors and revenge. All the powers of the earth, emperor, pope, princes, and legates, began to rise up against this humble friar of Erfurt, whose internal struggles we have already witnessed. "The kings of the earth set themselves, and the rulers take counsel together against the Lord, and against His Anointed."

Chapter 19
Melancthon

Before this letter and the brief had reached Germany, and while Luther was still afraid of being compelled to appear at Rome, a fortunate event brought consolation to his heart. He needed a friend into whose bosom he could pour out his sorrows, and whose faithful affection would comfort him in his hours of dejection. God gave him such a friend in Philipp Melancthon.

George Schwartzerd was a skillful master-armorer of Bretten, a small town in the palatinate. On February 14, 1497, his wife bore him a son, who was named Philipp, and who became famous in afteryears under the name of Melancthon. Philipp was not eleven years old when his father died. Two days before he expired, George called his son to his bedside and exhorted him to have the fear of God constantly before his eyes. "I foresee," said the dying armorer, "that terrible tempests are about to shake the world. I have witnessed great things, but greater still are preparing. May God direct and guide thee." After Philipp had received his father's blessing, he was sent to Speyer, that he might not be present at his parent's death. He departed weeping bitterly.

The lad's grandfather, the worthy bailiff Reuter, who himself had a son, performed a father's duty to Philipp, and took him and his brother George into his own house. Shortly after this he engaged John Hungarus to teach the three boys. The tutor was an excellent man, and in afteryears proclaimed the gospel with great energy, even to an advanced age. He overlooked nothing in the young man. He punished him for every fault, but with discretion: "It is thus," said Melancthon in 1554, "that he made a scholar of me. He loved me as a son; I loved him as a father; and we shall meet, I hope, in heaven."

Philipp was remarkable for the excellence of his understanding, and his facility in learning and explaining what he had learned. He could not remain idle and was always looking for someone to discuss with him the things he had heard. It frequently happened that well-educated foreigners passed through Bretten and visited Reuter. Immediately the bailiff's grandson should go up to them, enter into conversation, and press them so hard in the discussion that the hearers were filled with admiration. With strength of genius he united great gentleness, and thus won the favor of all. He stammered; but like the illustrious Grecian orator, he so diligently set about correcting this defect, that in afterlife no traces of it could be perceived.

On the death of his grandfather, the youthful Philipp, with his brother and his young uncle John, was sent to the school at Pforzheim. These lads resided with one of their relations, sister to the famous John Reuchlin, a learned doctor. Eager in the pursuit of knowledge, Philipp, under the tuition of George Simmler, made rapid progress in learning, and particularly in Greek, of which he was passionately fond. Reuchlin frequently came to Pforzheim. At his sister's house he became acquainted with her young boarders and was soon struck with Philipp's replies. He presented him with a Greek grammar and a Bible. These two books were to be the study of his whole life.

When Reuchlin returned from his second journey to Italy, his young relative, then twelve years old, celebrated the day of his arrival by representing before him, with the aid of some friends, a Latin comedy which he had himself composed. Reuchlin, charmed with the young man's talents, tenderly embraced him, called him his dear son, and placed sportively upon his head the red hat he had received when he had been made doctor. It was at this time that Reuchlin changed the name of *Schwartzerd* into that of *Melancthon;* both words, the one in German and the other in Greek, signifying *black earth.* Most of the learned men of that age thus translated their names into Greek or Latin.

Melancthon, at twelve years of age, went to the University of Heidelberg, and here he began to slake his ardent thirst for knowledge. He took his bachelor's degree at fourteen. In 1512, Reuchlin invited him to Tübingen, where many learned men were assembled. He attended by turns the lectures of the theologians, doctors, and lawyers. There was no branch of knowledge that he deemed unworthy his study. Praise was not his object, but the possession and the fruits of learning.

138

Philipp Melancthon, an engraving by Albrecht Dürer.

The Holy Scriptures especially engaged his attention. Those who frequented the church of Tübingen had remarked that he frequently held a book in his hands, which he was occupied in reading between the services. This unknown volume appeared larger than the prayer books, and a report was circulated that Philipp used to read profane authors during those intervals. But the suspected book proved to be a copy of the Holy Scriptures, printed shortly before at Basel by John Frobenius. All his life he continued this study with the most unceasing application. He always carried this precious volume with him, even to the public assemblies to which he was invited. Rejecting the empty systems of the school-men, he adhered to the plain work of the gospel. "I entertain the most distinguished and splendid expectations of Melancthon," wrote Erasmus to Oecolampadius about this time.

In 1514 he was made Doctor of Philosophy, and then began to teach. He was seventeen years old. The grace and charm that he imparted to his lessons formed the most striking contrast to the tasteless method which the doctors, and above all, the monks, had pursued till then. Agreeable in conversation, mild and elegant in his manners, beloved by all who knew him, he soon acquired great authority and solid reputation in the learned world.

It was at this time that the elector formed the design of inviting some distinguished scholar to the University of Wittenberg, as professor of the ancient languages. He applied to Reuchlin, who recommended Melancthon. Frederick foresaw the celebrity that this young man would confer on an institution so dear to him, and Reuchlin, charmed at beholding so noble a career opening before his young friend, wrote to him these words of the Almighty to Abraham: " 'Get thee out of thy country, and from thy kindred, and from thy father's house, and I will make thy name great, and thou shalt be a blessing.' Yea," continued the old man, "I hope that it will be so with thee, my dear Philipp, my handiwork and my consolation." In this invitation Melancthon acknowledged a call from God. At his departure the university was filled with sorrow; yet, it contained individuals who were jealous and envious of him. He left his native place, exclaiming, "The Lord's will be done!" He was then twenty-one years of age.

Melancthon traveled on horseback, in company with several Saxon merchants, as a traveler joins a caravan in the deserts. He arrived in Wittenberg on August 25, 1518, two days after Leo X had signed the brief addressed to Cajetan and the letter to the elector.

The Wittenberg professors did not receive Melancthon favorably. The first impression he made on them did not correspond with their expectations. They saw a young man, who appeared younger than he really was, of small stature, and with a feeble and timid air. Was this the illustrious doctor whom Erasmus and Reuchlin, the greatest men of the day, extolled so highly? Neither Luther, with whom he first became acquainted, nor his colleagues, entertained any great hopes of him when they saw his youth, his shyness, and his diffident manners.

On August 29, four days after his arrival, he delivered his inaugural discourse. All the university was assembled. This lad, as Luther calls him, spoke in such elegant Latinity and showed so much learning, an understanding so cultivated, and a judgment so sound, that all his hearers were struck with admiration.

When the speech was finished, all crowded round him with congratulations, but no one felt more joy than Luther. He hastened to impart to his friends the sentiments that filled his heart. "Melancthon," wrote he to Spalatin on August 31, "delivered, four days after his arrival, so learned and so beautiful a discourse, that every one listened with astonishment and admiration. We soon recovered from the prejudices excited by his stature and appearance; we now praise and admire his eloquence; we return our thanks to you and to the prince for the service you have done us. I ask for no other Greek master. But I fear that his delicate frame will be unable to support our mode of living, and that we shall be unable to keep him long on account of the smallness of his salary. I hear that the Leipzig people are already boasting of their power to take him from us. O my dear Spalatin, beware of despising his age and his personal appearance. He is a man worthy of every honor."

Melancthon began immediately to lecture on Homer and the Epistle of St. Paul to Titus. He was full of ardor. "I will make every effort," wrote he to Spalatin, "to conciliate the favor of all those in Wittenberg who love learning and virtue." Four days after his inauguration, Luther wrote again to Spalatin, "I most particularly recommend to you the very learned and very amiable Grecian, Philipp. His lecture room is always full. All the theologians in particular go to hear him. He is making every class, upper, lower, and middle, begin to read Greek."

Melancthon was able to respond to Luther's affection. He soon found in him a kindness of disposition, a strength of mind, a courage, a discretion, that he had never found till then in any man. "If there is any one," said he, "whom I dearly love, and whom I embrace with my whole heart, it is Martin Luther."

Thus did Luther and Melancthon meet; they were friends until death. We cannot too much admire the goodness and wisdom of God in bringing together two men so different, and yet so necessary to one another. Luther possessed warmth, vigor, and strength; Melancthon, clearness, discretion, and mildness. Luther gave energy to Melancthon; Melancthon moderated Luther. They were like substances in a state of positive and negative electricity, which mutually act upon each other. If Luther had been without Melancthon, perhaps the torrent would have overflowed its banks; Melancthon, when Luther was taken from him by death, hesitated and gave way, even where he should not have yielded. Luther did much by power; Melancthon perhaps did no less by following a gentler and more tranquil method. Both were upright, open-hearted, generous; both ardently loved the Word of eternal life and obeyed it with a fidelity and devotion that governed their whole lives.

Melancthon's arrival at Wittenberg effected a revolution not only in that university, but in the whole of Germany and in all the learned world. The attention he had bestowed on the Greek and Latin classics and on philosophy had given a regularity, clearness, and precision to his ideas, which shed a new light and an indescribable beauty on every subject that he took in hand. The mild spirit of the gospel fertilized and animated his meditations, and in his lectures the driest pursuits were clothed with a surpassing grace that captivated all hearers. The barrenness that scholasticism had cast over education was at an end. A new manner of teaching and of studying began with Melancthon. "Thanks to him," says an illustrious German historian, "Wittenberg became the school of the nation."

It was indeed highly important that a man who knew Greek thoroughly should teach in that university, where the new developments of theology called upon masters and pupils to study in their original language the earliest documents of the Christian faith.

From this time Luther zealously applied to the task. He had already found that the right understanding of a Greek word, which he had previously misunderstood, might suddenly clear up his theological ideas. What consolation and what joy had he not felt, for instance, when he saw that the Greek word *metanoia,* which, according to the Latin church, signifies a *penance,* a satisfaction required by the church, a human expiation, really meant in Greek *repentance,* a transformation or conversion of the heart. A thick mist was suddenly rolled away from before his eyes. The two significations given to this word suffice of themselves to characterize the two churches.

The impulse Melancthon gave to Luther in the translation of the Bible is one of the most remarkable circumstances of the friendship between these two great men. As early as 1517, Luther had made some attempts at translation. He had procured as many Greek and Latin books as were within his reach. And now, with the aid of his dear Philipp, he applied to his task with fresh energy. Luther compelled Melancthon to share in his researches; consulted him on the difficult passages; and the work, which was destined to be one of the great labors of the reformer, advanced more safely and more speedily.

Melancthon, on his side, became acquainted with the new theology. The beautiful and profound doctrine of justification by faith filled him with astonishment and joy, but he received with independence the system taught by Luther and molded it to the peculiar form of his mind; for, although he was only twenty-one years old, he was one of those precocious geniuses who attain early to a full possession of all their powers, and who think for themselves from the very first.

The zeal of the teachers was soon communicated to the disciples. It was decided to reform the method of instruction. With the elector's consent, certain courses that possessed a merely scholastic importance were suppressed; at the same time the study of the classics received a fresh impulse. The school of Wittenberg was transformed, and the contrast with other universities became daily more striking. All this, however, took place within the limits of the church, and none suspected they were on the eve of a great contest with the pope.

Chapter 20
Journey to Augsburg

A few days after Melancthon's arrival, and before the resolution of the pope transferring Luther's citation from Rome to Augsburg could be known, the latter wrote thus to Spalatin: "I do not require that our sovereign should do the least thing in defense of my theses; I am willing to be given up and thrown into the hands of my adversaries. Let him permit all the storm to burst upon me. What I have undertaken to defend, I hope to be able to maintain, with the help of Christ. As for violence, we must needs yield to that, but without abandoning the truth."

Luther's courage was infectious: the mildest and most timid men, as they beheld the danger that threatened this witness to the truth, found language full of energy and indignation. The prudent, the pacific Staupitz wrote to Spalatin on September 7: "Do not cease to exhort the prince, your master and mine, not to allow himself to be frightened by the roaring of the lions. Let him defend the truth, without anxiety either about Luther, Staupitz, or the order. Let there be one place at least where men may speak freely and without fear. I know that the plague of Babylon, I was nearly saying of Rome, is let loose against whoever attacks the abuses of those who sell Jesus Christ. I have myself seen a preacher thrown from the pulpit for teaching the truth; I saw him, although it was a festival, bound and dragged to prison. Others have witnessed still more cruel sights. For this reason, dearest Spalatin, prevail upon his highness to continue in his present sentiments."

At last the order to appear before the cardinal-legate at Augsburg arrived. It was now with one of the princes of the Roman church that Luther had to deal. All his friends entreated him not to set out. They feared that even during the journey snares might be laid for his life. Some busied themselves in finding an asylum for him. Staupitz himself, the timid Staupitz, was moved at the thought of the dangers to which brother Martin would be exposed, that brother whom he had dragged from the seclusion of the cloister, and whom he had launched on that agitated sea in which his life was now endangered. Alas, would it not have been better for the poor brother to have remained forever unknown? It was too late. At least he would do everything in his power to save him. Accordingly, he wrote from his convent at Salzburg, on September 15, soliciting Luther to flee and seek an asylum with him. "It appears to me," said he, "that the whole world is enraged and combined against the truth. The crucified Jesus was hated in like manner. I do not see that you have anything else to expect but persecution. Ere long no one will be able without the pope's permission to search the Scriptures and therein look for Jesus Christ, which Jesus Christ, however, commands. You have but few friends: I would to God that fear of your adversaries did not prevent those few from declaring themselves in your favor. The wisest course is for you to abandon Wittenberg for a season and come to me. Then we shall live and die together. This is also the prince's opinion," adds Staupitz.

From different quarters Luther received the most alarming intelligence. Count Albert of Mansfeldt bade him beware of undertaking the journey, for several powerful lords had sworn to seize his person and strangle or drown him. But nothing could frighten him. He had no intention of profiting by the vicar-general's offer. He would not go and conceal himself in the obscurity of a convent at Salzburg; he would remain faithfully on that stormy scene where the hand of God had placed him. It was by his persevering in spite of his adversaries, and proclaiming the truth aloud in the midst of the world, that the reign of this truth advanced. "I am like Jeremiah," said Luther at the time of which we are speaking, "a man of strife and contention; but the more their threats increase, the more my joy is multiplied. . . . They have already destroyed my honor and my reputation. One single thing remains; it is my wretched body: let them take it; they will thus shorten my life by a few hours. But as for my soul, they cannot take that. He who desires to proclaim the Word of Christ to the world must expect death at every moment, for our husband is a bloody husband to us."

The elector was then at Augsburg. Shortly before quitting the diet in that city, he had paid the legate a visit. The cardinal, highly flattered with this condescension from so illustrious a prince, promised Frederick that if the monk appeared before him, he would listen to him in a paternal manner and dismiss him kindly. Spalatin, by the prince's order, wrote to his friend that the pope had appointed a commission to hear him in Germany; that the elector would not permit him to be dragged to Rome; and that he must prepare for his journey to Augsburg. Luther resolved to obey. The notice he had received from the count of Mansfeldt induced him to ask a safe-conduct from Frederick. The latter replied that it was unnecessary and sent him only letters of recommendation to some of the most distinguished councilors of Augsburg. He also provided him with money for the journey; and the poor defenseless reformer set out on foot to place himself in the hands of his enemies.

He arrived at Weimar on September 28 and lodged in the Cordeliers' monastery. The elector of Saxony was then holding his court at Weimar, and it is on this account probably that the Cordeliers gave the doctor a welcome. The day following his arrival was the festival of St. Michael. Luther said mass and was invited to preach in the palace chapel. This was a mark of favor his prince loved to confer on him. He preached extempore, in the presence of the court, selecting his text (Matt. 18:1-11) from the gospel of the day. He spoke forcibly against hypocrites and those who boast of their own righteousness. But he said not a word about angels, although such was the custom on St. Michael's day.

The courage of the Wittenberg doctor, who was going quietly and on foot to answer a summons which had terminated in death to so many of his predecessors, astonished all who saw him. Interest, admiration, and sympathy prevailed by turns in their hearts. John Destner, purveyor to the Cordeliers, struck with apprehension at the thought of the dangers which awaited his guest, said to him, "Brother, in Augsburg you will meet with Italians who are learned men and subtle antagonists and who will give you enough to do. I fear you will not be able to defend your cause against them. They will cast you into the fire, and their flames will consume you."

Luther solemnly replied, "Dear friend, pray to our Lord God who is in heaven for me and for His dear Son Jesus, whose cause is mine, that He may be favorable to Him. If He maintain His cause, mine is maintained; but if He will not maintain it, of a truth it is not I who can maintain it, and it is He who will bear the dishonor."

Luther continued his journey on foot and arrived at Nuremberg. The letters he wrote from this city show the spirit which then animated him: "I have met," said he, "with pusillanimous men who wish to persuade me not to go to Augsburg, but I am resolved to proceed. The Lord's will be done. Even at Augsburg, even in the midst of His enemies, Christ reigns. Let Christ live; let Luther die, and every sinner, according as it is written. May the God of my salvation be exalted. Farewell; persevere, stand fast; for it is necessary to be rejected either by God or by man: but God is true, and man is a liar."

His faithful friend Wenceslas Link, preacher at Nuremberg, and an Augustinian monk named Leonard could not make up their minds to permit Luther to go alone to face the dangers that threatened him. They knew his disposition and were aware that, abounding as he did in determination and courage, he would probably be wanting in prudence. They therefore accompanied him. When they were about five leagues from Augsburg, Luther, whom the fatigues of the journey and the various agitations of his mind had probably exhausted, was seized with violent pains in the stomach. He thought he should die. His two friends in great alarm hired a wagon, in which they placed the doctor. On the evening of October 7, they reached Augsburg and alighted at the Augustinian convent. Luther was very tired, but he soon recovered. No doubt his faith and the vivacity of his mind speedily recruited his weakened body.

Immediately on his arrival, and before seeing anyone, Luther, desirous of showing the legate all due respect, begged Link to go and announce his presence. Link did so, and respectfully informed the cardinal, on the part of the Wittenberg doctor, that the latter was ready to appear before him whenever he should give the order. The legate was delighted at this news. At last he had this impetuous heretic within his reach, and promised himself that the reformer should not quit the walls of Augsburg as he had entered them.

The diet was over. The emperor and the electors had already separated. The emperor, it is true, had not yet quitted the place but was hunting in the neighborhood. The ambassador of Rome remained alone in Augsburg. If Luther had gone thither during the diet, he would have met with powerful supporters; but everything now seemed destined to bend beneath the weight of the papal authority.

The name of the judge before whom Luther was to appear was not calculated to encourage him. Thomas De Vio, surnamed Cajetan, from the town of Gaeta, in the kingdom of Naples, where he was born in 1469, had given great promise from his youth. At sixteen, he had entered the Dominican order, contrary to the express will of his parents. He had afterwards become general of his order and cardinal of the Roman church. But what was worse for Luther, this learned doctor was one of the most zealous defenders of that scholastic theology which the reformer had always treated so unmercifully. His mother, we are informed, had dreamed during her pregnancy that St. Thomas in person would instruct the child to which she was about to give birth and would introduce him into heaven. Accordingly Cajetan, when he became a Dominican, had changed his name from James to Thomas. He had zealously defended the prerogatives of the papacy and the doctrines of Thomas Aquinas, whom he looked upon as the pearl of theologians. Such was the man before whom the Wittenberg monk was about to appear.

Further, the legate's learning, the austerity of his disposition, and the purity of his morals insured him an influence and authority in Germany that other Roman courtiers would not easily have obtained. It was no doubt to this reputation for sanctity that he owed this mission. Rome perceived that it would admirably forward her designs. Thus even the good qualities of Cajetan rendered him still more formidable. Besides, the affair entrusted to him was by no means complicated. Luther was already declared a heretic. If he would not retract, the legate must send him to prison; and if he escaped, whoever would give him an asylum was to be excommunicated. This was what the dignitary of the church, before whom Luther was summoned, had to perform on behalf of Rome.

Luther had recovered his strength during the night. On Saturday morning, October 8, being already reinvigorated after his journey, he began to consider his strange position. He was resigned, and awaited the manifestation of God's will by the course of events. He had not long to wait. A person unknown to him sent to say—as if entirely devoted to him—that he was about to pay him a visit and that Luther should avoid appearing before the legate until after this interview. The message proceeded from an Italian courtier named Urban of Serra Longa, who had often visited Germany as envoy from the margrave of Montferrat. He had known the elector of Saxony, to whom he had been accredited, and after the margrave's death, he had attached himself to the Cardinal Cajetan.

The Italian soon arrived at the Augustinian monastery. The cardinal had sent him to sound the reformer and prepare him for the recantation expected from him. Serra Longa imagined that his sojourn in Germany had given him a great advantage over the other courtiers in the legate's train; he hoped to make short work with this German monk. He arrived attended by two domestics and professed to have come of his own accord, from friendship toward a favorite of the elector of Saxony and from attachment to the holy church. After having most cordially saluted Luther, the diplomatist added in an affectionate manner: "I am come to offer you good advice. Be wise, and become reconciled to the church. Submit to the cardinal without reserve. Retract your offensive language. Remember the Abbot Joachim of Florence: he had published, as you know, many heretical things, and yet he was declared no heretic because he retracted his errors."

Upon this Luther spoke of justifying what he had done.

Serra Longa: Beware of that. Would you enter the lists against the legate of his holiness?

Luther: If they convince me of having taught anything contrary to the Roman church, I shall be my own judge, and immediately retract. The essential point will be to know whether the legate relies on the authority of St. Thomas more than the faith will sanction. If he does so, I will not yield.

Serra Longa: Oh, oh, you intend to break a lance, then.

The Italian then began to use language which Luther styles horrible. He argued that one might maintain false propositions, provided they brought in money and filled the treasury; that all discussion in the universities against the pope's authority must be avoided; that, on the contrary, it should be asserted that the pope could, by a single nod, change or suppress articles of faith; and so he ran on, in a similar strain. But the wily Italian soon perceived that he was forgetting himself; and returning to his mild language, he endeavored to persuade Luther to submit to the legate in all things and to retract his doctrine, his oaths, and his theses.

The doctor, who was at first disposed to credit the fair professions of the orator Urban, as he calls him in his narrative, was now convinced that they were of little worth and that he was much more on the legate's side than on his. He consequently became less communicative and was content to say that he was disposed to render satisfaction in those things in which he might have erred. At these words Serra Longa exclaimed joyfully, "I shall hasten to the legate; you will follow me presently. Everything will go well, and all will soon be settled."

He was away. The Saxon monk had more discernment than the Roman courtier. Luther was in suspense between hope and fear; yet hope prevailed. The visit and the strange professions of Serra Longa, whom he afterwards called a bungling mediator, revived his courage.

The councilors and other inhabitants of Augsburg, to whom the elector had recommended Luther, were all eager to see the monk whose name already resounded throughout Germany. Peutinger, the imperial councilor, one of the most eminent patricians of the city, who frequently invited Luther to his table; the councilor Langemantel; Doctor Auerbach of Leipzig; the two brothers Adelmann, both canons; and many more repaired to the Augustinian convent. They cordially saluted this extraordinary man, who had undertaken so long a journey to place himself in the hands of the Roman agents. "Have you a safe-conduct?" asked they.

"No," replied the intrepid monk.

"What boldness!" they all exclaimed. "It was a polite expression," says Luther, "to designate my rashness and folly." All unanimously entreated him not to visit the legate before obtaining a safe-conduct from the emperor himself. It is probable the public had already heard something of the pope's brief, of which the legate was the bearer.

"But," replied Luther, "I set out for Augsburg without a safe-conduct and have arrived safely."

"The elector has recommended you to us; you ought therefore to obey us and do all that we tell you," answered Langemantel affectionately, but firmly.

Doctor Auerbach coincided with these views and added, "We know that at the bottom of his heart the cardinal is exceedingly irritated against you. One cannot trust these Italians."

The canon Adelmann urged the same thing: "You have been sent without protection, and they have forgotten to provide you with that which you needed most."

His friends undertook to obtain the requisite safe-conduct from the emperor. They then told Luther how many persons, even in elevated rank, had a leaning in his favor. "The minister of France himself, who left Augsburg a few days ago, has spoken of you in the most honorable manner." This remark struck Luther, and he remembered it afterwards. Thus several of the most respectable citizens in one of the first cities of the empire were already gained over to the Reformation.

The conversation had reached this point when Serra Longa returned. "Come," said he to Luther, "the cardinal is waiting for you. I will myself conduct you to him. But you must first learn how to appear in his presence: when you enter the room in which he is, you will prostrate yourself with your face to the ground; when he tells you to rise, you will kneel before him; and you will wait his further orders before you stand up. Remember, you are about to appear before a prince of the church. As for the rest, fear nothing: all will speedily be settled without difficulty."

Luther, who had promised to follow this Italian as soon as he was invited, found himself in a dilemma. However, he did not hesitate to inform him of the advice of his Augsburg friends and spoke of a safe-conduct.

"Beware of asking for anything of the kind," immediately replied Serra Longa; "you do not require one. The legate is kindly disposed toward you and ready to end this business in a friendly manner. If you ask for a safe-conduct, you will ruin everything."

"My gracious lord, the elector of Saxony," replied Luther, "recommended me to several honorable men in this city. They advise me to undertake nothing without a safe-conduct: I ought to follow their advice. For if I did not, and anything should happen, they will write to the elector, my master, that I would not listen to them."

Luther persisted in his determination, and Serra Longa was compelled to return to his chief and announce the shoal on which his mission had struck, at the very moment he flattered himself with success.

Thus terminated the conferences of that day with the orator of Montferrat.

The next day was Sunday, on which Luther obtained a little more repose. Yet he had to endure fatigues of another kind. All the talk in the city was about Doctor Luther. They crowded round him in his walks, and the good doctor smiled, no doubt, at this singular excitement.

The cardinal's people renewed their persuasions. "The cardinal," said they, "gives you assurances of his grace and favor: what are you afraid of?" They employed a thousand reasons to persuade him to wait upon Cajetan. "He is a very merciful father," said one of these envoys. But another approached and whispered in his ear, "Do not believe what they tell you. He never keeps his word." Luther persisted in his resolution.

On Monday morning, October 10, Serra Longa again returned to the charge. The courtier had made it a point of honor to succeed in his negotiation. He had scarcely arrived when he said in Latin, "Why do you not wait upon the cardinal? He is expecting you most indulgently: the whole matter lies in six letters: *Revoca,* retract. Come, you have nothing to fear."

Luther thought to himself that these six letters were very important ones; but without entering into any discussion on the merits of the things to be retracted, he replied, "I will appear as soon as I have a safe-conduct."

Serra Longa lost his temper on hearing these words. He insisted; he made fresh representations; but Luther was immovable. Becoming still more angry, he exclaimed, "You imagine, no doubt, that the elector will take up arms in your defense, and for your sake run the risk of losing the territories he received from his forefathers!"

Luther: God forbid.

Serra Longa: When all forsake you, where will you take refuge?

Luther (looking to heaven with an eye of faith): Under heaven.

Serra Longa was silent for a moment, struck with the sublimity of this unexpected answer. He then resumed the conversation: "What would you do if you held the legate, pope, and cardinals in your hands, as they have you now in theirs?"

Luther: I would show them all possible honor and respect. But with me, the Word of God is before everything.

Serra Longa (smiling, and snapping his fingers in the manner of Italians): Eh, eh; all honor. I do not believe a word of it.

He then went out, sprang into his saddle, and disappeared.

Serra Longa did not return to Luther; but he long remembered the resistance he had met with from the reformer and that which his master was soon after to experience in person. We shall find him at a later period loudly calling for Luther's blood.

Serra Longa had not long quitted the doctor when the safe-conduct arrived. Luther's friends had obtained it from the imperial councilors. It is probable that the latter had consulted the emperor on the subject, as he was not far from Augsburg. It would even appear from what the cardinal said afterward that from unwillingness to displease him, his consent also had been asked. Perhaps this was the reason that Serra Longa was set to work upon Luther, for open opposition to the security of a safe-conduct would have disclosed intentions that it was desirable to keep secret. It was a safer plan to induce Luther himself to desist from the demand. But they soon found out that the Saxon monk was not a man to give way.

Luther was now to appear. At this solemn moment he felt the need of communing once again with his friends, above all with Melancthon, who was so dear to his heart, and he took advantage of a few moments of leisure to write to him.

"Show yourself a man," said he, "as you do at all times. Teach our beloved youths what is upright and acceptable to God. As for me, I am going to be sacrificed for you and for them, if such is the Lord's will. I would rather die, and even—which would be my greatest misfortune—be forever deprived of your sweet society, than retract what I felt it my duty to teach, and thus ruin perhaps by my own fault the excellent studies to which we are now devoting ourselves.

"Italy, like Egypt in times of old, is plunged in darkness so thick that it may be felt. No one in that country knows anything of Christ, or of what belongs to Him; and yet they are our lords and our masters in faith and in morals. Thus the wrath of God is fulfilled among us; as the prophet saith: 'I will give children to be their princes, and babes shall rule over them.' Do your duty to God, my dear Philipp, and avert His anger by pure and fervent prayer."

The legate, being informed that Luther would appear before him on the morrow, assembled the Italians and Germans in whom he had the greatest confidence, in order to concert with them the method he should pursue with the Saxon monk. Their opinions were divided: we must compel him to retract, said one; we must seize him and put him in prison, said another; it would be better to put him out of the way, thought a third; they should try to win him over by gentleness and mildness, was the opinion of a fourth. The cardinal seems to have resolved on beginning with the last method.

Chapter 21
Before Cardinal Cajetan

The day fixed for the interview arrived at last, Tuesday, October 11. The legate, knowing that Luther had declared himself willing to retract everything that could be proved contrary to the truth, was full of hope; he doubted not that it would be easy for a man of his rank and learning to reclaim this monk to obedience to the church.

Luther repaired to the legate's residence, accompanied by the prior of the Carmelites, his host and his friend; by two friars of the same convent; by Doctor Link and an Augustinian, probably the one that had come from Nuremberg with him. He had scarcely entered the legate's palace when all the Italians who formed the train of this prince of the church crowded round him; everyone desired to see the famous doctor, and they thronged him so much that he could with difficulty proceed. Luther found the apostolic nuncio and Serra Longa in the hall where the cardinal was waiting for him. His reception was cold, but civil, and conformable with Roman etiquette. Luther, in accordance with the advice he had received from Serra Longa, prostrated himself before the cardinal; when the latter told him to rise, he remained on his knees; and at a fresh order from the legate, he stood up. Many of the most distinguished Italians in the legate's court found their way into the hall in order to be present during the interview; they particularly desired to see the German monk humble himself before the pope's representative.

The legate remained silent. He hated Luther as an adversary of the theological supremacy of St. Thomas and as the chief of a new, active, and hostile party in a rising university, whose first steps had disquieted the Thomists. He was pleased at seeing Luther fall down before him and thought, as a contemporary observes, that he was about to recant. The doctor on his part humbly waited for the prince to address him; but as he did not speak, Luther understood this silence as an invitation to begin, and he did so in these words:

"Most worthy father, in obedience to the summons of his papal holiness, and in compliance with the orders of my gracious lord the elector of Saxony, I appear before you as a submissive and dutiful son of the holy Christian church, and acknowledge that I have published the propositions and theses ascribed to me. I am ready to listen most obediently to my accusation, and if I have erred, to submit to instruction in the truth."

The cardinal, who had determined to assume the appearance of a tender and compassionate father toward an erring child, then adopted the most friendly tone; he praised and expressed his delight at Luther's humility, and said to him, "My dear son, you have disturbed all Germany by your dispute on indulgences. I understand that you are a very learned doctor in the Holy Scriptures, and that you have many followers. For this reason, if you desire to be a member of the church, and to find a gracious father in the pope, listen to me."

After this prelude, the legate did not hesitate to declare at once what he expected of him, so confident was he of Luther's submission. "Here are three articles," said he, "which, by the command of our holy father, Pope Leo X, I have set before you. First, you must bethink yourself, own your faults, and retract your errors, propositions, and sermons; secondly, you must promise to abstain in future from propagating your opinions; and thirdly, bind yourself to behave with greater moderation and avoid everything that may grieve or disturb the church."

Luther: Most holy father, I beg you will show me the pope's brief, by virtue of which you have received full powers to treat of this matter.

Cajetan: This request, my dear son, cannot be granted. You must confess your errors, keep a strict watch upon your words for the future, and not return like a dog to his vomit, so that we may sleep without anxiety or disturbance; then, in accordance with the order and authorization of our most holy father the pope, I will arrange the whole business.

Luther: Condescend, then, to inform me in what I have erred.

At this new request, the Italian courtiers, who had expected to see the poor German fall down on his knees and beg pardon, were still more astonished than before. None of them would have deigned to reply to so impertinent a question. But Cajetan, who thought it ungenerous to crush this petty monk with the weight of his authority, and who, besides, trusted to gain an easy victory by his learning, consented to tell Luther of what he was accused, and even to enter into discussion with him. We must do justice to the general of the Dominicans. We must acknowledge that he showed more equity, a greater sense of propriety, and less passion, than have been often shown in similar matters since. He replied in a condescending tone:

"Most dear son, here are two propositions that you have advanced and which you must retract before all: First, the treasure of indulgences does not consist of the sufferings and merits of our Lord Jesus Christ; second, the man who receives the holy sacrament must have faith in the grace that is presented to him."

Each of these propositions, in truth, struck a mortal blow at the Roman commerce. If the pope had not the power of dispensing at his pleasure the merits of the Savior; if, in receiving the drafts which the brokers of the church negotiated, men did not receive a portion of this infinite righteousness, this paper money would lose its value, and would be as worthless as a heap of rags. It was the same with the sacraments. Indulgences were more or less an extraordinary branch of Roman commerce; the sacraments were a staple commodity. The revenue they produced was of no small amount. To assert that faith was necessary before they could confer a real benefit on the soul of a Christian took away all their charms in the eyes of the people; for it is not the pope who gives faith: it is beyond his province; it proceeds from God alone. To declare its necessity was therefore depriving Rome both of the speculation and the profit. By attacking these two doctrines, Luther had imitated Jesus Christ, who at the very beginning of His ministry had overthrown the tables of the money-changers and driven the dealers out of the temple. "Make not my Father's house a house of merchandise," He had said.

"In confuting your errors," said Cajetan, "I will not appeal to the authority of St. Thomas and other doctors of the schools; I will rely entirely on Holy Scripture and talk with you in all friendliness."

But Cajetan had scarcely begun to bring forward his proofs before he departed from the rule he had declared that he would follow. He combatted Luther's first proposition by an Extravagance (a name applied to certain papal constitutions collected and subjoined to the body of the canon law) of Pope Clement, and the second by all sorts of opinions from the schoolmen. The discussion turned first on this papal constitution in favor of indulgences. Luther, indignant at hearing what authority the legate ascribed to a decree of Rome, exclaimed, "I cannot receive such constitutions as sufficient proofs on matters so important. For they pervert the Holy Scriptures and never quote them to the purpose."

Cajetan: The pope has power and authority over all things.

Luther (quickly): Except Scripture.

Cajetan (sneering): Except Scripture! Do you not know that the pope is above councils? He has recently condemned and punished the council of Basel.

Luther: The University of Paris has appealed from this sentence.

Cajetan: These Paris gentlemen will receive their deserts.

The dispute between the cardinal and Luther then turned upon the second point, namely, the faith that Luther declared necessary for the efficacy of the sacraments. Luther, according to his custom, quoted various passages of Scripture in favor of the opinion he maintained; but the legate treated them with ridicule. "It is of faith in general that you are speaking," said he. "No," replied Luther.

"As for indulgences," said Luther to the legate, "if it can be shown that I am mistaken, I am very ready to receive instruction. We may pass over that and yet be good Christians. But as to the article of faith, if I made the slightest concession, I should renounce Jesus Christ. I cannot, I will not yield on this point, and with God's grace I will never yield."

Cajetan (growing angry): Whether you will, or whether you will not, you must retract that article this very day, or upon that article alone I shall reject and condemn your whole doctrine.

Luther: I have no will but the Lord's. Let Him do with me as seemeth good to Him. But if I had four hundred heads, I would rather lose them all than retract the testimony which I have borne to the holy Christian faith.

Cajetan: I did not come here to dispute with you. Retract, or prepare to suffer the penalty you have deserved.

Luther saw clearly that it was impossible to put an end to the subject by a conference. His opponent sat before him as if he were himself pope and pretended that he would receive humbly and submissively all that was said to him; and yet he listened to Luther's replies, even when they were founded on Holy Scripture, with shrugging of shoulders and every mark of irony and contempt. He thought the wiser plan would be to answer the cardinal in writing. This means, thought he, gives at least one consolation to the oppressed. Others will be able to judge of the matter, and the unjust adversary, who by his clamors remains master of the field of battle, may be frightened at the consequences.

Luther having shown a disposition to retire, the legate said, "Do you wish me to give you a safe-conduct to go to Rome?"

Nothing would have pleased Cajetan better than the acceptance of this offer. He would thus have been freed from a task of which he now began to perceive the difficulties; and Luther with his heresy would have fallen into hands that would soon have arranged everything. But the reformer, who saw the dangers that surrounded him even in Augsburg, took care not to accept an offer that would have delivered him up, bound hand and foot, to the vengeance of his enemies. He therefore rejected it as often as Cajetan proposed it; and he did so very frequently. The legate dissembled his vexation at Luther's refusal; he took refuge in his dignity and dismissed the monk with a compassionate smile, under which he endeavored to conceal his disappointment, and at the same time with the politeness of a man who hopes for better success another time.

The noble and decided bearing of the Wittenberg doctor had greatly surprised the cardinal and his courtiers. Instead of a poor monk asking pardon as a favor, they had found a man of independence, a firm Christian, an enlightened doctor, who required that unjust accusations should be supported by proofs, and who victoriously defended his own doctrine. Everyone in Cajetan's palace cried out against the pride, obstinacy, and effrontery of the heretic. Luther and Cajetan had learned to know each other, and both prepared for their second interview.

A very agreeable surprise awaited Luther on his return to the Carmelite convent. The vicar-general of the Augustinian order, his friend and father, Staupitz, had arrived at Augsburg. Unable to prevent Luther's journey to that city, Staupitz gave his friend a new and touching proof of his attachment by going thither himself in the hope of being useful to him. This excellent man foresaw that the conference with the legate might have the most serious consequences. He was equally agitated by his fears and by his friendship for Luther. After so painful an interview, it was a great comfort to the doctor to embrace so dear a friend. He told him how impossible it had been to obtain an answer of any value, and how the cardinal had insisted solely upon a recantation, without having essayed to convince him. "You must positively," said Staupitz, "reply to the legate in writing."

After what he had learned of the first interview, Staupitz entertained but little hopes from another. He therefore resolved upon an act which he now thought necessary; he determined to release Luther from the obligations of his order. By this means Staupitz thought to attain two objects: if, as everything seemed to forebode, Luther should fail in this undertaking, he would thus prevent the disgrace of his condemnation from being reflected on the whole order; and if the cardinal should order him to force Luther to be silent or to retract, he would have an excuse for not doing so. The ceremony was performed with the usual formalities. Luther saw clearly what he must now expect. His soul was deeply moved at the breaking of those bonds which he had taken upon him in the enthusiasm of youth. The order he had chosen had rejected him; his natural protectors had forsaken him. He was already become a stranger among his brethren. But although his heart was filled with sadness at the thought, all his joy returned when he directed his eyes to the promises of a faithful God, who has said, "I will never leave thee, nor forsake thee."

The next day, Wednesday, October 12, both parties prepared for a second interview, which it seemed would be decisive. When Luther arrived at the cardinal's, he found a new adversary: this was the prior of the Dominicans of Augsburg, who sat beside his chief. Luther, conformably with the resolution he had taken, had written his answer. The customary salutations being finished, he read the following declaration with a loud voice:

"I declare that I honor the holy Roman church, and that I shall continue to honor her. I have sought after truth in my public disputations, and everything that I have said I still consider as right, true, and Christian. Yet I am but a man, and may be deceived. I am therefore willing to receive instruction and correction in those things wherein I may have erred. I declare myself ready to reply orally or in writing to all the objections and charges that the lord legate may bring against me. I declare myself ready to submit my theses to the four universities of Basel, Freiburg in Brisgau, Louvain, and Paris, and retract whatever they shall declare erroneous. In a word, I am ready to do all that can be required of a Christian. But I solemnly protest against the method that has been pursued in this affair, and against the strange pretension of compelling me to retract without having refuted me."

Undoubtedly nothing could be more reasonable than these propositions of Luther's, and they must have greatly embarrassed a judge who had been tutored beforehand as to the judgment he should pronounce. The legate, who had not expected this protest, endeavored to hide his confusion by affecting to smile at it, and by assuming an appearance of mildness. "This protest," said he to Luther, with a smile, "is unnecessary; I have no desire to dispute with you either privately or publicly, but I propose arranging this matter with the kindness of a parent." The sum of the cardinal's policy consisted in laying aside the stricter forms of justice, which protect the accused, and treating the whole affair as one of mere administration between a superior and an inferior: a convenient method that opens a wider field for arbitrary proceedings.

Continuing with the most affectionate air, Cajetan said, "My dear friend, abandon, I beseech you, so useless an undertaking; bethink yourself, acknowledge the truth, and I am prepared to reconcile you with the church and the sovereign bishop. Retract, my friend, retract; such is the pope's wish. Whether you will, or whether you will not, is of little consequence. It would be a hard matter for you to kick against the pricks."

Luther, who saw himself treated as if he were already a rebellious child and an outcast from the church, exclaimed, "I cannot retract; but I offer to reply, and that too in writing. We had debating enough yesterday."

Cajetan was irritated at this expression, which reminded him that he had not acted with sufficient prudence; but he recovered himself, and said with a smile, "Debated! my dear son, I have not debated with you; besides, I have no wish to debate; but to please the most serene Elector Frederick, I am ready to listen to you and to exhort you in a friendly and paternal manner."

Cajetan, who felt that in the presence of the respectable witnesses who attended this conference, he must at least appear anxious to convince Luther, reverted to the two propositions which he had pointed out as fundamental errors, being firmly resolved to permit the reformer to speak as little as possible. Availing himself of his Italian volubility, he overwhelmed the doctor with objections, without waiting for any reply. At one time he jeered, at another scolded; he declaimed with passionate warmth; mingled together the most heterogeneous matters; quoted St. Thomas and Aristotle; clamored, stormed against all who thought differently from himself. More than ten times did the latter try to speak, but the legate immediately interrupted him and overwhelmed him with threats. Retract, retract, this was all that was required of him. He raved; he domineered; he alone was permitted to speak. Staupitz took upon himself to check the legate. "Pray, allow brother Martin time to reply to you," said he. But Cajetan began again; he quoted the Extravagances and the opinions of St. Thomas; he had resolved to have all the talk to himself during this interview. If he could not convince, and if he dared not strike, he would do his best to stun by his violence.

Luther and Staupitz saw very clearly that they must renounce all hope not only of enlightening Cajetan by discussion but still more of making any useful confession of faith. Luther therefore reverted to the request he had made at the beginning of the sitting, and which the cardinal had then eluded. Since he was not permitted to speak, he begged that he might at least be permitted to transmit a written reply to the legate. Staupitz seconded this petition: several of the spectators joined their entreaties to his, and Cajetan, notwithstanding his repugnance to everything that was written, for he remembered that such writings are lasting, at length consented. We must give Cajetan credit for this mark of moderation and impartiality. The meeting broke up. The hopes that had been entertained of seeing the matter arranged at this interview were deferred; they must wait and see the issue of the next conference. Luther quitted the cardinal, delighted that his request had been granted.

It became more evident every day that the legate would hear no other words from Luther than these, "I retract," and Luther was resolved not to pronounce them. He beheld the sentence of excommunication suspended over his head, and doubted not that it would soon fall upon him. These prospects afflicted his soul, but he was not cast down. His trust in God was not shaken. He therefore began to prepare the protest that he intended presenting to the legate. It would appear that he devoted part of October 13 to this task.

On Friday, October 14, Luther returned to the cardinal, accompanied by the elector's councilors. The Italians crowded around him as usual, and were present at the conference in great numbers. Luther advanced and presented his protest to the cardinal: "You attack me on two points. First, you oppose to me the constitution of Pope Clement VI in which it is said that the treasure of indulgences is the merit of the Lord Jesus Christ and of the saints, which I deny in my theses.

"Panormitanus declares in his first book, that in whatever concerns the holy faith, not only a general council, but still further, each believer is above the pope, if he can bring forward the declarations of Scripture and allege better reasons than the pope. The voice of our Lord Jesus Christ is far above the voice of all men, whatever be the names they bear.

"My greatest cause of grief and of serious reflection is that this constitution contains doctrines entirely at variance with the truth. It declares that the merits of the saints are a treasure, while the whole of Scripture bears witness that God rewards us far more richly than we deserve. The prophet exclaims, 'Enter not into judgment with thy servant; for in thy sight shall no man living be justified' (Ps. 143:2). 'Woe be to men, however honorable and however praiseworthy their lives may have been,' says Augustine, 'if a judgment from which mercy was excluded should be pronounced upon them.'

"Thus the saints are not saved by their merits, but solely by God's mercy, as I have declared. I maintain this, and in it I stand fast. The words of Holy Scripture, which declare that the saints have not merit enough, must be set above the words of men, which affirm that they have an excess. For the pope is not above the Word of God, but below it."

Luther does not stop here: he shows that if indulgences cannot be the merits of the saints, they cannot any the more be the merits of Christ. He proves that indulgences are barren and fruitless, since their only effect is to exempt men from performing good works, such as prayer and almsgiving. "No," exclaims he, "the merits of Jesus Christ are not a treasure of indulgence exempting man from good works, but a treasure of grace which quickeneth. The merits of Christ are applied to the believer without indulgences, without the keys, by the Holy Ghost alone, and not by the pope. If any one has an opinion better founded than mine," adds he, terminating what referred to this first point, "let him make it known to me, and then will I retract."

"I affirm," said he, coming to the second article, "that no man can be justified before God if he has not faith, so that it is necessary for a man to believe with a perfect assurance that he has obtained grace. To doubt of this grace is to reject it. The faith of the righteous is his righteousness and his life."

Luther proves his proposition by a multitude of declarations from Scripture.

"Condescend, therefore, to intercede for me with our most holy father the pope," adds he, "in order that he may not treat me with such harshness. My soul is seeking for the light of truth. I am not so proud or so vainglorious as to be ashamed of retracting, if I have taught false doctrines. My greatest joy will be to witness the triumph of what is according to God's Word. Only let not men force me to do anything that is against the voice of my conscience."

The legate took the declaration from Luther's hands. After glancing over it, he said coldly, "You have indulged in useless verbiage; you have penned many idle words; you have replied in a foolish manner to the two articles, and have blackened your paper with a great number of passages from Scripture that have no connection with the subject." Then, with an air of contempt, Cajetan flung Luther's protest aside, as if it were of no value, and recommencing in the tone which had been so successful in the previous interview, he began to exclaim with all his might that Luther ought to retract. The latter was immovable. "Brother, brother," then cried Cajetan in Italian, "on the last occasion you were very tractable, but now you are very obstinate."

The cardinal then began a long speech, extracted from the writings of St. Thomas; he again extolled the constitution of Clement VI, and persisted in maintaining that by virtue of this constitution it is the very merits of Jesus Christ that are dispensed to the believer by means of indulgences. He thought he had reduced Luther to silence: the latter sometimes interrupted him; but Cajetan raved and stormed without intermission, and claimed, as on the previous day, the sole right of speaking.

"Retract," said Cajetan, "retract; or if you do not, I shall send you to Rome to appear before judges commissioned to take cognizance of your affair. I shall excommunicate you with all your partisans, and all who are or who may be favorable to you, and reject them from the church. All power has been given me in this respect by the holy apostolic see. Think you that your protectors will stop me? Do you imagine that the pope cares anything for Germany? The pope's little finger is stronger than all the German princes put together."

"Deign," replies Luther, "to forward to Pope Leo X, with my humble prayers, the answer which I have transmitted you in writing."

At these words, the legate, highly pleased at finding a moment's release, again assumed an air of dignity and said to Luther with pride and anger, "Retract, or return no more."

These words struck Luther. This time he would reply in another way than by speeches: he bowed and left the hall, followed by the elector's councilors. The cardinal and the Italians, remaining alone, looked at one another in confusion at such a result.

Thus the Dominican system, covered with the brilliancy of the Roman purple, had haughtily dismissed its humble adversary. But Luther was conscious that there was a power—the Christian doctrine, the truth—that no secular or spiritual authority could ever subdue. Of the two combatants, he who withdrew remained master of the field of battle.

This is the first step by which the church separated from the papacy.

Luther and Cajetan did not meet again; but the reformer had made a deep impression on the legate, which was never effaced. What Luther had said about faith, what Cajetan read in the subsequent writings of the Wittenberg doctor, greatly modified the cardinal's opinions. The theologians of Rome beheld with surprise and discontent the sentiments he advanced on justification in his commentary on the Epistle to the Romans. The Reformation did not recede, did not retract; but its judge, he who had not ceased from crying, "Retract, retract," changed his views, and indirectly retracted his errors. Thus was crowned the unshaken fidelity of the reformer.

Luther returned to the monastery where he had been entertained. He had stood fast; he had given testimony to the truth; he had done his duty. God would perform the rest. His heart overflowed with peace and joy.

Chapter 22
Return from Augsburg

The legate soon repented of his violence; he felt that he had gone beyond his part, and endeavored to retrace his steps. Staupitz had scarcely finished his dinner—on the morning of the interview, and the dinner hour was noon—before he received a message from the cardinal, inviting him to his palace. Staupitz went thither attended by Wenceslas Link. The vicar-general found the legate alone with Serra Longa. Cajetan immediately approached Staupitz and addressed him in the mildest language. "Endeavor," said he, "to prevail upon your monk and induce him to retract. Really, in other respects, I am well pleased with him, and he has no better friend than myself."

Staupitz: I have already done so, and I will again advise him to submit to the church in all humility.

Cajetan: You will have to reply to the arguments he derives from the Holy Scriptures.

Staupitz: I must confess, my lord, that is a task beyond my abilities; for Doctor Martin Luther is superior to me both in genius and knowledge of the Holy Scriptures.

The cardinal smiled, no doubt at the vicar-general's frankness. Besides, he knew himself how difficult it would be to convince Luther. He continued, addressing both Staupitz and Link: "Are you aware that, as partisans of a heretical doctrine, you are yourselves liable to the penalties of the church?"

Staupitz: Condescend to resume the conference with Luther and order a public discussion on the controverted points.

Cajetan (alarmed at the very thought): I will no longer dispute with that beast, for it has deep eyes and wonderful speculations in its head.

Staupitz at length prevailed on the cardinal to transmit to Luther in writing what he was required to retract.

The vicar-general returned to Luther. Staggered by the representations of the cardinal, he endeavored to persuade him to come to an arrangement. "Refute, then," said Luther, "the declarations of Scripture that I have advanced."

"It is beyond my ability," said Staupitz.

"Well, then," replied Luther, "it is against my conscience to retract so long as these passages of Scripture are not explained differently. What!" continued he, "the cardinal professes, as you inform me, that he is desirous of arranging this affair without any disgrace or detriment to me. Ah, these are Roman expressions, which signify in good German that it will be my eternal shame and ruin. What else can he expect who, through fear of men and against the voice of his conscience, denies the truth?"

Staupitz did not persist; he only informed Luther that the cardinal had consented to transmit to him in writing the points which he would be required to retract. He then, no doubt, informed him also of his intention of quitting Augsburg, where he had no longer anything to do. Luther communicated to him a plan he had formed for comforting and strengthening their souls. Staupitz promised to return, and they separated for a short time.

Alone in his cell, Luther turned his thoughts toward the friends dearest to his heart. His ideas wandered to Weimar and to Wittenberg. He desired to inform the elector of what was passing; and fearful of being indiscreet by addressing the prince himself, he wrote to Spalatin and begged the chaplain to inform his master of the state of affairs. He detailed the whole transaction, even to the promise given by the legate to send him the controverted points in writing, and finished by saying, "This is the posture of affairs, but I have neither hope nor confidence in the legate. I will not retract a syllable. I will publish the reply I gave him in order that, if he should proceed to violence, he may be covered with shame in all Christendom."

The doctor then profited by the few moments that still remained to write to his Wittenberg friends.

"Peace and happiness," wrote he to Doctor Carlstadt. "Accept these few words as if they were a long letter, for time and events are pressing. At a better opportunity I will write to you and others more fully. Three days my business has been in hand, and matters are now at such a point that I have no longer any hope of returning to you, and I have nothing to look for but excommunication. The legate positively will not allow me to dispute either publicly or privately. He desires not to be a judge, says he, but a father to me; and yet he will hear no other words from me than these: 'I retract, and acknowledge my error.' And these I will not utter.

"The dangers of my cause are so much the greater that its judges are not only implacable enemies but, still further, men incapable of understanding it. Yet the Lord God lives and reigns: to His protection I commit myself, and I doubt not that, in answer to the prayers of a few pious souls, He will send me deliverance; I imagine I feel them praying for me.

"Either I shall return to you without having suffered any harm, or else, struck with excommunication, I shall have to seek a refuge elsewhere.

"However that may be, conduct yourself valiantly, stand fast, and glorify Christ boldly and joyfully.

"The cardinal always styles me his dear son. I know how much I must believe of that. I am nevertheless persuaded that I should be the most acceptable and dearest man to him in the world if I would pronounce the single word *Revoco,* 'I retract.' But I will not become a heretic by renouncing the faith by which I became a Christian. I would rather be exiled, accursed, and burned to death.

"Farewell, my dear doctor; show this letter to our theologians . . . in order that you may pray for me and also for yourselves; for it is your cause that I am pleading here. It is that of faith in the Lord Jesus Christ and in the grace of God."

The next day Luther waited for the articles the legate was to send him; but not receiving any message, he begged his friend Wenceslas Link to go to the cardinal. Cajetan received Link in the most affable manner and assured him that he had no desire but to act like a friend. He said, "I no longer regard Luther as a heretic. I will not excommunicate him this time unless I receive further orders from Rome. I have sent his reply to the pope by an express." And then to show his friendly intentions, he added, "If Doctor Luther would only retract what concerns indulgences, the matter would soon be finished; for, as to what concerns faith in the sacraments, it is an article that each one may understand and interpret in his own fashion." Spalatin, who records these words, adds this shrewd but just remark: "It follows clearly that Rome looks to money, rather than to the holy faith and the salvation of souls."

Link returned to Luther: he found Staupitz with him and gave them an account of his visit. When he came to the unexpected concession of the legate, "It would have been well," said Staupitz, "if Doctor Wenceslas had had a notary and witnesses with him to take down these words in writing; for if such a proposal were made known, it would be very prejudicial to the Romans."

However, in proportion to the mildness of the prelate's language, the less confidence did these worthy Germans place in him. Many of the good men to whom Luther had been recommended held counsel together: "The legate," said they, "is preparing some mischief by this courier of whom he speaks, and it is very much to be feared that you will all be seized and thrown into prison."

Staupitz and Wenceslas therefore resolved to quit the city; they embraced Luther, who persisted in remaining at Augsburg, and departed hastily for Nuremberg by two different roads, not without much anxiety respecting the fate of the courageous witness they were leaving behind them.

Sunday passed off quietly enough. But Luther in vain waited for the legate's message: the latter sent none. At last he determined to write. Staupitz and Link, before setting out, had begged him to treat the cardinal with all possible respect. Luther had not yet made trial of Rome and of her envoys: this was his first experiment. If deference did not succeed, he would take a warning from it. Now at least he must make the attempt. He took up his pen and, with a sentiment of the most respectful good will, wrote to the cardinal.

Luther received no answer to his letter. Cajetan and his courtiers, after being so violently agitated, had suddenly become motionless. What could be the reason? Might it not be the calm that precedes the storm? Some persons felt sure that the legate intended to arrest Luther, but that, not daring to proceed to such extremities on his own account because of the imperial safe-conduct, he was waiting a reply from Rome to his message. Others could not believe that the cardinal would delay so long. The Emperor Maximilian, said they—and this may really be the truth—would have no more scruple to deliver Luther over to the judgment of the church, notwithstanding the safe-conduct, than Sigismund had to surrender Huss to the Council of Constance. The legate was perhaps even then negotiating with the emperor. Maximilian's authorization might arrive every minute. The more he was opposed to the pope before, the more would he seem to flatter him now, until the imperial crown encircle his grandchild's head. There was not a moment to be lost. "Draw up an appeal to the pope," said the noble-minded men who surrounded Luther, "and quit Augsburg without delay."

Luther, whose presence in this city had been useless during the last four days, yielded at length to his friends' solicitations. But first he resolved to inform Cajetan of his intention: he wrote to him on Tuesday, the eve of his departure.

"Most worthy father in God," wrote he to Cajetan, "your paternal kindness has witnessed—I repeat it, witnessed and sufficiently acknowledged my obedience. I have undertaken a long journey, through great dangers, in great weakness of body, and despite my extreme poverty; at the command of our most holy lord Leo X, I have appeared in person before your eminence. Lastly, I have thrown myself at the feet of his holiness, and I now wait his good pleasure, ready to submit to his judgment, whether he should condemn or acquit me. I therefore feel that I have omitted nothing which it becomes an obedient child of the church to do.

"I think, consequently, that I ought not uselessly to prolong my sojourn in this town; besides, it would be impossible; my resources are failing me; and your paternal goodness has loudly forbidden me to appear before you again, unless I will retract.

"I therefore depart in the name of the Lord, desiring, if possible, to find some spot where I may dwell in peace. Many persons of greater importance than myself have requested me to appeal from your paternal kindness and even from our most holy lord Leo X, ill informed, to the pope when better informed. Although I know that such an appeal will be far more acceptable to our most serene highness the elector than a retraction, nevertheless, if I had consulted my own feelings only, I should not have done so. I have committed no fault; I ought therefore to fear nothing."

Luther having written this letter, which was not given to the legate until after his departure, prepared to quit Augsburg. God had preserved him till this hour, and he praised the Lord for it with all his heart; but he must not tempt God. On Wednesday, before daybreak, he was up and ready to set out. His friends had recommended him to take every precaution, for fear that he should be prevented if his intentions were known. He followed their advice as far as possible. A pony that Staupitz had left for him was brought to the door of the convent. Once more he bid his brethren adieu; he then mounted and set off, without a bridle for his horse, without boots or spurs, and unarmed. The magistrate of the city had sent him as a guide one of the horse-police who was well acquainted with the roads. This servant conducted him in the dark through the silent streets of Augsburg. They directed their course to a small gate in the wall of the city. At length Luther and his guide arrived at the little gate; they passed through. They were out of Augsburg, and soon they put their horses to a gallop and rode speedily away.

Luther, on his departure, had left his appeal to the pope in the hands of the prior of Pomesaw. His friends had recommended that it should not be transmitted to the legate. The prior was commissioned to have it posted upon the cathedral gates two or three days after the doctor's departure, in the presence of a notary and witnesses. This was done.

In this paper, Luther declares that he appeals from the most holy father the pope, ill informed, to the most holy lord and father in Christ, Leo X of that name, by the grace of God, better informed. This appeal had been drawn up in the customary form and style, by aid of the imperial notary, Gall of Herbrachtingen, in presence of two Augustinian monks, Bartholomew Uzmair and Wenzel Steinbies. It was dated October 16.

When the cardinal was informed of Luther's departure, he was thunderstruck, and even frightened and alarmed, as he assured the elector in his letter. Indeed, there was good cause to be annoyed. This departure, which so abruptly terminated the negotiations, disconcerted the hopes with which he had so long flattered his pride. He had been ambitious of the honor of healing the wounds of the church, of restoring the tottering influence of the pope in Germany; and the heretic had escaped not only unpunished, but even without being humbled. The conference had served only to exhibit in a stronger light, on the one hand, Luther's simplicity, integrity, and firmness; and on the other, the imperious and unreasonable proceedings of the pope and his ambassador. Since Rome had gained nothing, she had lost; her authority, not having been strengthened, had received a fresh check. What would they say in the Vatican? What messages would be received from Rome? The difficulties of his position would be forgotten; the unlucky issue of this affair would be attributed to his want of skill. Serra Longa and the Italians were furious at seeing themselves, with all their dexterity, outwitted by a German monk. Cajetan could hardly conceal his irritation. Such an insult called for vengeance.

Luther and his guide continued their flight far from the walls of Augsburg. He spurred his horse and galloped as fast as the poor animal's strength would permit. Now that he was free, now that he inhaled the fresh breezes of the country, traversed the villages and rural districts, and beheld himself wonderfully delivered by the arm of the Lord, his whole being returned thanks to the Almighty. It was truly he who could now say, "Our soul is escaped as a bird out of the snare of the fowlers: the snare is broken, and we are escaped. Our help is in the name of the Lord, who made heaven and earth" (Ps. 124:7-8). Thus was Luther's heart overflowing with joy. But his thoughts were turned on Cajetan also: "The cardinal would have liked to have me in his hands to send me to Rome. He is vexed, no doubt, at my escape. He imagined I was in his power at Augsburg; he thought he had me, but he was holding an eel by the tail. Is it not disgraceful that these people set so high a value upon me? They would give a heap of crowns to have me in their clutches, while our Lord Jesus Christ was sold for thirty pieces of silver."

The first day he traveled fourteen leagues. When he reached the inn where he was to pass the night, he was so fatigued—his horse was a very hard trotter, a historian tells us—that, when he dismounted, he could not stand upright, and lay down upon a bundle of straw. He nevertheless obtained some repose. On the morrow he continued his journey. At Nuremberg he met with Staupitz, who was visiting the convents of his order. It was in this city that he first saw the brief sent by the pope to Cajetan about him. He was indignant at it, and it is very probable that if he had seen this brief before leaving Wittenberg, he would have never gone to the cardinal. "It is impossible to believe," said he, "that anything so monstrous could have proceeded from any sovereign pontiff."

He hastened forward, desiring to be at Wittenberg on October 31, under the impression that the elector would be there for the Festival of All Saints, and that he should see him. The brief which he had read at Nuremberg had disclosed to him all the perils of his situation. In fact, being already condemned at Rome, he could not hope either to stay at Wittenberg, to obtain an asylum in a convent, or to find peace and security in any other place. The elector's protection might perhaps be able to defend him, but he was far from being sure of it. The elector was not sufficiently acquainted with the doctrine of the gospel to encounter manifest danger for its sake. Luther thought, however, that he could not do better than to return to Wittenberg and there await what the eternal and merciful God would do with him. If, as many expected, he were left unmolested, he resolved to devote himself entirely to study and to the education of youth.

Luther reentered Wittenberg on October 30. All his expedition had been to no purpose. Neither the elector nor Spalatin had come to the feast. His friends were overjoyed at seeing him again among them. He hastened to inform Spalatin of his arrival. "I returned to Wittenberg today safe and sound, by the grace of God," said he, "but how long I shall stay here I do not know. I am filled with joy and peace and can hardly conceive that the trial which I endure can appear so great to so many distinguished personages."

Cajetan had not waited long after Luther's departure to pour forth all his indignation to the elector. His letter breathes vengeance. He gives Frederick an account of the conference with an air of assurance. "Since brother Martin," says he in conclusion, "cannot be induced by paternal measures to acknowledge his error and remain faithful to the Catholic church, I beg your highness will send him to Rome or expel him from your states. Be assured that this difficult, mischievous, and envenomed business cannot be protracted much longer; for so soon as I have informed our most holy lord of all this artifice and wickedness, it will be brought to an end." In a postscript, written with his own hand, the cardinal entreats the elector not to tarnish his honor and that of his illustrious ancestors for the sake of a miserable little friar.

Never perhaps did Luther's soul feel a nobler indignation than when he read the copy of this letter forwarded to him by the elector. He gave, in his turn, an account of the Augsburg conference; and after describing the cardinal's behavior, he continued thus:

"It is thus I would reply, most excellent prince.

"Let the reverend legate, or the pope himself, specify my errors in writing; let them give their reasons; let them instruct me, for I am a man who desires instruction, who begs and longs for it, so that even a Turk would not refuse to grant it. If I do not retract and condemn myself when they have proved that the passages which I have cited ought to be understood in a different sense from mine, then, most excellent elector, let your highness be the first to prosecute and expel me; let the university reject me and overwhelm me with its anger. Nay, more, and I call heaven and earth to witness, may the Lord Jesus Christ cast me out and condemn me. The words that I utter are not dictated by vain presumption but by an unshaken conviction. I am willing that the Lord God withdraw His grace from me, and that every one of God's creatures refuse me his countenance if, when a better doctrine has been shown me, I do not embrace it.

"If they despise me on account of my low estate, me a poor little mendicant friar, and if they refuse to instruct me in the way of truth, then let your highness entreat the legate to inform you in writing wherein I have erred; and if they refuse even your highness this favor, let them write their views either to his imperial majesty, or to some archbishop of Germany. What can I, or what ought I to say more?

"Let your highness listen to the voice of your conscience and of your honor and not send me to Rome. No man can require you to do so, for it is impossible I can be safe in Rome. The pope himself is not safe there. It would be commanding you to betray Christian blood. They have paper, pens, and ink: they have also notaries without number. It is easy for them to write wherein and wherefore I have erred. It will cost them less to instruct me when absent by writing, than to put me to death by stratagem when among them.

"I resign myself to banishment. My adversaries are laying their snares on every side, so that I can nowhere live in security. In order that no evil may happen to you on my account, I leave your territories in God's name. I will go wherever the eternal and merciful God will have me. Let Him do with me according to His pleasure.

"Thus then, most serene elector, I reverently bid you farewell. I commend you to the everlasting God and give you eternal thanks for all your kindness toward me. Whatever be the people among whom I shall dwell in future, I shall ever remember you and pray continually and gratefully for the happiness of yourself and of your family. I am still, thanks be to God, full of joy, and praise Him because Christ, the Son of God, thinks me worthy to suffer in such a cause. May He ever protect your illustrious highness. Amen."

This letter made a deep impression on the elector. "He was shaken by a very eloquent letter," says Maimbourg. Never could he have thought of surrendering an innocent man to the hands of Rome; perhaps he would have desired Luther to conceal himself for a time, but he resolved not to appear to yield in any manner to the legate's menaces. He wrote to his councilor Pfeffinger, who was at the emperor's court, telling him to inform this prince of the real state of affairs and to beg him to write to Rome so that the business might be concluded, or at least that it might be settled in Germany by impartial judges.

A few days after, the elector replied to the legate: "Since Doctor Martin has appeared before you at Augsburg, you should be satisfied. We did not expect that you would endeavor to make him retract without having convinced him of his errors. None of the learned men in our principality have informed me that Martin's doctrine is impious, anti-Christian, or heretical." The prince refused, moreover, to send Luther to Rome, or to expel him from his states.

This letter, which was communicated to Luther, filled him with joy. "Gracious God," wrote he to Spalatin, "with what delight I have read it again and again! I know what confidence may be put in these words, at once so forcible and moderate. I fear that the Romans will not understand their full hearing, but they will at least understand that what they think already finished is as yet hardly begun. Pray return my thanks to the prince."

What had doubtless encouraged the elector to reply to the legate in a tone the latter had not expected was a letter addressed to him by the University of Wittenberg. It had good reason to declare in the doctor's favor, for it flourished daily more and more and was eclipsing all the other schools. A crowd of students flocked thither from all parts of Germany to hear this extraordinary man, whose teaching appeared to open a new era to religion and learning. These youths, who came from every province, halted as soon as they discovered the steeples of Wittenberg in the distance; they raised their hands to heaven and praised God for having caused the light of truth to shine forth from this city, as from Zion in times of old, and whence it spread even to the most distant countries.

Chapter 23
A New Envoy from Rome

Luther, imagining he might soon be expelled from Germany, was engaged in publishing a report of the Augsburg conference. He desired that it should remain as a testimony of the struggle between him and Rome. He saw the storm ready to burst but did not fear it. He waited from day to day for the anathemas that were to be sent from Italy, and he put everything in order, that he might be prepared when they arrived. "Having tucked up my robe, and girt my loins," said he, "I am ready to depart, like Abraham, without knowing whither I go; or rather, well knowing, since God is everywhere." He intended leaving a farewell letter behind him. "Be bold enough," wrote he to Spalatin, "to read the letter of an accursed and excommunicated man."

The moment seemed to have come at last. The prince informed Luther that he desired him to leave Wittenberg. The wishes of the elector were too sacred for him not to hasten to comply with them. He therefore made preparations for his departure, without well knowing whither he should direct his steps. He desired, however, to see his friends once more around him, and with this intent prepared a farewell repast. Seated at the same table with them, he enjoyed their sweet conversation, their tender and anxious friendship. A letter was brought to him from the court. He opened it and read; it contained a fresh order for his departure. The prince inquired "why he delays so long." His soul was overwhelmed with sadness. The Reformation seemed to hang upon a thread, and at the moment Luther quit the walls of Wittenberg, would not this thread break? Luther and his friends said little. But shortly after, a new messenger arrived. Luther opened the letter, not doubting that it contained a fresh order. But everything was changed. "Since the pope's new envoy hopes that all may be arranged by a conference, remain for the present."

Luther then published his "Report of the Conference at Augsburg." "I send you my Report," wrote he to Link. "It is keener, no doubt, than the legate expects, but my pen is ready to produce much greater things. I do not know myself whence these thoughts arise. In my opinion, the work is not yet begun, so far are the great ones at Rome mistaken in looking for the end. I will send you what I have written, in order that you may judge whether I have guessed rightly that the antichrist of whom St. Paul speaks now reigns in the court of Rome. I think I shall be able to show that he is worse nowadays than the Turks themselves."

At Rome they were much displeased with Cajetan. The vexation felt at the ill success of this business was at first vented on him. Why did he exasperate Luther by insults and threats, instead of alluring him by the promise of a rich bishopric, or even of a cardinal's hat? These mercenaries judged of the reformer by themselves. Still the failure must be retrieved. On the one hand, Rome must declare herself; on the other, she must conciliate the elector, who might be very serviceable to her in the choice they would soon have to make of an emperor. As it was impossible for Roman ecclesiastics to suspect whence Luther derived his courage and his strength, they imagined that the elector was implicated more deeply in the affair than he really was.

The pope therefore resolved to pursue another course. He caused a bull to be published in Germany by his legate, in which he confirmed the doctrine of indulgences precisely in the points attacked, but in which he made no mention either of Luther or of the elector. As the reformer had always declared that he would submit to the decision of the Roman church, the pope imagined that he would now either keep his word or exhibit himself openly as a disturber of the peace of the church and a condemner of the holy apostolic see. In either case the pope could not but gain. No advantage, however, is derived by obstinately opposing the truth. In vain had the pope threatened with excommunication whoever should teach otherwise than he ordained; the light is not stopped by such orders. It would have been wiser to moderate by certain restrictions the pretensions of the sellers of indulgences. This decree from Rome was therefore a new fault. By legalizing crying abuses, it irritated all wise men and rendered Luther's reconciliation impossible. "It was thought," says a Roman Catholic historian, "that this bull had been issued solely for the benefit of the pope and the begging of the friars, who began to find that no one would purchase their indulgences."

Cardinal Cajetan published the decree at Lintz, in Austria, on December 13, 1518; but Luther had already placed himself beyond its reach. On November 28, he had appealed, in the chapel of Corpus Christi at Wittenberg, from the pope to a general council of the church. He foresaw the storm that was about to burst upon him; he knew that God alone could disperse it, but he did what it was his duty to do. He must, no doubt, quit Wittenberg, if only on the elector's account, as soon as the Roman anathemas arrived: he would not, however, leave Saxony and Germany without a striking protest. He therefore drew one up that it might be ready for circulation as soon as the Roman thunders reached him. This bold protest was soon circulated everywhere. In it Luther declared anew that he had no intention of saying anything against the holy church or the authority of the apostolic see, and of the pope when well advised. "But," continued he, "seeing that the pope, who is God's vicar upon earth, may, like any other man, err, sin, and lie, and that an appeal to a general council is the only means of safety against that injustice which it is impossible to resist, I am obliged to have recourse to this step."

The appeal of the Wittenberg doctor to a general council was a new assault upon the papal power. A bull of Pius II had pronounced the greater excommunication even against the emperors who should dare be guilty of such an act of revolt. Frederick of Saxony, as yet weak in the evangelical doctrine, was ready to banish Luther from his states. A new message from Leo X would therefore have driven the reformer among strangers who might have feared to compromise themselves by receiving a monk under the anathema of Rome. And if any of the nobles had drawn the sword in his defense, these simple knights, despised by the mighty princes of Germany, would soon have been crushed in their perilous enterprise.

But at the very moment that the courtiers of Leo X were urging him to measures of severity, and when another blow would have placed his adversary in his hands, this pope suddenly changed his policy and entered upon a course of conciliation and apparent mildness. We may reasonably presume that he was deceived as to the elector's sentiments and thought them more favorable to Luther than they really were; we may admit that the public voice and the spirit of the age—powers then quite new—appeared to surround Luther with an impregnable rampart; we may suppose, as one of his historians has done, that he followed the impulses of his judgment and of his heart, which inclined to mildness and moderation; but this new mode of action adopted by Rome at such a moment is so strange that it is impossible not to recognize in it a higher and a mightier hand.

A Saxon noble, the pope's chamberlain and canon of Mentz, Treves, and Meissen, was then at the Roman court. He had contrived to make himself of importance. He boasted of being distantly related to the Saxon princes, so that the Roman courtiers sometimes gave him the title of duke of Saxony. In Italy, he made a foolish display of his German nobility; in Germany, he was an awkward imitator of the elegance and manners of the Italians. He was fond of wine, and his residence at the court of Rome had increased this vice. The Roman courtiers, however, entertained great expectations of him. His German origin, his insinuating manners, his skill in business, all led them to hope that Charles of Miltitz—for such was his name—would by his prudence succeed in arresting the mighty revolution that threatened to shake the world.

It was of importance to conceal the real object of the mission of the Roman chamberlain. This was effected without difficulty. Four years previously, the pious elector had petitioned the pope for the Golden Rose. This rose, the most beautiful of flowers, represented the body of Jesus Christ; it was consecrated yearly by the sovereign pontiff and sent to one of the chief princes in Europe. It was resolved to give it this year to the elector. Miltitz departed with a commission to examine the state of affairs and to gain over Spalatin and Pfeffinger, the elector's councilors. He carried private letters for them. In this manner, by seeking to conciliate those who surrounded the prince, Rome hoped erelong to have her formidable adversary in her power.

The new legate, who arrived in Germany in December 1518, was engaged during his journey in sounding the public opinion. To his great surprise he found that wherever he went the majority of the inhabitants were partisans of the Reformation. They spoke of Luther with enthusiasm. For one person favorable to the pope, there were three favorable to the reformer. Luther has transmitted to us one of the incidents of his mission. "What do you think of the papal chair?" the legate would frequently ask the landladies and maidservants at the inns. On one occasion one of these poor women artlessly replied, "What can we know of the papal chair, whether it is of wood or of stone?"

The mere rumor of the new legate's arrival filled the elector's court, the university and town of Wittenberg, and the whole of Saxony, with suspicion and distrust. It was affirmed that the Roman legate had received orders to get Luther into his power either by violence or stratagem. Miltitz indeed came bearing letters for the elector, for his councilors, and for the bishops and the burgomaster of Wittenberg. He brought with him seventy apostolical briefs. If Frederick delivered Luther into his hands, these seventy briefs were, in some measure, to serve as passports. He would produce and post up one in each of the cities through which he would have to pass, and by this means he hoped to succeed in dragging his prisoner to Rome without opposition.

The pope appeared to have taken every precaution. Already, in the electoral court, they did not know what course to adopt. They would have resisted violence; but how could they oppose the head of Christendom, who spoke with so much mildness and with so great an appearance of reason? Would it not be desirable, they said, for Luther to conceal himself until the storm had passed over? An unexpected event extricated Luther, the elector, and the Reformation from this difficult position. The aspect of the world suddenly changed.

On January 12, 1519, Maximilian, emperor of Germany, expired. Frederick of Saxony, in conformity with the Germanic constitution, became administrator of the empire. Henceforth the elector no longer feared the projects of nuncios. New interests began to agitate the court of Rome, which forced it to be cautious in its negotiations with Frederick and arrested the blow that Miltitz and Cajetan undoubtedly were meditating.

The pope earnestly desired to prevent Charles of Austria, already king of Naples, from filling the imperial throne. He thought that a neighboring king was more to be feared than a German monk. Desirous of securing the elector, who might be a great use to him in this affair, he resolved to let the monk rest that he might better oppose the king; but both advanced in spite of him. Thus changed Leo X.

181

Miltitz, who had reached Saxony before the death of Maximilian, had hastened to visit his old friend Spalatin; but he had no sooner begun his complaints against Luther than Spalatin broke out against Tetzel. He made the nuncio acquainted with the falsehoods and blasphemies of the indulgence merchant and declared that all Germany ascribed to the Dominican the divisions by which the church was rent.

Miltitz was astonished. Instead of being the accuser, he found himself the accused. All his anger was immediately directed against Tetzel. He summoned him to appear at Altenburg to justify his conduct.

The Dominican, as cowardly as he was boastful, fearing the people whom his impositions had exasperated, had discontinued passing from town to town and had hidden himself in the college of St. Paul at Leipzig. He turned pale on receiving Miltitz's letter. Even Rome had abandoned him. Tetzel refused to obey the nuncio's summons. "Certainly," wrote he to Miltitz on December 31, 1518, "I should not care about the fatigue of the journey, if I could leave Leipzig without danger to my life; but the Augustinian Martin Luther has so excited and aroused the men of power against me, that I am nowhere safe. A great number of Luther's partisans have sworn my death; I cannot, therefore, come to you."

Miltitz had been ordered to employ persuasive measures in the first instance, and it was only when these failed that he was to produce his seventy briefs, and at the same time make use of all the favors of Rome to induce the elector to restrain Luther. He therefore intimated his desire to have an interview with the reformer. Their common friend Spalatin offered his house for that purpose, and Luther quitted Wittenberg on January 2 or 3 to visit Altenburg.

In this interview, Miltitz exhausted all the cunning of a diplomatist and of a Roman courtier. "My dear Martin," said the pope's chamberlain in a fawning tone, "I thought you were an old theologian who, seated quietly at his fireside, was laboring under some theological crotchet; but I see you are still a young man and in the prime of life. Do you know," continued he, assuming a graver tone, "that you have drawn away everybody from the pope and attached them to yourself? If I had an army of 25,000 men," added he, "I do not think I should be able to carry you to Rome."

The nuncio, believing he had now prepared his adversary's mind, continued in these terms: "Bind up the wound that you yourself have inflicted on the church and that you alone can heal. Beware," said he, "of raising a tempest that would cause the destruction of Christendom." He then gradually proceeded to hint that a retractation alone could repair the mischief, but he immediately softened down whatever was objectionable in this word by giving Luther to understand that he felt the highest esteem for him and by storming against Tetzel. "If, at the outset, the archbishop of Mentz had spoken to me in this manner," said the reformer afterward, "this business would not have created so much disturbance."

Luther then replied and set forth with calmness, but with dignity and force, the just complaints of the church; he did not conceal his great indignation against the archbishop of Mentz and complained in a noble manner of the unworthy treatment he had received from Rome, notwithstanding the purity of his intentions. Miltitz, who had not expected to hear such decided language, was able, however, to suppress his anger.

"I offer," resumed Luther, "to be silent for the future on this matter and to let it die away of itself, provided my opponents are silent on their part; but if they continue attacking me, a serious struggle will soon arise out of a trifling quarrel. My weapons are quite prepared."

"I will do still more," he added a moment after. "I will write to his holiness, acknowledging I have been a little too violent, and I will declare to him that it is as a faithful son of the church that I opposed discourses which drew upon them the mockeries and insults of the people. I even consent to publish a writing desiring all those who read my works not to see in them any attacks upon the Roman church and to continue under its authority. Yes, I am willing to do and to bear everything; but as for a retraction, never expect one from me."

Miltitz saw by Luther's firm tone that the wisest course would be to appear satisfied with what the reformer so readily promised. He merely proposed they should choose an archbishop to arbitrate on some points that were still to be discussed. "Be it so," said Luther; "but I am very much afraid that the pope will not accept any judge; in that case I will not abide by the pope's decision, and then the struggle will begin again. The pope will give the text, and I shall make my own comments upon it."

Thus ended the first interview between Luther and Miltitz. They had a second meeting, in which the truce, or rather the peace, was signed. Luther immediately informed the elector of what had taken place. "Most serene prince and most gracious lord," wrote he, "I hasten most humbly to acquaint your electoral highness that Charles of Miltitz and myself are at last agreed, and have terminated this matter by deciding upon the following articles:

"First, both parties are forbidden to preach, write, or do anything further in the discussion that has been raised.

"Second, Miltitz will immediately inform the holy father of the state of affairs. His holiness will empower an enlightened bishop to investigate the matter and to point out the erroneous articles I should retract. If they prove me to be in error, I shall willingly recant and will do nothing derogatory to the honor or authority of the holy Roman church."

When the agreement had been thus effected, Miltitz appeared overjoyed. "These hundred years past," exclaimed he, "no question has occasioned more anxiety to the cardinals and Roman courtiers than this. They would rather have given ten thousand ducats than consent to its being prolonged."

Miltitz gave Luther an invitation to supper, which the latter accepted. His host laid aside all the severity connected with his mission, and Luther indulged in all the cheerfulness of his disposition. The repast was joyous, and when the moment of departure was come, the legate opened his arms to the heretical doctor and kissed him. "A Judas kiss," thought Luther. "I pretended not to understand these Italian artifices," wrote he to Staupitz.

Was that kiss destined to reconcile Rome and the dawning Reformation? Miltitz hoped so and was delighted at the thought, for he had a nearer view than the Roman courtiers of the terrible consequences the papacy might suffer from the Reformation. If Luther and his adversaries are silenced, thought he, the dispute will be ended; and Rome, by calling up favorable circumstances, will regain all her former influence. It appeared, then, that the termination of the contest was at hand. Rome had opened her arms, and the reformer seemed to have cast himself into them. But this work was not of man, but of God. The error of Rome was in seeing a mere dispute with a monk in what was an awakening of the church. The kisses of a papal chamberlain could not check the renewal of Christendom.

Miltitz being of opinion that he would by this means reclaim the erring Lutherans, behaved most graciously to all of them, accepted their invitation, and sat down to table with the heretics; but soon becoming inebriated—it is a pope who relates this—the pontifical nuncio was no longer master of his tongue. The Saxons led him to speak of the pope and the court of Rome; and Miltitz, confirming the old proverb, *in vina veritas* ("When the wine is in, the wit is out"), gave an account in the openness of his heart of all the practices and disorders of the papacy. His companions smiled, urging and pressing him to continue; everything was exposed; they took notes of what he said; and these scandals were afterward made matter of public reproach against the Romans at the Diet of Worms in the presence of all Germany. Pope Paul III complained, alleging they had put things in his envoy's mouth that were utterly destitute of foundation, and in consequence ordered his nuncios, whenever they were invited out, to make a pretense of accepting the invitations, to behave graciously, and to be guarded in their conversation.

Miltitz, faithful to the arrangement he had just concluded, went from Altenburg to Leipzig, where Tetzel was residing. There was no necessity to silence him, for sooner than speak he would have concealed himself, if possible, in the center of the earth. But the nuncio resolved to vent all his anger on him. As soon as he reached Leipzig, he summoned the wretched Tetzel before him, overwhelmed him with reproaches, accused him of being the author of all his trouble, and threatened him with the pope's displeasure. This was not enough. An agent from the house of Fugger, who was then in the city, was confronted with him. Miltitz laid before the Dominican the accounts of this establishment, the papers he had himself signed, and proved that he had squandered or stolen considerable sums of money. The unhappy man, whom in the day of his triumph nothing could alarm, bent under the weight of these just accusations: he fell into despair, his health suffered, he knew not where to hide his shame.

Luther was informed of the wretched condition of his old adversary, and he alone was affected by it. "I am sorry for Tetzel," wrote he to Spalatin. He did not confine himself to words: it was not the man, but his actions that he hated. At the very moment that Rome was venting her wrath on the Dominican, Luther sent him a letter full of consolation. But all was unavailing. Tetzel, a prey to remorse, terrified by the reproaches of his best friends, and dreading the pope's anger, died very miserably not long after. It was believed that grief accelerated his death.

The reformer made a better use of his time than his powerful adversary. While Leo X was occupied with his interests as a temporal prince and was making every exertion to exclude a formidable neighbor from the throne, Luther grew each day in knowledge and in faith. He studied the papal decrees, and the discoveries he made therein greatly modified his ideas. "I am reading the decrees of the pontiffs," wrote he to Spalatin, "and—I whisper this in your ear—I do not know whether the pope is antichrist himself, or his apostle, so greatly is Christ misrepresented and crucified in them."

Yet he still felt esteem for the ancient church of Rome and had no thought of separating from it. "That the Roman church," said he in the explanation which he had promised Miltitz to publish, "is honored by God above all others, is what we cannot doubt. St. Peter, St. Paul, forty-six popes, many hundreds of thousands of martyrs, have shed their blood in its bosom and have overcome hell and the world, so that God's eye regards it with especial favor. Although everything is now in a very wretched state there, this is not a sufficient reason for separating from it. On the contrary, the worse things are going on within it, the more should we cling to it; for it is not by separation that we shall make it better. We must not desert God on account of the Devil; or abandon the children of God who are still in the Roman communion, because of the multitude of the ungodly. There is no sin, there is no evil that should destroy charity or break the bond of union. For charity can do all things, and to unity nothing is difficult."

These declarations, which were published by Luther at the end of February, did not entirely satisfy Miltitz and Cajetan. These two had retired within the ancient walls of Treves. There, assisted by the prince-archbishop, they hoped to accomplish together the object in which each of them had failed separately. The two nuncios felt clearly that nothing more was to be expected from Frederick, now invested with supreme power in the empire. They saw that Luther persisted in his refusal to retract. The only means of success was to deprive the heretical monk of the elector's protection and entice him into their hands. Once at Treves, in the states of an ecclesiastical prince, the reformer would be very skillful if he escaped without having fully satisfied the demands of the sovereign pontiff. They immediately applied themselves to the task. "Luther," said Miltitz to the elector-archbishop of Treves, "has accepted your grace as arbitrator. Summon him before you." The elector of Treves accordingly wrote on May 3 to the elector of Saxony, requesting him to send Luther to him. Cajetan, and afterwards Miltitz himself, wrote also to Frederick, informing him that the Golden Rose had arrived at Augsburg. This, thought they, was the moment for striking a decisive blow.

But circumstances had changed: neither Frederick nor Luther permitted himself to be shaken. The elector comprehended his new position. He no longer feared the pope, much less his agents. The reformer, seeing Miltitz and Cajetan united, foresaw the fate that awaited him if he complied with their invitation. "Everywhere," said he, "and in every manner they seek after my life." Besides, he had appealed to the pope, and the pope, busied in intrigues with crowned heads, had not replied. Luther wrote to Miltitz, "How can I set out without an order from Rome, in the midst of the troubles by which the empire is agitated? How can I encounter so many dangers and incur such heavy expense, seeing that I am the poorest of men?"

The elector of Treves, a prudent and moderate man, and a friend of Frederick, was desirous of keeping on good terms with the latter. Besides, he had no desire to interfere in this matter unless he was positively called upon. He therefore arranged with the elector of Saxony to put off the inquiry until the next diet, which did not take place until two years after, when it assembled at Worms.

While a providential hand thus warded off, one by one, the dangers by which Luther was threatened, he himself was boldly advancing toward a goal which he did not suspect. It was no longer in Germany alone that the reformer's voice was heard. It had passed the frontiers of the empire and begun to shake, among the different nations of Europe, the foundations of Roman Catholic power. Frobenius, a celebrated printer at Basel, had published a collection of Luther's works. It was rapidly circulated.

Frederick III ("the Wise"), Elector of Saxony, an engraving by Albrecht Dürer. The ruler of Luther's home territory, Frederick moved from cautious sympathy to firm support of the Reformation.

Erasmus was at Louvain when Luther's writings reached the low countries. The prior of the Augustinians of Antwerp, who had studied at Wittenberg and who, according to the testimony of Erasmus, was a follower of true primitive Christianity, read them with eagerness, as did other Belgians. Frobenius sent six hundred copies of these works into France and Spain. They were sold publicly in Paris. The doctors of the Sorbonne, as it would appear, read them with approbation. "It is high time," said some of them, "that those who devote themselves to biblical studies should speak out freely." In England these books were received with still greater eagerness. Some Spanish merchants translated them into their mother tongue and forwarded them from Antwerp to their own country.

Calvi, a learned bookseller of Pavia, carried a great number of copies to Italy and circulated them in all the transalpine cities. It was not the love of gain that inspired this man of letters, but a desire of contributing to the revival of piety. The energy with which Luther maintained the cause of Christ filled him with joy. "All the learned men of Italy," wrote he, "will unite with me, and we will send you verses composed by our most distinguished writers."

Frobenius, in transmitting a copy of his publication to Luther, related all these joyful tidings and added, "I have sold every copy, except ten; and I have never made so good a speculation." Other letters informed Luther of the joy caused by his works. "I am delighted," said he, "that the truth is so pleasing, although she speaks with so little learning and in so barbarous a tone."

Such was the commencement of the awakening in the various countries of Europe. If we except Switzerland, and even France, where the gospel had already been preached, the arrival of the Wittenberg doctor's writings everywhere forms the first page in the history of the Reformation. A printer of Basel scattered the first germs of truth. At the very moment when the Roman pontiff thought to stifle the work in Germany, it began in France, the low countries, Italy, Spain, England, and Switzerland. What mattered it, even should Rome cut down the parent stem? The seeds were already scattered over every land.

Chapter 24
Eck Challenges Luther

While the combat was beginning beyond the confines of the empire, it appeared dying away within. The papal partisans were mute: Tetzel was no longer in a condition to fight. Luther was entreated by his friends not to continue the discussion, and he had promised compliance. The theses were passing into oblivion. This treacherous peace rendered the eloquence of the reformer powerless. The Reformation appeared checked. "But," said Luther somewhat later, when speaking of this epoch, "men imagine vain things; for the Lord awoke to judge the people."

Eck the scholastic, Luther's old friend and author of the "Obelisks," was the man who recommenced the combat. He was sincerely attached to the papacy, but seems to have had no true religious sentiments, and to have been one of that class of men, so numerous in every age, who look upon science, and even theology and religion, as the means of acquiring worldly reputation. Vainglory lies hid under the priest's cassock, no less than under the warrior's coat of mail. Eck had studied the art of disputation according to the rules of the schoolmen and had become a master in this sort of controversy. While the knights of the Middle Ages and the warriors, in the time of the Reformation, sought for glory in the tournament, the schoolmen struggled for it in syllogistic disputation—a spectacle of frequent occurrence in the universities. Eck, who entertained no mean idea of himself and was proud of his talents, of the popularity of his cause, and of the victories he had gained in eight universities of Hungary, Lombardy, and Germany, ardently desired to have an opportunity of trying his strength and skill against the reformer. We shall see what circumstances afforded the Ingolstadt doctor the means of entering the lists with his importunate rival.

The zealous but too ardent Carlstadt was still on friendly terms with Luther. These two theologians were closely united by their attachment to the doctrine of grace and by their admiration for St. Augustine. Carlstadt was inclined to enthusiasm and possessed little discretion; he was not a man to be restrained by the skill and policy of a Miltitz. He had published some theses in reply to Dr. Eck's "Obelisks," in which he defended Luther and their common faith. Eck had answered him; but Carlstadt did not let him have the last word. The discussion grew warm. Eck, desirous of profiting by so favorable an opportunity, had thrown down the gauntlet, and the impetuous Carlstadt had taken it up. God made use of the passions of these two men to accomplish His purposes. Luther had not interfered in their disputes, and yet he was destined to be the hero of the fight. It was agreed that the discussion should take place at Leipzig. Such was the origin of that Leipzig disputation which became so famous.

Eck cared little for disputing with and even conquering Carlstadt: Luther was his great aim. He therefore made every exertion to allure him to the field of battle, and with this view published thirteen theses, which he pointed expressly against the chief doctrines already set forth by the reformer.

Luther, who had reluctantly consented to remain silent, was deeply moved as he read these propositions. He saw that they were aimed at him, and felt that he could not honorably avoid the contest. "This man," said he, "calls Carlstadt his antagonist, and at the same time attacks me. But God reigns. He knows what He will bring out of this tragedy. It is neither Doctor Eck nor myself that will be at stake. God's purpose will be accomplished. Thanks to Eck, this affair, which hitherto has been mere play, will become serious and inflict a deadly blow on the tyranny of Rome and of the Roman pontiff."

Rome herself had broken the truce. She did more; in renewing the signal of battle, she began the contest on a point that Luther had not yet attacked. It was the papal supremacy to which Doctor Eck drew the attention of his adversaries. In this he followed the dangerous example that Tetzel had already set. Rome invited the blows of the gladiator; and if she left some of her members quivering on the arena, it was because she had drawn upon herself his formidable arm.

Luther, who had set a rare example of moderation by remaining silent so long, fearlessly replied to the challenge of his antagonist.

John Eck

"God knows," wrote he to the elector, "that I was firmly resolved to keep silence, and that I was glad to see this struggle terminated at last. I have so strictly adhered to the treaty concluded with the papal commissary that I have not replied to Sylvester Prierio, notwithstanding the insults of my adversaries and the advice of my friends. But now Doctor Eck attacks me, and not only me, but the University of Wittenberg also. I cannot suffer the truth to be thus covered with opprobrium."

At the same time Luther wrote to Carlstadt: "Most excellent Andrew, I would not have you enter upon this dispute, since they are aiming at me. I shall joyfully lay aside my serious occupations to take my part in the sports of these flatterers of the Roman pontiff." Then addressing his adversary, he cried disdainfully from Wittenberg to Ingolstadt, "Now, my dear Eck, be brave, and gird thy sword upon thy thigh, thou mighty man. If I could not please thee as mediator, perhaps I shall please thee better as antagonist. Not that I imagine I can vanquish thee, but because, after all the triumphs thou hast gained in Hungary, Lombardy, and Bavaria—if at least we are to believe thee—I shall give thee opportunity of gaining the title of conqueror of Saxony and Misnia, so that thou shalt forever be hailed with the glorious title of August."

All Luther's friends did not share in his courage, for no one had hitherto been able to resist the sophisms of Doctor Eck. But their greatest cause of alarm was the subject of the discussion, the pope's primacy. The courtiers of the elector were alarmed. Spalatin, the prince's confidant and Luther's intimate friend, was filled with anxiety. Frederick was uneasy. The reformer alone did not blanch. "The Lord," thought he, "will deliver him into my hands." The faith by which he was animated gave him the means of encouraging his friends. "I entreat you, my dear Spalatin," said he, "do not give way to fear. You well know that if Christ had not been on my side, all that I have hitherto done must have been my ruin. . . .

"O my poor Spalatin, it is impossible to speak with truth of the Scriptures and of the church without arousing the beast. Never expect to see me free from danger, unless I abandon the teaching of sound divinity. If this matter be of God, it will not come to an end before all my friends have forsaken me, as Christ was forsaken by His disciples. Truth will stand alone and will triumph by its own right hand, not by mine, nor yours, nor any other man's. If I perish, the world will not perish with me. But, wretch that I am, I fear I am unworthy to die in such a cause."

Luther wrote letter upon letter to Duke George, begging this prince, in whose states Leipzig was situated, to give him permission to go and take part in the disputation; but he received no answer. The grandson of the Bohemian king, alarmed by Luther's proposition on the papal authority, and fearing the recurrence of those wars in Saxony of which Bohemia had so long been the theater, would not consent to the doctor's request. He positively refused the sanction required by the reformer to take a share in the disputation, allowing him only to be present as a spectator. This annoyed Luther very much: yet he had but one desire, to obey God. He resolved to go, to look on, and to wait his opportunity.

At the same time, the prince forwarded to his utmost ability the disputation between Eck and Carlstadt. George was attached to the old doctrine; but he was upright, sincere, a friend to free inquiry, and did not think that every opinion should be judged heretical simply because it was offensive to the court of Rome. More than this, the elector used his influence with his cousin; and George, gaining confidence from Frederick's language, ordered that the disputation should take place.

Adolphus, bishop of Merseburg, in whose diocese Leipzig was situated, saw more clearly than Miltitz and Cajetan the danger of leaving such important questions to the chances of single combat. Rome dared not expose to such hazard the hard-earned fruits of many centuries. All the Leipzig theologians felt no less alarm and entreated their bishop to prevent the discussion. Upon this, Adolphus made the most energetic representations to Duke George, who very sensibly replied, "I am surprised that a bishop should have so great a dread of the ancient and praiseworthy custom of our fathers, the investigation of doubtful questions in matters of faith. If your theologians refuse to defend their doctrines, it would be better to employ the money spent on them in maintaining old women and children, who at least could spin while they were singing."

The timid Erasmus was alarmed at the very idea of a combat, and his prudence would have prevented the discussion. "If you would take Erasmus' word," wrote he to Melancthon, "you would labor rather in cultivating literature, than in disputing with its enemies. I think that we should make greater progress by this means. Above all, let us never forget that we ought to conquer not only by our eloquence, but also by mildness and moderation." Neither the alarm of the priests nor the discretion of the pacificators could any longer prevent the combat. Each man got his arms ready.

While the electors were meeting at Frankfurt to choose an emperor in June of 1519, the theologians assembled at Leipzig for an act unnoticed by the world at large, but whose importance was destined to be quite as great for posterity.

Eck came first to the rendezvous. On June 21, he entered Leipzig with Poliander, a young man whom he had brought from Ingolstadt to write an account of the disputation. Every mark of respect was paid to the scholastic doctor. Robed in his sacerdotal garments and at the head of a numerous procession, he paraded the streets of the city on the festival of Corpus Christi. All were eager to see him: the inhabitants were on his side, he tells us himself; "yet," adds he, "a report was current in the town that I should be beaten in this combat."

On the day succeeding the festival, Friday, June 24, which was the feast of St. John, the Wittenbergers arrived. Carlstadt, who was to contend with Doctor Eck, sat alone in his carriage, and preceded all the rest. Duke Barnim of Pomerania, who was then studying at Wittenberg, and who had been named honorary rector of the university, came next in an open carriage: at each side were seated the two great divines, the fathers of the Reformation, Luther and Melancthon.

John Lange, vicar of the Augustinians, many doctors in law, several masters of arts, two licentiates in theology, and other ecclesiastics, among whom was Nicholas Amsdorff, closed the procession. Amsdorff, sprung from a noble family, valuing little the brilliant career to which his illustrious birth might have called him, had dedicated himself to theology. The theses on indulgences had brought him to a knowledge of the truth. He had immediately made a bold confession of faith. Possessing a strong mind and an ardent character, Amsdorff frequently excited Luther, who was naturally vehement enough, to acts that were perhaps imprudent. Born in exalted rank, he had no fear of the great, and he sometimes spoke to them with a freedom bordering on rudeness. "The gospel of Jesus Christ," said he one day before an assembly of nobles, "belongs to the poor and afflicted; not to you, princes, lords, and courtiers, who live continually in luxury and pleasures."

But these persons alone did not form the procession from Wittenberg. A great number of students followed their teachers: Eck affirms that they amounted to two hundred. Armed with pikes and halberds, they surrounded the carriages of the doctors, ready to defend them and proud of their cause.

Such was the order in which the *cortège* of the reformers arrived in Leipzig. They had already entered by the Grimma gate and advanced as far as St. Paul's cemetery when one of the wheels of Carlstadt's carriage gave way. The archdeacon, whose vanity was delighted at so solemn an entry, rolled into the mud. He was not hurt but was compelled to proceed to his lodgings on foot. Luther's carriage, which followed next, rapidly outstripped him and bore the reformer in safety to his quarters.

Adolphus of Merseburg was not idle. As soon as he heard of the approach of Luther and Carlstadt, and even before they had alighted from their carriages, he ordered placards to be posted upon the doors of all the churches, forbidding the opening of the disputation under pain of excommunication. Duke George, astonished at this audacity, commanded the town council to tear down the placards and committed to prison the bold agent who had ventured to execute the bishop's order. George had repaired to Leipzig, attended by all his court, and made the customary presents to the respective combatants. "The duke," observed Eck with vanity, "gave me a fine deer; but he only gave a fawn to Carlstadt."

Immediately on hearing of Luther's arrival, Eck went to visit the Wittenberg doctor. "What is this?" asked he; "I am told that you refuse to dispute with me."

Luther: How can I, since the duke has forbidden me?

Eck: If I cannot dispute with you, I care little about meeting Carlstadt. It was on your account I came here. [Then after a moment's silence he added,] If I can procure you the duke's permission, will you enter the lists with me?

Luther (joyfully): Procure it for me, and we will fight.

Eck immediately waited on the duke and endeavored to remove his fears. He represented to him that he was certain of victory and that the papal authority, far from suffering in the dispute, would come forth covered with glory. The ringleader must be attacked: if Luther remained standing, all stood with him; if he fell, everything would fall with him. George granted the required permission.

The duke had caused a large hall to be prepared in his palace of the Pleissenburg. Two pulpits had been erected opposite each other, tables were placed for the notaries commissioned to take down the discussion, and benches had been arranged for the spectators. The pulpits and benches were covered with handsome hangings. Over the pulpit of the Wittenberg doctor was suspended the portrait of Saint Martin, whose name he bore; over that of Doctor Eck, a representation of Saint George the champion. "We shall see," said the presumptuous Eck, as he looked at this emblem, "whither I shall not ride over my enemies." Everything announced the importance that was attached to this contest.

On June 25, both parties met at the palace to hear the regulations that were to be observed during the disputation. Eck, who had more confidence in his declamations and gestures than in his arguments, exclaimed, "We will dispute freely and extemporaneously, and the notaries shall not take down our words in writing."

Carlstadt: It has been agreed that the disputation should be reported, published, and submitted to the judgment of all men.

Eck: To take down everything that is said is dispiriting to the combatants, and prolongs the battle. There is an end to that animation which such a discussion requires. Do not check the flow of eloquence.

The friends of Doctor Eck supported his proposition, but Carlstadt persisted in his objections. The champion of Rome was obliged to give way.

Eck: Be it so; it shall be taken down. But do not let the notes be published before they have been submitted to the examination of chosen judges.

Luther: Does then the truth of Doctor Eck and his followers dread the light?

Eck: We must have judges.

Luther: What judges?

Eck: When the disputation is finished, we will arrange about selecting them.

The object of the partisans of Rome was evident. If the Wittenberg divines accepted judges, they were lost; for their adversaries were sure beforehand of those who would be applied to. If they refused these judges, they would be covered with shame, for their opponents would circulate the report that they were afraid to submit their opinions to impartial arbitrators.

The judges whom the reformers demanded were not any particular individual whose opinion had been previously formed, but all Christendom. They appealed to this universal suffrage. Besides, it was a slight matter to them if they were condemned, if, while pleading their cause before the whole world, they brought a few souls to the knowledge of the truth. "Luther," says a Catholic historian, "required all men for his judges; that is, such a tribunal that no urn could have been vast enough to contain the votes."

They separated. "See what artifices they employ," said Luther and his friends one to another. "They desire, no doubt, to have the pope or the universities for judges."

In fact, on the next morning the Roman Catholic divines sent one of their number to Luther, who was commissioned to propose that their judge should be—the pope! "The pope," said Luther; "how can I possibly agree to this?"

"Beware," exclaimed all his friends, "of acceding to conditions so unjust." Eck and his party held another council. They gave up the pope and proposed certain universities.

"Do not deprive us of the liberty which you had previously granted," answered Luther.

"We cannot give way on this point," replied they.

"Well then," exclaimed Luther, "I will take no part in the discussion."

Again the parties separated, and this matter was a general topic of conversation throughout the city. "Luther," everywhere exclaimed the Roman Catholics, "will not dispute. . . . He will not acknowledge any judge." His words were commented on and misrepresented, and his adversaries endeavored to place them in the most unfavorable light.

"What, does he really decline the discussion?" said the reformer's best friends. They went to him and expressed their alarm. "You refuse to take any part in the discussion," cried they. "Your refusal will bring everlasting disgrace on your university and on your cause."

This was attacking Luther on his weakest side. "Well, then," replied he, his heart overflowing with indignation, "I accept the conditions imposed upon me, but I reserve the right of appeal."

Chapter 25
The Leipzig Disputation (Part 1)

June 27 was the day appointed for the opening of the discussion. Early in the morning the two parties assembled in the college of the university and thence went in procession to the church of St. Thomas, where a solemn mass was performed by order and at the expense of the duke. After the service, they proceeded to the ducal palace. At their head were Duke George and the duke of Pomerania; after them came counts, abbots, knights, and other persons of distinction, and last of all the doctors of the two parties. A guard composed of seventy-six citizens armed with halberds accompanied the train, with banners flying and to the sound of martial music. It halted at the castle gates.

The procession having reached the palace, each took his station in the hall appointed for the discussion. Duke George, the hereditary Prince John, Prince George of Anhalt, then twelve years old, and the duke of Pomerania occupied the seats assigned them.

Mosellanus ascended the pulpit to remind the theologians, by the duke's order, in what manner they were to dispute. "If you fall to quarrelling," said the speaker, "what difference will there be between a theologian in discussion and a shameless duelist? What is your object in gaining the victory, if it be not to recover a brother from the error of his ways? It appears to me that each of you should desire less to conquer than to be conquered."

When this address was terminated, sacred music resounded through the halls of the Pleissenburg; all the assembly knelt down, and the ancient hymn of invocation to the Holy Ghost, *Veni, Sancte Spiritus* ("Come, Holy Spirit"), was sung. This was a solemn moment in the annals of the Reformation. Thrice the invocation was repeated, and while this solemn strain was heard, the defenders of the old doctrine and the champions of the new, the churchmen of the Middle Ages and those who sought to restore the church of the apostles, here assembled and confounded with one another, humbly bent their heads to the earth. The ancient tie of one and the same communion still bound together all those different minds; the same prayer still proceeded from all those lips, as if pronounced by one heart.

These were the last moments of outward, of dead unity: a new unity of spirit and of life was about to begin. The Holy Ghost was invoked upon the church and was preparing to answer and to renovate Christendom.

The singing and the prayers being ended, they all rose up. The discussion was about to open; but as it was past the hour of noon, it was deferred until two o'clock.

The duke invited to his table the principal persons who were to be present at the discussion. After the repast, they returned to the castle. The great hall was filled with spectators. Disputations of this kind were the public meetings of that age. It was here that the representatives of their day agitated the questions that occupied all minds. The speakers were soon at their posts. That the reader may form a better idea of their appearance, we will give their portraits as drawn by one of the most impartial witnesses of the contest.

"Martin Luther is of middle stature and so thin, in consequence of his studies, that his bones may almost be counted. He is in the prime of life and has a clear and sonorous voice. His knowledge and understanding of the Holy Scriptures is unparalleled; he has the Word of God at his fingers' ends. Besides this, he possesses great store of arguments and ideas. One might perhaps desire a little more judgment in arranging his subjects. In conversation he is pleasing and affable; there is nothing harsh or austere about him; he can accommodate himself to every one; his manner of speaking is agreeable and unembarrassed. He displays firmness and has always a cheerful air, whatever may be his adversaries' threats; so that it is difficult to believe that he could undertake such great things without the divine protection. He is blamed, however, for being more caustic, when reproving others, than becomes a theologian, particularly when putting forward novelties in religion.

"Carlstadt is of shorter stature; his complexion is dark and sunburnt, his voice unpleasing, his memory less trustworthy than Luther's; and he is more inclined to anger. He possesses, however, though in a smaller degree, the qualities that distinguish his friend.

"Eck is tall, broad-shouldered, and has a strong and thorough German voice. He has good lungs, so that he would be heard well in a theater and would even make an excellent town crier. His accent is rather vulgar than elegant. He has not that gracefulness so much extolled by Fabius and Cicero. His mouth, his eyes, and his whole countenance give you the idea of a soldier or a butcher rather than of a divine. He has an excellent memory, and if he had only as much understanding, he would be really a perfect man. But he is slow of comprehension and is wanting in judgment, without which all other qualities are useless. Hence, in disputing, he heaps together, without selection or discernment, a mass of passages from the Bible, quotations from the Fathers, and proofs of all kinds. He has, besides, an impudence almost beyond conception. If he is embarrassed, he breaks off from the subject he is treating of and plunges into another; he sometimes even takes up his adversary's opinion, clothing it in other words, and with extraordinary skill attributes to his opponent the absurdity he had been himself defending."

Such, according to Mosellanus, were the men at that time attracting the attention of the crowd which thronged the great hall of the Pleissenburg.

The dispute began between Eck and Carlstadt.

Eck's eyes were fixed for a moment on certain objects that lay on the desk of his adversary's pulpit and which seemed to disturb him; they were the Bible and the holy Fathers. "I decline the discussion," exclaimed he suddenly, "if you are permitted to bring your books with you." Surprising that a divine should have recourse to books in order to dispute! Eck's astonishment was still more marvellous.

"It is the fig-leaf which this Adam makes use of to hide his shame," said Luther. "Did not Augustine consult his books when arguing with the Manicheans?" Eck's partisans raised a great clamor. The other side did the same. At last it was arranged, according to the wish of the chancellor of Ingolstadt, that each should rely upon his memory and his tongue only.

"Thus, then," said many, "the object of this disputation will not be to discover the truth, but what praise is to be conferred on the tongue and the memory of the disputants."

As we are unable to give the details of this discussion, which lasted seventeen days, we shall, as a historian expresses it, imitate the painters who, when they have to represent a battle, set the most memorable actions in the foreground and leave the others in the distance.

The subject of discussion between Eck and Carlstadt was important. "Man's will, before his conversion," said Carlstadt, "can perform no good work: every good work comes entirely and exclusively from God, who gives man first the will to do and then the power of accomplishing." This truth had been proclaimed by Scripture, which says, "It is God which worketh in you both to will and to do of his good pleasure" (Phil. 2:13); and by St. Augustine, who, in his dispute with the Pelagians, had enunciated it in nearly the same terms. Every work in which the love of God and obedience toward him do not exist is deprived, in the eyes of the Almighty, of all that can render it good, even should it originate in the best of human motives. Now there is in man a natural opposition to God, an opposition that the unaided strength of man cannot surmount. He has neither the will nor the power to overcome it. This must therefore be effected by the divine will.

This is the whole question of free will, so simple and yet so decried by the world. Such had been the doctrine of the church. But the schoolmen had so explained it that it was not recognizable. Undoubtedly, said they, the natural will of man can do nothing really pleasing to God; but it can do much toward rendering men meet to receive the grace of God and more worthy to obtain it. They called these preparations a merit of congruity: "because it is *congruous*," said Thomas Aquinas, "that God should treat with particular favor him who makes a good use of his own will." And as regards the conversion to be effected in man, undoubtedly it must be accomplished by the grace of God, which, according to the schoolmen, should bring it about, but not to the exclusion of his natural powers. These powers, said they, were not destroyed by sin: sin only opposes an obstacle to their development; but so soon as this obstacle is removed—and it was this, in their opinion, that the grace of God had to effect—the action of these powers begins again. The bird, to use one of their favorite comparisons, that has been tied for some time has in this state neither lost its ability nor forgotten the art of flying; but some hand must loose the bonds in order that he may again make use of his wings. This is the case with man, said they.

Such was the question agitated between Eck and Carlstadt. At first, Eck had appeared to oppose all Carlstadt's propositions on this subject; but finding his position untenable, he said, "I grant that the will has not the power of doing a good work, and that it receives this power from God."

"Do you acknowledge, then," asked Carlstadt, overjoyed at obtaining so important a concession, "that every good work comes entirely from God?"

"The *whole* good work really proceeds from God, but not *wholly,*" cunningly replied the scholastic doctor. "An entire apple," continued Eck, "is produced by the sun, but not entirely and without the cooperation of the plant." Most certainly it has never yet been maintained that an apple is produced solely by the sun.

Well then, said the opponents, plunging deeper into this important and delicate question of philosophy and religion, let us inquire how God acts upon man and how man conducts himself under this action. "I acknowledge," said Eck, "that the first impulse in man's conversion proceeds from God, and that the will of man in this instance is entirely passive." Thus far the two parties were agreed. "I acknowledge," said Carlstadt, "that after this first impulse which proceeds from God, something must come on the part of man, something that St. Paul denominates *will,* and which the Fathers entitle *consent.*" Here again they were both agreed, but from this point they diverged.

"This consent of man," said Eck, "comes partly from our natural will, and partly from God's grace."

"No," said Carlstadt, "God must entirely create this will in man."

Upon this, Eck manifested anger and astonishment at hearing words so fitted to make man sensible of his nothingness. "Your doctrine," exclaimed he, "converts a man into a stone, a log, incapable of any reaction."

"What?" replied the reformers. "The faculty of receiving this strength which God produces in him, this faculty which, according to us, man possesses, does not sufficiently distinguish him from a log or a stone?"

"But," said their antagonist, "by denying that man has any natural ability, you contradict all experience."

"We do not deny," replied they, "that man possesses a certain ability and that he has the power of reflection, meditation, and choice. We consider this power and ability as mere instruments that can produce no good work until the hand of God has set them in motion. They are like a saw in the hands of a sawyer."

A trivial circumstance interrupted the discussion. We learn from Eck that Carlstadt had prepared a number of arguments; and, like many public speakers of our own day, he was reading what he had written. Eck saw in this the tactics of a mere learner and objected to it. Carlstadt, embarrassed, and fearing that he should break down if he were deprived of his papers, persisted. "Ah," exclaimed the schoolman, proud of the advantage he thought he had obtained, "his memory is not so good as mine." The point was referred to the arbitrators, who permitted the reading of extracts from the Fathers, but decided that in other respects the disputants should speak extempore.

This first part of the disputation was often interrupted by the noise of the spectators. They were in commotion and frequently raised their voices. Any proposition that offended the ears of the majority immediately excited their clamors, and then, as in our own days, the galleries were often called to order. The disputants themselves were sometimes carried away by the heat of discussion.

Near Luther sat Melancthon, who attracted almost as much attention as his neighbor. He was of small stature and appeared little more than eighteen years old. Luther was a head taller. "To look at Melancthon," wrote a Swiss theologian who studied at Wittenberg, "you would say he was a mere boy; but in understanding, learning, and talent, he is a giant, and I cannot comprehend how such heights of wisdom and genius can be found in so small a body." Between the sittings, Melancthon conversed with Carlstadt and Luther. He aided them in preparing for the combat and suggested the arguments with which his extensive learning furnished him; but during the discussion he remained quietly seated among the spectators and carefully listened to the words of the theologians. From time to time, however, he came to the assistance of Carlstadt; and when the latter was near giving way under the powerful declamation of the chancellor of Ingolstadt, the young professor whispered a word or slipped him a piece of paper on which the answer was written. Eck having perceived this on one occasion and feeling indignant that this grammarian, as he called him, should dare interfere in the discussion, turned toward him and said haughtily, "Hold your tongue, Philipp; mind your studies and do not disturb me." Perhaps Eck at that time foresaw how formidable an opponent he would afterward find in this young man. Luther was offended at the gross insult directed against his friend. "Philipp's judgment," said he, "has greater weight with me than that of a thousand Doctor Ecks." Each party claimed the victory. Eck strained every nerve to appear the conqueror. As the points of divergence almost touched each other, he frequently exclaimed that he had convinced his opponent; or else he suddenly turned round, put forth Carlstadt's opinions in other words, and asked him, with a tone of triumph, if he did not find himself compelled to yield. And the unskillful auditors, who could not detect the maneuver of the sophist, applauded and exulted with him.

In many respects they were not equally matched. Carlstadt was slow, and on some occasions did not reply to his adversary's objections until the next day. Eck, on the contrary, was a master in his science and found whatever he required at the very instant. He entered the hall with a disdainful air; ascended the rostrum with a firm step; and there he tossed himself about, paced to and fro, spoke at the full pitch of his sonorous voice, had a reply ready for every argument, and bewildered his hearers by his memory and skill.

Three or four days after the opening of the conference, the disputation was interrupted by the festival of Peter and Paul the apostles.

On this occasion the duke of Pomerania requested Luther to preach before him in his chapel. Luther cheerfully consented. But the place was soon crowded, and as the number of hearers kept increasing, the assembly was transferred to the great hall of the castle in which the discussion was held. Luther chose his text from the gospel of the day and preached on the grace of God and the power of St. Peter. What Luther ordinarily maintained before an audience composed of men of learning he then set before the people. Christianity causes the light of truth to shine upon the humblest as well as the most elevated minds; it is this which distinguishes it from every other religion and from every system of philosophy. The theologians of Leipzig, who had heard Luther preach, hastened to report to Eck the scandalous words with which their ears had been shocked. "You must reply," exclaimed they; "you must publicly refute these subtle errors." Eck desired nothing better. All the churches were open to him, and four times in succession he went into the pulpit to cry down Luther and his sermon. Luther's friends were indignant at this. They demanded that the Wittenberg divine should be heard in his turn. But it was all in vain. The pulpits were open to the adversaries of the evangelical doctrine; they were closed against those who proclaimed it. "I was silent," said Luther, "and was forced to suffer myself to be attacked, insulted, and calumniated without even the power of excusing or defending myself."

It was not only the ecclesiastics who manifested their opposition to the evangelical doctors: the citizens of Leipzig were, in this respect, of the same opinion as the clergy. The principal inhabitants did not visit either Luther or Carlstadt. If they met them in the street, they did not salute them, and endeavored to traduce their characters with the duke. But on the contrary, they paid frequent visits to the doctor of Ingolstadt and ate and drank with him. The latter feasted with them, entertaining them with a description of the costly banquets to which he had been invited in Germany and Italy, sneering at Luther who had imprudently rushed upon his invincible sword, slowly quaffing the beer of Saxony, the better to compare it with that of Bavaria. His manners, which were rather free, did not give a favorable idea of his morals. Those who were favorably disposed toward Luther concealed their feelings from the public; many, like Nicodemus of old, visited him stealthily and by night.

The greatest agitation prevailed in the city. The two parties were like two hostile camps, and they sometimes came to blows. Frequent quarrels took place in the taverns between the students of Leipzig and those of Wittenberg. It was generally reported, even in the meetings of the clergy, that Luther carried a devil about with him shut up in a little box. "I don't know whether the Devil is in the box, or merely under his frock," said Eck; "but he is certainly in one or the other."

Several doctors of the two parties had lodgings during the disputation in the house of the printer Herbipolis. They became so outrageous that their host was compelled to station a police officer armed with a halberd at the head of the table, with orders to prevent the guests from coming to blows. One day Baumgartner, an indulgence merchant, quarrelled with a gentleman, a friend of Luther, and gave way to such a violent fit of anger that he expired. "I was one of those who carried him to his grave," said Froschel, who relates the circumstance. In this manner did the general ferment in men's minds display itself. Then, as in our own times, the speeches in the pulpits found an echo in the drawing room and in the streets.

Chapter 26
The Leipzig Disputation (Part 2)

On July 4 the discussion between Eck and Luther commenced. Everything seemed to promise that it would be more violent, more decisive, and more interesting than that which had just concluded and which had gradually thinned the hall. The two combatants entered the arena resolved not to lay down their arms until victory declared in favor of one or the other. The general expectation was aroused, for the papal primacy was to be the subject of discussion.

Christianity has two great adversaries: hierarchism and rationalism. Rationalism, in its application to the doctrine of man's ability, had been attacked by the reformers in the previous part of the Leipzig disputation. Hierarchism, considered in what is at once its summit and its base—the doctrine of papal authority—was to be contested in the second. On the one side appeared Eck, the champion of the established religion, vaunting of the discussions he had maintained as a general boasts of his campaigns. On the other side advanced Luther. On his features might be seen the traces of the storms his soul had encountered and the courage with which he was prepared to meet fresh tempests. These combatants, both sons of peasants and the representatives of the two tendencies that still divide Christendom, were about to enter upon a contest on which depended, in great measure, the future prospects of the state and of the church.

At seven in the morning the two disputants were in their pulpits, surrounded by a numerous and attentive assembly.

Luther stood up, and with a necessary precaution, he said modestly: "In the name of the Lord, Amen, I declare that the respect I bear to the sovereign pontiff would have prevented my entering upon this discussion, if the excellent Dr. Eck had not dragged me into it."

Eck: In thy name, gentle Jesus, before descending into the lists, I protest before you, most noble lords, that all that I may say is in submission to the judgment of the first of all sees and of him who is its possessor.

After a brief silence, Eck continued: "There is in the church of God a primacy that cometh from Christ Himself. The church militant was formed in the image of the church triumphant. Now, the latter is a monarchy in which the hierarchy ascends step by step up to God, its sole chief. For this reason Christ has established a similar order upon earth. What a monster the church would be if it were without a head!"

Luther (turning toward the assembly): When Dr. Eck declares that the universal church must have a head, he says well. If there is any one among us who maintains the contrary, let him stand up. As for me, it is no concern of mine.

Eck: If the church militant has never been without a head, I should like to know who it can be, if not the Roman pontiff?

Luther: The head of the church militant is Christ Himself, and not a man. I believe this on the testimony of God's Word. "He must reign," says Scripture, "till he hath put all enemies under his feet" (I Cor. 15:25). Let us not listen to those who banish Christ to the church triumphant in heaven. His kingdom is a kingdom of faith. We cannot see our Head, and yet we have one.

Eck, who did not consider himself beaten, had recourse to other arguments and resumed: "It is from Rome, according to Saint Cyprian, that sacerdotal unity has proceeded."

Luther: For the Western church, I grant it. But is not this same Roman church the offspring of that of Jerusalem? It is the latter, properly speaking, that is the nursing-mother of all the churches.

Eck: Saint Jerome declares that if an extraordinary power, superior to all others, were not given to the pope, there would be in the churches as many sects as there were pontiffs.

Luther: Given; that is to say, if all the rest of believers consent to it, this power might be conceded to the chief pontiff *by human right.* And I will not deny, that if all the believers in the world agree in recognizing as first and supreme pontiff either the bishop of Rome, or of Paris, or of Magdeburg, we should acknowledge him as such from the respect due to this general agreement of the church; but that has never been seen yet, and never will be seen. Even in our own days, does not the Greek church refuse its assent to Rome?

Luther was at that time prepared to acknowledge the pope as chief magistrate of the church, freely elected by it; but he denied that he was pope of divine right. It was not till much later that he denied that submission was in any way due to him; and this step he was led to take by the Leipzig disputation. Eck had ventured on ground better known to Luther than to himself. The nearer the discussion approached the primitive ages of the church, the greater was Luther's strength. Eck appealed to the Fathers; Luther replied to him from the Fathers, and all the bystanders were struck with his superiority over his rival.

"That the opinions I set forth are those of Saint Jerome," said he, "I prove by the epistle of St. Jerome himself to Evagrius: 'Every bishop,' says he, 'whether at Rome, Eugubium, Constantinople, Rhegium, Tanis, or Alexandria, is partaker of the same merit and of the same priesthood. The power of riches, the humiliation of poverty, are the only things that make a difference in the rank of the bishops.' "

From the writings of the Fathers, Luther passed to the decisions of the councils, which consider the bishop of Rome as only the first among his peers.

"We read," said he, "in the decree of the Council of Africa, 'The bishop of the first see shall neither be called prince of the pontiffs, nor sovereign pontiff, nor by any other name of that kind; but only bishop of the first see.' If the monarchy of the bishop of Rome was of divine right," continued Luther, "would not this be an heretical injunction?"

Eck replied by one of those subtle distinctions that were so familiar to him: "The bishop of Rome, if you will have it so, is not universal bishop, but bishop of the universal church."

Luther: I shall make no reply to this: let our hearers form their own opinion of it. Certainly, this is an explanation very worthy of a theologian and calculated to satisfy a disputant who thirsts for glory. It is not for nothing, it seems, that I have remained at great expense at Leipzig, since I have learnt that the pope is not, in truth, the universal bishop, but the bishop of the universal church.

Eck: Well, then, I will come to the point. The worthy doctor calls upon me to prove that the primacy of the church of Rome is of divine right. I will prove it by this expression of Christ: "Thou art Peter, and on this rock will I build my church." St. Augustine, in one of his epistles, has thus explained the meaning of this passage: "Thou art Peter, and on this *rock,*" that is to say, *on Peter,* "I will build my church." It is true that in another place the same father has explained that by this *rock* we should understand Christ Himself, but he has not retracted his former exposition.

Luther: If the reverend doctor desires to attack me, let him first reconcile these contradictions in St. Augustine. For it is most certain that Augustine has said *many times* that the *rock* was Christ, and perhaps not more than *once* that it was Peter himself. But even should St. Augustine and all the Fathers say that the apostle is the rock of which Christ speaks, I would resist them single-handed in reliance upon the Holy Scriptures, that is, on divine right; for it is written, "Other foundation can no man lay than that is laid, which is Jesus Christ" (I Cor. 3:11). Peter himself terms Christ "the chief corner stone," and a "living stone," on which we are built up a spiritual house (I Pet. 2:4-6).

Eck: I am surprised at the humility and modesty with which the reverend doctor undertakes to oppose, alone, so many illustrious Fathers and pretends to know more than the sovereign pontiffs, the councils, the doctors, and the universities! . . . It would be surprising, no doubt, if God had hidden the truth from so many saints and martyrs until the advent of the reverend father.

Luther: The Fathers are not against me. St. Augustine and St. Ambrose, both most excellent doctors, teach as I teach. "The church is founded on that article of faith," says St. Ambrose, when explaining what is meant by the rock on which the church is built. Let my opponent then set a curb upon his tongue. To express himself as he does will only serve to excite contention, and not be to discuss like a true doctor.

Eck had no idea that his opponent's learning was so extensive and that he would be able to extricate himself from the toils that were drawn around him. "The reverend doctor," said he, "has come well armed into the list. I beg your lordships to excuse me, if I do not exhibit such accuracy of research. I came here to discuss, and not to make a book."

Eck was surprised but not beaten. As he had no more arguments to adduce, he had recourse to a trick which, if it did not vanquish his antagonist, must at least embarrass him greatly. If the accusation of being Bohemian, a heretic, a Hussite, could be fixed upon Luther, he was vanquished; for the Bohemians were objects of abhorrence in the church. The scene of combat was not far from the frontiers of Bohemia; Saxony, after the sentence pronounced on John Huss by the Council of Constance, had been exposed to all the horrors of a long and ruinous war; it was its boast to have resisted the Hussites at that time. The University of Leipzig had been founded in opposition to the tendencies of John Huss; and this discussion was going on in the presence of princes, nobles, and citizens whose fathers had fallen in that celebrated contest. To insinuate that Luther and Huss were of one mind would be to inflict a most terrible blow on the former.

It is to this stratagem that the Ingolstadt doctor now had recourse: "From the earliest times, all good Christians have acknowledged that the church of Rome derives its primacy direct from Christ Himself and not from human right. I must confess, however, that the Bohemians, while they obstinately defended their errors, attacked this doctrine. I beg the worthy father's pardon, if I am an enemy of the Bohemians because they are enemies of the church, and if the present discussion has called these heretics to my recollection; for, in my humble opinion, the doctor's conclusions are in every way favorable to these errors. It is even asserted that the Hussites are loudly boasting of it."

Eck had calculated well: his partisans received this perfidious insinuation with the greatest favor. There was a movement of joy among the audience. "These insults," said the reformer afterward, "tickled them much more agreeably than the discussion itself."

Luther: I do not like, and I never shall like a schism. Since on their own authority the Bohemians have separated from our unity, they have done wrong, even if the divine right had pronounced in favor of their doctrines; for the supreme divine right is charity and oneness of mind.

It was during the morning sitting of July 5 that Luther had made use of this language. The meeting broke up shortly after, as it was the hour of dinner. Luther felt ill at ease. Had he not gone too far in thus condemning the Christians of Bohemia? Did they not hold doctrines that Luther was now maintaining? He saw all the difficulties of his position. Should he rise up against a council that condemned John Huss, or should he deny that sublime idea of a universal Christian church which had taken full possession of his mind? Accordingly, when the assembly met again at two in the afternoon, he was the first to speak.

He said with firmness, "Among the articles of faith held by John Huss and the Bohemians, there are some that are most Christian. This is a positive certainty. Here, for instance, is one: 'That there is but one universal church'; and here is another: 'It is not necessary for salvation to believe the Roman church superior to all others.' It is of little consequence to me whether these things were said by Wycliffe or by Huss; they are truth."

Luther's declaration produced a great sensation among his hearers. Huss, Wycliffe—those odious names pronounced with approbation by a monk in the midst of a Catholic assembly! An almost general murmur ran round the hall. Duke George himself felt alarmed. He fancied he saw that banner of civil war upraised in Saxony which had for so many years desolated the states of his maternal ancestors. Unable to suppress his emotion, he placed his hands on his hips, shook his head, and exclaimed aloud, so that all the assembly heard him, "He is carried away by rage!" The whole meeting was agitated: they rose up, each man speaking to his neighbor. Those who had given way to drowsiness awoke. Luther's friends were in great perplexity, while his enemies exulted. Many who had thus far listened to him with pleasure began to entertain doubts of his orthodoxy. The impression produced on Duke George's mind by these words was never effaced; from this moment he looked upon the reformer with an evil eye and became his enemy.

Luther did not suffer himself to be intimidated by these murmurs. One of his principal arguments was that the Greeks had never recognized the pope, and yet they had never been declared heretics; that the Greek church had existed, still existed, and would exist without the pope, and that it as much belonged to Christ as the church of Rome did. Eck, on the contrary, impudently maintained the Christian and the Roman church were one and the same; that the Greeks and Orientals, in abandoning the pope, had also abandoned the Christian faith and were indisputably heretics. "What!" exclaimed Luther, "are not Gregory of Nazianzum, Basil the Great, Epiphanius, Chrysostom, and an immense number besides of Greek bishops—are they not saved? And yet they did not believe that the church of Rome was above the other churches. . . . It is not in the power of the Roman pontiffs to make new articles of faith. The

Christian believer acknowledges no other authority than Holy Scripture. This alone is the *right divine*. I beg the worthy doctor to concede that the Roman pontiffs were men and that he will not make them gods."

Eck then resorted to one of those jests which give a specious air of triumph to him who employs them. "The reverend father is a very poor cook," said he; "he has made a terrible hodgepodge of Greek saints and heretics; so that the odor of sanctity in the one prevents us from smelling the poison of the other."

Luther (interrupting Eck with warmth): The worthy doctor is becoming abusive. In my opinion, there can be no communion between Christ and Belial.

Luther had made a great stride in advance. In 1516 and 1517, he had attacked only the sermons of the indulgence hawkers and the scholastic doctrines but had respected the papal decrees. Somewhat later he had rejected these decrees and had appealed to a council. Now he had thrown off even this latter authority, declaring that no council could lay down a new article of faith and claim to be infallible. Thus had all human authorities fallen successively before him; the sands that the rain and the torrents carry with them had disappeared, and for rebuilding the ruined house of the Lord nothing remained but the everlasting rock of the Word of God. "Reverend father," said Eck, "if you believe that a council, regularly assembled, can err, you are in my eyes nothing better than a heathen and a publican."

The discussion on the papal primacy had lasted five days. On July 8, they proceeded to the doctrine of purgatory. This spread over a little more than two days. Luther still admitted this doctrine, but denied that it was taught in Scripture, or in the Fathers, in the manner that his opponent and the schoolmen pretended. "Our Doctor Eck," said he, alluding to the superficial character of his adversary's mind, "has this day skimmed over Scripture almost without touching it, as a spider runs upon water."

On July 11, they came to indulgences. "It was a mere joke," said Luther; "the dispute was ridiculous. The indulgences fell outright, and Eck was nearly of my opinion." Eck himself said, "If I had not disputed with Doctor Martin on the papal supremacy, I should almost have agreed with him."

The discussion next turned on repentance, absolution of the priest, and satisfactions. Eck, according to his usual practice, quoted the scholastic doctors, the Dominicans, and the pope's canons. Luther closed the disputation with these words: "The reverend doctor flees from the Scriptures as the Devil from before the cross. As for me, with all due respect to the Fathers, I prefer the authority of holy writ, and this test I would recommend to our judges."

Here ended the dispute between Eck and Luther. Carlstadt and the Ingolstadt doctor kept up the discussion two days longer on human merits in good works. On July 16 the business was concluded, after having lasted twenty days, by a speech from the rector of the university. As soon as he had finished, loud music was heard, and the solemnity was concluded by singing the *Te Deum.*

But during the chanting of this solemn thanksgiving, men's minds were no longer as they had been during the *Veni Spiritus* at the opening of the discussion. Already the presentiments of many had been realized. The blows that the champions of the two doctrines had aimed at each other had inflicted a deep wound upon the papacy.

Chapter 27
The Aftermath of Leipzig

These theological disputes had been followed and listened to for twenty successive days with great attention: laymen, knights, and princes had manifested a constant interest. Duke Barnim of Pomerania and Duke George were remarkably regular in their attendance. But, on the contrary, some of the Leipzig theologians, friends of Doctor Eck, slept soundly, as an eyewitness informs us. It was necessary to wake them up at the close of the disputation for fear they should lose their dinners.

Luther quitted Leipzig first; Carlstadt followed him, but Eck remained several days after their departure.

No decision had been come to on the discussion. Everyone commented on it according to his own feelings. "At Leipzig," said Luther, "there was great loss of time, but no seeking after truth. We have been examining the doctrines of our adversaries these two years past, so that we have counted all their bones. Eck, on the contrary, has hardly grazed the surface; but he made more noise in one hour than we have in two long years."

Eck and the Leipzig divines loudly vaunted of what they called *their victory*. They circulated false reports in every direction. All the mouthpieces of their party repeated their self-congratulations. "You see," said Luther to Spalatin, "that they are singing a new *Iliad* and a new *Aeneid*. They are so kind as to make a Hector or a Turnus of me, while Eck, in their eyes, is Achilles or Aeneas. They have but one doubt remaining, whether the victory was gained by the arms of Eck or by those of Leipzig. All that I can say to clear up the subject is this: Doctor Eck never ceased bawling, and the Leipzig divines did nothing but hold their tongues."

The Leipzig disputation was not destined, however, to evaporate in smoke. Every work performed with devotion bears fruit. Luther's words had sunk with irresistible power into the minds of his hearers. Many of those who daily thronged the hall of the castle were subdued by the truth. It was especially in the midst of its most determined adversaries that its victories were gained. Doctor Eck's secretary, familiar friend, and disciple, Poliander, was won to the Reformation; and in the year 1522, he publicly preached the gospel at Leipzig. John Cellarius, professor of Hebrew, a man violently opposed to the reformed doctrines, was touched by the words of the eloquent doctor and began to search the Scriptures more deeply. Ere long he gave up his station and went to Wittenberg to study humbly at Luther's feet. Some time after, he was pastor at Frankfurt and at Dresden.

Among those who had taken their seats on the benches reserved for the count, and who surrounded Duke George, was a young prince, twelve years old, descended from a family celebrated for their combats against the Saracens—it was George of Anhalt. He was then studying at Leipzig under a private tutor. An eager desire for learning and an ardent thirst for truth had already distinguished this illustrious youth. The discussion at Leipzig awakened serious reflections in this boy and excited a decided partiality for Luther. On the death of his pious mother, who was secretly well disposed toward Luther, he became possessed of all the reformer's writings. Convinced and carried away, he fearlessly ranged himself on the side of the gospel. In vain did his guardians, and particularly Duke George, besiege him with entreaties and remonstrances. He was inflexible, and George exclaimed, half convinced by the reasoning of his ward, "I cannot answer him; but I will still remain in my own church, for it is a hard matter to break in an old dog." This amiable prince preached in person to his subjects the words of everlasting life, and to him has been applied the saying of Dion on the Emperor Marcus Antoninus: "He was consistent during the whole of his life; he was a good man, one in whom there was no guile."

But it was the students in particular who received Luther's words with enthusiasm. They felt the difference between the spirit and energy of the Wittenberg doctor and the sophistical distinctions, the empty speculations of the chancellor of Ingolstadt. They saw that Luther relied upon the Word of God and that Eck's opinions were grounded on human tradition. The effect was instantaneous. The lecture rooms of the University of Leipzig were speedily deserted after the disputation. One circumstance, indeed, contributed to this result: the plague seemed on the point of breaking out in that city. But there were other universities to which the students might have gone. The power of truth drew them to Wittenberg, where the number of students was soon doubled.

The Leipzig disputation bore still greater fruits. Here it was that the theologian of the Reformation received his call. Melancthon sat modest and silent listening to the discussion, in which he took very little part. Till that time literature had been his sole occupation. The conference gave him a new impulse and launched the eloquent professor into the career of divinity. From that hour his extensive learning bowed before the Word of God. He received the evangelical truth with the simplicity of a child, explained the doctrine of salvation with the grace and perspicuity that charmed all his hearers, and trod boldly in that path so new to him, for, said he, "Christ will never abandon his followers."

Henceforward the two friends walked together, contending for liberty and truth—the one with the energy of St. Paul, the other with the meekness of St. John. Luther has admirably expressed the difference of their callings. "I was born," said he, "to contend on the field of battle with faction and with wicked spirits. This is why my works abound with war and tempests. It is my task to uproot the stock and the stem, to clear away the briars and underwood, to fill up the pools and the marshes. I am the rough woodman who has to prepare the way and smooth the road. But Philipp advances quietly and softly; he tills and plants the ground, sows and waters it joyfully, according to the gifts that God has given him with so liberal a hand."

If Melancthon, the tranquil sower, was called to the work by the disputation of Leipzig, Luther, the hardy woodman, felt his arm strengthened by it and his courage reinvigorated. The greatest effect of this discussion was that wrought in Luther himself. "The scales of scholastic theology," said he, "fell then entirely from before my eyes, under the triumphant presidence of Dr. Eck." The veil which the school and the church had conjointly drawn before the sanctuary was rent for the reformer from top to bottom.

Driven to new inquiries, he arrived at unexpected discoveries. With as much indignation as astonishment, he saw the evil in all its magnitude. Searching into the annals of the church, he discovered that the supremacy of Rome had no other origin than ambition on the one hand and ignorant credulity on the other. The narrow point of view under which he had hitherto looked upon the church was succeeded by a deeper and more extended range. He recognized in the Christians of Greece and of the East true members of the universal church; and instead of a visible chief, seated on the banks of the Tiber, he adored, as sole chief of the people of God, an invisible and eternal Redeemer, who, according to His promise, is daily in the midst of every nation upon earth, with all who believe in His name. The Latin church was no longer, in Luther's estimation, the universal church; he saw the narrow barriers of Rome fall down and exulted in discovering beyond them the glorious dominions of Christ. From that time he comprehended how a man might be a member of Christ's church without belonging to the pope's.

But above all, the writings of John Huss produced a deep impression upon him. He there found, to his great surprise, the doctrine of St. Paul and of St. Augustine—that doctrine at which he himself had arrived after so many struggles. "I believed and I taught all the doctrines of John Huss without being aware of it; and so did Staupitz. In short, although unconscious of it, we are all Hussites. Paul and Augustine were so themselves. I am confounded and know not what to think. Oh, how terribly have men deserved the judgments of God, seeing that the gospel truth, which has been unveiled and published this century past, has been condemned, burned, and stifled. . . . Woe, woe to the world."

Luther has pointed to this moment as that of his emancipation from the papal yoke. "Learn from me," said he, "how difficult a thing it is to throw off errors confirmed by the example of all the world and which, through long habit, have become a second nature to us. I had then been seven years reading and publicly explaining the Holy Scriptures with great zeal, so that I knew them almost by heart. I had also all the first fruits of knowledge and faith in our Lord Jesus Christ; that is to say, I knew that we are justified and saved not by our works, but by faith in Christ; and I even maintained openly that the pope is not the head of the Christian church by divine right. And yet I could not see the consequences that flowed from this; namely, that the pope is necessarily and certainly of the Devil. For what is not of God must needs be of the Devil." Luther adds further on, "I no longer permit myself to be indignant against those who are still attached to the pope, since I, who had for so many years studied the Holy Scriptures so attentively, still clung with so much obstinacy to popery."

Eck gave way to all the intoxication of what he wished to represent as a victory. He inveighed against Luther; heaped charge upon charge against him; wrote to Frederick; and desired, like a skillful general, to take advantage of the confusion that always follows a battle, to obtain important concessions from that prince. While waiting for the measures that were to be taken against his adversary's person, he called down fire upon his writings, even on those he had not read. He begged the elector to summon a provincial council: "Let us exterminate these vermin," said the coarse doctor, "before they multiply beyond all bounds." It was not upon Luther alone that he vented his anger. Eck took up the pen against Melancthon, "that grammarian of Wittenberg, who was not ignorant, indeed, of Latin and Greek, but who had dared to publish a letter in which he had insulted him—Dr. Eck."

Melancthon replied, and this was his first theological writing. Laying down the fundamental principles of hermeneutics (the art of interpreting the Holy Scriptures), he showed that we ought not to interpret Scripture by the Fathers, but the Fathers by Scripture. "How often has not Jerome been mistaken," said he; "how frequently Augustine, how frequently Ambrose; how often their opinions are different, and how often they retract their errors! There is but one Scripture, inspired by the Holy Ghost, and pure and true in all things.

" 'Luther does not follow certain ambiguous explanations of the ancients,' say they; and why should he? When he explains the passage of Saint Matthew, 'Thou art Peter, and upon this rock I will build my church,' he says the same thing as Origen, who alone is a host; as Augustine in his homily; and as Ambrose in his sixth book upon Saint Luke: I will mention no others. What, then, will you say the Fathers contradict one another? And is there anything astonishing in that? I believe in the Fathers, because I believe in Scripture. The meaning of Scripture is one and simple, like heavenly truth itself. It is obtained by comparing Scripture with Scripture: it is deduced from the thread and connection of the discourse. There is a philosophy that is enjoined us as regards the divine Scriptures, and that is to bring all human opinions and maxims to it, as to a touchstone by which to try them."

The weaker Eck was, the louder he clamored. By his boastings and his accusations he hoped to secure the victory that he had lost in his discussions. The monks and all the partisans of Rome reechoed his clamors. From every part of Germany, reproaches were poured upon Luther; but he remained unaffected by them. "The more I find my name covered with opprobrium, the more do I glory in it," said he at the conclusion of the explanations he published on the Leipzig propositions. "The truth, that is to say, Christ, must needs increase, and I must decrease. The voice of the bride and the Bridegroom causes me a joy that far surpasses the terrors inspired by their clamors. Men are not the authors of my sufferings, and I entertain no hatred toward them. It is Satan, the prince of wickedness, who desires to terrify me. But He who is within us is mightier than he that is in the world. The judgment of our contemporaries is bad; that of posterity will be better."

If the Leipzig disputation augmented Luther's enemies in Germany, it also increased the number of his friends in foreign countries. "What Huss was in Bohemia in other days, you are now in Saxony, dear Martin," wrote the Bohemian brethren to him; "for this reason, pray and be strong in the Lord."

While new friends and enemies sprang up around Luther, his old friends seemed to be deserting him. Staupitz, who had brought the reformer from the obscurity of his cloister at Erfurt, began to evince some coolness toward him. Luther had soared too high for Staupitz, who could not follow him. "You abandon me," wrote Luther to him. "All day long I have been very sad on your account, as a weaned child cries after its mother. I dreamed of you last night," continues the reformer: "you were leaving me, while I groaned and shed bitter tears. But you stretched out your hand, bade me be calm, and promised to return to me again."

Luther, far from retreating, advanced daily. His adversaries compelled him to advance more quickly than he would have done without them. At this period Eck incited the Franciscans of Jüter-bock to attack him again. Luther, in his reply, not content with repeating what he had already taught, attacked errors that he had newly discovered. "I should like to know," said he, "in what part of Scripture the power of canonizing the saints has been given to the popes; and also what necessity, what utility there is in canonizing them. For that matter," added he sarcastically, "let them canonize as much as they like."

Luther's new attacks remained unanswered. The blindness of his enemies was as favorable to him as his own courage. They passionately defended secondary matters, and when Luther laid his hand on the foundations of the Roman doctrine, they saw them shaken without uttering a word. They busied themselves in defending the outward, while their intrepid adversary was advancing into the body of the place and there boldly planting the standard of truth. Accordingly, they were afterward astonished when they beheld the fortress were defending undermined and on fire and crumbling into ruins in the midst of the flames, while they were flattering themselves that it was impregnable and were still braving those who led the assault. Thus are all great catastrophes effected.

The Elector Frederick invited the doctor to a splendid banquet which he gave the Spanish ambassador, and there Luther valiantly contended against Charles's minister. The elector had begged him, through his chaplain, to defend his cause with moderation. "Too much folly is displeasing to men," replied Luther to Spalatin; "but too much discretion is displeasing to God. The gospel cannot be defended without tumult and without scandal. The Word of God is a sword, a war, a ruin, a stumbling block, a destruction, a poison; and as Amos says, it meets us like a bear in the road or a lioness in the forest. I seek nothing; I ask nothing. There is one greater than I, who seeketh and asketh. If He should fall, I lose nothing; if He stand, I am profited nothing."

Everything announced that Luther would need faith and courage now more than ever. Eck was forming plans of revenge. Instead of the laurels that he had reckoned on gaining, the Leipzig gladiator had become the laughingstock of all the sensible men of his nation. What a disappointment for the chancellor of Ingolstadt. His fellow-countrymen abandoned him. He prepared to cross the Alps to seek foreign support. Wherever he went, he vented his threats against Luther, Melancthon, Carlstadt, and the elector himself. "From his lofty language," said the Wittenberg doctor, "one might take him to be God Almighty." Inflamed with anger and the desire of revenge, Eck set out for Italy to receive the reward of his pretended triumphs and to forge in Rome, under the shadow of the papal capitol, more powerful thunderbolts than the frail weapons of the schoolmen that had shivered in his hands.

Luther foresaw all the perils that his opponent's journey might draw upon him, but he feared not. Spalatin, in alarm, begged him to propose peace. "No," replied Luther, "so long as he continues his clamors, I cannot withdraw my hands from the contest. I trust everything to God. I consign my bark to the winds and to the waves. The battle is the Lord's. Why should you imagine that Christ will advance His cause by peace? Did He not fight with His own blood, and all the martyrs after Him?"

Such, at the opening of the year 1520, was the position of the combatants of Leipzig. The one was rousing all the papacy to crush his rival; the other waited for war with the same calmness that men look for peace. The new year was destined to see the storm burst forth.

—

Chapter 28
Charles V and the Nobility

A new actor was about to appear on the stage. God designed to bring the Wittenberg monk face to face with the most powerful monarch that had appeared in Christendom since the days of Charlemagne. He selected a prince in the vigor of youth, and to whom everything seemed to announce a long reign—a prince whose scepter extended over a considerable part of the Old World and even the New, so that, according to a celebrated saying, the sun never went down on his vast dominions; and to him He opposed that lowly Reformation, begun in the secluded cell of a convent at Erfurt by the anguish and sighs of a poor monk.

The history of this monarch and of his reign was destined, it would seem, to teach the world an important lesson. It was to show the nothingness of all the strength of man when it presumes to measure itself with the weakness of God. If a prince, a friend to Luther, had been called to the imperial throne, the success of the Reformation might have been ascribed to his protection. If even an emperor opposed to the new doctrines, but yet a weak ruler, had worn the diadem, the triumph of this work might have been accounted for by the weakness of the monarch. But it was the haughty conqueror at Pavia who was destined to veil his pride before the power of God's Word; and the whole world beheld the man who found it an easy task to drag Francis I a prisoner to Madrid, obliged to lower his sword before the son of a poor miner.

The Emperor Maximilian was dead, and the electors had met at Frankfurt to choose a successor. This was an important event for all Europe under the existing circumstances. All Christendom was occupied with this election. Maximilian had not been a great prince, but his memory was dear to the people. They were delighted to call to recollection his presence of mind and his good nature. Luther used often to converse with his friends about this and one day related the following anecdote of this monarch:

A mendicant was once following him and begging alms, calling him *brother;* "for," said he, "we are both descended from the same father, Adam. I am poor," continued he, "but you are rich, and you ought therefore to help me."

The emperor turned round at these words, and said to him, "There is a penny for you; go to all your other brothers, and if each one gives you as much, you will be richer than I am."

It was not a good-natured Maximilian that was destined to wear the imperial crown. The times were changing; men of overweening ambition were about to dispute the throne of the emperors of the West; a strong hand was to grasp the reins of the empire, and long and bloody wars were on the point of succeeding a profound peace.

Three kings claimed the crown of the Caesars from the assembly at Frankfurt. A youthful prince, grandson of the last emperor, born in the first year of the century, and consequently nineteen years old, appeared first. His name was Charles, and he was born at Ghent. His paternal grandmother, Mary, daughter of Charles the Bold, had bequeathed to him Flanders and the rich domains of Burgundy. His mother, Joanna, daughter of Ferdinand of Aragon and Isabella of Castile, and wife of Philip, the emperor Maximilian's son, had transmitted to him the united crowns of the two Spains, Naples, and Sicily, to which Christopher Columbus had recently added a New World. His grandfather's death now put him in possession of the hereditary states of Austria.

This young prince, endowed with great intelligence, and amiable whenever it pleased him to be so, joined to a taste for military exercises, in which the famous dukes of Burgundy had long distinguished themselves, an extensive knowledge of public affairs which he had acquired under the direction of Chiévres; for, from the age of fifteen years, he had attended all the deliberations of his councils. Qualities so various were covered and concealed, as it were, by his Spanish taciturnity and reserve; there was an air of melancholy in his long visage. "He was pious and silent," said Luther; "I will wager that he does not talk so much in a year as I do in a day." If Charles had grown up under free and Christian influences, he would perhaps have been one of the most meritorious princes recorded in history; but politics absorbed his whole life and blighted his naturally amiable character.

The youthful Charles, not content with the scepters he already grasped in his hand, aspired to the imperial dignity. "It is a beam of sunshine that casts a splendor upon the house on which it falls," said many; "but stretch forth the hand to seize it, and you find nothing." Charles, on the contrary, looked upon it as the summit of all earthly grandeur and a means of obtaining a magical influence over the minds of nations.

Francis I, king of France, was the second candidate. The young paladins of the court of this chivalrous sovereign were ever repeating that he ought, like Charlemagne, to be emperor of all the West and, reviving the exploits of the knights of old, attack the Crescent that threatened the empire, crush the infidels, and recover the holy sepulcher.

"You should convince the dukes of Austria that the imperial crown is not hereditary," said the ambassadors of Francis to the electors. "Besides, in the present state of affairs, Germany requires not a youth of nineteen, but a prince who with a tried judgment combines talents already proved. Francis will unite the arms of France and Lombardy with those of Germany to make war on the Muslims. As sovereign of the duchy of Milan, he is already a member of the empire." The French ambassadors strengthened their arguments by four hundred thousand crowns which they expended in buying votes and in banquets which the guest generally quitted in a state of inebriation.

Lastly, Henry VIII of England, jealous of the influence the choice of the electors would give Francis or Charles, also entered the lists; but he soon left these two powerful rivals to dispute the crown between them.

The electors were not very favorably disposed toward either. "Our people," thought they, "will consider the king of France as a foreign master, and this master may wrest even from us that independence of which the great lords of his own kingdom have recently been deprived." As for Charles, it was an old maxim with the electors never to select a prince who already played an important part in the empire. The pope participated in these fears. He was opposed to the king of Naples, his neighbor, and to the king of France, whose enterprising spirit alarmed him. "Choose rather one of yourselves," was the advice he sent to the electors. The elector of Treves proposed to nominate Frederick of Saxony, and the imperial crown was laid at the feet of this friend to Luther.

Such a choice would have gained the approbation of the whole of Germany. Frederick's wisdom and love for the people were well known. During the revolt of Erfurt, he had been advised to take the city by storm. He refused, that he might avoid bloodshed.

"But it will not cost five men," was the reply.

"A single man would be too many," answered the prince.

It appeared that the election of the protector of the Reformation would secure the triumph of that work. Ought not Frederick to have seen a call from God in this wish of the electors? Who could have been better suited to preside over the destinies of the empire than this wise prince? Who could have been stronger against the Turks than a truly Christian emperor? The refusal of the elector of Saxony, so extolled by historians, may have been a fault on the part of this prince. Perhaps to him must be partly ascribed the contests that devastated Germany in afterdays. But it is a difficult matter to decide whether Frederick deserves to be blamed for want of faith or honored for his humility. He thought that the very safety of the empire required him to refuse the crown. "We need an emperor more powerful than myself to preserve Germany," said this modest and disinterested prince. "The Turk is at our gates. The king of Spain, whose hereditary possessions of Austria border on the threatened frontier, is its natural defender."

The Roman legate, seeing that Charles would be elected, declared that the pope withdrew his objections; and on June 28, the grandson of Maximilian was nominated emperor. "God," said Frederick not long after, "hath given him to us in His favor and in His anger." The Spanish envoys offered thirty thousand gold florins to the elector of Saxony as a testimonial of their master's gratitude, but this prince refused them and forbade his ministers to accept any present. At the same time, he secured the liberties of Germany by a capitulation to which Charles's envoys swore in his name. The circumstances under which the latter assumed the imperial crown seemed, moreover, to give a stronger pledge than these oaths in favor of German liberty and the work of the Reformation. This youthful prince was jealous of the laurels that his rival Francis I had gathered at Marignan. The struggle would still be continued in Italy, and the interval thus employed would doubtless suffice for the

Reformation to gain strength. Charles quitted Spain in May 1520, and was crowned at Aix-la-Chapelle on October 22.

Luther had foreseen that the cause of the Reformation would soon be carried before the new emperor. He wrote to Charles while this prince was yet at Madrid: "If the cause that I defend," said he, "is worthy of appearing before the throne of the majesty of heaven, it ought not to be unworthy of engaging the attention of a prince of this world. O Charles, first of the kings of the earth, I throw myself a suppliant at the feet of your most serene majesty. Deign to receive under the shadow of your wings, not me, but the cause of that eternal truth, for the defense of which God has entrusted you with the sword." The young monarch laid aside this singular letter from a German monk and made no reply to it.

While Luther was vainly turning toward Madrid, the storm seemed to increase around him. It was particularly in the direction of Rome that the storm was gathering. Valentine Teutleben, a Thuringian nobleman, vicar to the archbishop of Mentz, and a zealous partisan of the papacy, was the elector of Saxony's representative at the papal court. Teutleben, ashamed of the protection accorded by his master to an heretical monk, was impatient at seeing his mission paralyzed by this imprudent conduct. He imagined that, by alarming the elector, he would induce him to abandon the rebellious divine. "They will not listen to me here," wrote he to his master, "because of the protection you show to Luther."

But the Romans were deceived if they thought to frighten the prudent Frederick. This prince was aware that the will of God and the movements of nations were more irresistible than the decrees of the papal chancery. He ordered his envoy to intimate to the pope that, far from defending Luther, he had always left him to defend himself; besides, he had already called upon him to quit Saxony and the university; that the doctor had declared his willingness to obey, and that he would not then be in the electoral states if the legate himself, Charles of Miltitz, had not entreated the prince to keep him near at hand, for fear that, by going to other countries, Luther would act with greater liberty than even in Saxony.

Frederick went farther than this: he desired to enlighten Rome. "Germany," continues he in his letter, "now possesses a great number of learned men, well taught in every language and science; the laity themselves begin to have understanding and to love the

Holy Scriptures; if, therefore, the reasonable conditions of Dr. Luther are rejected, there is great cause to fear that peace will never be reestablished. Luther's doctrine has struck deep root into many hearts. If, instead of refuting it by the testimony of the Bible, you strive to destroy him by the thunderbolts of the ecclesiastical authority, great scandals will arise, and ruinous and terrible revolts will be excited."

The warning the elector had given Rome through his envoy was not without foundation. Luther's words had found an echo everywhere—in cottages and convents, in the homes of the citizens and in the castles of the nobles, in the universities and in the palaces of kings. "If my life," he had said to Duke John of Saxony, "has been instrumental to the conversion of a single man, I shall willingly consent to see all my books perish." It was not one man, it was a great multitude that had found the light in the writings of the humble doctor. Everywhere, accordingly, were men to be found ready to protect him. The sword intended to slay him was forging in the Vatican, but heroes were springing up in Germany to shield him with their bodies. At the moment when the bishops were chafing with rage, when princes kept silence, when the people were in expectation, and when the first murmurs of the thunder were beginning to be heard from the Seven Hills, God aroused the German nobles to make a rampart for His servant.

Sylvester of Schaumburg, one of the most powerful knights of Franconia, sent his son to Wittenberg at this time with a letter for the reformer. "Your life is in danger," wrote he. "If the support of the electors, princes, or magistrates fail you, I entreat you to beware of going to Bohemia, where in former times learned men have had much to undergo; rather come to me. God willing, I shall soon have collected more than a hundred gentlemen, and with their help I shall be able to protect you from every danger."

Franz von Sickingen, the hero of his age, loved the reformer because he found him worthy of being loved, and also because he was hated by the monks. "My services, my goods, and my body, all that I possess," wrote he to Luther, "are at your disposal. You desire to maintain the Christian truth: I am ready to aid you in the work." Harmurth of Cronberg held the same language. Lastly, Ulrich von Hutten, the poet and valiant knight of the sixteenth century, never ceased speaking in Luther's favor. But what a contrast between

Knight, Death, and the Devil by Albrecht Dürer. Some art historians believe that Dürer's inspiration for the figure of the knight was Franz von Sickingen, the German knight who dedicated his military forces to the defense of Luther and the Reformation.

these two men! Hutten wrote to the reformer: "It is with swords and with bows, with javelins and bombs, that we must crush the fury of the Devil."

Luther of receiving these letters exclaimed, "I will not have recourse to arms and bloodshed in defense of the gospel. By the Word the earth has been subdued; by the Word the church has been saved; and by the Word also it shall be reestablished."

"I do not despise his offer," said he at another time on receiving Schaumburg's letter, which we have mentioned above, "but I will rely upon nothing but Jesus Christ."

Hutten felt the difference between his cause and Luther's, and he accordingly wrote to him with noble-mindedness: "As for me, I am busied with the affairs of men; but you soar far higher and are occupied solely with those of God." He then set out to win, if possible, Charles and Ferdinand to the side of truth.

Luther at this time met with a still more illustrious protector. Erasmus, whom the Roman Catholics so often quote against the Reformation, raised his voice and undertook the reformer's defense, after his own fashion, however, that is to say, without any show of defending him. On November 1, 1519, this patriarch of learning wrote to Albert, elector of Mentz and primate of all Germany, a letter in which, after describing in vivid colors the corruption of the church, he says, "This is what stirred up Luther and made him oppose the intolerable imprudence of certain doctors. For what other motive can we ascribe to a man who seeks not honors, and who cares not for money? Luther has dared doubt the virtue of indulgences, but others before him had most unblushingly affirmed it. He feared not to speak, certainly with little moderation, against the power of the Roman pontiff; but others before him had extolled it without reserve. He has dared condemn the decrees of St. Thomas, but the Dominicans had set them almost above the gospel. He has dared give utterance to his scruples about confession, but the monks continually made use of this ordinance as a net in which to catch and enslave the consciences of men. Pious souls were grieved at hearing that in the universities there was little mention of the evangelical doctrine; that in the assemblies of Christians very little was heard of Christ; that nothing was there talked of, except the power of the pontiff and the opinions of the Roman Catholic doctors; and that the whole sermon was a mere matter of lucre, flattery, ambition, and imposture. It is to such a state of affairs that we should ascribe Luther's violent language." Such was Erasmus' opinion on the state of the church and on the reformer. This letter, which was published by Ulrich von Hutten, then residing at the court of Mentz, made a profound impression.

Thus at one time Luther's enemies oppress him, at another his friends spring up to defend him. Luther felt that he was not alone; his words had borne fruit, and this thought filled him with fresh courage. The fear of compromising the elector no longer checked him when he found other defenders ready to brave the anger of Rome. He became more free and, if possible, more determined. This is an important epoch in the development of Luther's character. "Rome ought to understand," wrote he at this period to the elector's chaplain, "that, even should she succeed by her threats in expelling me from Wittenberg, she would only injure her cause. It is not in Bohemia, but in the very heart of Germany that those are to be found who are ready to defend me against the thunders of the papacy. If I have not done my enemies all the harm I am preparing for them, they must ascribe it neither to my moderation nor to their tyranny, but to the elector's name and to the interests of the University of Wittenberg, which I feared to compromise: now that I have such fears no longer, they will see me fall with fresh vigor upon Rome and upon her courtiers."

And yet it was not on the great that Luther fixed his hopes. He had been often solicited to dedicate a book to Duke John, the elector's brother. He had not done so. "I am afraid," said he, "that the suggestion comes from himself. Holy Scripture should subserve the glory of God's name alone." Luther now recovered from his fears and dedicated his *Sermon on Good Works* to Duke John. This is one of the writings in which the reformer lays down with the greatest force the doctrine of justification by faith—that powerful truth whose strength he sets far above the sword of Hutten, the army of Sickingen, and the protection of dukes and electors.

"The first, the noblest, the sublimest of all works," says he, "is faith in Jesus Christ. It is from this work that all other works must proceed: they are but the vassals of faith and receive their efficacy from it alone. . . .

"Consequently I have always extolled faith. But in the world it is otherwise. There, the essential thing is to have many works—works high and great and of every dimension, without caring whether they are quickened by faith. Thus, men build their peace, not on God's good pleasure, but on their own merits, that is to say, on sand (Matt. 7:27).

"To preach faith, it has been said, is to prevent good works; but if a man should possess the strength of all men united, or even of all creatures, this sole obligation of living in faith would be a task too great for him ever to accomplish. If I say to a sick man, 'Be well, and thou shalt have the use of thy limbs,' will any one say that I forbid him to use his limbs? Must not health precede labor? It is the same when we preach faith: it should go before works, in order that the works themselves should exist.

"Where then, you will say, can we find this faith; and how can we receive it? This is in truth what it is most important to know. Faith comes solely from Jesus, who was promised and given freely."

As we cannot notice all Luther's writings, we have quoted a few short passages from this discourse on good works, in consequence of the opinion the reformer himself entertained of it. "In my own judgment," said he, "it is the best I ever published." And he added immediately this deep reflection: "But I know that when I please myself with what I write, the infection of that bad leaven hinders it from pleasing others." Melancthon, in forwarding this discourse to a friend, accompanied it with these words: "There is no one among all the Greek and Latin writers who has come nearer than Luther to the spirit of St. Paul."

Chapter 29
The *Appeal to the German Nobility*

But there was another evil in the church besides the substitution of a system of meritorious works for the grand idea of grace and amnesty. A haughty power had arisen in the midst of the shepherds of Christ's flock. Luther prepared to attack this usurped authority. Already a vague and distant rumor announced the success of Dr. Eck's intrigues at Rome. This rumor aroused the militant spirit of the reformer, who, in the midst of all his troubles, had studied in his retirement the rise, progress, and usurpations of the papacy. His discoveries had filled him with surprise. He no longer hesitated to make them known and to strike the blow which, like Moses' rod in ancient times, was to awaken a people who had long slumbered in captivity. "The time to be silent is past," exclaimed he; "the time to speak is come. At last, we must unveil the mysteries of antichrist." On June 23, 1520, he published his famous *Appeal to His Imperial Majesty, and to the Christian Nobility of the German Nation, on the Reformation of Christianity*. This work was the signal of the attack that was to decide both the rupture and the victory.

"It is not through presumption," said he at the opening of this address, "that I, a man of the people, venture to speak to your lordships. The misery and oppression that at this hour weigh down all the states of Christendom, and particularly Germany, extort from me a cry of distress. I must call for help; I must see if God will not give His Spirit to some man in our own country, and thus stretch forth His hand to save our wretched nation. God has placed over us a young and generous prince [the emperor Charles V] and has thus filled our hearts with great expectations. But on our parts we must do everything that lies in our power.

"Now the first requisite is not to trust in our own strength or in our lofty wisdom. If we begin a good work with confidence in ourselves, God overthrows and destroys it. Frederick I, Frederick II, and many other emperors besides, before whom the world trembled, have been trodden under foot by the popes because they trusted more in their own strength than in God. Therefore they could not but fall. It is against the powers of hell that we have to contend in this struggle. Hoping nothing from the strength of arms, humbly trusting in the Lord, looking more to the distress of Christendom than to the crimes of the wicked—*this* is how we must set to work. Otherwise the work will have a prosperous look at the beginning; but suddenly, in the midst of the contest, confusion will enter in, evil minds will cause incalculable disasters, and the whole world will be deluged with blood. The greater our power, the greater also is our danger, if we do not walk in the fear of the Lord."

After this prelude, Luther continues:

"The Romans have raised around themselves three walls to protect them against every kind of reformation. Have they been attacked by the temporal power? They have asserted that it had no authority over them and that the spiritual power was superior to it. Have they been rebuked by Holy Scripture? They have replied that no one is able to interpret it except the pope. Have they been threatened with a council? No one, said they, but the sovereign pontiff has authority to convoke one.

"They have thus despoiled us of the three rods destined to correct them and have given themselves up to every wickedness. But now may God be our helper and give us one of those trumpets that overthrew the walls of Jericho. With our breath let us throw down those barriers of paper and straw which the Romans have built around them, and upraise the rods which punish the wicked by exposing the wiles of the Devil."

"It has been said," writes Luther, "that the pope, the bishops, the priests, and all those who people the convents form the spiritual or ecclesiastical state; and that the princes, the nobility, the citizens, and peasants form the secular or lay estate. This is a fine story. Let no person, however, be startled at it. All Christians belong to the spiritual state, and there is no other difference between them than that arising from the functions which they discharge. We have all one baptism, one faith; and this it is which constitutes the spiritual man. The unction, the tonsure, ordination, consecration by the bishop or the pope may make a hypocrite, but never a spiritual man.

"We are all consecrated priests by baptism. As St. Peter says, 'Ye are priests and kings,' although it does not belong to all to exercise such offices, for no one can take what is common to all without the consent of the community. But if we possess not this divine consecration, the pope's anointing can never make a priest. If ten brothers, sons of a king, having equal claims to the inheritance, select one of them to administer it for them, they would all be kings, and yet only one of them would be the administrator of their common power. So it is with the church. If a few pious laymen were banished to a desert place, and if, not having among them a priest consecrated by a bishop, they should agree to choose one of their own number, married or not, this man would be as truly a priest as if all the bishops in the world had consecrated him. Thus Augustine, Ambrose, and Cyprian were elected.

"Hence it follows that laymen and priests, princes and bishops, or, as they say, the clergy and laity, have nothing but their functions to distinguish them. They have all the same estate but have not all the same work to perform.

"If this be true, why should not the magistrate chastise the clergy? The secular power was established by God to punish the wicked and to protect the good. And it must be allowed to act throughout all Christendom, whomsoever it may touch, be he pope, bishop, priest, monk, or nun. St. Paul says to all Christians, 'Let every one,' and consequently the pope also, 'be subject unto the higher powers; for they bear not the sword in vain.' "

Luther, having in like manner overthrown the two other walls, passes in review all the corruptions of Rome. He begins with the pope. "It is a horrible thing," says he, "to behold the man who styles himself Christ's vicegerent, displaying a magnificence that no emperor can equal. Is this being like the poor Jesus or the humble Peter? He is, say they, the lord of the world! But Christ, whose vicar he boasts of being, has said, 'My kingdom is not of this world.' Can the dominions of a vicar extend beyond those of his superior?"

Luther now proceeds to describe the effects of the papal rule. "Do you know what is the use of cardinals? I will tell you. Italy and Germany have many convents, religious foundations, and richly endowed benefices. How can this wealth be drawn to Rome? Cardinals have been created; these cloisters and prelacies have been given to them; and now. . . Italy is almost deserted, the convents are in ruins, the bishoprics devoured, the cities decayed, the inhabitants corrupted, religious worship is expiring, and preaching abolished. . . . And why is this? Because all the wealth of the churches must go to Rome. The Turk himself would never have so ruined Italy.

"And now that they have thus sucked all the blood of their own nation, they come into Germany: they begin tenderly; but let us be on our guard, or Germany will ere long be like Italy. We have already a few cardinals. Before the dull Germans comprehend our design, think they, they will no longer have either bishopric, convent, or benefice, penny, or farthing left. . . .

"What, shall we Germans endure such robberies and such extortions from the pope? If the kingdom of France has been able to defend itself, why should we permit ourselves to be thus ridiculed and laughed at? Oh, if they only despoiled us of our goods. But they lay waste the churches, fleece the sheep of Christ, abolish religious worship, and annihilate the Word of God."

Luther here exposes "the practices of Rome" to obtain the money and the revenues of Germany. He says, "Let us endeavor to check such desolation and wretchedness. If we desire to march against the Turks, let us march against those who are the worst Turks of all. If we hang thieves and decapitate highway robbers, let us not permit Roman avarice to escape, which is the greatest of thieves and robbers, and that too in the name of St. Peter and of Jesus Christ. Who can suffer this? Who can be silent? All that the pope possesses, has he not gained by plunder? For he has neither bought it, nor inherited it from St. Peter, nor gained it by the sweat of his brow. Whence then has he all this?"

Luther proposes remedies for these evils and calls energetically upon the nobility of Germany to put an end to these Roman Catholic depredations. He then comes to the reformation of the pope himself: "Is it not ridiculous," says he, "that the pope pretends to be the lawful heir to the empire? Who gave it him? Was it Jesus Christ, when He said, 'The kings of the Gentiles exercise lordship over them, . . . but ye shall not be so' (Luke 22:25-26)? How is it possible to govern an empire, and at the same time preach, pray, study, and take care of the poor? Jesus Christ forbade His ministers to carry with them either gold or two coats, because they would be unable to discharge the duties of their ministry if they were not free from all other care; and yet the pope would govern the empire and still remain pope."

After having called the pope to his bar, he summons before him all the corruptions that form the papal train and purposes sweeping from the floor of the church the rubbish by which it was encumbered. He begins with the monks:

"And now then I come to that sluggish troop which promises much but does little. Do not be angry, my dear sirs; my intentions are good: what I have to say is a truth at once sweet and bitter; namely, no more cloisters must be built for mendicant friars. We have, indeed, too many already, and would to God that they were all pulled down. Strolling through a country like beggars never has done and never can do good."

The marriage of the clergy now has its turn, and this is the first time Luther speaks of it:

"To what a sad state have the clergy fallen, and how many priests do we not find burdened with women, and children, and remorse, and yet no one comes to their aid. It is all very well for the pope and the bishops to let things go on as before, and for that to continue lost which is lost; but I am determined to save my conscience and to open my mouth freely: after that, let the pope, the bishops, and any one who pleases, take offense at it. . . . I assert, then, that according to the appointment of Christ and His apostles, each city should have a pastor or bishop, and that this pastor may have a wife as St. Paul writes to Timothy, 'A bishop then must be . . . the husband of one wife' (I Tim. 3:2), and as is still practiced in the Greek church.

"But the Devil has persuaded the pope, as the same apostle says to Timothy (I Tim. 4:1-3), to forbid the clergy to marry; and hence have proceeded miseries so numerous that we cannot mention all. What is to be done? How can we save so many pastors in whom we have no fault to find, except that they live with a woman to whom they would with all their heart be legitimately married? Ah, let them quiet their consciences; let them take this woman as their lawful wife, and let them live virtuously with her, not troubling themselves whether the pope is pleased or not. The salvation of your soul is of greater consequence to you than tyrannical and arbitrary laws that do not emanate from the Lord."

The reformer continues: "Let all festivals be abolished, and let none but Sunday be observed; or if people desire to keep the great

Christian festivals, let them be celebrated only in the morning, and let the rest of the day be like any other working day. For as on those days men do nothing but drink, gamble, indulge in every sin, or remain idle, they offend God on the festivals more than at other times."

He not only desires to put an end to abuses, he wishes also to put away schism. After proposing some excellent means of reconciliation, he adds, "We must convince heretics by Scripture, as did the ancient Fathers, and not subdue them by fire. In this latter system, the executioners would be the most learned doctors in the world. . . . Oh, would to God that on both sides we stretched forth our hands in brotherly humility instead of being inflexible in the sentiment of our strength and of our right. Charity is more necessary than the papacy of Rome. I have now done all that is in my power. If the pope and his adherents oppose this, the responsibility will fall on them. The pope should be ready to renounce his papacy, all his possessions, and all his honors, if he could by that means save a single soul. But he would rather see all the world perish than bate even a hair's breadth of the power he has usurped. . . . I am clear of these things."

Luther next proceeds to the universities and schools:

"I am much afraid that the universities will prove to be the great gates of hell, unless they diligently labor in explaining the Holy Scriptures and engraving them in the hearts of youth. I advise no one to place his child where the Scriptures do not reign paramount. Every institution in which men are not unceasingly occupied with the Word of God must become corrupt."

Luther concludes this courageous appeal in these words:

"I can very well imagine that I have pitched my song too high, proposed many things that will seem impossible, and attacked many errors rather too violently. But what can I do? Let the world be offended with me, rather than God. . . . They can but take away my life. I have often proposed peace to my adversaries. But God, by their instrumentality, has compelled me continually to cry louder and louder against them. . . .

"If my cause is just, it will be condemned by all the world and justified only by Christ in heaven. Let them come on then, pope, bishops, priests, monks, and doctors; let them put forth all their zeal;

let them give the rein to all their fury. These are, in truth, the men who ought to persecute the truth, as every age has witnessed."

This exhortation, which was addressed to the German nobility, soon reached all those for whom it had been written. It circulated through Germany with inconceivable rapidity. Luther's friends trembled; Staupitz and those who desired to employ mild measures found the blow too severe. "In our days," replied Luther, "everything that is handled gently falls into oblivion, and no one cares about it."

The *Appeal to the German Nobility* was published on June 26, 1520; in a short time four thousand copies were sold, a number unprecedented in those days. The astonishment was universal. This writing produced a powerful sensation among the people, who felt at last that he who spoke to them loved them also. Even the elector's court, so circumspect and timid, did not disapprove of the reformer; it waited patiently. But the nobility and the people did not wait. The nation was reanimated. Luther's voice had shaken it; it was won over and rallied round the standard that he had uplifted. Nothing could have been more advantageous to the reformer than this publication. In the palaces and castles, in the homes of the citizens and the cottages of the peasants, all were now prepared, and defended as it were with a breastplate against the sentence of condemnation that was about to fall upon this prophet of the people. All Germany was on fire.

Chapter 30
"Arise, O Lord"—The Papal Bull

Every preparation was made at Rome for condemning the defender of the liberty of the church. That church had long been living in a state of haughty security. For several years the monks had been accusing Leo X of caring only for luxury and pleasure, of occupying himself solely with the chase, the theater, and music, while the church was tottering to its fall. At length, aroused by the clamors of Dr. Eck, who had come from Leipzig to invoke the power of the Vatican, pope, cardinals, monks, and all Rome awoke and thought of saving the papacy.

Rome indeed was compelled to have recourse to the severest measures. The gauntlet had been thrown down; the combat must be to the death. Luther did not attack the abuses of the Roman pontificate, but the pontificate itself. At his command he would have had the pope to descend humbly from his throne and become a simple pastor or bishop on the banks of the Tiber. All the dignitaries of the Roman hierarchy were to renounce their wealth and their worldly glory and become elders and deacons of the churches of Italy. All that splendor and power which for ages had dazzled the West was to vanish and give place to the humble simplicity of the primitive Christian worship. God might have brought this about; He will do so in His own time, but it could not be expected from man. And even should any pope have been so disinterested or bold as to be willing to overthrow the ancient and costly edifice of the Roman church, thousands of priests and bishops would have stretched out their hands to prevent its fall. The pope had received his power on the express condition of maintaining what was confided to him.

Rome thought herself divinely appointed to the government of the church. We cannot therefore be astonished that she prepared to strike the most terrible blows. And yet she hesitated at first. Many cardinals and the pope himself were opposed to violent measures. The skillful Leo saw clearly that a decision, the execution of which depended on the very doubtful compliance of the civil power, might seriously compromise the authority of the church. He was aware, besides, that the violent measures hitherto employed had served only to aggravate the mischief. Is it not possible to gain over this Saxon monk? asked the Roman politicians of one another. Will all the power of the church, will all the craft of Italy fail? They must negotiate still.

Eck accordingly met with powerful obstacles. He neglected nothing that might prevent such impious concessions. In every quarter of Rome he vented his rage and called for revenge. The fanatical portion of the monks soon leagued with him. Strengthened by their alliance, he assailed the pope and cardinals with fresh courage. In his opinion, every attempt at conciliation would be useless. These, said he, are idle dreams with which you soothe yourselves at a distance from the danger. He knew the peril, for he had contended with the audacious monk. He saw that there should be no delay in cutting off this gangrened limb, for fear the disease should infect the whole body. The impetuous disputant of Leipzig parried objection after objection and with difficulty persuaded the pope. He desired to save Rome in spite of herself. He made every exertion, passing many hours together in deliberation in the pontiff's cabinet. He excited the court and the cloisters, the people and the church. "Eck is stirring up the bottomless pit against me," said Luther; "he is setting fire to the forests of Lebanon."

At the same time, the theologians of Cologne, Louvain, and other universities, and even princes of Germany, either by letter or through their envoys, daily urged the pope in private by the most pressing entreaties. But the most earnest solicitations proceeded from a banker who, by his wealth, possessed great influence at Rome, and who was familiarly styled "the king of crowns." The papacy has always been more or less in the hands of those who have lent it money. This banker was Fugger, the treasurer of the indulgences. Inflamed with anger against Luther and very uneasy about his profits and his wares, the Augsburg merchant strained every nerve to exasperate the pope: "Employ force against Luther," said he, "and I will promise you the alliance and support of several princes." It would even appear that it was he who had sent Eck to Rome.

246

This gave the decisive blow. The "king of crowns" was victor in the pontifical city. It was not the sword of the Gaul, but well-stored purses that were on this occasion thrown into the balance. Eck prevailed at last. Leo gave way, and Luther's condemnation was resolved upon. Eck breathed again. His pride was flattered by the thought that it was he who had decided the destruction of his heretical rival and thus saved the church. "It was fortunate," said he, "that I came to Rome at this time, for they were but little acquainted with Luther's errors. It will one day be known how much I have done in this cause."

Few were more active in supporting Dr. Eck than Sylvester Mazzolini de Prierio, master of the sacred palace. He had just published a work in which he laid down that not only did the infallible decision of all controverted points belong to the pope alone, but that the papal dominion was the fifth monarchy prophesied by Daniel, and the only true monarchy; that the pope was the first of all ecclesiastical princes, the father of all secular rulers, the chief of the world, and essentially the world itself. In another writing, he affirmed that the pope is as much superior to the emperor as gold is more precious than lead; that the pope may elect and depose both emperors and electors, establish and annul positive rights; and that the emperor, though backed by all the laws and nations of Christendom, cannot decide the least thing against the pope's will. Such was the voice that issued from the palace of the sovereign pontiff; such was the monstrous fiction which, combined with the scholastic doctrines, pretended to extinguish the dawning truth. If this fable had not been unmasked as it has been, and even by learned men in the Roman Catholic communion, there would have been neither true religion nor true history. The papacy is not only a lie in the face of the Bible, it is so even in the face of the annals of all nations. Thus the Reformation, by breaking its charm, emancipated not only the church but also kings and people. It has been said that the Reformation was a political work: in this sense it is true; but this is only a secondary sense.

Thus did God send forth a spirit of infatuation on the Roman doctors. The separation between truth and error had now become necessary, and error was the instrument of its accomplishment. If they had come to an agreement, it could only have been at the expense of truth; but to take away the smallest part of itself is to prepare the way for its complete annihilation. It is like the insect which is said to die if one of its antennae be removed. Truth requires to be entire in all its members in order to display that energy by which it is enabled to gain wide and salutary victories, and to propagate itself through future ages. To mingle a little error with truth is like throwing a grain of poison into a well-filled dish; this one grain is sufficient to change the nature of the food and will cause death, slowly perhaps, but surely. Luther, however great his courage, would probably have kept silence if Rome had been silent herself and had affected to make a few apparent concessions. But God had not abandoned the Reformation to the weak heart of man. Luther was in the hands of one more farsighted than himself. The pontifical bull was the letter of divorcement that Rome gave to the pure church of Jesus Christ in the person of him who was then its humble but faithful representative; and the church accepted it, from that hour, to depend solely on her Head who is in heaven.

Luther's condemnation being once resolved upon, new difficulties were raised in the consistory. The theologians were of opinion that the fulmination should be issued immediately; the lawyers, on the contrary, that it should be preceded by a summons. "Was not Adam first summoned?" said they to their theological colleagues; "so too was Cain: 'Where is thy brother Abel?' demanded the Almighty." To these singular arguments drawn from the Holy Scriptures, the canonists added motives derived from the natural law: "The evidence of a crime," said they, "cannot deprive a criminal of his right of defense."

But these scruples were not to the taste of the divines in the assembly, who, instigated by passion, thought only of going immediately to work. One man in particular then came forward whose opinions must of necessity have had great influence: this was Cardinal Cajetan, still laboring under extreme vexation at his defeat in Augsburg and the little honor or profit he had derived from his German mission. Cajetan, who had returned to Rome in ill health, was carried to the assembly on his couch. Although defeated at Augsburg, he desired to take part at Rome in condemning this indomitable monk, before whom he had witnessed the failure of all his learning, skill, and authority. Luther was not there to reply: Cajetan thought himself invincible. "I have seen enough to know," said he, "that if the Germans are not kept under by fire and sword, they will entirely throw off the yoke of the Roman church." A final conference, which Eck attended, was held in the pope's presence at his villa of Malliano. On June 15, the sacred college decided on the condemnation and sanctioned the famous bull.

"Arise, O Lord," said the Roman pontiff, speaking at this solemn moment as God's vicegerent and head of the church, "arise, judge Thy cause, and call to mind the opprobrium which madmen continually heap on Thee. Arise, O Peter; remember thy holy Roman church, mother of all churches, and queen of the faith. Arise, O Paul, for behold, a new Porphyry attacks thy doctrines and the holy popes, our predecessors. Lastly, arise, ye assembly of saints, the holy church of God, and intercede with the Almighty!"

The pope then proceeds to quote from Luther's works forty-one pernicious, scandalous, and poisonous propositions, in which the latter set forth the holy doctrines of the gospel. "So soon as this bull shall be published," continues the pope, "the bishops shall make diligent search after the writings of Martin Luther that contain these errors and burn them publicly and solemnly in the presence of the clergy and laity. As for Martin himself, what have we not done? Imitating the long-suffering of God Almighty, we are still ready to receive him again into the bosom of the church, and we grant him sixty days in which to forward us his recantation in a paper, sealed by two prelates; or else, which would be far more agreeable to us, for him to come to Rome in person, in order that no one may entertain any doubts of his obedience. Meanwhile, and from this very moment, he must give up preaching, teaching, and writing and commit his works to the flames. And if he does not retract in the space of sixty days, we by these presents condemn both him and his adherents as open and obstinate heretics." The pope then pronounces a number of excommunications, maledictions, and interdicts against Luther and his partisans, with orders to seize their persons and send them to Rome. We may easily conceive what would have become of these noble-minded confessors of the gospel in the papal dungeons.

Thus was the tempest gathering over Luther's head. The bull was published, and for centuries Rome had not pronounced a sentence of condemnation that her arm had not followed up with death. This murderous message was about to leave the Seven Hills and reach the Saxon monk in his cell. The moment was aptly chosen. It might be supposed that the new emperor, who had so many reasons for courting the pope's friendship, would be eager to deserve it by sacrificing to him an obscure monk. Already Leo X, the cardinals, nay, all Rome, exulted in their victory and fancied they saw their enemy at their feet.

Chapter 31
The Babylonian Captivity of the Church

Terrible combats awaited Luther. Rome was brandishing the sword with which she was about to strike the gospel. The rumor of the condemnation that was about to fall upon him, far from dispiriting the reformer, augmented his courage. It was at this time that Luther preached his sermon on the mass at Wittenberg. In this discourse he inveighs against the numerous sects of the Roman Catholic Church and reproaches it, with reason, for its want of unity. "The multiplicity of spiritual laws," says he, "has filled the world with sects and divisions. Priests, monks, and laymen have come to hate each other more than the Christians hate the Turks. What do I say? Priests against priests, and monks against monks, are deadly enemies. Each one is attached to his own sect and despises all others. The unity and charity of Christ are at an end."

He next attacks the doctrine that the mass is a sacrifice and has some virtue in itself. "What is most precious in every sacrament, and consequently in the eucharist," says he, "is the promises and the Word of God. Without faith in this Word and these promises, the sacrament is dead: it is a body without a soul, a cup without wine, a purse without money, a type without fulfillment, a letter without spirit, a casket without jewels, a scabbard without a sword."

Luther's voice was not, however, confined to Wittenberg; God had provided a missionary of a new kind. The printing press was the successor of the evangelists. This was the breaching battery employed against the Roman fortress. Luther had prepared a mine, the explosion of which shook the edifice of Rome to its lowest foundations. This was the publication of his famous book *The Babylonian Captivity of the Church,* which appeared on October 6, 1520.

In this work he first sets forth with irony all the advantages for which he is indebted to his enemies: "Whether I will it or not," says he, "I become wiser every day, urged on as I am by so many illustrious masters. Two years ago, I attacked indulgences, but with so much indecision and fear, that I am now ashamed of it. It is not, however, to be wondered at, for I was alone when I set this stone rolling." He thanks his adversaries: "I denied," continues he, "that the papacy was of divine origin, but I granted that it was of human right. Now, after reading all the subtleties on which these gentry have set up their idol, I know that the papacy is none other than the kingdom of Babylon and the violence of Nimrod the mighty hunter. I therefore beseech all my friends and all the booksellers to burn the books that I have written on this subject, and to substitute this one proposition in their place: *The papacy is a general chase led by the Roman bishop, to catch and destroy souls.*"

Luther next proceeds to attack the prevailing errors on the sacraments, monastic vows, etc. He reduces the seven sacraments of the church to three: baptism, penance, and the Lord's supper. After explaining the true nature of this supper, he passes on to baptism; and it is here especially that he lays down the excellence of faith and vigorously attacks Rome. "God," says he, "has preserved this sacrament alone free from human traditions. God has said, 'He that believeth and is baptized shall be saved.' This promise of God should be preferred to the glory of all works, vows, satisfactions, indulgences, and all inventions of man. Now on this promise, received by faith, depends our salvation. If we believe, our hearts are strengthened by the divine promise; and though the believer should be forsaken of all, this promise in which he believes will never forsake him. With it he will resist the adversary who assaults his soul, and be prepared to meet death and stand before the judgment seat of God. It will be his consolation in all his trials to say, God's promises never deceive; of their truth I received a pledge at my baptism; if God is for me, who shall be against me? Oh, how rich is the baptized Christian! Nothing can destroy him, except he refuse to believe.

"Perhaps to what I have said on the necessity of faith, the baptism of little children may be objected. But as the Word of God is mighty to change the heart of a wicked man, who is not less deaf nor less helpless than an infant; so the prayers of the church, to which all things are possible, change the little child, by the faith it pleases God to place in his heart, and thus purifies and renews it."

Portrait of Martin Luther published on the title page of *The Babylonian Captivity of the Church* (1520)

We state Luther's doctrine upon baptism without pretending to approve it. The very scriptural idea that no sacrament can be useful without faith led Luther to declare "that children themselves believe in baptism; that they have a faith peculiar to them;" and when it was objected to him, that not having reason they could not have faith, he replied, "What has reason to do with faith, and with the Word of God? Does it not, on the contrary, resist them? No man can attain to faith unless he becomes a fool, without reason, without intelligence, and like a little child." We must not be afraid to point out errors in the leaders of the Reformation: we do not pay them honors like those which Rome pays to its saints; we defend neither Calvin nor Luther but only Christ and His Word.

After having thus explained the doctrine of baptism, Luther wields it as a weapon against the papacy. In fact, if the Christian finds all his salvation in the renewal of his baptism by faith, what need has he of the Roman ordinances?

"For this reason, I declare," says Luther, "that neither pope, nor bishop, nor any man living, has authority to impose the least thing on a Christian without his own consent. All that is done without it is an act of tyranny. We are free from all men. The vow that we made at our baptism is sufficient of itself, and more than we can ever fulfill. All other vows, then, may be abolished. Let every man who enters the priesthood, or any religious order, be assured that the works of a monk or of a priest differ in no respect before God from those of a peasant who tills his fields, or of a woman who manages her house. God estimates all things by the standard of faith. And it often happens that the simple labor of a serving-man or maiden is more acceptable to God than the fasts and works of a monk, because the latter are void of faith. . . . Christians are God's true people, led captive to Babylon, and there stripped of what they had acquired by their baptism."

Luther terminates *The Babylonian Captivity* with these words: "I hear that new papal excommunications are about to be fabricated against me. If it be true, this present book must be considered as part of my future recantation. The remainder will soon follow, to prove my obedience; and the complete work will form, with Christ's aid, such a whole as Rome has never heard or seen the like."

After such a publication, all hope of reconciliation between Luther and the pope must of necessity have vanished. The incompatibility of the reformer's faith with the doctrines of the church must have struck the least discerning, but precisely at that very time fresh negotiations had been opened. Five weeks before the publication of *The Babylonian Captivity,* at the end of August 1520, the general chapter of the Augustinian monks was held at Eisleben. The venerable Staupitz there resigned the general vicarship of the order, and it was conferred on Wenceslas Link, the same who had accompanied Luther to Augsburg.

The indefatigable Miltitz suddenly arrived in the midst of the proceedings. He was ardently desirous of reconciling Luther with the pope. Eck and his boastings annoyed him; he knew that the Ingolstadt doctor had been decrying him at Rome, and he would have made every sacrifice to baffle, by a peace that should be promptly concluded, the schemes of this importunate rival. The interests of religion were mere secondary matters in his eyes. One day, as he relates, he was dining with the bishop of Leissen. The guests had already made pretty copious libations, when a new work of Luther's was laid before them. It was opened and read; the bishop grew angry; the official swore; but Miltitz burst into a hearty laugh. He dealt with the Reformation as a man of the world; Eck, as a theologian.

Aroused by the arrival of Dr. Eck, Miltitz addressed the chapter of the Augustinians in a speech, delivered with a strong Italian accent, thinking thus to impose on his simple fellow countrymen. "The whole Augustinian order," said he, "is compromised in this affair. Show me the means of restraining Luther."

"We have nothing to do with the doctor," replied the fathers, "and cannot give you advice." They relied, no doubt, on the release from the obligations to his order which Staupitz had given Luther at Augsburg.

Miltitz persisted: "Let a deputation from this venerable chapter wait upon Luther, and entreat him to write to the pope, assuring him that he has never plotted against his person. That will be sufficient to put an end to the matter." The chapter complied with the nuncio's demand, and commissioned, no doubt at his own request, the former vicar-general and his successor, Staupitz and Link, to speak to Luther. This deputation immediately set out for Wittenberg, bearing a letter from Miltitz to the doctor, filled with expressions of the greatest respect. "There is no time to lose," said he; "the thunderstorm, already gathering over the reformer's head, will soon burst forth; and then all will be over."

Neither Luther nor the deputies who shared in his sentiments expected any success from a letter to the pope, but that was an additional reason for not refusing to write one. Such a letter could only be a mere matter of form, which would set the justice of Luther's cause in a still stronger light. But not long after, the doctor was informed of the arrival of the bull in Germany; on October 3, he told Spalatin that he would not write to the pope, and on October 6, he published *The Babylonian Captivity of the Church.*

Even after Luther had been informed of the bull, the intriguing Miltitz was not discouraged. He requested to have a conference with Luther at Lichtemberg. The elector ordered the latter to go there; but his friends, and above all, the affectionate Melancthon, opposed it. "What," thought they, "accept a conference with the nuncio in so distant a place, at the very moment when the bull is to appear which commands Luther to be seized and carried to Rome? Is it not clear that, as Dr. Eck is unable to approach the reformer on account of the open manner in which he has shown his hatred, the crafty chamberlain has taken upon himself to catch Luther in his toils?"

These fears had no power to stop the Wittenberg doctor. The prince had commanded, and he would obey. "I am setting out for Lichtemberg," he wrote to the chaplain on October 11; "pray for me." His friends would not abandon him. Toward evening of the same day, he entered Lichtemberg on horseback, accompanied by thirty cavaliers, among whom was Melancthon. The papal nuncio arrived about the same time, with a train of four persons.

Miltitz was very pressing in his solicitation, assuring Luther that the blame would be thrown on Eck and his foolish vaunting, and that all would be concluded to the satisfaction of both parties. "Well then," replied Luther, "I offer to keep silence henceforward, provided my adversaries are silent likewise. For the sake of peace, I will do everything in my power."

Luther had now to fulfill his promise of writing to the pope. The following is Luther's letter:

"To the most holy father in God, Leo X, pope at Rome, be all health in Christ Jesus our Lord. Amen.

"From the midst of the violent battle which for three years I have been fighting against dissolute men, I cannot hinder myself from sometimes looking toward you, O Leo, most holy father in God. And although the madness of your impious flatterers has constrained me to appeal from your judgment to a future council, my heart has never been alienated from your holiness, and I have never ceased praying constantly and with deep groaning for your prosperity, and for that of your pontificate.

"It is true that I have attacked certain anti-Christian doctrines and have inflicted a deep wound upon my adversaries, because of their impiety. I do not repent of this, for I have the example of Christ before me. What is the use of salt, if it hath lost its pungency; or of the edge of the sword, if it cuts not? Cursed be the man who does the Lord's work coldly. Most excellent Leo, far from ever having entertained an evil thought in your respect, I wish you the most precious blessings for eternity. I have done but one thing—upheld the Word of truth. I am ready to submit to you in everything; but as for this Word, I will not, I cannot, abandon it. He who thinks differently from me thinks erroneously.

"It is true that I have attacked the court of Rome; but neither you nor any man on earth can deny that it is more corrupt than Sodom and Gomorrah, and that the impiety prevailing there is past all hope of cure. Yes, I have been filled with horror at seeing that under your name the poor people of Christ have been made a sport of. This I opposed, and I will oppose it again: not that I imagine I shall be able, despite the opposition of flatterers, to prosper in anything connected with this Babylon, which is confusion itself; but I owe it to my brethren, in order that some may escape, if possible, from these terrible scourges.

"You are aware that Rome for many years past has inundated the world with all that could destroy both body and soul. The church of Rome, once the foremost in sanctity, is become the most licentious den of robbers, the most shameless of all brothels, the kingdom of sin, of death, and of hell, which Antichrist himself, if he were to appear, could not increase in wickedness. All this is clearer than the sun at noonday.

"And yet, O Leo, you sit like a lamb in the midst of wolves, like Daniel in the lions' den. What can you do alone against such monsters? Perhaps there are three or four cardinals who combine learning with virtue. But what are they against so great a number? You would all die of poison before being able to make trial of any remedy. The fate of the court of Rome is decreed; God's wrath is upon it, and will consume it. It hates good advice, dreads reform, will not mitigate the fury of its impiety, and thus deserves that men should speak of this city as of its mother: 'We would have healed Babylon, but she is not healed: forsake her' (Jer. 51:9). It was for you and your cardinals to have applied the remedy; but the sick man mocks the physician, and the horse will not obey the rein.

"Full of affection for you, most excellent Leo, I have always regretted that you, who are worthy of better times, should have been raised to the pontificate in such days as these. Rome merits you not nor those who resemble you; she deserves to have Satan himself for her king. So true it is that he reigns more than you in that Babylon. Would to God that, laying aside that glory which your enemies so loudly extol, you would exchange it for some small living, or would support yourself on your paternal inheritance; for none but Iscariots deserve such honor. . . . O my dear Leo, Leo, you are the most unhappy of men, and you sit on the most dangerous of thrones. I tell you the truth because I mean you well.

"Is it not true, that under the spreading firmament of heaven there is nothing more corrupt or more detestable than the Roman court? It infinitely exceeds the Turks in vices and corruption. Once it was the gate of heaven; now it is the mouth of hell—a mouth which the wrath of God keeps open so wide, that on witnessing the unhappy people rushing into it, I cannot but utter a warning cry, as in a tempest, that some at least may be saved from the terrible gulf.

"Behold, O Leo, my father, why I have inveighed against this death-dealing see. Far from rising up against your person, I thought I was laboring for your safety, by valiantly attacking that prison, or rather that hell, in which you are shut up. To inflict all possible mischief on the court of Rome is performing *your* duty. To cover it with shame is to do Christ honor; in a word, to *be* a Christian is *not to be* a Roman. . . .

"O Leo, my father, listen not to those flattering sirens who would persuade you that you are not a mere man, but a demi-god, and can command and require whatever you please. You are the servant of servants, and the place where you are seated is the most dangerous and miserable of all. Believe those who depreciate you, and not those who extol you. I am perhaps too bold in presuming to teach so exalted a majesty, which ought to instruct all men. But I see the dangers that surround you at Rome; I see you driven to and fro, like the waves of the sea in a storm. Charity urges me, and it is my duty to utter a cry of warning and of safety.

"That I may not appear empty-handed before your holiness, I present you a small book which I have dedicated to you, and which will inform you of the subjects on which I should be engaged, if your parasites permitted me. It is a little matter, if its size be considered; but a great one, if we regard its contents; for the sum of the Christian life is therein contained. I am poor, and have nothing else to offer you; besides, have you need of any other than spiritual gifts? I commend myself to your holiness, whom may the Lord Jesus preserve forever. Amen."

The little book which Luther presented to the pope was his discourse on *Christian Liberty*, in which the reformer demonstrates incontrovertibly how, without infringing the liberty given by faith, a Christian may submit to all external ordinances in a spirit of liberty and charity. Two truths serve as a foundation to the whole argument: "The Christian is free, and master in all things. The Christian is in bondage, and a servant in all and to all. He is free, and a master by faith; he is a servant, and a slave by love."

He first explains the power of faith to make a Christian free. "Faith unites the soul to Christ, as a wife to her husband," says Luther to the pope. "All that Christ has becomes the property of the believing soul; all that the soul has becomes the property of Christ. Christ possesses every blessing and eternal salvation; they are henceforward the property of the soul. The soul possesses every vice and sin; they become henceforth the property of Christ. It is then the blessed exchange commences: Christ who is God and man, Christ who has never sinned, and whose holiness is immaculate, Christ the Almighty and Everlasting, appropriating by His nuptial ring, that is, by faith, all the sins of the believer's soul, these sins are swallowed up and lost in Him; for there is no sin that can stand before His infinite righteousness. Thus, by means of faith, the soul is delivered from every sin and clothed with the eternal righteousness of her husband, Jesus Christ.

"Blessed union! the rich, noble, and holy spouse, Jesus Christ, unites in marriage with that poor, guilty, and despised wife, delivers

THE TRIUMPH OF TRUTH

her from every ill, and adorns her with the most costly blessings. . . . Christ, a priest and king, shares this honor and glory with every Christian. The Christian is a king, and consequently possesses all things; he is a priest, and consequently possesses God. And it is faith, and not works, that brings him to such honor. The Christian is free of all things, above all things, faith giving him abundantly of everything."

In the second part of his discourse, Luther gives another view of the truth. "Although the Christian is thus made free, he voluntarily becomes a slave, to act toward his brethren as God has acted toward him through Jesus Christ. I desire," says he, "to serve freely, joyfully, and gratuitously a Father who has thus lavished upon me all the abundance of His blessings: I wish to become all things for my neighbor, as Christ has become all things for me."

"From faith," continues Luther, "proceeds the love of God; from love proceeds a life full of liberty, charity, and joy. Oh, how noble and elevated is the Christian life. But alas, no one knows it, no one preaches it. By faith the Christian ascends to God; by love, he descends even to man, and yet he abides ever with God. This is true liberty—a liberty which surpasses all others as much as the heavens are above the earth."

Such is the work with which Luther accompanied his letter to Leo.

Chapter 32
"It Is Christ Who Has Begun These Things"

While the reformer was thus addressing the Roman pontiff for the last time, the bull which anathematized him was already in the hands of the chiefs of the German church and at the threshold of Luther's dwelling place. It would appear that no doubts were entertained at Rome of the success of the step just taken against the Reformation. The pope had commissioned two high functionaries of his court, Caraccioli and Aleander, to bear it to the archbishop of Mentz, desiring him to see it put in execution. But Eck himself appeared in Saxony as the herald and agent of the great pontifical work.

The doctor of Ingolstadt had felt more than any other man the force of Luther's attack; he had seen the danger and stretched forth his hand to steady the tottering edifice of Rome. He was, in his own opinion, the Atlas destined to bear on his sturdy shoulders the ancient Roman world now threatening to fall to ruins. Proud of the success of his journey to Rome—proud of the commission he had received from the sovereign pontiff—proud of appearing in Germany with the new title of protonotary and pontifical nuncio—proud of the bull he held in his hands, and which contained the condemnation of his indomitable rival, Eck saw in his present mission a more magnificent triumph than all the victories he had gained in Hungary, Bavaria, Lombardy, and Saxony, and from which he had previously derived so much renown.

But this pride was soon to be brought low. The pope, by confiding the publication of the bull to Eck, had committed a fault destined to destroy its effect. So great a distinction accorded to a man not filling an elevated station in the church offended all sensible men. The bishops, accustomed to receive the bulls direct from the Roman pontiff, were displeased that this should be published in their dioceses by a nuncio created for the occasion. Luther considered this judgment brought by his implacable opponent as an act of personal revenge; this condemnation was, in his idea, the treacherous dagger of a mortal enemy, and not the lawful axe of a Roman lictor. This paper was no longer regarded as the bull of the supreme pontiff, but as the bull of Doctor Eck. Thus the edge was blunted and weakened beforehand by the very man who had prepared it.

The chancellor of Ingolstadt had made all haste to Saxony. It was there he had fought; it was there he wished to publish his victory. He succeeded in posting up the bull at Meissen, Merseburg, and Brandenburg, toward the end of September. But in the first of these cities it was stuck up in a place where no one could read it, and the bishops of the three sees did not press its publication. Even his great protector, Duke George, forbade the council of Leipzig to make it generally known before receiving an order from the Bishop of Merseburg; and this order did not come till the following year. "These difficulties are merely for form's sake," thought John Eck at first; for everything in other respects seemed to smile upon him. Duke George himself sent him a gilt cup filled with ducats.

But ere long the Ingolstadt doctor observed that the wind was changing. A great alteration had taken place in Leipzig during the past year. On St. Michael's day, some students posted up placards in ten different places, in which the new nuncio was sharply attacked. In alarm he fled to the cloister of St. Paul, in which Tetzel had already taken refuge, refused to see any one, and prevailed upon the rector to bring these youthful adversaries to account. But poor Eck gained little by this. The students wrote a ballad upon him, which they sang in the streets; Eck heard it from his retreat. Upon this he lost all his courage; the formidable champion trembled in every limb. Each day he received threatening letters. One hundred and fifty students arrived from Wittenberg, boldly exclaiming against the papal envoy. The wretched apostolical nuncio could hold out no longer. "I have no wish to see him killed," said Luther, "but I am desirous that his schemes should fail."

Eck quitted his asylum by night, escaped secretly from Leipzig, and hid himself at Coburg. Miltitz, who relates this, boasted of it more than the reformer. This triumph was not of long duration; all the conciliatory plans of the chamberlain failed, and he came to a melancholy end. Miltitz, being intoxicated, fell into the Rhine at Mentz and was drowned.

Gradually, however, Eck's courage revived. He repaired to Erfurt, whose theologians had given the Wittenberg doctor several proofs of their jealousy. He insisted that the bull should be published in this city; but the students seized the copies, tore them in pieces, and—playing on the word *bulla* (which means a *bubble,* the seal appended to the bull, and hence the *bull* itself)—flung the fragments into the river, saying, "Since it is a bull," a bubble, "let it float!"

Eck did not dare to appear at Wittenberg; he sent the bull to the rector, threatening to destroy the university if he did not conform to it. At the same time he wrote to Duke John, Frederick's brother and coregent: "Do not misconstrue my proceedings," said he; "for I am fighting on behalf of the faith, which costs me much care, toil, and money."

The Bishop of Brandenburg could not, even had he so wished, act in Wittenberg; for the university was protected by its privileges. Luther and Carlstadt, both condemned by the bull, were invited to be present at the deliberations that took place on its contents. The rector declared, that as the bull was not accompanied by a letter from the pope, he would not publish it. The university already enjoyed in the surrounding countries a greater authority than the pontiff himself. Its declaration served as a model for the elector's government. Thus the spirit that was in Luther triumphed over the bull of Rome.

In truth, what signified all this resistance of students, rectors, and priests? If the mighty hand of Charles united with the pope's, would they not crush these scholars and grammarians? Who could withstand the power of the pontiff of Christendom and of the emperor of the West? At this solemn moment, the reformer did not conceal from himself the perils that surrounded him. He cast his looks to heaven. "What will happen?" said he. "I know not, and I care not to know, feeling sure that He who sitteth in heaven hath foreseen from all eternity the beginning, continuation, and end of all this affair. Wherever the blow may reach me, I fear not. The leaf of a tree does not fall to the ground without the will of our Father; how much less we ourselves. . . . It is a little matter to die for the Word, since this Word, which was made flesh for us, died itself at first. We shall arise with it, if we die with it, and passing where it has gone before, we shall arrive where it has arrived, and abide with it through all eternity."

On October 3, he was informed of the papal brief. "It is come at last, this Roman bull," said he. "I despise and attack it as impious, false, and in every respect worthy of Eck. It is Christ Himself who is condemned therein. No reasons are given in it: I am cited to Rome, not to be heard, but that I may eat my words. I shall treat it as a forgery, although I believe it true. O that Charles V would act like a man, and that for the love of Christ he would attack these wicked spirits. I rejoice in having to bear such ills for the best of causes. Already I feel greater liberty in my heart; for at last I know that the pope is antichrist, and that his throne is that of Satan himself."

Luther at first pretended to doubt the authenticity of the bull. "I hear," says he in the first of his writings on the subject, "that Eck has brought a new bull from Rome, which resembles him so much that it might be called *Doctor Eck,* so full is it of falsehood and error. He would have us believe that it is the pope's doing, while it is only a forgery." After having set forth the reasons for his doubts, Luther concludes by saying, "I must see with my own eyes the lead, the seal, the strings, the clause, the signature of the bull, in fact the whole of it, before I value all these clamors even at a straw."

But no one doubted, not even Luther himself, that it really emanated from the pope. Germany waited to see what the reformer would do. Would he stand firm? All eyes were fixed on Wittenberg. Luther did not keep his contemporaries long in suspense. He replied with a terrible discharge of artillery, publishing on November 4, 1520, his treatise *Against the Bull of Antichrist.*

"What errors, what deceptions," says he, "have crept among the poor people under the mantle of the church and of the pretended infallibility of the pope! How many souls have thus been lost; how much blood spilt; how many murders committed; how many king-doms devastated!"

"I can pretty clearly distinguish," says he ironically, a little further on, "between skill and malice, and I set no high value on a malice so unskillful. To burn books is so easy a matter that even children can do it; much more, then, the holy father and his doctors. It would be well for them to show greater ability than that which is required to burn books. . . . Besides, let them destroy my works. I desire nothing better; for all my wish has been to lead souls to the Bible, so that they might afterwards neglect my writings. Great God, if we had a knowledge of Scripture, what need would there be of any books of mine? . . . I am free, by the grace of God, and bulls neither console nor alarm me. My strength and my consolation are in a place where neither men nor devils can reach them."

Luther's tenth proposition, condemned by the pope, was thus drawn up: "No man's sins are forgiven, unless he believes they are forgiven when the priest absolves him." By condemning this, the pope denied that faith was necessary in the sacrament. "They pretend," exclaims Luther, "that we must not believe our sins are forgiven when we receive absolution from the priest. And what then ought we to do? . . . Listen, Christians, to this news from Rome. Condemnation is pronounced against that article of faith which we profess when we say, 'I believe in the Holy Ghost, the holy Catholic church, the forgiveness of sins.' If I were certain that the pope had really issued this bull at Rome"—and he had no doubt about it—"and that it was not invented by Eck, that prince of liars, I should like to proclaim to all Christians that they ought to consider the pope as the real Antichrist spoken of in Scripture. And if he would not discontinue publicly to proscribe the faith of the church, then . . . let even the temporal sword resist *him,* rather than the Turk . . . for the Turk permits us to believe, but the pope forbids it."

While Luther was speaking thus forcibly, his dangers were increasing. His enemies' plan was to expel him from Wittenberg. If Luther and Wittenberg could be separated, Luther and Wittenberg would be ruined. One blow would thus free Rome both from the heretical doctor and the heretical university. Duke George, the bishop of Merseburg, and the Leipzig theologians secretly applied themselves to the task. These intrigues were not entirely ineffectual: Adrian, Hebrew professor at Wittenberg, suddenly turned against the doctor. Great strength of faith was required to bear up against the blow inflicted by the court of Rome. There are some characters that will go along with the truth only to a certain point. Such was Adrian. Alarmed by this condemnation, he quitted Wittenberg, and repaired to Dr. Eck at Leipzig.

The bull was beginning to be carried into execution. The voice of the pontiff of Christendom was not powerless. For ages, fire and sword had taught submission to his decrees. The burning piles were erected at his voice. Everything seemed to announce that a terrible catastrophe would shortly put an end to the daring revolt of this Augustinian monk. In October 1520, Luther's books were taken away from all the booksellers' shops in Ingolstadt and put under seal. The elector archbishop of Mentz, moderate as he was, felt obliged to banish Ulrich von Hutten from his court and to imprison his printer. The papal nuncios had besieged the youthful emperor: Charles declared that he would protect the old religion; and in some of his hereditary possessions scaffolds were erected, on which the writings of the heretic were to be reduced to ashes. Princes of the church and councilors of state were present at these *autos-da-fé*.

Eck behaved with insolence, in every quarter threatening the great and the learned, and "filling everything with his smoke," as Erasmus says. "The pope," said Eck, "who has overthrown so many counts and dukes, will know how to bring these wretched grammarians to their senses. We must tell the Emperor Charles himself, *You are but a cobbler.*" And his colleague Aleander, frowning like a schoolmaster who threatens his pupils with the rod, said to Erasmus, "We shall know how to get at this Duke Frederick and teach him reason." Aleander was quite elated with his success. To hear the haughty nuncio talk, one would have thought that the fire which consumed Luther's books at Mentz was "the beginning of the end."

It was so with many timid and superstitious minds; but even in the hereditary states of Charles, the only places in which they dared carry out the bull, the people, and sometimes the nobles, often replied to these pontifical demonstrations by ridicule, or by expressions of indignation. "Luther," said the doctors of Louvain, when they appeared before Margaret, governor of the Netherlands, "is overturning the Christian faith."

"Who is Luther?" asked the princess.

"An ignorant monk."

"Well, then," replied she, "do you who are so wise and so numerous write against him. The world will rather believe many wise men than an isolated and unlearned man."

The Louvain doctors preferred an easier method. They erected a vast pile at their own expense. A great multitude thronged the place of execution. Students and citizens might be seen hastily traversing the crowd bearing large volumes under their arms, which they threw into the flames. Their zeal edified both monks and doctors; but the trick was afterwards discovered—it was the *Sermones Discipuli, Tartaretus,* and other scholastic and papistical works they had been throwing into the fire, instead of Luther's writings.

The Count of Nassau, viceroy of Holland, replied to the Dominicans who solicited permission to burn the doctor's books, "Go and preach the gospel with as much purity as Luther does, and you will have to complain of nobody." As the conversation turned upon the reformer at a banquet when the leading princes of the empire were present, the Lord of Ravenstein said aloud, "In the space of four centuries, a single Christian has ventured to raise his head, and him the pope wishes to put to death."

Luther, sensible of the strength of his cause, remained tranquil in the midst of the tumult the bull had created. "If you did not press me so earnestly," said he to Spalatin, "I should keep silence, well knowing that the work must be accomplished by the counsel and power of God." The timid man was for speaking out; the strong desired to remain silent. Luther discerned a power that escaped the eyes of his friend. "Be of good cheer," continued the reformer. "It is Christ who has begun these things, and it is He that will accomplish them, whether I be banished or put to death. Jesus Christ is here present, and He who is within us is greater than he who is in the world."

Chapter 33
Luther Responds to the Bull

Duty obliged Luther to speak that the truth might be manifested to the world. Rome had struck the blow; he would show how he had received it. The pope had put him under the ban of the church; he would put the pope under the ban of Christendom. He prepared to make a fresh appeal to a general council. An appeal from the pope to a council was a crime. It was therefore by a new attack on the pontifical power that Luther presumed to justify those by which it had been preceded.

On November 17, a notary and five witnesses met at ten o'clock in the morning in one of the halls of the Augustinian convent where Luther resided. There the public officer, Sarctor of Eisleben, immediately proceeded to draw up the minute of his protest. The reformer in presence of these witnesses said with a solemn tone of voice:

"Considering that a general council of the Christian church is above the pope, especially in matters of faith:

"Considering that the power of the pope is not above, but inferior to Scripture; and that he has no right to slaughter the sheep of Christ's flock and throw them into the jaws of the wolf:

"I, Martin Luther, an Augustinian friar, doctor of the Holy Scriptures at Wittenberg, appeal by these presents, in behalf of myself and of those who are or who shall be with me, from the most holy pope Leo to a future general and Christian council.

"I appeal from the said pope, first as an unjust, rash, and tyrannical judge, who condemns me without hearing, and without giving any reasons for his judgment; secondly as a heretic and an apostate, misled, hardened, and condemned by the Holy Scriptures, who commands me to deny that Christian faith is necessary in the use of the sacraments; thirdly as an enemy, an antichrist, an adversary, an oppressor of Holy Scripture, who dares set his own words in opposition to the Word of God; fourthly as a despiser, a calumniator, a blasphemer of the holy Christian church, and of a free council, who maintains that a council is nothing of itself.

"For this reason, with all humility, I entreat the most serene, most illustrious, excellent, generous, noble, strong, wise, and prudent lords, namely, Charles emperor of Rome, the electors, princes, counts, barons, knights, gentlemen, councilors, cities, and communities of the whole German nation, to adhere to my protest, and to resist with me the anti-Christian conduct of the pope for the glory of God, the defense of the church and of the Christian doctrine, and for the maintenance of the free councils of Christendom; and Christ our Lord will reward them bountifully by His everlasting grace. But if there be any who scorn my prayer and continue to obey that impious man the pope rather than God, I reject by these presents all responsibility, having faithfully warned their consciences, and I abandon them to the supreme judgment of God, with the pope and his adherents."

Such was Luther's bill of divorce—such was his reply to the pontiff's bull. This protest was circulated through Germany and sent to most of the courts of Christendom.

Luther had, however, a still more daring step in reserve, although this which he had just taken appeared the extreme of audacity. He would in no respect be behindhand with Rome. The monk of Wittenberg would do all that the sovereign pontiff dared do. On December 10, a placard was posted on the walls of the University of Wittenberg, inviting the professors and students to be present at nine o'clock in the morning, at the eastern gate, near the holy cross. A great number of doctors and students assembled, and Luther, walking at their head, conducted the procession to the appointed place. A scaffold had been prepared. One of the oldest masters of arts set fire to it. As the flames rose high into the air, the formidable Augustinian, wearing his frock, approached the pile, carrying the canon law, the decretals, the Clementines, the papal extravagants, some writings by Eck and Emser, and the pope's bull. The decretals having been first consumed, Luther held up the bull, and said, "Since thou hast vexed the holy One of the Lord, may everlasting fire vex and consume thee." He then flung it into the flames.

After this Luther calmly returned to the city, and the crowd of doctors, professors, and students, testifying their approval by loud cheers, reentered Wittenberg with him. "My enemies," said he on another occasion, "have been able, by burning my books, to injure the cause of truth in the minds of the common people, and destroy their souls; for this reason, I consumed their books in return. A serious struggle has just begun. Hitherto I have been only playing with the pope. I began this work in God's name; it will be ended without me, and by His might. If they dare burn my books, in which more of the gospel is to be found—I speak without boasting—than in all the books of the pope, I can with much greater reason burn theirs, in which no good can be discovered."

If Luther had commenced the Reformation in this manner, such a step would undoubtedly have entailed the most deplorable results. Fanaticism might have been aroused by it, and the church thrown into a course of violence and disorder. But the reformer had preluded his work by seriously explaining the lessons of Scripture. The foundation had been wisely laid. Now, a powerful blow, such as he had just given, might accelerate the moment in which Christendom would throw off its bonds. Luther thus solemnly declared that he separated from the pope and his church. He burnt his ships upon the beach, thus imposing on himself the necessity of advancing and of combating.

Luther had reentered Wittenberg. On the morrow, the lecture room was more crowded than usual. All minds were in a state of excitement; a solemn feeling pervaded the assembly; they waited, expecting an address from the doctor. He lectured on the Psalms—a course that he had commenced in the month of March in the preceding year. Having finished his explanations, he remained silent a few minutes and then continued energetically, "Be on your guard against the laws and statutes of the pope. I have burnt his decretals, but this is merely child's play. It is time, and more than time, that the pope were burnt; that is," explaining himself immediately, "the see of Rome, with all its doctrines and abominations. . . .

"If you reject it, you must expect to incur every kind of danger, and even to lose your lives. But it is far better to be exposed to such perils in this world than to keep silence. So long as I live, I will denounce to my brethren the sore and the plague of Babylon, for fear that many who are with us should fall back like the rest into the bottomless pit."

This discourse and the act by which it was crowned mark an important epoch in the Reformation. The dispute at Leipzig had inwardly detached Luther from the pope. But the moment in which he burnt the bull was that in which he declared in the most formal manner his entire separation from the bishop of Rome and his church and his attachment to the universal church, such as it had been founded by the apostles of Jesus Christ. At the eastern gate of the city he lit a fire that has been burning for centuries.

"The pope," said he, "has three crowns, and for this reason: the first is against God, for he condemns religion; the second against the emperor, for he condemns the secular power; the third is against society, for he condemns marriage." When he was reproached with inveighing too severely against the papacy, "Alas," replied he, "would that I could speak against it with a voice of thunder, and that each of my words were a thunderbolt."

This firmness spread to Luther's friends and fellow countrymen. A whole nation rallied around him. The University of Wittenberg in particular grew daily more attached to this hero, to whom it was indebted for its importance and glory. Carlstadt then raised his voice against that "furious lion of Florence," which tore all human and divine laws, and trampled underfoot the principles of eternal truth. Melancthon, also, about this time addressed the states of the empire in a writing characterized by the elegance and wisdom peculiar to this amiable man. Melancthon says, "It matters little to Luther whether our riches, that is to say, the treasures of Europe, are sent to Rome; but the great cause of his grief and ours is that the laws of the pontiffs and the reign of the pope not only endanger the souls of men, but ruin them entirely. Each one may judge for himself whether it is becoming or not to contribute his money for the maintenance of Roman luxury; but to judge of religion and its sacred mysteries is not within the scope of the commonalty. It is on this ground, then, that Luther appeals to your faith and zeal, and that all pious men unite with him—some aloud, others with sighs and groans. . . . That same spirit which animated Jehu against the priests of Baal, urges you, by this precedent, to abolish the Roman superstition, which is much more horrible than the idolatry of Baal."

A few cries of alarm were heard among the friends of the Reformation. Timid minds inclined to extreme measures of conciliation, and Staupitz, in particular, expressed the deepest anxiety. "All this matter has been hitherto mere play," wrote Luther to him. "You have said yourself, that if God does not do these things, it is impossible they can be done. The tumult becomes more and more tumultuous, and I do not think it will ever be appeased, except at the last day."

"The papacy," continued he, "is no longer what it was yesterday and the day before. Let it excommunicate and burn my writings; . . . let it slay me; . . . it shall not check that which is advancing."

Luther was overwhelmed with reproaches. "Who knows," replied Luther, sensible of the call that was addressed to him from on high, "if God has not chosen and called me, and if they ought not to fear that, by despising me, they despise God Himself? Moses was alone at the departure from Egypt; Elijah was alone in the reign of King Ahab; Isaiah alone in Jerusalem; Ezekiel alone in Babylon. . . . God never selected as a prophet either the high priest or any other great personage; but ordinarily He chose low and despised men, once even the shepherd Amos. In every age, the saints have had to reprove the great, kings, princes, priests, and wise men, at the peril of their lives. . . . And was it not the same under the New Testament? Ambrose was alone in his time; after him, Jerome was alone; later still, Augustine was alone. . . . I do not say that I am a prophet, but I say that they ought to fear, precisely because I am alone and that they are many. I am sure of this, that the Word of God is with me and that it is not with them. . . .

"I am accused of rejecting the holy doctors of the church. I do not reject them; but, since all these doctors endeavor to prove their writings by Holy Scripture, Scripture must be clearer and surer than they are. Who would think of proving an obscure passage by one that was obscurer still? Thus, then, necessity obliges me to have recourse to the Bible, as all the doctors have done, and to call upon it to pronounce upon their writings; for the Bible alone is lord and master."

The courageous doctor, although he protests, still retracts some of his propositions. Our astonishment will cease when we see the manner in which he does it. After quoting the four propositions on indulgences condemned by the bull, he simply adds:

"In submission to the holy and learned bull, I retract all that I have ever taught concerning indulgences. If my books have been justly burnt, it is certainly because I made concessions to the pope on the doctrine of indulgences; for this reason I condemn them myself to the flames."

He retracts also with respect to John Huss: "I now say that not a *few* articles, but *all* the articles of John Huss are wholly Christian. By condemning John Huss, the pope has condemned the gospel. I have done five times more than he, and yet I much fear I have not done enough. Huss said only that a wicked pope is not a member of Christendom; but if Peter himself were now sitting at Rome, I should deny that he was pope by divine appointment."

Chapter 34
Political Maneuvering

The mighty words of the reformer sank deep into men's hearts and contributed to their emancipation. The sparks that flew from every one of them were communicated to the whole nation. But still a greater question remained to be solved. Would the prince in whose states Luther was residing favor or oppose the execution of the bull? The reply appeared doubtful. The elector, as well as all the princes of the empire, was at Aix-la-Chapelle. Here the crown of Charlemagne was placed on the head of the youngest but most powerful monarch of Christendom. An unusual pomp and magnificence were displayed in this ceremony. Charles V, Frederick, princes, ministers, and ambassadors repaired immediately to Cologne. Aix-la-Chapelle, where the plague was raging, seemed to pour its whole population into this ancient city on the banks of the Rhine.

Among the crowd of strangers who thronged this city were the two papal nuncios, Marino Caraccioli and Jerome Aleander. Caraccioli, who had already been ambassador at the court of Maximilian, was commissioned to congratulate the new emperor and to treat with him on political matters. But Rome had discovered that to succeed in extinguishing the Reformation, it was necessary to send into Germany a nuncio specially accredited for this work, and of a character, skill, and activity fitted for its accomplishment. Aleander had been selected. His knowledge of Greek, Hebrew, Chaldee, and Arabic gained him the reputation of being the most learned man of his age. He devoted himself with his whole heart to everything he undertook. The zeal with which he studied languages was by no means inferior to that which he exerted afterwards in persecuting the Reformation. Leo X attached him to his own service. Some historians speak of his epicurean manners; Roman Catholics of the integrity of his life. It would appear that he was fond of luxury, parade, and amusement. All are agreed in confessing that he was violent, prompt in his actions, full of ardor, indefatigable, imperious, and devoted to the pope. Eck was the fiery and intrepid champion of the schools; Aleander the haughty ambassador of the proud court of the pontiffs. He seemed born to be a nuncio.

Rome had made every preparation to destroy the monk of Wittenberg. The duty of attending the coronation of the emperor as the pope's representative was a mere secondary mission in Aleander's eyes, yet calculated to facilitate his task by the respect it secured for him. But he was specially charged to prevail upon Charles to crush the rising Reformation.

As soon as Aleander arrived at Cologne, he and Caraccioli set every wheel in motion to have Luther's heretical works burnt throughout the empire, but particularly under the eyes of the German princes assembled in that city. Charles V had already given his consent with regard to his hereditary states. The agitation of men's minds was excessive. "Such measures," said they to Charles's ministers and the nuncios themselves, "far from healing the wound, will only increase it. Do you imagine that Luther's doctrines are found only in those books that you are throwing into the fire? They are written, where you cannot reach them, in the hearts of the nation. . . . If you desire to employ force, it must be that of countless swords unsheathed to massacre a whole nation. A few logs of wood piled up to burn a few sheets of paper will effect nothing; and such arms are unbecoming the dignity of an emperor and of a pontiff."

The nuncio defended his burning piles. "These flames," said he, "are a sentence of condemnation written in colossal characters, equally intelligible to those who are near and those who are afar off, to the learned and ignorant, and even to those who cannot read."

But it was not, in reality, papers and books that the nuncio wanted; it was Luther himself. "These flames," resumed he, "are not sufficient to purify the infected air of Germany. If they terrify the simple, they do not punish the wicked. We require an imperial edict against Luther's person."

Aleander did not find the emperor so compliant when the reformer's life was in question, as when his books only were concerned. "As I have but recently ascended the throne," said he to Aleander, "I cannot without the advice of my councilors and the consent of the princes strike such a blow as this against a numerous faction surrounded by so many powerful defenders. Let us first learn what our father the elector of Saxony thinks of this matter; we shall afterwards see what reply we can make to the pope." The nuncios therefore proceeded to make trial of their artifices and eloquence on the elector.

The first Sunday in November, Frederick having attended mass in the Greyfriars' convent, Caraccioli and Aleander begged an audience. He received them in the presence of the bishop of Trent and several of his councilors. Caraccioli first presented the papal brief. Of a milder disposition than Aleander, he thought it his duty to win over the prince by his flatteries, and began by eulogizing him and his ancestors. "It is to you," said he, "that we look for the salvation of the Roman church and of the empire."

But the impetuous Aleander, wishing to come to the point, hastily stepped forward and interrupted his colleague, who modestly gave way: "It is to me and Eck," said he, "that this business of Martin's has been entrusted. Look at the imminent dangers into which this man is plunging the Christian republic. If we do not make haste to apply some remedy, the empire is ruined. . . . You cannot remain united to Luther without separating from Jesus Christ. I require two things of you, in the name of his holiness: first, that you will burn Luther's writings; secondly, that you will inflict on him the punishment he deserves, or at least that you will deliver him up to the pope. The emperor and all the princes of the empire have declared their willingness to accede to our request; you alone hesitate still."

Frederick replied, through the medium of the bishop of Trent, "This matter is too serious to be settled now. We will let you know our determination."

The situation in which Frederick was placed was a difficult one. What part ought he to take? On the one side were the emperor, the princes of the empire, and the supreme pontiff of Christendom, whose authority the elector had as yet no idea of throwing off; on the other, a monk, a feeble monk; for it was he only that they demanded. Charles's reign had just commenced. Ought Frederick, the oldest and wisest of all the princes of Germany, to sow disunion in the empire? Besides, how could he renounce that ancient piety which led him even to the sepulcher of Christ?

In the midst of this general agitation, one man alone remained tranquil: it was Luther. While it was sought to preserve him by the influence of the great, the monk in his cloister at Wittenberg thought that it was rather for him to save the great ones of this world. "If the gospel," wrote he to Spalatin, "were of a nature to be propagated or maintained by the powers of this world, God would not have entrusted it to fishermen. It belongs not to the princes and pontiffs of this age to defend the Word of God. They have enough to do to shelter themselves from the judgments of the Lord and of His Anointed. If I speak, it is in order that they may attain a knowledge of the divine Word, and that by it they may be saved."

Luther's expectation was not to be deceived. That faith which a convent at Wittenberg concealed exerted its power in the palaces of Cologne. Frederick's heart, shaken perhaps for a moment, grew stronger by degrees. He was indignant that the pope, in defiance of his earnest entreaties to examine into the matter in Germany, had decided upon it at Rome at the request of a personal enemy of the reformer, and that in his absence this opponent should have dared publish in Saxony a bull that threatened the existence of the university and the peace of his subjects. Besides, the elector was convinced that Luther was wronged. He shuddered at the thought of delivering an innocent man into the hands of his cruel enemies. Justice was the principle on which he acted, and not the wishes of the pope. He came to the determination of not giving way to Rome.

On November 4, his councilors replied on his behalf to the Roman nuncios. The elector said that neither his imperial majesty nor any other person had shown that Luther's writings had been refuted and that they only deserved to be thrown into the fire. He requested that Doctor Luther should be furnished with a safe-conduct, so that he might appear before a tribunal of learned, pious, and impartial judges.

After this declaration, Aleander, Caraccioli, and their followers retired to deliberate. This was the first time that the elector had publicly made known his intentions with regard to the reformer. The nuncios had expected quite a different course from him. Being readmitted into the presence of the elector's councilors, the imperious Aleander said, "I should like to know what the elector would think, if one of his subjects would choose the king of France, or any other foreign prince, for judge." Seeing that nothing could shake the Saxon councilors, he said, "We will execute the bull; we will hunt out and burn Luther's writings. As for his person," added he, affecting a contemptuous indifference, "the pope is not desirous of staining his hands with the blood of the wretched man."

The news of the reply the elector had made to the nuncios having reached Wittenberg, Luther's friends were filled with joy. "The German nobility," said Melancthon, "will direct their course by the example of this prince, whom they follow in all things, as their Nestor. If Homer styled his hero *the bulwark of the Greeks,* why should we not call Frederick *the bulwark of the Germans?*"

The oracle of courts, the torch of the schools, the light of the world, Erasmus, was then at Cologne. Many princes had invited him, to be guided by his advice. At the epoch of the Reformation, Erasmus was the leader of the moderates; at least he imagined himself to be so, but without just cause; for when truth and error meet face to face, justice lies not between them. He was the chief of that philosophical and academical party which, for ages, had attempted to correct Rome, but had never succeeded; he was the representative of human wisdom, but that wisdom was too weak to batter down the high places of Roman Catholicism. It needed that wisdom from God which men often call foolishness, but at whose voice mountains crumble into dust.

Erasmus would neither throw himself into the arms of Luther, nor sit at the pope's feet. He hesitated, and often wavered between these two powers, attracted at one time toward Luther, then suddenly repelled in the direction of the pope. "The last spark of Christian piety seems nearly extinguished," said he in his letter to Albert; "and it is this which has moved Luther's heart. He cares neither for money nor honors." But this letter, which the imprudent Ulrich von Hutten had published, caused Erasmus so much annoyance that he determined to be more cautious in future. Besides, he was accused of being Luther's accomplice, and the latter offended him by his imprudent language. "Almost all good men are for Luther," said he; "but I see that we are tending toward a revolt. . . . I would not have my name joined with his. That would injure me without serving him." "So be it," replied Luther; "since that annoys you, I promise never to make mention either of you or of your friends."

The elector, knowing that the opinion of a man so much respected as Erasmus would have great influence, invited the illustrious Dutchman to visit him. Erasmus obeyed the order. This was on December 5. Luther's friends could not see this step without secret uneasiness. The elector was standing before the fire, with Spalatin at his side, when Erasmus was introduced.

"What is your opinion of Luther?" immediately demanded Frederick.

The prudent Erasmus, surprised at so direct a question, sought at first to elude replying. He screwed up his mouth, bit his lips, and said not a word. Upon this the elector, raising his eyebrows, as was his custom when he spoke to people from whom he desired to have a precise answer, says Spalatin, fixed his piercing glance on Erasmus. The latter, not knowing how to escape from his confusion, said at last, in a half jocular tone, "Luther has committed two great faults: he has attacked the crown of the pope and the bellies of the monks."

The elector smiled, but gave his visitor to understand that he was in earnest. Erasmus then laying aside his reserve, said, "The cause of all this dispute is the hatred of the monks toward learning and the fear they have of seeing their tyranny destroyed. What weapons are they using against Luther? clamor, cabals, hatred, and libels. The more virtuous a man is, the greater his attachment to the gospel, the less is he opposed to Luther. The severity of the bull has aroused the indignation of all good men, and no one can recognize in it the gentleness of a vicar of Christ. Two only out of all the universities have condemned Luther; and they have only *condemned* him, not *proved* him in the wrong. Do not be deceived; the danger is greater than some men imagine. Arduous and difficult things are pressing on. To begin Charles's reign by so odious an act as Luther's imprisonment would be a mournful omen. The world is thirsting for evangelical truth; let us beware of setting up a blamable opposition. Let this affair be inquired into by serious men, men of sound judgment; this will be the course most consistent with the dignity of the pope himself."

Spalatin was delighted. He went out with Erasmus and accompanied him as far as the house of the Count of Nuenar, provost of Cologne, where Erasmus was residing. The latter, in an impulse of frankness, on retiring to his study, took a pen, sat down, wrote a summary of what he had said to the elector, and forwarded the paper to Spalatin; but ere long the fear of Aleander came over the timid Erasmus; the courage that the presence of the elector and his chaplain had communicated to him had evaporated; and he begged Spalatin to return the too daring paper, for fear it should fall into the hands of the terrible nuncio. But it was too late.

The elector, feeling reassured by the opinion of Erasmus, spoke to the emperor in a more decided tone. Erasmus himself endeavored, in nocturnal conferences, like those of Nicodemus of old, to persuade Charles's councilors that the whole business would be referred to impartial judges. But at the same time, and not to lose his credit at Rome, he wrote the most submissive letters to Leo, who replied with a kindness that seriously mortified Aleander. Erasmus communicated these letters from the pontiff, and they added still more to his credit. The nuncio complained of it to Rome. "Pretend not to notice this man's wickedness," was the reply; "prudence enjoins this: we must leave a door open to repentance."

Charles at the same time adopted a "see-saw" system, which consisted in flattering the pope and the elector, and appearing to incline by turns toward each, according to the necessities of the moment. One of his ministers, whom he had sent to Rome on Spanish business, arrived at the very moment that Doctor Eck was clamorously urging on Luther's condemnation. The wily ambassador immediately saw what advantage his master might derive from the Saxon monk. "Your majesty," he wrote on May 12, 1520, to the emperor, who was still in Spain, "ought to go into Germany, and show some favor to a certain Martin Luther, who is at the Saxon court, and who by the sermons he preaches gives much anxiety to the court of Rome."

Such from the commencement was the view Charles took of the Reformation. It was of no importance for him to know on which side truth or error might be found, or to discern what the great interests of the German nation required. His only question was what policy demanded and what should be done to induce the pope to support the emperor. And this was well known at Rome. Charles's ministers intimated to Aleander the course their master intended following. "The emperor," said they, "will behave toward the pope as he behaves toward the emperor; for he has no desire to increase the power of his rivals, and particularly of the king of France."

At these words the imperious nuncio gave way to his indignation. "What!" replied he. "Supposing the pope should abandon the emperor, must the latter renounce his religion? If Charles wishes to avenge himself thus . . . let him tremble; this baseness will turn against himself." But the nuncio's threats did not shake the imperial diplomatists.

Chapter 35
The Diet of Worms Convenes

The Reformation, commenced by the struggles of a humble spirit in the cell of a cloister at Erfurt, had continually increased. An obscure individual, bearing in his hand the Word of Life, had stood firm before the mighty ones of the world, and they had shaken before him. He had wielded this arm of the Word of God, first against Tetzel and his numerous army; and those greedy merchants, after a brief struggle, had fled away. He next employed it against the Roman legate at Augsburg; and the legate in amazement had allowed the prey to escape him. Somewhat later with its aid he contended against the champions of learning in the halls of Leipzig; and the astonished theologians had beheld their syllogistic weapons shivered in their hands. Lastly, with this single arm, he had opposed the pope, when the latter, disturbed in his slumbers, had risen on his throne to blast the unfortunate monk with his thunders; and this same Word had paralyzed all the power of this head of Christendom. A final struggle remained to be undergone. The Word was destined to triumph over the emperor of the West, over the kings and princes of the earth; and then, victorious over all the powers of the world, to rise in the church and reign as the very Word of God.

The entire nation was agitated. Princes and nobles, knights and citizens, clergy and laity, town and country—all participated in the struggle. A mighty religious revolution, of which God Himself was the prime mover, but which was also deeply rooted in the lives of the people, threatened to overthrow the long-venerated chief of the Roman hierarchy. A new generation, of a serious, deep, active, and energetic spirit, filled the universities, cities, courts, castles, rural districts, and frequently even the cloisters. A presentiment that a great transformation of society was at hand inspired all minds with holy enthusiasm. What would be the position of the emperor with regard to this movement of the age; and what would be the end of this formidable impulse by which all men were carried along?

A solemn diet was about to be opened: this was the first assembly of the empire over which Charles was to preside. As Nuremberg, where it should have been held, in accordance with the Golden Bull, was suffering from the plague, it was convoked to meet at Worms on January 6, 1521. Never before had so many princes met together in diet; each one was desirous of participating in this first act of the young emperor's government and was pleased at the opportunity of displaying his power. The youthful landgrave Philip of Hesse, among others, arrived at Worms about the middle of January with six hundred horsemen, among whom were warriors celebrated for their valor.

But a much stronger motive inclined the electors, dukes, archbishops, landgraves, margraves, counts, bishops, barons, and lords of the empire, as well as the deputies of the towns, and the ambassadors of the kings of Christendom, to throng with their brilliant trains the roads that led to Worms. It had been announced that among other important matters to be laid before the diet, would be the nomination of a council of regency to govern the empire during Charles's absence, and the jurisdiction of the imperial chamber; but public attention was more particularly directed to another question, which the emperor had also mentioned in his letters of convocation—that of the Reformation. The great interests of worldly policy grew pale before the cause of the monk of Wittenberg. It was this which formed the principal topic of conversation between the noble personages who arrived at Worms.

Everything announced that the diet would be stormy and difficult to manage. Charles, who was hardly twenty years of age, was pale, of weak health, and yet a graceful horseman, able to break a lance like others of his time. His character was as yet undeveloped; his air was grave and melancholy, although of a kindly expression, and he had not hitherto shown any remarkable talent, and did not appear to have adopted any decided line of conduct. Numerous ambitions here met; many passions came into collision; the Spaniards and the Belgians vied with each other in their exertions to creep into the counsels of the young prince; the nuncios multiplied their intrigues; the German princes spoke out boldly. It might easily be foreseen that the underhanded practices of parties would have a principal share in the struggle.

Emperor Charles V of the Holy Roman Empire in 1531, from an engraving by Bartel Beham

But over all these scenes of agitation hovered a terrible will—the Roman papacy, which, inflexible as the destiny of the ancients, had unceasingly crushed for ages past every doctor, king, or people that had opposed its tyrannous progress. We shall soon behold Rome busy at her task.

Charles opened the diet on January 28, 1521, the festival of Charlemagne. His mind was filled with the high importance of the imperial dignity. He said, in his opening discourse, that no monarchy could be compared with the Roman Empire, to which nearly the whole world had submitted in former times; that unfortunately this empire was a mere shadow of what it once had been; but that, by means of his kingdoms and powerful alliances, he hoped to restore it to its ancient glory.

But numerous difficulties immediately presented themselves to the young emperor. What must he do, placed between the papal nuncio and the elector to whom he was indebted for his crown? How can he avoid displeasing either Aleander or Frederick? The first entreated the emperor to execute the pope's bull, and the second besought him to take no steps against the monk until he had been heard. Desirous of pleasing both parties, the young prince, during his stay at Oppenheim, had written to the elector to bring Luther with him to the diet, assuring him that no injustice would be shown to the reformer, that no violence should be used toward him, and that learned men should confer with him.

This letter threw the elector into great perplexity. At every moment the alliance of the pope might become necessary to the young and ambitious emperor, and then Luther's fate was sealed. If Frederick should take the reformer to Worms, he might be leading him to the scaffold. And yet Charles's orders were precise.

Luther's friends were alarmed, but he himself did not tremble. His health was at that time very weak; but that was a trifling matter for him. "If I cannot go to Worms in good health," replied he to the elector, "I will be carried there, sick as I am. For if the emperor calls me, I cannot doubt that it is the call of God Himself. If they desire to use violence against me, and that is very probable—for it is not for their instruction that they order me to appear—I place the matter in the Lord's hands. He still lives and reigns who preserved the three young men in the burning fiery furnace. If He will not save me, my life is of little consequence. Let us only prevent the gospel from being exposed to the scorn of the wicked, and let us shed our blood for it, for fear they should triumph. It is not for me to decide whether my life or my death will contribute most to the salvation of all. Let us pray God that our young emperor may not begin his reign by dipping his hands in my blood. . . . You may expect everything from me . . . except flight and recantation. Fly I cannot, and still less retract."

Before receiving Luther's reply, the elector had formed his resolution. This prince, who was advancing in the knowledge of the gospel, now became more decided in his conduct. He felt that the conference at Worms would not have a favorable result. "It appears a difficult matter," he wrote in reply to Charles, "to bring Luther with me to Worms; I beseech you to relieve me from this anxiety. Furthermore, I have never been willing to defend his doctrine, but only to prevent his being condemned without a hearing. The legates, without waiting for your orders, have permitted themselves to take a step at once dishonoring Luther and myself; and I much fear that they thus dragged Luther to commit a very imprudent act, which might expose him to great danger if he were to appear before the diet." The elector alluded to the burning of the papal bull.

But the rumor of Luther's coming was already current through the city. Men eager for novelty were delighted; the emperor's courtiers were alarmed; but none showed greater indignation than the papal legate. On his journey, Aleander had been able to discover how far the gospel announced by Luther had found an echo in all classes of society. Men of letters, lawyers, nobles, the inferior clergy, the regular orders, and the people, were gained over to the Reformation. These friends of the new doctrine walked boldly with heads erect; their language was fearless and daring; an invincible terror froze the hearts of the partisans of Rome. The papacy was still standing, but its buttresses were tottering; for their ears already distinguished a presage of destruction, like that indistinct murmur heard ere the mountain falls and crumbles into dust.

Aleander on the road to Worms was frequently unable to contain himself. If he desired to dine or sleep in any place, neither the learned, the nobles, nor the priests, even among the supposed partisans of Rome, dared receive him; and the haughty nuncio was obliged to seek a lodging at inns of the lowest class. Aleander was frightened and began to think his life in danger. Thus he arrived at

Worms, and to his Roman fanaticism was then superadded the feeling of the personal indignities he had suffered. He immediately used every exertion to prevent the appearance of the bold and formidable Luther. "Would it not be scandalous," said he, "to behold laymen examining anew a cause already condemned by the pope?"

Aleander pressed Charles closely: he entreated, threatened, and spoke as the nuncio of the head of the church. Charles submitted, and wrote to the elector that the time accorded to Luther having already elapsed, this monk lay under the papal excommunication; so that, if he would not retract what he had written, Frederick must leave him behind at Wittenberg. But this prince had already quitted Saxony without Luther. "I pray the Lord to be favorable to our elector," said Melancthon, as he saw him depart. "It is on him all our hopes for the restoration of Christendom repose. His enemies will dare anything, (and they will not leave a stone unturned); but God will confound the counsels of Ahithophel. As for us, let us maintain our share of the combat by our teaching and by our prayers." Luther was deeply grieved at being forbidden to come to Worms.

It was not sufficient for Aleander that Luther did not appear at Worms; he desired his condemnation. He was continually soliciting the princes, prelates, and different members of the diet; he accused the Augustinian monk not only of disobedience and heresy, but even of sedition, rebellion, impiety, and blasphemy. But the very tone of his voice betrayed the passions by which he was animated. Some persons observed to him that the papal bull had only condemned Luther conditionally; others could not altogether conceal the joy they felt at this humiliation of the haughtiness of Rome. The emperor's ministers on the one hand, the ecclesiastical electors on the other, showed a marked coldness: the former, that the pope might feel the necessity of leaguing with their master; the latter, that the pontiff might purchase their support at a dearer price. A feeling of Luther's innocence predominated in the assembly; and Aleander could not contain his indignation.

But the coldness of the diet made the legate less impatient than the coldness of Rome. Rome, which had had so much difficulty in taking a serious view of this quarrel of a "drunken German," did not imagine that the bull of the sovereign pontiff would be ineffectual to humiliate and reduce him. She had resumed all her carelessness, and sent neither additional bulls nor money. But how could they bring this matter to an issue without money? Rome must be awakened. Aleander uttered a cry of alarm. "Germany is separating from Rome," wrote he to the Cardinal de Medici; "the princes are separating from the pope. Yet a little more delay, yet a little more negotiation, and hope will be gone. Money, money, or Germany is lost."

Rome awoke at this cry; the vassals of the papacy, emerging from their torpor, hastily forged their redoubtable thunderbolts in the Vatican. The pope issued a new bull; and the excommunication, with which the heretical doctor had as yet been only threatened, was decidedly pronounced against him and all his adherents. Rome, by breaking the last tie which still bound him to the church, augmented Luther's liberty, and with increased liberty came an increase of strength. Cursed by the pope, he took refuge with fresh love at the feet of Christ. Ejected from the outward courts of the temple, he felt more strongly that he was himself a temple in which dwelt the living God.

Rome rejected him with violence. The reformer and all his partisans were accursed, whatever their rank and power, and dispossessed, with their inheritors, of all their honors and goods. Every faithful Christian who valued the salvation of his soul, was to flee at the sight of this accursed band. Wherever the heresy had been introduced, the priests were enjoined, on Sundays and festivals, at the hour when the churches were thronged with worshipers, to publish the excommunication with due solemnity. The altars were to be stripped of their ornaments and sacred vessels; the cross to be laid on the ground; twelve priests holding tapers in their hands were first to light them, and immediately dashing them violently to the earth, to extinguish them under their feet; the bishop was then to proclaim the condemnation of these unbelievers; all the bells were to be rung; the bishops and priests were to utter their anathemas and maledictions and preach boldly against Luther and his adherents.

The excommunication had been published in Rome twenty-two days, but probably had not yet reached Germany, when Luther, being informed that there was another talk of summoning him to Worms, wrote a letter to the elector, drawn up in such a manner that Frederick might show it to the diet. Luther was desirous of correcting the erroneous ideas of the princes, and of frankly laying before this august tribunal the true nature of a cause so misunderstood. "I rejoice with all my heart, most serene lord," says he, "that his imperial majesty desires to summon me before him touching this affair. I call Jesus Christ to witness, that it is the cause of the whole German nation, of the universal church, of the Christian world, nay, of God Himself . . . and not of an individual, especially such a one as myself. I am ready to go to Worms, provided I have a safe-conduct, and learned, pious, and impartial judges. I am ready to answer . . . for it is not from a presumptuous spirit, nor to derive any advantage that I have taught the doctrine with which I am reproached: it is in obedience to my conscience and to my oath as doctor of the Holy Scriptures; it is for the glory of God, for the salvation of the Christian church, for the good of the German nation, and for the extirpation of so much superstition, abuse, evil, scandal, tyranny, blasphemy, and impiety."

Chapter 36
Conflict and Controversy at Worms

But all this was of little consequence to politicians. However noble might have been the idea Charles had formed of the imperial dignity, Germany was not the center of his interests and of his policy. He understood neither the spirit nor the language of Germany. He was always a duke of Burgundy, who to many other scepters had united the first crown of Christendom. It was a remarkable circumstance that, at the moment of its most intimate transformation, Germany should elect a foreign prince, to whom the necessities and tendencies of the nation were but of secondary importance.

Undoubtedly the emperor was not indifferent to the religious movement, but it had no meaning in his eyes except so far as it threatened the pope. War between Charles and Francis I was inevitable; the principal scene of that war would be Italy. The alliance of the pope became therefore daily more necessary to Charles's projects. He would have preferred detaching Frederick from Luther or satisfying the pope without offending Frederick. Many of his courtiers manifested in the affair of the Augustinian monk that disdainful coldness which politicians generally affect when there is any question of religion. "Let us avoid all extreme measures," said they. "Let us entangle Luther by negotiations and reduce him to silence by some trifling concessions. The proper course is to stifle, and not to fan the flame."

Charles's confessor, John Glapio, a man of great weight, a skillful courtier, and a wily monk, took upon himself the execution of the scheme. Glapio possessed the full confidence of Charles; and this prince, imitating the Spanish customs in this particular, entrusted him almost entirely with the care of matters pertaining to religion. As soon as Charles had been named emperor, Leo hastened to win over Glapio by favors which the confessor very gratefully acknowledged. He could make no better return to the pontiff's generosity than by crushing this heresy, and he applied himself to the task.

Among the elector's councilors was Gregory Bruck, or Pontanus, the chancellor, a man of intelligence, decision, and courage, who was a better theological scholar than many doctors, and whose wisdom was capable of resisting the wiles of the monks in Charles's court. Glapio, knowing the chancellor's influence, requested an interview with him, and introducing himself as if he had been a friend of the reformer, said with an air of kindness, "I was filled with joy, in reading Luther's first writings; I thought him a vigorous tree, which had put forth goodly branches, and gave promise to the church of the most precious fruit. Many people, it is true, have entertained the same views before his time; yet no one but himself has had the noble courage to publish the truth without fear. But when I read his book *The Babylonian Captivity,* I felt like one overwhelmed with blows from head to foot. I do not think," added the monk, "that brother Martin will acknowledge himself to be the author of it; I do not find in it either his usual style or learning." After some discussion, the confessor continued, "Introduce me to the elector, and in your presence I will show him Luther's errors."

The chancellor replied that the business of the diet left his highness no leisure, and besides, he did not mix himself up with this matter. "Nevertheless," continued the chancellor, "since you say there is no evil without a remedy, explain yourself."

Assuming a confidential air, the confessor replied, "The emperor earnestly desires to see a man like Luther reconciled with the church; for his books, previous to the publication of *The Babylonian Captivity,* were rather agreeable to his majesty. . . . The irritation caused by the bull no doubt excited Luther to write the latter work. Let him then declare that he had no intention of troubling the repose of the church, and the learned of every nation will side with him. . . . Let Luther deny that he wrote *The Babylonian Captivity.*"

The Chancellor: But the pope's bull condemns all his other writings.

The Confessor: That is because of his obstinacy. If he disclaims this book, the pope in his omnipotence can easily pardon him. What hopes may we not entertain, now that we have so excellent an emperor?

Perceiving that these words had produced some effect on the chancellor, the monk hastily added, "Luther always desires to argue from the Bible. The Bible . . . it is like wax; you may stretch it and bend it as you please. I would undertake to find in the Bible opinions more extravagant even than Luther's. He is mistaken when he changes every word of Christ into a commandment." And then wishing to act upon the fears of his hearers, he added, "What would be the result, if today or tomorrow the emperor should have recourse to arms? Reflect upon this." He then permitted Pontanus to retire.

"What an excellent book is that of Luther's on Christian liberty," said the confessor to the chancellor, whom he saw again a few days after; "what wisdom, what talent, what wit; it is thus that a real scholar ought to write. . . . Let both sides choose men of irreproachable character, and let the pope and Luther refer the whole matter to their decision. There is no doubt that Luther would come off victorious on many points. I will speak about it to the emperor. Believe me, I do not mention these things solely on my own authority. I have told the emperor that God would chastise him and all the princes if the church, which is the spouse of Christ, be not cleansed from all the stains that defile her. I added that God Himself had sent Luther and commissioned him to reprove men from their offenses, employing him as a scourge to punish the sins of the world."

The chancellor, on hearing these words, which reflected the feelings of the age and showed the opinion entertained of Luther even by his adversaries, could not forbear expressing his astonishment that his master was not treated with more respect. "There are daily consultations with the emperor on this affair," said he, "and yet the elector is not invited to them. He thinks it strange that the emperor, who is not a little indebted to him, should exclude him from his councils."

The Confessor: I have been present only once at these deliberations, and then heard the emperor resist the solicitations of the nuncios. Five years hence it will be seen what Charles has done for the reformation of the church.

"The elector," answered Pontanus, "is unacquainted with Luther's intentions. Let him be summoned and have a hearing."

The confessor replied with a deep sigh, "I call God to witness how ardently I desire to see the reformation of Christendom accomplished."

Such were the maneuvers resorted to by the courtiers. They were disconcerted by the firmness of Pontanus. That just man was immovable as a rock during all these negotiations. Not only were the artifices of the confessor ineffectual, but his admissions still more confirmed Frederick in his opinion that Luther was right and that it was his duty to protect him.

Aleander grew uneasy and displayed unusual energy. It was no longer against the elector and Luther alone that he had to contend. He beheld with horror the secret negotiations of the confessor, the proposition of the prior, the consent of Charles's ministers, the extreme coldness of Roman piety, even among the most devoted friends of the pontiff, "so that one might have thought," says Pallavicini, "that a torrent of iced water had gushed over them." He had at length received from Rome the money he had demanded; he held in his hand the energetic briefs addressed to the most powerful men in the empire. Fearing to see his prey escape, he felt that now was the time to strike a decisive blow. He forwarded the briefs, scattered the money profusely, and made the most alluring promises; "and armed with this threefold weapon," says the historian Cardinal Pallavicini, "he made a fresh attempt to bias the wavering assembly of electors in the pope's favor."

But around the emperor in particular he laid his snares. He took advantage of the dissensions existing between the Belgian and Spanish ministers. He besieged the monarch unceasingly. All the partisans of Rome, awakened by his voice, solicited Charles. "Daily deliberations," wrote the elector to his brother John, "are held against Luther; they demand that he shall be placed under the ban of the pope and of the emperor; they endeavor to injure him in every way. Those who parade in their red hats, the Romans, with all their followers, display indefatigable zeal in this task."

Aleander was in reality pressing for the condemnation of the reformer with a violence that Luther characterizes as marvelous fury. The apostate nuncio, as Luther styles him, transported by anger beyond the bounds of prudence, one day exclaimed, "If you Germans pretend to shake off the yoke of obedience to Rome, we will act in such a manner that, exterminated by mutual slaughter, you shall perish in your own blood." "This is how the pope feeds Christ's sheep," adds the reformer.

Charles V could not resist the solicitation of the nuncio. The pope had addressed him in a brief, entreating him to give the power of law to the bull by an imperial edict. "To no purpose will God have invested you with the sword of the supreme power," said he, "if you do not employ it, not only against the infidels, but against the heretics also, who are far worse than they." Accordingly, one day at the beginning of February, at the moment when everyone in Worms was making preparations for a splendid tournament, and the emperor's tent was already erected, the princes, who were arming themselves to take part in the brilliant show, were summoned to the imperial palace. After listening to the reading of the papal bull, a stringent edict was laid before them, enjoining its immediate execution. "If you can recommend any better course," added the emperor, following the usual custom, "I am ready to hear you."

An animated debate immediately took place in the assembly. "This monk," wrote a deputy from one of the free cities of Germany, "gives us plenty of occupation. Some would like to crucify him, and I think that he will not escape; only it is to be feared that he will rise again the third day." The emperor had imagined that he would be able to publish his edict without opposition from the states, but such was not the case. Their minds were not prepared. It was necessary to gain over the diet. "Convince this assembly," said the youthful monarch to the nuncio. This was all that Aleander desired, and he was promised to be introduced to the diet on February 13.

The nuncio prepared for this solemn audience. This was an important duty, but Aleander was not unworthy of it. Ambassador from the sovereign pontiff and surrounded with all the splendor of his high office, he was also one of the most eloquent men of his age. The friends of the Reformation looked forward to this sitting with apprehension. The elector, pretending indisposition, was not present; but he gave some of his councilors orders to attend and take notes of the nuncio's speech.

When the day arrived, Aleander proceeded toward the assembly of the princes. Never had Rome been called to make its defense before so august an assembly. The nuncio placed before him the documents that he had judged necessary, namely, Luther's works and the papal bulls; and as soon as the diet was silent he began:

"Most august emperor, most mighty princes, most excellent deputies—I appear before you in defense of a cause for which my heart glows with the most ardent affection. It is to retain on my master's head that triple crown which you all adore; to maintain that papal throne for which I should be willing to deliver my body to the flames, if the monster that has engendered this growing heresy that I am now to combat could be consumed at the same stake, and mingle his ashes with mine.

"No, the whole difference between Luther and the pope does not turn on the papal interests. I have Luther's books before me, and a man only needs have eyes in his head to see that he attacks the holy doctrines of the church. He teaches that those alone communicate worthily whose consciences are overwhelmed with sorrow and confusion because of their sins; and that no one is justified by baptism, if he has not faith in the promise of which baptism is the pledge. He denies the necessity of works to obtain heavenly glory. He denies that we have the liberty and power of obeying the natural and divine law. He asserts that we sin of necessity in every one of our actions. Has the arsenal of hell ever sent forth weapons better calculated to break the bonds of decency? ... He preaches in favor of the abolition of monastic vows. Can we imagine any greater sacrilegious impiety? ...

"Shall I enumerate all the crimes of this Augustinian monk? He sins against the dead, for he denies purgatory; he sins against heaven, for he says that he would not believe even an angel from heaven; he sins against the church, for he maintains that all Christians are priests; he sins against the saints, for he despises their venerable writings; he sins against councils, for he designates that of Constance an assembly of devils; he sins against the world, for he forbids the punishment of death to be inflicted on any who have not committed a deadly sin. Some of you may say that he is a pious man. ... I have no desire to attack his life, but only to remind this assembly that the Devil often deceives people in the garb of truth."

Aleander, after having thus accused Luther, proceeded to the second point, which was to justify Rome:

"At Rome, says Luther, the mouth promises one thing, the hand does another. If this were true, must we not come to the very opposite conclusion? If the ministers of a religion live conformably to its precepts, it is a sign that the religion is false. Such was the religion of the ancient Romans. . . . Such is that of Mohammed and of Luther himself, but such is not the religion which the Roman pontiffs teach us. Yes, the doctrine they profess condemns them all, as having committed faults; many, as guilty; and some—I will speak frankly—as criminal. . . . This doctrine exposes their actions to the censure of men during their lives, to the brand of history after their death. Now I would ask what pleasure or profit could the popes have found in inventing such a religion?

"The church, it may be said, was not governed by the Roman pontiffs in the primitive ages. What conclusion shall we draw from this? With such arguments we might persuade men to feed on acorns, and princesses to wash their own linen."

But his adversary, the reformer, was the special object of the nuncio's hatred. "Luther will not allow himself to be instructed by anyone. The pope had already summoned him to Rome, and he did not comply. Next, the pope cited him before the legate at Augsburg, and he did not appear until he had procured a safe-conduct, that is to say, after the legate's hands were tied, and his tongue alone was left unfettered."

"Ah," said Aleander, turning toward Charles V, "I entreat your imperial majesty to do nothing that may lead to your reproach. Do not interfere in a matter which does not concern the laity. Perform your own duties. Let Luther's doctrines be interdicted by you throughout the length and breadth of the empire; let his writings be burnt everywhere. Fear not. In Luther's errors there is enough to burn a hundred thousand heretics. . . . And what have we to fear? The multitude? . . . Its insolence makes it appear terrible before the conflict, but in the battle its cowardice renders it contemptible. Foreign princes? . . . But the king of France has forbidden the introduction of Luther's doctrines into his kingdom, and the king of England is preparing an assault with his own royal hand. You know what are the sentiments of Hungary, Italy, and Spain; and there is not one of your neighbors, however much he may hate you, who wishes you so much evil as this heresy would cause you. For if our adversary's house adjoins our own, we may desire it to be visited with fever, but not with the plague. . . .

"What are all these Lutherans? A crew of insolent pedagogues, corrupt priests, dissolute monks, ignorant lawyers, and degraded nobles, with the common people, whom they have misled and perverted. How far superior to them is the Catholic party in number, ability, and power. A unanimous decree from this illustrious assembly will enlighten the simple, warn the imprudent, decide the waverers, and give strength to the weak. . . . But if the axe is not put to the roots of this poisonous tree, if the deathblow is not struck, then . . . I see it overshadowing the heritage of Jesus Christ with its branches, changing our Lord's vineyard into a gloomy forest, transforming the kingdom of God into a den of wild beasts, and reducing Germany into that frightful state of barbarism and desolation which has been brought upon Asia by the superstition of Mohammed."

The nuncio was silent. He had spoken for three hours. The enthusiasm of his language had produced a deep impression on the assembly. No one rose to speak. The assembly remained under the impression produced by this speech; and agitated and transported, showed itself ready to extirpate Luther's heresy by force from the soil of the empire.

Nevertheless, it was a victory only in appearance. A few days were sufficient to dissipate the first impression, as is ever the case when an orator conceals the emptiness of his arguments by high-sounding words.

The majority of the princes were ready to sacrifice Luther, but no one desired to immolate the rights of the empire and the grievances of the Germanic nation. They were very ready to give up the insolent monk who had dared to speak so boldly, but they were the more resolved to make the pope feel the justice of a reform demanded by the chiefs of the nation. It was accordingly Luther's most determined personal enemy, Duke George of Saxony, who spoke with the greatest energy against the encroachments of Rome.

This grandson of Podiebrad, king of Bohemia, although offended by the doctrine of grace preached by the reformer, had not yet lost the hope of a moral and ecclesiastical reform. The principal cause of his irritation against the monk of Wittenberg was that by his despised doctrines he was spoiling the whole affair. But now, seeing the nuncio affecting to involve Luther and the reform of the church in one and the same condemnation, George suddenly rose in the assembly of the princes, to the great astonishment of those who knew his hatred of the reformer.

"The diet, " said he, "must not forget its grievances against the court of Rome. How many abuses have crept into our states: the annats, which the emperor granted voluntarily for the good of Christianity, now exacted as a due; the Roman courtiers daily inventing new regulations to monopolize, sell, and ease the ecclesiastical benefices; a multitude of transgressions connived at; rich transgressors undeservedly tolerated, while those who have no money to purchase impunity are punished without mercy; . . . stalls for the sale of indulgences set up in every street and public place of our cities—stalls of St. Anthony, of the Holy Ghost, of St. Hubert, of St. Cornelius, of St. Vincent, and so forth; companies purchasing at Rome the right to hold such markets, then buying permission of their bishop to display their wares, and squeezing and draining the pockets of the poor to obtain money; the indulgence, that ought only to be granted for the salvation of souls, and that should be earned by prayer, fasting, and works of charity, sold according to a tariff; the bishops' officials oppressing the lowly with penances for blasphemy, adultery, debauchery, and the violation of any festival, but not even reprimanding the clergy who commit similar crimes; penalties imposed on those who repent, and devised in such a manner that they soon fall again into the same error and give more money; . . . these are some of the abuses that cry out against Rome.

"All shame has been put aside, and their only object is . . . money, money, money, . . . so that the preachers who should teach the truth utter nothing but falsehoods, and are not only tolerated, but rewarded, because the greater their lies, the greater their gain. It is from this foul spring that such tainted waters flow. . . . Alas, it is the scandal caused by the clergy that hurls so many poor souls into eternal condemnation. A general reform must be effected. An ecumenical council must be called to bring about this reform. For these reasons, most excellent princes and lords, I humbly entreat you to take this matter into your immediate consideration." Duke George then handed in a list of the grievances he had enumerated. This was some days after Aleander's speech.

Even Luther had not spoken with greater force against the abuses of Rome, but he had done something more. The duke pointed out the evil; Luther had pointed out both the cause and the remedy. He had demonstrated that the sinner receives the true indulgence, that which cometh from God, solely by faith in the grace and merits of Jesus Christ; and this simple but powerful doctrine had over-thrown all the markets established by the priests. "How can a man become pious?" asked he one day. "A gray friar will reply, 'By putting on a gray hood and girding yourself with a cord.' A Roman will answer, 'By hearing mass and by fasting.' But a Christian will say, 'Faith in Christ alone justifies and saves. Before works, we must have eternal life. But when we are born again and made children of God by the word of grace, then we perform good works.'" The duke's speech was that of a secular prince; Luther's, that of a reformer.

Chapter 37
Luther Summoned to Worms

The duke's speech produced a proportionally greater impression, as his hostility to Luther was notorious. Other members of the diet brought forward their respective grievances, which received the support of the ecclesiastical princes themselves. "We have a pontiff who loves only the chase and his pleasures," said they; "the benefices of the German nation are given away at Rome to gunners, falconers, footmen, donkey-drivers, grooms, guardsmen, and other people of this class, ignorant, inexperienced, and strangers to Germany."

The diet appointed a committee to draw up all these grievances; they were found to amount to a hundred and one. A deputation composed of secular and ecclesiastical princes presented the report to the emperor, conjuring him to see them rectified, as he had engaged to do in his capitulation. "What a loss of Christian souls," said they to Charles V; "what depredations, what extortions, on account of the scandals by which the spiritual head of Christendom is surrounded. It is our duty to prevent the ruin and dishonor of our people. For this reason we most humbly but most urgently entreat you to order a general reformation, and to undertake its accomplishment."

Charles could not be insensible to the remonstrances of the empire. Neither he nor the nuncio had expected them. Even his confessor had threatened him with the vengeance of heaven, unless he reformed the church. The emperor immediately recalled the edict commanding Luther's writings to be burnt throughout the empire, and substituted a provisional order to deliver these books into the keeping of the magistrates.

This did not satisfy the assembly, which desired the appearance of the reformer. It is unjust, said his friends, to condemn Luther without a hearing and without learning from his own mouth whether he is the author of the books that are ordered to be burnt. His doctrines, said his adversaries, have so taken hold of men's minds that it is impossible to check their progress, unless we hear them from himself. There shall be no discussion with him; and if he avows his writings and refuses to retract them, then we will all with one accord, electors, princes, estates of the holy empire, true to the faith of our ancestors, assist your majesty to the utmost of our power in the execution of your decrees.

The man who thus moved all the powers of the earth seemed alone undisturbed. The news from Worms was alarming. Luther's friends were terrified. "There remains nothing for us but your good wishes and prayers," wrote Melancthon to Spalatin. "Oh that God would deign to purchase at the price of our blood the salvation of the Christian world." But Luther was a stranger to fear; shutting himself up in his quiet cell, he there meditated on and applied to himself those words in which Mary the mother of Jesus exclaims, "My soul doth magnify the Lord, and my spirit hath rejoiced in God my Savior. . . . For he that is mighty hath done to me great things; and holy is his name. . . . He hath showed strength with his arm; . . . he hath put down the mighty from their seats, and exalted them of low degree . . ." (Luke 1:46-55). These are some of the reflections that filled Luther's heart: *He that is mighty . . . says Mary. What great boldness on the part of a young girl. With a single word she brands all the strong with weakness, all the mighty with feebleness, all the wise with folly, all those whose name is glorious upon earth with disgrace, and casts all strength, all might, all wisdom, and all glory at the feet of God.

"*His arm,* continues she, meaning by this the power by which He acts of Himself, without the aid of any of His creatures; by mysterious power, . . . which is exerted in secrecy and in silence until His designs are accomplished. Destruction is at hand, when no one has seen it coming; relief is there, and no one had suspected it. He leaves His children in oppression and weakness, so that every man says, They are lost. . . . But it is then He is strongest; for where the strength of men ends, there begins that of God. Only let faith wait upon Him. . . . And on the other hand, God permits His adversaries to increase in grandeur and power. He withdraws His support, and suffers them to be puffed up with their own. He empties them of His eternal wisdom and lets them be filled with their own, which is but for a day. And while they are rising in the brightness of their power, the arm of the Lord is taken away, and their work vanishes as a bubble bursting in the air."

It was on March 10, at the very moment when the imperial city of Worms was filled with dread at his name, that Luther concluded this explanation of the *Magnificat.*

He was not left quiet in his retreat. Spalatin, in conformity with the elector's orders, sent him a note of the articles which he would be required to retract. "Fear not," wrote he to Spalatin, "that I shall retract a single syllable, since their only argument is that my works are opposed to the rites of what they call the church. If the Emperor Charles summons me only that I may retract, I shall reply that I will remain here, and it will be the same as if I had gone to Worms and returned. But on the contrary, if the emperor summons me that I may be put to death as an enemy of the empire, I am ready to comply with his call; for with the help of Christ, I will never desert the Word on the battlefield. I am well aware that these bloodthirsty men will never rest until they have taken away my life. Would that it were the papists alone that would be guilty of my blood."

At last the emperor made up his mind. Luther's appearance before the diet seemed the only means calculated to terminate an affair which engaged the attention of all the empire. Charles V resolved to summon him, but without granting him a safe-conduct. Here Frederick was again compelled to assume the character of a protector. The dangers by which the reformer was threatened were apparent to all. Luther's friends feared that he would be delivered into the pope's hands, or that the emperor himself would put him to death, as undeserving, on account of his heresy, that any faith should be kept with him. On this question there was a long and violent debate between the princes. Struck at last by the extensive agitation then stirring up the people in every part of Germany, and fearing that during Luther's journey some unexpected tumult or dangerous commotion might burst forth in favor of the reformer, the princes thought the wisest course would be to tranquilize the public feelings on this subject; and not only the emperor, but also the elector of Saxony, Duke George, and the landgrave of Hesse, through whose territories he would have to pass, gave him each a safe-conduct.

On March 6, 1521, Charles V signed the following summons addressed to Luther:

Honorable, well-beloved, and pious—We and the states of the holy empire here assembled, having resolved to institute an inquiry touching the doctrine and the books that thou hast lately published, have issued, for thy coming hither and thy return to a place of security, our safe-conduct and that of the empire, which we sent thee herewith. Our sincere desire is that thou shouldst prepare immediately for this journey, in order that within the space of the twenty-one days fixed by our safe-conduct, thou mayest without fail be present before us. Fear neither injustice nor violence. We will firmly abide by our aforesaid safe-conduct, and expect that thou wilt comply with our summons. In so doing, thou wilt obey our earnest wishes.

Given in our imperial city of Worms, the sixth day of March, in the year of our Lord 1521, and the second of our reign.

CHARLES

Gaspard Sturm was commissioned to bear this message to the reformer and accompany him to Worms. The elector, apprehending an outburst of public indignation, wrote on March 12 to the magistrates of Wittenberg to provide for the security of the emperor's officer and to give him a guard, if it was judged necessary. The herald departed.

Thus were God's designs fulfilled. It was His will that this light, which He had kindled in the world, should be set upon a hill; and emperor, kings, and princes immediately began to carry out his purpose without knowing it. It costs Him little to elevate what is lowliest. A single act of His power sufficed to raise the humble native of Mansfeldt from an obscure cottage to the palaces in which kings were assembled. In His sight there is neither small nor great, and in His good time Charles and Luther met.

But would Luther comply with this citation? His best friends were doubtful about it. "Doctor Martin has been summoned here," wrote the elector to his brother on March 25, "but I do not know whether he will come. I cannot augur any good from it." Three weeks later, on April 16, this excellent prince, seeing the danger increase, wrote again to Duke John, "Orders against Luther are placarded on the walls. The cardinals and bishops are attacking him very harshly; God grant that all may turn out well. Would to God that I could procure him a favorable hearing."

It was now March 24. At last the imperial herald had passed the gate of the city in which Luther resided. Gaspard Sturm waited upon the doctor and delivered the citation from Charles V. What a serious and solemn moment for the reformer! All his friends were in consternation. No prince, without exception Frederick the Wise, had declared for him. The knights, it is true, had given utterance to their threats; but them the powerful Charles despised.

Luther, however, was not discomposed. "The papists," said he, on seeing the anguish of his friends, "do not desire my coming to Worms, but my condemnation and my death. It matters not. Pray not for me, but for the Word of God. Before my blood has grown cold, thousands of men in the whole world will have become responsible for having shed it. The most holy adversary of Christ, the father, the master, the generalissimo of murderers, insists on its being shed. So be it. Let God's will be done. Christ will give me His Spirit to overcome these ministers of error. I despise them during my life; I shall triumph over them by my death. They are busy at Worms about compelling me to retract; and this shall be my retraction: I said formerly that the pope was Christ's vicar; now I assert that he is our Lord's adversary, and the Devil's apostle."

At this time there arrived at Wittenberg a man who, like Melancthon, was destined to be Luther's friend all his life, and to comfort him at the moment of his departure. This was a priest named Bugenhagen, thirty-six years of age, who had fled from the severities which the bishop of Camin and Prince Bogislas of Pomerania exercised on the friends of the gospel, whether ecclesiastics, citizens, or men of letters. Sprung from a senatorial family, and born at Wollin in Pomerania, Bugenhagen had been teaching at Treptow from the age of twenty years. He diligently studied the Holy Scriptures, praying God to enlighten him.

One day toward the end of December 1520, Luther's book *The Babylonian Captivity of the Church* was put into his hands as he sat at supper with several of his friends. "Since the death of Christ," said he, after running his eye over the pages, "many heretics have infested the church; but never yet has there existed such a pest as the author of this work." Having taken the book home and perused it two or three times, all his opinions were changed; truths quite new to him presented themselves to his mind; and on returning some days after to his colleagues, he said, "The whole world has fallen into the thickest darkness. This man alone sees the light." Several priests, a deacon, and the abbot himself, received the pure doctrine of salvation; and in a short time, by the power of their preaching, they led their hearers, says a historian, back from human superstitions to the sole and effectual merits of Jesus Christ. Upon this a persecution broke out. Already the prisons reechoed with the groans of many individuals. Bugenhagen fled from his enemies and arrived at Wittenberg. "He is suffering for love to the gospel," wrote Melancthon to the elector's chaplain. "Whither could he fly, but to our asylum, and to the protection of our prince?"

But no one welcomed Bugenhagen with greater joy than Luther. It was agreed between them that immediately after the departure of the reformer Bugenhagen should begin to lecture on the Psalms. It was thus divine Providence led this able man to supply in some measure the place of him whom Wittenberg was about to lose. A year later, Bugenhagen was placed at the head of the church in this city, over which he presided thirty-six years. Luther styled him in a special manner "the Pastor."

Luther was about to depart. His friends, in alarm, thought that if God did not interpose in a miraculous manner, he was going to certain death. Melancthon desired to accompany Luther in his dangers; but their common friends, and no doubt the doctor himself, opposed his wishes. Ought not Philipp to fill his friend's place? and if the latter never returned, who then would there be to direct the work of the Reformation? Melancthon, resigned yet disappointed, said, "Would to God that he had allowed me to go with him."

The impetuous Amsdorff immediately declared that he would accompany the doctor. His strong mind found pleasure in confronting danger. His boldness permitted him to appear fearlessly before an assembly of kings. The elector had invited to Wittenberg, as professor of jurisprudence, Jerome Schurff, son of a physician at St. Gall, a celebrated man, of gentle manners, and who was very intimate with Luther. "He has not yet been able to make up his mind," said Luther, "to pronounce sentence of death on a single malefactor." This timid man, however, desired to assist the doctor by his advice in this perilous journey. A young Danish student, Peter Suaven, who resided with Melancthon, and who afterwards became celebrated by his evangelical labors in Pomerania and Denmark, likewise declared that he would accompany his master. The youth of the schools were also to have their representative at the side of the champion of truth.

Germany was moved at the sight of the perils that menaced the representative of her people. She found a suitable voice to give utterance to her fears. Ulrich von Hutten shuddered at the thought of the blow about to be inflicted on his country. On April 1, he wrote to Charles V himself: "Most excellent emperor," said he, "you are on the point of destroying us, and yourself with us. What is proposed to be done in this affair of Luther's, except to ruin our liberty, and to crush your power? In the whole extent of the empire there is not a single upright man that does not feel the deepest interest in this matter. The priests alone set themselves against Luther, because he has opposed their enormous power, their scandalous luxury, and their depraved lives; and because he has pleaded, in behalf of Christ's doctrine, for the liberty of our country and for purity of morals.

"O Emperor, discard from your presence these Roman ambassadors, bishops, and cardinals, who desire to prevent all reformation. Did you not observe the sorrow of the people as they saw you arrive on the banks of the Rhine, surrounded by these red-hatted gentry, . . . and by a band of priests, instead of a troop of valiant warriors? . . .

"Do not surrender your sovereign majesty to those who desire to trample it under foot. Have pity on us. Do not drag yourself and the whole nation into one common destruction. Lead us into the midst of the greatest dangers, under the weapons of your soldiers, to the cannon's mouth; let all nations conspire against us; let every army assail us, so that we can show our valor in the light of day, rather than that we should be thus vanquished and enslaved obscurely and stealthily, like women, without arms, and unresisting. . . . Alas, we had hoped that you would deliver us from the Roman yoke and overthrow the tyranny of the pontiff. God grant that the future may be better than these beginnings.

"All Germany falls prostrate at your feet; with tears we entreat and implore your help, your compassion, your faithfulness; and by the holy memory of those Germans who, when all the world owned the Roman sway, did not bow their heads before that haughty city, we conjure you to save us, to restore us to ourselves, to deliver us from bondage and take revenge upon our tyrants."

Thus, by the mouth of this knight, spoke the German nation to Charles V. The emperor paid no attention to this epistle. He was a Fleming, and not a German. His personal aggrandizement, and not the liberty and glory of the empire, was the object of all his desires.

Chapter 38
Luther Journeys to Worms

It was now April 2, and Luther had to take leave of his friends. After apprising Lange, by a note, that he would spend the Thursday or Friday following at Erfurt, he bade farewell to his colleagues. Turning to Melancthon, he said with an agitated voice, "My dear brother, if I do not return, and my enemies put me to death, continue to teach, and stand fast in the truth. Labor in my stead, since I shall no longer be able to labor for myself. If you survive, my death will be of little consequence." Then committing his soul to the hands of Him who is faithful, Luther got into the car, and quitted Wittenberg.

The town council had provided him with a modest conveyance, covered with an awning, which the travelers could set up or remove at pleasure. The imperial herald, wearing his robe of office, and carrying the imperial eagle, rode on horseback in front, attended by his servant. Next came Luther, Schurff, Amsdorff, and Suaven, in the car. The friends of the gospel and the citizens of Wittenberg were deeply agitated, and invoking God's aid, burst into tears. Thus Luther began his journey.

He soon discovered that gloomy presentiment filled the hearts of all he met. At Leipzig no respect was shown him, and the magistrates merely presented him with the customary cup of wine. At Naumburg he met a priest, probably J. Langer, a man of stern zeal, who carefully preserved in his study a portrait of the famous Jerome Savonarola, who was burnt at Florence in 1498 by order of Pope Alexander VI, as a martyr to freedom and morality, as well as a confessor of the evangelical truth. Having taken down the portrait of the Italian martyr, the priest approached Luther, and held it out to him in silence. The latter understood what this mute representation was intended to announce, but his intrepid soul remained firm. "It is Satan," said he, "that would prevent, by these terrors, the confession of the truth in the assembly of princes, for he foresees the blow it would inflict upon his kingdom."

"Stand firm in the truth thou hast proclaimed," said the priest solemnly, "and God will as firmly stand by thee."

After passing the night at Naumburg, where he had been hospitably entertained by the burgomaster, Luther arrived the next evening at Weimar. He had hardly been a minute in the town, when he heard loud cries in every direction; it was the publication of his condemnation. "Look there," said the herald. He turned his eyes, and with astonishment saw the imperial messengers going from street to street, everywhere posting up the emperor's edict commanding his writings to be deposited with the magistrates. Luther doubted not that this unseasonable display of severity was intended to frighten him from undertaking the journey, so that he might be condemned as having refused to appear. "Well, doctor, will you proceed?" asked the imperial herald in alarm.

"Yes," replied Luther; "although interdicted in every city, I shall go on. I rely upon the emperor's safe-conduct."

At Weimar, Luther had an audience with Duke John, brother to the elector of Saxony, who resided there. The prince invited him to preach, and the reformer consented. Words of life flowed from the doctor's agitated heart. A Franciscan monk, who heard him, by name John Voit, the friend of Frederick Myconius, was then converted to the evangelical doctrine. He left his convent two years after, and somewhat later became professor of theology at Wittenberg. The duke furnished Luther with the money necessary for his journey.

From Weimar the reformer proceeded to Erfurt. This was the city of his youth. Here he hoped to meet his friend Lange, if, as he had written to him, he might enter the city without danger. When about three or four leagues from the city, near the village of Nora, he perceived a troop of horsemen approaching in the distance. Were they friends, or enemies? In a short time, Crotus rector of the university, Eobanus Hesse the friend of Melancthon, and whom Luther styled the prince of poets, Euricius Cordus, John Draco, and others, to the number of forty, all members of the senate, the university, or of the burghers, greeted him with acclamations. A multitude of the inhabitants of Erfurt thronged the road and gave utterance to their joy. All were eager to see the man who had dared to declare war against the pope.

A man about twenty-eight years old, named Justus Jonas, had outstripped the cavalcade. Jonas, after studying the law at Erfurt, had been appointed rector of that university in 1519. Receiving the light of the gospel, which was shining forth in every direction, he had entertained the desire of becoming a theologian. "I think," wrote Erasmus to him, "that God has elected you as an instrument to make known the glory of His Son Jesus." All his thoughts were turned toward Wittenberg and Luther.

Some years before, when he was as yet a law student, Jonas, who was a man of active and enterprising spirit, had set out on foot in company with a few friends, and had crossed forests infested with robbers, and cities devastated by the plague, in order to visit Erasmus, who was then at Brussels. Should he now hesitate to confront other dangers by accompanying the reformer to Worms? He earnestly begged the favor to be granted him, and Luther consented.

Thus met these two doctors, who were to labor together all their lives in the talk of renovating the church. Divine Providence gathered round Luther men who were destined to be the light of Germany—Melancthon, Amsdorff, Bugenhagen, and Jonas. On his return from Worms, Jonas was elected provost of the church of Wittenberg and Doctor of Divinity. "Jonas," said Luther, "is a man whose life is worth purchasing at a large price, in order to retain him on earth." No preacher ever surpassed him in his power of captivating his hearers. Said Melancthon, "I am a dialectician; Jonas is an orator. Words flow from his lips with admirable beauty, and his eloquence is full of energy. But Luther surpasses us all." It appears that about this time a friend of Luther's childhood, and also one of his brothers, increased the number of his escort.

The deputation from Erfurt had turned their horses' heads. Luther's carriage entered within the walls of the city surrounded by horsemen and pedestrians. At the gate, in the public places, in the streets where the poor monk had so often begged his bread, the crowd of spectators was immense. Luther alighted at the convent of the Augustinians, where the gospel had first given consolation to his heart. Lange joyfully received him; Usingen, and some of the elder fathers, showed him much coldness. There was a great desire to hear him preach; the pulpit had been forbidden him, but the herald, sharing the enthusiasm of those about him, gave his consent.

On the Sunday after Easter, the church of the Augustinians of Erfurt was filled to overflowing. This friar, who had been accustomed in former times to unclose the doors and sweep out the church, went up to the pulpit and opening the Bible, read these words: "Peace be unto you. And when he had so said, he showed unto them his hands and his side" (John 20:19-20). "Philosophers, doctors, and writers," said he, "have endeavored to teach men the way to obtain everlasting life, and they have not succeeded. I will now tell it to you."

"There are two kinds of works," continued the reformer, "works not of ourselves, and these are good; our own works, and they are of little worth. One man builds a church; another goes on a pilgrimage to St. Jago of Compostella or St. Peter's; a third fasts, prays, takes the cowl, and goes barefoot; another does something else. All these works are nothingness and will come to naught; for our own works have no virtue in them. But I am now going to tell you what is the true work. God has raised one man from the dead, the Lord Jesus Christ, that He might destroy death, extirpate sin, and shut the gates of hell. This is the work of salvation. The Devil thought he had the Lord in his power when he saw Him hanging between two thieves, suffering the most disgraceful martyrdom, accursed of God and of men. . . . But the Godhead displayed its power, and destroyed death, sin, and hell. . . .

"Christ has vanquished! This is the joyful news; and we are saved by His work, and not by our own. The pope says differently; but I affirm that the holy mother of God herself was saved, neither by her virginity, nor by her maternity, nor by her purity, nor by her works, but solely by the instrumentality of faith and the works of God."

While Luther was speaking, a sudden noise was heard; one of the galleries cracked, and it was feared that it would break down under the pressure of the crowd. This incident occasioned a great disturbance in the congregation. Some ran out from their places; other stood motionless through fright. The preacher stopped a moment, and then stretching out his hand, exclaimed with a loud voice, "Fear nothing; there is no danger: it is thus the Devil seeks to hinder me from proclaiming the gospel, but he will not succeed." At these words, those who were flying halted in astonishment and surprise; the assembly again became calm, and Luther, undisturbed, continued thus: "You say a great deal about faith, you may perhaps reply to me: show us how we may obtain it. Well, I will teach you. Our Lord Jesus Christ said, 'Peace be unto you; behold my hands'; that is to say, Behold, O man, it is I, I alone, who have taken away thy sin, and ransomed thee; and now thou hast peace, saith the Lord."

"I have not eaten of the fruit of the forbidden tree," resumed Luther, "nor have you; but we have all partaken of the sin that Adam has transmitted to us and have gone astray. In like manner, I have not suffered on the cross, neither have you; but Christ has suffered for us; we are justified by God's work, and not by our own. . . . I am, saith the Lord, thy righteousness and thy redemption.

"Let us believe in the gospel and in the epistles of St. Paul, and not in the letters and decretals of the popes."

After proclaiming faith as the cause of the sinner's justification, Luther proclaims works as the consequence and manifestation of salvation.

"Since God has saved us," continues he, "let us so order our works that they may be acceptable to Him. Art thou rich? let thy goods administer to the necessities of the poor. Art thou poor? let thy services be acceptable to the rich. If thy labor is useful to thyself alone, the service that thou pretendest to render unto God is a lie."

In the whole of this sermon there is not a word about himself; not a single allusion to the circumstances in which he is placed: nothing about Worms, or Charles, or the nuncios; he preaches Christ, and Christ only. At this moment, when the eyes of all the world are upon him, he has no thought of himself: this stamps him as a true servant of God.

Luther departed from Erfurt and passed through Gotha, where he preached another sermon. The doctor slept at the convent of the Benedictines at Reinhardsbrunn, and from thence proceeded to Eisenach, where he felt indisposed. Amsdorff, Jonas, Schurff, and all his friends were alarmed. He was bled; they tended him with the most affectionate anxiety, and John Oswald, the mayor of the town, brought him a cordial. Luther having drunk a portion, fell asleep, and reinvigorated by this repose, he was enabled to continue his journey on the following morning.

His progress resembled that of a victorious general. The people gazed with emotion on this daring man, who was going to lay his head at the feet of the emperor and the empire. An immense crowd flocked eagerly around him. "Ah," said some, "there are so many bishops and cardinals at Worms. . . . They will burn you, and reduce your body to ashes, as they did with John Huss." But nothing frightened the monk. "Though they should kindle a fire," said he, "all the way from Worms to Wittenberg, the flames of which reached to heaven, I would walk through it in the name of the Lord; I would appear before them; I would enter the jaws of this behemoth and break his teeth, confessing the Lord Jesus Christ."

The doctor arrived at Frankfurt on Sunday, April 14. Already the news of Luther's journey had reached Worms. As soon as Luther arrived in Frankfurt, he took some repose, and afterwards gave intelligence of his approach to Spalatin, who was then at Worms with the elector. This was the only letter he wrote during his journey. "I am coming," said he, "although Satan endeavored to stop me on the road by sickness. Since I left Eisenach I have been in a feeble state, and am still as I never was before. I learn that Charles has published an edict to frighten me. But Christ lives, and I shall enter Worms in spite of all the gates of hell, and of the powers of the air. Have the goodness, therefore, to prepare a lodging for me."

The next day Luther went to visit the school of the learned William Nesse, a celebrated geographer of that period. "Apply to the study of the Bible, and to the investigation of truth," said he to the pupils. And then putting his right hand on one of the children, and his left upon another, he pronounced a benediction on the whole school.

If Luther blessed the young, he was also the hope of the aged. Catherine of Holzhausen, a widow far advanced in years, and who served God, approached him, and said, "My parents told me that God would raise up a man who would oppose the papal vanities and preserve His Word. I hope thou art that man, and I pray for the grace and Holy Spirit of God upon thy work."

These were far from being the general sentiments in Frankfurt. John Cochloeus, dean of the church of Our Lady, was one of the most devoted partisans of the papacy. He could not repress his apprehensions when he saw Luther pass through Frankfurt on his road to Worms. He thought that the church had need of devoted champions. It is true no one had summoned him, but that mattered not. Luther had scarcely quitted the city, when Cochloeus followed him, ready, he said, to sacrifice his life in defense of the honor of the church.

Luther had arrived at Oppenheim. His safe-conduct was available for only three days more. He saw a troop of horsemen approaching him, and at their head soon recognized Bucer, with whom he had held such intimate conversations at Heidelberg. "These cavaliers belong to Franz von Sickingen," said Bucer, after the first interchange of friendship; "he has sent me to conduct you to his castle. The emperor's confessor desires to have an interview with you. His influence over Charles is unlimited; everything may yet be arranged. But beware of Aleander." Jonas, Schurff, and Amsdorff knew not what to think. Bucer was pressing, but Luther felt no hesitation. "I shall continue my journey," replied he to Bucer; "and if the emperor's confessor has anything to say to me, he will find me at Worms. I go whither I am summoned."

In the meanwhile, Spalatin himself began to be anxious and to fear. Surrounded at Worms by the enemies of the Reformation, he heard it said that the safe-conduct of a heretic ought not to be respected. He grew alarmed for his friend. At the moment when the latter was approaching the city, a messenger appeared before him, with this advice from the chaplain: "Do not enter Worms." But Luther, undismayed, turned his eyes on the messenger and replied, "Go and tell your master, that even should there be as many devils in Worms as tiles on the housetops, still I would enter it."

Chapter 39
"Here I Stand"

At length, on the morning of April 16, Luther discovered the walls of the ancient city. All were expecting him. One absorbing thought prevailed in Worms. Some young nobles, Bernard of Hirschfeldt, Albert of Lendenau, with six knights and other gentlemen in the train of the number of a hundred—if we may believe Pallavicini—unable to restrain their impatience, rode out on horseback to meet him and surrounded him to form an escort at the moment of his entrance. He drew near. Before him pranced the imperial herald, in full costume. Luther came next in his modest car. Jonas followed him on horseback, and the cavaliers were on both sides of him. A great crowd was waiting for him at the gates. It was near midday when he passed those walls, from which so many persons had predicted he would never come forth alive. Everyone was at table; but as soon as the watchman on the tower of the cathedral sounded his trumpet, all ran into the streets to see the monk. Luther was now in Worms.

Two thousand persons accompanied him through the streets of the city. The citizens eagerly pressed forward to see him; every moment the crowd was increasing. It was much greater than at the public entry of the emperor. On a sudden, says a historian, a man dressed in a singular costume and bearing a large cross, such as is employed in funeral processions, made way through the crowd, advanced toward Luther, and then with a loud voice, and in that plaintive, measured tone in which mass is said for the repose of the soul, he sang these words as if he were uttering them from the abode of the dead: "At last thou art come, long looked-for one, whom we have waited for in the darkness of the grave." Thus a *requiem* was Luther's welcome to Worms. It was the court-fool of one of the dukes of Bavaria, who, if the story be true, gave Luther one of those warnings, replete at once with sagacity and irony, of which so many examples have been recorded of these personages. But the shouts of the multitude soon drowned the *De Profundis* of the cross-bearer.

The procession made its way with difficulty through the crowd. At last, the herald of the empire stopped before the hotel of the knights of Rhodes. There resided the two councilors of the elector, Frederick of Thun and Philip of Feilitsch, as well as the marshal of the empire, Ulrich of Pappenheim. Luther alighted from his car and said as he touched the ground, "God will be my defense." "I entered Worms in a covered wagon and in my monk's gown," said he at a later period. "All the people came out into the streets to get a sight of Friar Martin."

Charles V immediately summoned his council. The emperor's privy-councilors hastily repaired to the palace, for the alarm had reached them also. "Luther is come," said Charles; "what must we do?"

Modo, bishop of Palermo and chancellor of Flanders, replied, if we may credit the testimony of Luther himself, "We have long consulted on this matter. Let your imperial majesty get rid of this man at once. Did not Sigismund cause John Huss to be burnt? We are not bound either to give or to observe the safe-conduct of a heretic."

"No," said Charles, "we must keep our promise." They submitted, therefore, to the reformer's appearance before the diet.

While the councils of the great were thus agitated on account of Luther, there were many persons in Worms who were delighted at the opportunity of at length beholding this illustrious servant of God. Capito, chaplain and councilor to the archbishop of Mentz, was the foremost among them. This remarkable man, who shortly before had preached the gospel in Switzerland with great freedom, thought it becoming to the station he filled to act in a manner which led to his being accused of cowardice by the Evangelicals and of dissimulation by the Catholics. While proclaiming the new doctrine, Capito attempted to keep friends with those who persecuted it. He flattered himself, as others did who shared in his opinions, that he might in this way be of great service to the church. Cochloeus, dean of Frankfurt, who reached Worms about the same time as Luther, immediately waited on Capito. The latter, who was outwardly at least, on very friendly terms with Aleander, presented Cochloeus to him, thus serving as a link between the two greatest enemies of the reformer. Capito no doubt thought he was advancing Christ's cause by all these temporizing expedients, but we cannot find that they led to any good result.

Meantime the crowd still continued round the hotel of Rhodes, where Luther had alighted. To some he was a prodigy of wisdom, to others a monster of iniquity. All the city longed to see him. They left him, however, the first hours after his arrival to recruit his strength and to converse with his most intimate friends. But as soon as the evening came, counts, barons, knights, gentlemen, ecclesiastics, and citizens flocked about him. All, even his greatest enemies, were struck with the boldness of his manner, the joy that seemed to animate him, the power of his language, and that imposing elevation and enthusiasm which gave this simple monk an irresistible authority. But while some ascribed this grandeur to something divine, the friends of the pope loudly exclaimed that he was possessed by a devil. Visitors rapidly succeeded each other, and this crowd of curious individuals kept Luther from his bed until a late hour of the night.

On the next morning, Wednesday, April 17, the hereditary marshal of the empire, Ulrich of Pappenheim, cited him to appear at four in the afternoon before his imperial majesty and the states of the empire. Luther received this message with profound respect.

Thus everything was arranged; he was about to stand for Jesus Christ before the most august assembly in the world. Encouragements were not wanting to him. The impetuous knight Ulrich von Hutten was then in the castle of Ebernburg. Unable to visit Worms—for Leo X had called upon Charles V to send him bound hand and foot to Rome—he resolved at least to stretch out the hand of friendship to Luther; and on this very day, April 17, he wrote to him, adopting the language of a king of Israel: " 'The Lord hear thee in the day of trouble; the name of the God of Jacob defend thee; Send thee help from the sanctuary, and strengthen thee out of Zion; . . . Grant thee according to thine own heart, and fulfil all thy counsel.' Dearly beloved Luther, my venerable father, . . . fear not, and stand firm. The counsel of the wicked has beset you, and they have opened their mouths against you like roaring lions. But the Lord will arise against the unrighteous and put them to confusion. Fight therefore valiantly in Christ's cause. As for me, I too will combat boldly. Would to God that I were permitted to see how they

319

frown. But the Lord will purge His vineyard, which the wild boar of the forest has laid waste. . . . May Christ preserve you." Bucer did what Hutten was unable to do: he came from Ebernburg to Worms and did not leave his friend during the time of his sojourn in that city.

Four o'clock arrived. The marshal of the empire appeared; Luther prepared to set out with him. He was agitated at the thought of the solemn congress before which he was about to appear. The herald walked first; after him the marshal of the empire; and the reformer came last. The crowd that filled the streets was still greater than on the preceding day. It was impossible to advance; in vain were orders given to make way; the crowd still kept increasing. At length the herald, seeing the difficulty of reaching the town hall, ordered some private houses to be opened and led Luther through the gardens and private passages to the place where the diet was sitting. The people who witnessed this rushed into the houses after the monk of Wittenberg, ran to the windows that overlooked the gardens, and a great number climbed on the roofs. The tops of the houses and the pavements of the streets, above and below, all were covered with spectators.

Having reached the town hall at last, Luther and those who accompanied him were again prevented by the crowd from crossing the threshold. They cried, "Make way, make way," but no one moved. Upon this the imperial soldiers by main force cleared a road, through which Luther passed. As the people rushed forward to enter with him, the soldiers kept them back with their halberds. Luther entered the interior of the hall; but even there, every corner was crowded. In the antechambers and embrasures of the windows there were more than five thousand spectators—Germans, Italians, Spaniards, and others.

Luther advanced with difficulty. At last, as he drew near the door which was about to admit him into the presence of his judges, he met a valiant knight, George of Freundsberg. The old general, seeing Luther pass, tapped him on the shoulder and, shaking his head, blanched in many battles, said kindly, "Poor monk, poor monk, thou art now going to make a nobler stand than I or any other captains have ever made in the bloodiest of our battles. But if thy cause is just, and thou art sure of it, go forward in God's name and fear nothing. God will not forsake thee."

At length the doors of the hall were opened. Luther went in, and with him entered many persons who formed no portion of the diet. Never had man appeared before so imposing an assembly. The Emperor Charles V, whose sovereignty extended over great part of the Old and New Worlds; his brother the Archduke Ferdinand; six electors of the empire; twenty-four dukes, the majority of whom were independent sovereigns over countries more or less extensive; eight margraves; thirty archbishops, bishops, and abbots; seven ambassadors, including those from the kings of France and England; the deputies of ten free cities; a great number of princes, counts, and sovereign barons; the papal nuncios—in all, two hundred and four persons: such was the imposing court before which appeared Martin Luther.

This appearance was of itself a signal victory over the papacy. The pope had condemned the man, and he was now standing before a tribunal which, by this very act, set itself above the pope. The pope had laid him under an interdict and cut him off from all human society; and yet he was summoned in respectful language and received before the most august assembly in the world. The pope had condemned him to perpetual silence, and he was now about to speak before thousands of attentive hearers drawn together from the farthest parts of Christendom. An immense revolution had thus been effected by Luther's instrumentality. Rome was already descending from her throne, and it was the voice of a monk that caused this humiliation.

Some of the princes, when they saw the emotion of this son of the lowly miner of Mansfeldt in the presence of this assembly of kings, approached him kindly, and one of them said to him, "Fear not them which kill the body, but are not able to kill the soul." And another added, "When ye shall be brought before governors and kings for my sake, the Spirit of your Father shall speak in you." Thus was the reformer comforted with his Master's words by the princes of this world.

Meanwhile, the guards made way for Luther. He advanced and stood before the throne of Charles V. The sight of so august an assembly appeared for an instant to dazzle and intimidate him. All eyes were fixed on him. The confusion gradually subsided, and a deep silence followed. "Say nothing," said the marshal of the empire to him, "before you are questioned." Luther was left alone.

After a moment of solemn silence, the chancellor of the arch-bishop of Treves, John ab Eck, the friend of Aleander who must not be confounded with the theologian of the same name, rose and said with a loud and clear voice, first in Latin and then in German, "Martin Luther, his sacred and invincible imperial majesty has cited you before his throne, in accordance with the advice and counsel of the states of the Holy Roman Empire, to require you to answer two questions: first, do you acknowledge these books to have been written by you?" At the same time the imperial speaker pointed with his finger to about twenty volumes placed on a table in the middle of the hall, directly in front of Luther. "Secondly," continued the chancellor, "are you prepared to retract these books and their contents; or do you persist in the opinions you have advanced in them?"

Luther was about to answer the first of these questions in the affirmative, when his counsel, Jerome Schurff, hastily interrupting him, exclaimed aloud, "Let the titles of the books be read."

The chancellor approached the table and read the titles. There were among their number many devotional works quite foreign to the controversy. Their enumeration being finished, Luther said first in Latin, and then in German:

"Most Gracious emperor—Gracious princes and lords:

"As to the first, I acknowledge as mine the books that have just been named: I cannot deny them.

"As to the second, seeing that it is a question which concerns faith and the salvation of souls, and in which the Word of God, the greatest and most precious treasure either in heaven or earth, is interested, I should act imprudently were I to reply without reflection. I might affirm less than the circumstance demands, or more than truth requires, and so sin against this saying of Christ: 'Whosoever shall deny me before men, him will I also deny before my Father which is in heaven.' For this reason I entreat your imperial majesty, with all humility, to allow me time, that I may answer without offending against the Word of God."

This reply, far from giving grounds to suppose Luther felt any hesitation, was worthy of the reformer and of the assembly. Luther restrained his own naturally impetuous disposition; he controlled his tongue, ever too ready to speak; he checked himself at a time when all the feelings by which he was animated were eager for utterance. And yet, because he had spoken in a respectful manner, and in a low tone of voice, many thought that he hesitated, and even that he was dismayed. Charles, impatient to know the man whose words had stirred the empire, had not taken his eyes off him. He turned to one of his courtiers and said disdainfully, "Certainly this man will never make a heretic of me." Then rising from his seat, the youthful emperor withdrew with his ministers into a council room; the electors with the princes retired into another; and the deputies of the free cities into a third. When the diet assembled again, it was agreed to comply with Luther's request.

"Martin Luther," said the Chancellor of Treves, "his imperial majesty, of his natural goodness, is very willing to grant you another day, but under condition that you make your reply orally, and not in writing."

The imperial herald now stepped forward and conducted Luther back to his hotel. Menaces and shouts of joy were heard by turns on his passage. The most sinister rumors circulated among Luther's friends. "The diet is dissatisfied," said they; "the papal envoys have triumphed; the reformer will be sacrificed."

Men's passions were inflamed. Many gentlemen hastened to Luther's lodgings. "Doctor," said they, with emotion, "what is this? It is said they are determined to burn you!"

"If they do so," continued these knights, "it will cost them their lives." "And that certainly would have happened," said Luther, as, twenty years after, he quoted these words at Eisleben.

On the other hand, Luther's enemies exulted. "He has asked for time," said they; "he will retract. At a distance his speech was arrogant; now his courage fails him. . . . He is conquered."

Perhaps Luther was the only man who felt tranquil at Worms. Shortly after his return from the diet, he wrote to Cuspianus, the imperial councilor: "I write to you from the midst of the tumult"— alluding probably to the noise made by the crowd in front of the hotel. "I have just made my appearance before the emperor and his brother. . . . I confessed myself the author of my books and declared that I would reply tomorrow touching my retraction. With Christ's help, I shall never retract one tittle of my works."

The emotion of the people and of the foreign soldiers increased every hour. While the opposing parties were proceeding calmly in the diet, they were breaking out into acts of violence in the streets.

The insolence of the haughty and merciless Spanish soldiers offended the citizens. One of these followers of Charles, finding in a bookseller's shop the pope's bull with a commentary written by Hutten, took the book and tore it in pieces, and then throwing the fragments on the ground, trampled them underfoot. Others having discovered several copies of Luther's writing *The Babylonian Captivity* took them away and destroyed them. The indignant people fell upon the soldiers and compelled them to take to flight. At another time, a Spaniard on horseback pursued, sword in hand, through one of the principal streets of Worms, a German who fled before him; and the affrighted people dared not stop the furious man.

Some politicians thought they had found means of saving Luther. "Retract your doctrinal errors," said they; "but persist in all that you have said against the pope and his court, and you are safe." Aleander shuddered with alarm at this counsel. But Luther, immovable in his resolution, declared that he had no great opinion of a political reform that was not based upon faith.

Glapio, the chancellor ab Eck, and Aleander, by Charles's order, met early on the morning of April 18 to concert the measures to be taken with regard to Luther. At four o'clock the herald appeared and conducted him to the place where the diet was sitting. The curiosity of the people had increased, for the answer was to be decisive. As the diet was occupied, Luther was compelled to wait in the court in the midst of an immense crowd, which swayed to and fro like the sea in a storm, and pressed the reformer with its waves. Two long hours elapsed, while the doctor stood in this multitude so eager to catch a glimpse of him. The night began to fall. Torches were lighted in the hall of the assembly. Their glimmering rays shone through the ancient windows into the court. Everything assumed a solemn aspect. At last the doctor was introduced. Many persons entered with him, for everyone desired to hear his answer. Men's minds were on the stretch; all impatiently awaited the decisive moment that was approaching. The princes having taken their seats, though not without some difficulty, for many of their places had been occupied, and the monk of Wittenberg finding himself again standing before Charles V, the chancellor of the elector of Treves began by saying:

"Martin Luther, yesterday you begged for a delay that has now expired. Assuredly it ought not to have been conceded, as every man, and especially you, who are so great and learned a doctor in the Holy Scriptures, should always be ready to answer any questions touching his faith. . . . Now, therefore, reply to the question put by his majesty, who has behaved to you with so much mildness. Will you defend your books as a whole, or are you ready to disavow some of them?"

"Most serene emperor, illustrious princes, gracious lords," said Luther, turning his eyes on Charles and on the assembly, "I appear before you this day, in conformity with the order given me yesterday, and by God's mercies I conjure your majesty and your august highnesses to listen graciously to the defense of a cause which I am assured is just and true. If, through ignorance, I should transgress the usages and proprieties of courts, I entreat you to pardon me; for I was not brought up in the palaces of kings, but in the seclusion of a convent.

"Yesterday, two questions were put to me on behalf of his imperial majesty: the first, if I was the author of the books whose titles were enumerated; the second, if I would retract or defend the doctrine I had taught in them. To the first question I then made answer, and I persevere in that reply.

"As for the second, I have written works on many different subjects. There are some in which I have treated of faith and good works, in a manner at once so pure, so simple, and so scriptural that even my adversaries, far from finding anything to censure in them, allow that these works are useful and worthy of being read by all pious men. The papal bull, however violent it may be, acknowledges this. If therefore I were to retract these, what should I do? . . . Wretched man! among all men, I alone should abandon truths that friends and enemies approve, and I should oppose what the whole world glories in confessing. . . .

"Secondly, I have written books against the papacy, in which I have attacked those who, by their false doctrine, their evil lives, or their scandalous example, afflict the Christian world and destroy both body and soul. The complaints of all who fear God are confirmatory of this. Is it not evident that the human doctrines and laws of the pope entangle, torment, and vex the consciences of believers; while the crying and perpetual extortions of Rome swallow up the wealth and the riches of Christendom, and especially of this illustrious nation? . . .

"Were I to retract what I have said on this subject, what should I do but lend additional strength to this tyranny and open the floodgates to a torrent of impiety? Overflowing with still greater fury than before, we should see these insolent men increase in number, behave more tyrannically, and domineer more and more. And not only would the yoke that now weighs upon the Christian people be rendered heavier by my retraction, but it would become, so to speak, more legitimate, for by this very retraction it would have received the confirmation of your most serene majesty, and of all the states of the holy empire. Gracious God, I should thus become a vile cloak to cover and conceal every kind of malice and tyranny. . . .

"Lastly, I have written books against individuals who desired to defend the Roman tyranny and to destroy the faith. I frankly confess that I may have attacked them with more acrimony than is becoming my ecclesiastical profession. I do not consider myself a saint; but I cannot disavow these writings, for by so doing I should sanction the impiety of my adversaries, and they would seize the opportunity of oppressing the people of God with still greater cruelty.

"Yet I am but a mere man, and not God; I shall therefore defend myself as Christ did. 'If I have spoken evil, bear witness of the evil' (John 18:23), said He. How much more should I, who am but dust and ashes, and who may so easily go astray, desire every man to state his objections to my doctrine?

"For this reason, by the mercy of God, I conjure you, most serene emperor, and you, most illustrious princes and all men of every degree, to prove from the writings of the prophets and apostles that I have erred. As soon as I am convinced of this, I will retract every error and be the first to lay hold of my books and throw them into the fire. . . .

"If I say these things, it is not because I think that such great princes need my poor advice, but because I desire to render unto Germany what she has a right to expect from her children. Thus, commending myself to your august majesty and to your most serene highnesses, I humbly entreat you not to suffer the hatred of my enemies to pour out upon me an indignation that I have not merited."

Luther had pronounced these words in German; he was ordered to repeat them in Latin. The emperor did not like the German tongue. The imposing assembly that surrounded the reformer, the noise, and his own emotion, had fatigued him. "I was in a great perspiration," said he, "heated by the tumult, standing in the midst of the princes." Frederick of Thun, privy councilor to the elector of Saxony, who was stationed by his master's orders at the side of the reformer, to watch over him that no violence might be employed against him, seeing the condition of the poor monk, said, "If you cannot repeat what you have said, that will do, doctor." But Luther, after a brief pause to take breath, began again, and repeated his speech in Latin with the same energy as at first.

When he had ceased speaking, the Chancellor of Treves, the orator of the diet, said indignantly, "You have not answered the question put to you. You were not summoned hither to call in question the decisions of councils. You are required to give a clear and precise answer. Will you, or will you not, retract?"

Upon this Luther replied without hesitation, "Since your most serene majesty and your high mightinesses require from me a clear, simple, and precise answer, I will give you one, and it is this: I cannot submit my faith either to the pope or to the councils, because it is clear as the day that they have frequently erred and contradicted each other. Unless therefore I am convinced by the testimony of Scripture, or by the clearest reasoning—unless I am persuaded by means of the passages I have quoted, and unless they thus render my conscience bound by the Word of God, *I cannot and I will not retract,* for it is unsafe for a Christian to speak against his conscience." And then, looking round on this assembly before which he stood, and which held his life in its hands, he said, *"Here I stand; I can do no other; may God help me. Amen."*

The assembly was thunderstruck. Many of the princes found it difficult to conceal their admiration. The emperor, recovering from his first impression, exclaimed, "This monk speaks with an intrepid heart and unshaken courage." The Spaniards and Italians alone felt confounded and soon began to ridicule a greatness of soul which they could not comprehend.

"If you do not retract," said the chancellor, as soon as the diet had recovered from the impression produced by Luther's speech, "the emperor and the states of the empire will consult what course to adopt against an incorrigible heretic." At these words Luther's friends began to tremble; but the monk repeated, "May God be my helper; for I can retract nothing."

After this Luther withdrew, and the princes deliberated. Luther was again called in, and the orator of the diet said to him, "Martin, you have not spoken with the modesty becoming your position. The distinction you have made between your books was futile; for if you retracted those that contained your errors, the emperor would not allow the others to be burnt. It is extravagant in you to demand to be refuted by Scripture, when you are reviving heresies condemned by the general Council of Constance. The emperor, therefore, calls upon you to declare simply, yes or no, whether you presume to maintain what you have advanced, or whether you will retract a portion?"

"I have no other reply to make than that which I have already made," answered Luther calmly. His meaning was understood. He had said *no* to the church and to the empire. Charles V arose, and all the assembly with him: "The diet will meet again tomorrow to hear the emperor's opinion," said the chancellor with a loud voice.

Chapter 40
Attempts at Compromise

Night had closed in. Each man retired to his home in darkness. Two imperial officers formed Luther's escort. Some persons imagined that his fate was decided, that they were leading him to prison, whence he would never come forth but to mount the scaffold: an immense tumult broke out. Several gentlemen exclaimed, "Are they taking him to prison?"

"No," replied Luther, "they are accompanying me to my hotel." At these words the agitation subsided. Some Spanish soldiers of the emperor's household followed this bold man through the streets by which he had to pass, with shouts and mockery, while others howled and roared like wild beasts robbed of their prey. But Luther remained calm and firm.

Such was the scene at Worms. The intrepid monk, who had hitherto boldly braved all his enemies, spoke on this occasion, when he found himself in the presence of those who thirsted for his blood, with calmness, dignity, and humility. In the hall of the diet there was one greater than Charles and than Luther. "And ye shall be brought before governors and kings for my sake, . . . but when they deliver you up, take no thought how or what ye shall speak," saith Jesus Christ, ". . . for it is not ye that speak" (Matt. 10:18-20). Never perhaps had this promise been more clearly fulfilled.

Luther had returned to his hotel, seeking to recruit his body fatigued by so severe a trial. Spalatin and other friends surrounded him, and all together gave thanks to God. A messenger from the elector of Saxony came with orders for Spalatin to come to him immediately. Frederick had gone to the diet filled with great uneasiness. He had imagined that in the presence of the emperor Luther's courage would fail him, and hence he had been deeply moved by the resolute bearing of the reformer. He was proud of being the protector of such a man. When the chaplain arrived, the table was spread; the elector was just sitting down to supper with his court, and already the servants had brought in the water for their hands. As he saw Spalatin enter, he motioned him to follow; and as soon as he was alone with the chaplain in his bedchamber, he said, "Oh, how father Luther spoke before the emperor, and before all the states of the empire! I only trembled lest he should be too bold." Frederick then formed the resolution of protecting the doctor more courageously in future.

Aleander saw the impression Luther had produced; there was no time to lose; he must induce the emperor to act with vigor. The opportunity was favorable: war with France was imminent. Leo X, desirous of enlarging his states, and caring little for the peace of Christendom, was secretly negotiating two treaties at the same time—one with Charles against Francis, the other with Francis against Charles. In the former, he claimed of the emperor, for himself, the territories of Parma, Placentia, and Ferrara; in the second, he stipulated with the king for a portion of the kingdom of Naples, which would thus be taken from Charles. The latter felt the importance of gaining Leo to his side, in order to have his alliance in the war against his rival of France. It was a mere trifle to purchase the mighty pontiff's friendship at the cost of Luther's life.

On the day following Luther's appearance, Friday, April 19, the emperor ordered a message to be read to the diet, which he had written in French with his own hand. "Descended from the Christian emperors of Germany," said he, "from the Catholic kings of Spain, from the archdukes of Austria, and from the dukes of Burgundy, who have all been renowned as defenders of the Roman faith, I am firmly resolved to imitate the example of my ancestors. A single monk, misled by his own folly, has risen against the faith of Christendom. To stay such impiety, I will sacrifice my kingdoms, my treasures, my friends, my body, my blood, my soul, and my life. I am about to dismiss the Augustinian Luther, forbidding him to cause the least disorder among the people; I shall then proceed against him and his adherents as contumacious heretics, by excommunication, by interdict, and by every means calculated to destroy them. I call on the members of the states to behave like faithful Christians."

This address did not please everyone. Charles, young and hasty, had not complied with the usual forms; he should first have consulted with the diet. Two extreme opinions immediately declared themselves. The creatures of the pope, the elector of Brandenburg, and several ecclesiastical princes, demanded that the safe-conduct given to Luther should not be respected. "The Rhine," said they, "should receive his ashes, as it had received those of John Huss a century ago."

So horrible a proposition filled the elector and all Luther's friends with dismay. "The punishment of John Huss," said the elector-palatine, "has brought too many misfortunes on the German nation for us ever to raise such a scaffold a second time." "The princes of Germany," exclaimed even George of Saxony, Luther's inveterate enemy, "will not permit a safe-conduct to be violated. This diet, the first held by our new emperor, will not be guilty of so base an action. Such perfidy does not accord with the ancient German integrity." The princes of Bavaria, though attached to the church of Rome, supported this protest. The prospect of death that Luther's friends had already before their eyes appeared to recede.

The rumor of these discussions, which lasted two days, circulated through the city. Party spirit ran high. Some gentlemen, partisans of the reform, began to speak firmly against the treachery solicited by Aleander. "The emperor," said they, "is a young man whom the papists and bishops by their flatteries manage at their will." Pallavicini speaks of four hundred nobles ready to enforce Luther's safe-conduct with the sword. On Saturday morning placards were seen posted at the gates of houses and in the public places—some against Luther, and others in his favor. On one of them might be read merely these expressive words of the preacher: "Woe to thee, O land, when thy king is a child" (Eccles. 10:16). Sickingen, it was reported, had assembled at a few leagues from Worms, behind the impregnable ramparts of his stronghold, many knights and soldiers, and was only waiting to know the result of the affair before proceeding to action.

The enthusiasm of the people, not only in Worms, but also in the most distant cities of the empire; the intrepidity of the knights; the attachment felt by many princes to the cause of the reformer, were all of a nature to show Charles and the diet that the course suggested by the Roman Catholics might compromise the supreme authority, excite revolts, and even shake the empire. It was only the burning of a simple monk that was in question; but the princes and the partisans of Rome had not, all together, sufficient strength or courage to do this.

There can be no doubt, also, that Charles V, who was then young, feared to commit perjury. This would seem to be indicated by a saying, if it is true, which, according to some historians, he uttered on this occasion: "Though honor and faith should be banished from all the world, they ought to find a refuge in the hearts of princes." But other motives besides may have influenced the emperor. The Florentine Vettori, the friend of Leo X and of Machiavelli, asserts that Charles spared Luther only that he might thus keep the pope in check.

In the sitting of Saturday, the violent propositions of Aleander were rejected. On Monday, April 22, the princes went in a body to ask permission to make a last attempt. "I will not depart from what I have determined," replied the emperor. "I will authorize no one to communicate officially with Luther. But," added he, to Aleander's great vexation, "I will grant that man three days for reflection; during which time, you may exhort him privately." This was all that they required. The reformer, thought they, elevated by the solemnity of his appearance before the diet, would give way in a more friendly conference, and perhaps would be saved from the abyss into which he was about to fall.

The elector of Saxony knew the contrary, and hence was filled with apprehension. "If it were in my power," wrote he the next day to his brother Duke John, "I should be ready to defend Luther. You cannot imagine how far the partisans of Rome carry their attacks against me. Were I to tell you all, you would hear some most astonishing matters. They are resolved upon his destruction; and whoever manifests any interest for his safety is immediately set down as a heretic. May God, who never abandons the cause of justice, bring all things to a happy end."

Richard of Greiffenklau, archbishop of Treves, had with the permission of Charles V undertaken the office of mediator. Richard, who was on very intimate terms with the elector of Saxony, and a good Roman Catholic, desired by settling this affair to render a service to his friend as well as to his church. On Monday evening, April 22, just as Luther was sitting down to table, a messenger came from the archbishop, informing him that this prelate desired to see him on the next morning but one, Wednesday, at six o'clock.

The chaplain and Sturm the imperial herald waited on Luther before six o'clock on that day. But as early as four in the morning,

Aleander had sent for Cochloeus. The nuncio had soon discovered in the man whom Capito had introduced to him a devoted instrument of the court of Rome, on whom he might count as upon himself. As he could not be present at this interview, Aleander desired to find a substitute. "Go to the residence of the archbishop of Treves," said he to the dean of Frankfurt; "do not enter into discussion with Luther, but listen attentively to all that is said, so as to give me a faithful report."

The reformer with some of his friends arrived at the archbishop's, where he found the prelate surrounded by Joachim, margrave of Brandenburg, Duke George of Saxony, the bishops of Brandenberg and Augsburg, with several nobles, deputies of the free cities, lawyers, and theologians, among whom were Cochloeus and Jerome Wehe, chancellor of Baden. This skillful lawyer was anxious for a reformation in morals and discipline; he even went further: "The Word of God," said he, "that has been so long hidden under a bushel, must reappear in all its brightness." It was this conciliatory person who was charged with the conference. Turning kindly to Luther, he said, "We have not sent for you to dispute with you, but to exhort you in a fraternal tone. You know how carefully the Scriptures call upon us to beware of 'the arrow that flieth by day, and the destruction that wasteth at noonday.' That enemy of mankind has excited you to publish many things contrary to true religion. Reflect on your own safety and that of the empire. Beware lest those whom Christ by His blood has redeemed from eternal death should be misled by you and perish everlastingly. . . . Do not oppose the holy councils. If we did not uphold the decrees of our fathers, there would be nothing but confusion in the church. The eminent princes who hear me feel a special interest in your welfare; but if you persist, then the emperor will expel you from the empire, and no place in the world will offer you asylum. . . . Reflect on the fate that awaits you."

"Most serene princes," replied Luther, "I thank you for your solicitude on my account; for I am but a poor man, and too mean to be exhorted by such great lords." He then continued, "I have not blamed all the councils, but only that of Constance, because by condemning this doctrine of John Huss, 'That the Christian church is the assembly of all those who are predestined to salvation,' it has condemned this article of our faith, 'I believe in the holy catholic church,' and the Word of God itself. It is said my teaching is a cause of offense," added he; "I reply, that the gospel of Christ cannot be preached without offense. Why then should the fear or apprehension of danger separate me from the Lord, and from that divine Word which alone is truth? No; I would rather give up my body, my blood, and my life."

The princes and doctors having deliberated, Luther was again called in, and Wehe mildly resumed: "We must honor the powers that be, even when they are in error, and make great sacrifices for the sake of charity." And then with greater earnestness of manner, he said, "Leave it to the emperor's decision, and fear not."

Luther: I consent with all my heart that the emperor, the princes, and even the meanest Christian, should examine and judge my works; but on one condition, that they take the Word of God for their standard. Men have nothing to do but to obey it. Do not offer violence to my conscience, which is bound and chained up with the Holy Scriptures.

The Elector of Brandenburg: If I rightly understand you, doctor, you will acknowledge no other judge than the Holy Scriptures?

Luther: Precisely so, my lord, and on them I take my stand.

Upon this the princes and doctors withdrew. The partisans of the papacy felt Luther's superiority and attributed it to there being no one present capable of answering him. "If the emperor had acted wisely," says Cochloeus, "when summoning Luther to Worms, he would also have invited theologians to refute his errors."

The archbishop of Treves repaired to the diet and announced the failure of his mediation. The astonishment of the young emperor was equal to his indignation. "It is time to put an end to this business," said he. The archbishop pressed for two days more; all the diet joined in the petition; Charles V gave way. Aleander, no longer able to restrain himself, burst out into violent reproaches.

While these scenes were passing in the diet, Cochloeus burned to gain a victory in which kings and prelates had been unsuccessful. Although he had from time to time dropped a few words at the archbishop's, he was restrained by Aleander's injunction to keep silence. He resolved to find compensation, and as soon as he had rendered a faithful account of his mission to the papal nuncio, he called on Luther. He went up to him in the most friendly manner and expressed the vexation he felt at the emperor's resolution. After dinner, the conversation became animated. Cochloeus urged Luther to retract. The latter shook his head. Several nobles who were at table with him could hardly contain themselves. They were indignant that the partisans of Rome should insist, not upon convincing Luther by Scripture, but on constraining him by force. "Well then," said Cochloeus to Luther, impatient under these reproaches, "I offer to dispute publicly with you, if you will renounce your safe-conduct."

All that Luther demanded was a public disputation. What ought he to do? To renounce the safe-conduct would be to endanger his life; to refuse this challenge would appear to throw doubts on the justice of his cause. His guests perceived in this proposal a plot formed with Aleander, whom the dean of Frankfurt had just quitted. One of them, Vollrat of Watzdorf by name, extricated Luther from the embarrassment occasioned by so difficult a choice. This fiery lord, indignant at a snare, the sole object of which was to deliver Luther into the hands of the executioner, rose hastily, seized the frightened priest, and pushed him out of the room; and blood no doubt would have been spilt, if the other guests had not left the table at the same moment, and mediated between the furious knight and Cochloeus, who trembled with alarm. The latter retired in confusion from the hotel of the knights of Rhodes. Most probably it was in the heat of discussion that these words had fallen from the dean, and there had been no preconcerted plan formed between him and Aleander to entice Luther into so treacherous a snare.

On the morning of Thursday, April 25, the Chancellor Wehe and Doctor Peutinger of Augsburg, the emperor's councilor, who had shown great affection for Luther at the period of his interview with Cajetan, repaired to the hotel of the knights of Rhodes. Wehe and Peutinger would willingly have made every sacrifice to prevent the division that was about to rend the church. They urged the reformer pressingly. Luther, wearied out, rose and dismissed them, saying, "I will never permit any man to set himself above the Word of God."

"Reflect upon our proposal," said they, as they withdrew; "we will return in the evening."

They came; but feeling convinced that Luther would not give way, they brought a new proposition. Luther had refused to acknowledge, first the pope, then the emperor, and lastly the diet; there still remained one judge whom he himself had once demanded—a general council. Doubtless such a proposal would have offended

Rome, but it was their last hope of safety. The delegates offered a council to Luther. The latter might have accepted it without specifying anything. Years would have passed away before the difficulties could have been set aside which the convocation of a council would have met with on the part of the pope. To gain time was for the reformer and the Reformation to gain everything. God and the lapse of years would have brought about great changes. But Luther set plain dealing above all things; he would not save himself at the expense of truth, even were silence alone necessary to dissemble it. "I consent," replied he, "but"—and to make such a request was to refuse a council—"on condition that the council shall decide only according to Scripture."

Peutinger and Wehe, not imagining that a council could decide otherwise, ran quite overjoyed to the archbishop. "Doctor Martin," said they, "submits his books to a council." The archbishop was on the point of carrying these glad tidings to the emperor, when he felt some doubt, and ordered Luther to be brought to him.

Richard of Greiffenklau was alone when the doctor arrived. "Dear doctor," said the archbishop, with great kindness and feeling, "my doctors inform me that you consent to submit unreservedly your cause to a council."

"My lord," replied Luther, "I can endure everything, but I cannot abandon the Holy Scriptures."

The bishop perceived that Wehe and Peutinger had stated the matter incorrectly. Rome could never consent to a council that decided only according to Scripture. "It was like telling a short-sighted man," says Pallavicini, "to read very small print, and at the same time refusing him a pair of spectacles." The worthy archbishop sighed: "It was a fortunate thing that I sent for you," said he. "What would have become of me, if I had immediately carried this news to the emperor?"

"Well, then," said the venerable prelate to Luther, "point out a remedy yourself."

Luther (after a moment's silence): My lord, I know no better than this of Gamaliel: "If this work be of men, it will come to naught; but if it be of God, ye cannot overthrow it; lest haply ye be found even to fight against God." Let the emperor, the electors, the princes, and states of the empire, write this answer to the pope.

The Archbishop: Retract at least some articles.

Luther: Provided they are none of those which the Council of Constance has already condemned.

The Archbishop: I am afraid it is precisely those that you would be called upon to retract.

Luther: In that case I would rather lose my life—rather have my arms and legs cut off, than forsake the clear and true Word of God.

The archbishop understood Luther at last. "You may retire," said he, still with the same kind manner.

"My lord," resumed Luther, "may I beg you to have the goodness to see that his majesty provides me with the safe-conduct necessary for my return."

"I will see to it," replied the good archbishop, and so they parted. Thus ended these negotiations.

Luther withdrew in company with Spalatin, who had arrived at the archbishop's during the interview. John Minkwitz, councilor to the elector of Saxony, had fallen ill at Worms. The two friends went to visit him. Luther gave the sick man the most affectionate consolations. "Farewell," said he, as he retired; "tomorrow I shall leave Worms."

Luther was not deceived. Hardly had he returned three hours to the hotel of the knights of Rhodes, when the chancellor ab Eck, accompanied by the imperial chancellor and a notary, appeared before him.

The chancellor said to him, "Martin Luther, his imperial majesty, the electors, princes, and states of the empire, having at sundry times and in various forms exhorted you to submission, but always in vain, the emperor, in his capacity of advocate and defender of the Catholic faith, finds himself compelled to resort to other measures. He therefore commands you to return home in the space of twenty-one days, and forbids you to disturb the public peace on your road, either by preaching or by writing."

Luther felt clearly that this message was the beginning of his condemnation: "As the Lord pleases," answered he meekly, "blessed be the name of the Lord." He then added, "Before all things, humbly and from the bottom of my heart do I thank his majesty, the electors, princes, and other states of the empire, for having listened to me so kindly. I desire, and have ever desired but one thing—a reformation of the church according to Holy Scripture. I am ready to do and to suffer everything in humble obedience to the emperor's will. Life or death, evil or good report, it is all the same to me, with one reservation—the preaching of the gospel; for, says St. Paul, the Word of God must not be bound." The deputies retired.

On the morning of Friday, April 26, the friends of the reformer with several lords met at Luther's hotel. As it struck ten, Luther issued from the hotel with the friends who had accompanied him to Worms. Twenty gentlemen on horseback surrounded his car. A great crowd of people accompanied him beyond the walls of the city. Some time after, he was overtaken by Sturm the imperial herald at Oppenheim, and on the next day they arrived at Frankfurt.

Chapter 41
Captured

Thus had Luther escaped from these walls of Worms, that seemed destined to be his sepulcher. With all his heart he gave God the glory. "The Devil himself," said he, "guarded the pope's citadel; but Christ has made a wide breach in it, and Satan was constrained to confess that the Lord is mightier than he."

Luther, who reached Frankfurt on the evening of Saturday, April 27, took advantage the next day of a leisure moment, the first that he had enjoyed for a long time, to write a familiar and expressive note to his friend at Wittenberg, the celebrated painter Lucas Cranach. "Your servant, dear gossip Lucas," said he. "I thought his majesty would have assembled some fifty doctors at Worms to convict the monk outright. But not at all. Are these your books? Yes. Will you retract them? No. Well, then, begone. There's the whole history. O blind Germans, . . . how childishly we act, to allow ourselves to be the dupes and sport of Rome. . . . But a day of redemption is coming for us also, and then will we sing hallelujah. . . . For a season we must suffer in silence. 'A little while, and ye shall not see me: and again, a little while, and ye shall see me,' said Jesus Christ (John 16:16). I hope that it will be the same with me. Farewell. I commend you all to the Lord. May He preserve in Christ your understanding and your faith against the attacks of the wolves and the dragons of Rome. Amen."

After having written this letter, Luther, as the time pressed, immediately set out for Friedberg, which is six leagues distant from Frankfurt. On the next day Luther again collected his thoughts. He desired to write once more to Charles, as he had no wish to be confounded with guilty rebels. In his letter to the emperor he set forth clearly what is the obedience due to kings, and that which is due to God, and what is the limit at which the former should cease and give place to the latter.

"God, who is the searcher of hearts, is my witness," says Luther, "that I am ready most earnestly to obey your majesty, in honor or in dishonor, in life or in death, and with no exception save the Word of God, by which man lives. In all the affairs of this present life, my fidelity shall be unshaken, for here to lose or to gain is of no consequence to salvation. But when eternal interests are concerned, God wills not that man should submit unto man. For such submission in spiritual matters is a real worship, and ought to be rendered solely to the Creator."

As we read this epistle, we are involuntarily reminded of the words of Napoleon: "My dominion ends where that of conscience begins." Luther wrote also, but in German, a letter addressed to the states of the empire. Its contents were nearly similar to that which he had just written to the emperor. In it he related all that had passed at Worms.

Early the next day Luther wrote a note to Spalatin, enclosing the two letters he had written the evening before: he sent back to Worms the herald Sturm, won over to the cause of the gospel; and after embracing him, departed hastily for Grünberg.

On Tuesday, about two leagues from Hirschfeldt, he met the chancellor of the prince-abbot of that town, who came to welcome him. Soon after, there appeared a troop of horsemen with the abbot at their head. The latter dismounted, and Luther got out of his wagon. The prince and the reformer embraced, and afterwards entered Hirschfeldt together. The senate received them at the gates of the city. The princes of the church came out to meet a monk anathematized by the pope, and the chief men of the people bent their heads before a man under the ban of the emperor.

"At five in the morning we shall be at church," said the prince at night as he rose from the table to which he had invited the reformer. The abbot insisted on his sleeping in his own bed. The next day Luther preached, and this dignitary of the church with all his train escorted him on his way.

In the evening Luther reached Eisenach, the scene of his childhood. All his friends in this city surrounded him, entreating him to preach, and the next day accompanied him to the church. Upon this the priest of the parish appeared, attended by a notary and witnesses; he came forward trembling, divided between the fear of losing his place and of opposing the powerful man that stood before him. "I protest against the liberty that you are taking," said the priest at last, in an embarrassed tone. Luther went up into the pulpit, and that voice which, twenty-three years before, had sung in the streets of this town to procure a morsel of bread, sounded beneath the arched roof of the ancient church those notes that were beginning to agitate the world. After the sermon, the priest with confusion went up to Luther. The notary had drawn up the protest, the witnesses had signed it, all was properly arranged to secure the incumbent's place. "Pardon me," said he to the doctor humbly; "I am acting thus to protect me from the resentment of the tyrants who oppress the church."

And there were in truth strong grounds for apprehension. The aspect of affairs at Worms was changed: Aleander alone seemed to rule there. "Banishment is Luther's only prospect," wrote Frederick to his brother Duke John; "nothing can save him. If God permits me to return to you, I shall have matters to relate that are almost beyond belief. It is not only Annas and Caiaphas, but Pilate and Herod also, that have combined against him." Frederick had little desire to remain longer at Worms; he departed, and the elector Palatine did the same. The elector-archbishop of Cologne also quitted the diet. Their example was followed by many princes of inferior rank. As they deemed it impossible to avert the blow, they preferred—and in this perhaps they were wrong—abandoning the place. The Spaniards, the Italians, and the most ultramontane German princes alone remained.

The field was now free—Aleander triumphed. He laid before Charles the outline of an edict intended by him as a model of that which the diet ought to issue against the monk. The nuncio's project pleased the exasperated emperor. He assembled the remaining members of the diet in his chamber, and there had Aleander's edict read over to them; it was accepted by all who were present.

The next day, which was a great festival, the emperor went to the cathedral, attended by all the lords of his court. When the religious ceremonies were over, and a crowd of people still thronged the sanctuary, Aleander, robed in all the insignia of his dignity, approached Charles V. He held in his hand two copies of the edict against Luther, one in Latin, the other in German, and kneeling before his imperial majesty, entreated him to affix to them his signature and the seal of the empire. It was at the moment when the sacrifice had been offered, when the incense still filled the temple, while the sacred chants were still reechoing through its long-drawn aisles, and as it were in the presence of the Deity, that the destruction of the enemy of Rome was to be sealed. The emperor, assuming a very gracious air, took the pen and wrote his name. Aleander withdrew in triumph, immediately sent the decree to the printers and forwarded it to every part of Christendom. This edict, although bearing date of May 8, was not signed till later; but it was antedated to make it appear that the signature was affixed at a period when all the members of the diet were assembled.

"We, Charles the fifth," said the emperor, and then came his titles, "to all electors, princes, prelates, and others whom it may concern:

"The Almighty having confided to us, for the defense of the holy faith, more kingdoms and greater authority than He has ever given to any of our predecessors, we purpose employing every means in our power to prevent our holy empire from being polluted by any heresy.

"The Augustinian monk, Martin Luther, notwithstanding our exhortation, has rushed like a madman on our holy church and attempted to destroy it by books overflowing with blasphemy. He has shamefully polluted the indestructible law of holy matrimony; he has endeavored to excite the laity to dye their hands in the blood of the clergy; and setting at naught all authority, has incessantly urged the people to revolt, schism, war, murder, robbery, incendiarism, and to the utter ruin of the Christian faith. . . . In a word, not to mention his many other evil practices, this man, who is in truth not a man, but Satan himself under the form of a man and dressed in a monk's frock, has collected into one stinking slough all the vilest heresies of past times, and has added to them new ones of his own. . . .

"We have therefore dismissed from our presence this Luther, whom all pious and sensible men deem a madman, or one possessed by the Devil; and we enjoin you, moreover, to seize him or cause him to be seized, wherever you may find him, to bring him before us without any delay, or to keep him in safe custody, until you have learned from us in what manner you are to act toward him, and have received the reward due to your labors in so holy a work.

"As for his adherents, you will apprehend them, confine them, and confiscate their property.

"As for his writings, if the best nutriment becomes the detestation of all men as soon as one drop of poison is mingled with it, how much more ought such books, which contain a deadly poison for the soul, to be not only rejected, but destroyed? You will therefore burn them, or utterly destroy them in any other manner.

"As for the authors, poets, printers, painters, buyers or sellers of placards, papers, or pictures, against the pope or the church, you will seize them, body and goods, and will deal with them according to your good pleasure.

"And if any person, whatever be his dignity, should dare to act in contradiction to the decree of our imperial majesty, we order him to be placed under the ban of the empire.

"Let every man behave according to this decree."

Such was the edict signed in the cathedral of Worms. It was more than a bull of Rome, which, although published in Italy, could not be executed in Germany. The emperor himself had spoken, and the diet had ratified his decree. All the partisans of Rome burst into a shout of triumph. "It is the end of the tragedy," exclaimed they. "In my opinion," said Alphonso Valdez, a Spaniard at Charles's court, "it is not the end, but only the beginning." Valdez perceived that the movement was in the church, in the people, and in the age, and that, even should Luther perish, his cause would not perish with him. But no one was blind to the imminent and inevitable danger in which the reformer himself was placed; and the great majority of superstitious persons were filled with horror at the thought of that incarnate devil, covered with a monk's hood, whom the emperor pointed out to the nation.

The man against whom the mighty ones of the earth were thus forging their thunderbolts had quitted the church of Eisenach, and was preparing to bid farewell to some of his dearest friends. He did not take the road to Gotha and Erfurt, but proceeded to the village of More, his father's native place, once more to see his aged grandmother, who died four months after, and to visit his uncle, Henry Luther, and some other relations. Schurff, Jonas, and Suaven set out for Wittenberg; Luther got into the wagon with Amsdorff, who still remained with him, and entered the forests of Thuringia.

The same evening he arrived at the village of his sires. The poor old peasant clasped in her arms that grandson who had withstood Charles the emperor and Leo the pope. Luther spent the next day with his relations; happy, after the tumult at Worms, in this sweet tranquility. On the next morning he resumed his journey, accompanied by Amsdorff and his brother James. In this lonely spot the reformer's fate was to be decided.

They skirted the woods of Thuringia, following the road to Waltershausen. As the wagon was moving through a hollow way, near the deserted church of Glisbach, at a short distance from the castle of Altenstein, a sudden noise was heard, and immediately five horsemen, masked and armed from head to foot, sprung upon the travelers. His brother James, as soon as he caught sight of the assailants, leaped from the wagon and ran away as fast as his legs would carry him, without uttering a single word. The driver would have resisted. "Stop!" cried one of the strangers with a terrible voice, falling upon him and throwing him to the ground. A second mask laid hold of Amsdorff and kept him at a distance.

Meanwhile the three remaining horsemen seized upon Luther, maintaining a profound silence. They pulled him violently from the wagon, threw a military cloak over his shoulders, and placed him on a led horse. The two other masks now quitted Amsdorff and the wagoner; all five leaped to their saddles—one dropped his hat, but they did not even stop to pick it up—and in the twinkling of an eye vanished with their prisoner into the gloomy forest. At first they took the road to Broderade but soon retraced their steps by another path; and without quitting the wood, made so many windings in every direction as utterly to baffle any attempt to track them. Luther, little accustomed to being on horseback, was soon overcome with fatigue. They permitted him to alight for a few minutes: he lay down near a beech tree, where he drank some water from a spring which is still called after his name.

His brother James, continuing his flight, arrived at Waltershausen in the evening. The affrighted wagoner jumped into the car, which Amsdorff had again mounted and, whipping his horses, drove rapidly away from the spot and conducted Luther's friend to Wittenberg. At Waltershausen, at Wittenberg, in the country, villages, and towns along their road, they spread the news of the violent abduction of the doctor. This intelligence, which delighted some, struck the greater number with astonishment and indignation. A cry of grief soon resounded through all Germany: "Luther has fallen into the hands of his enemies."

As soon as it grew dark, and no one could track their footsteps, Luther's guards took a new road. About one hour before midnight they reached the foot of a mountain. The horses ascended slowly. On the summit was an old castle, surrounded on all sides, save that by which it was approached, by the black forests that cover the mountains of Thuringia.

It was to this lofty and isolated fortress, named the Wartburg, where in former times the ancient landgraves had sheltered themselves, that Luther was conducted. The bolts were drawn back, the iron bars fell, the gates opened; the reformer crossed the threshold; the doors were closed behind him. He dismounted in the court. One of the horsemen, Burkhardt of Hund, lord of Altenstein, withdrew; another, John of Berlepsch, provost of the Wartburg, led the doctor into the chamber that was to be his prison, and where he found a knight's uniform and a sword. The three other cavaliers, the provost's attendants, took away his ecclesiastical robes and dressed him in the military garments that had been prepared for him, enjoining him to let his beard and hair grow, in order that no one in the castle might discover who he was. The people in the Wartburg were to know the prisoner only by the name Knight George. Luther scarcely recognized himself in his new dress. At last he was left alone, and his mind could reflect by turns on the astonishing events that had just taken place at Worms, on the uncertain future that awaited him, and on his new and strange residence. From the narrow loopholes of his turret, his eye roamed over the gloomy, solitary, and extensive forests that surrounded him.

Frederick of Thun, Philip Feilitsch, and Spalatin, in a private conversation they had with Luther at Worms by the elector's orders, had not concealed from him that his liberty must be sacrificed to the anger of Charles and of the pope. And yet this abduction had been so mysteriously contrived that even Frederick was for a long time ignorant of the place where Luther was shut up. The grief of the friends of the Reformation was prolonged. The spring passed away; summer, autumn, and winter succeeded; the sun had accomplished its annual course, and still the walls of the Wartburg enclosed their prisoner. Truth had been interdicted by the diet; its defender, confined within the ramparts of a castle, had disappeared from the stage of the world, and no one knew what had become of him.

Wartburg Castle was part prison, part refuge for Martin Luther. To shield the reformer from his enemies, Luther's friends kidnapped him and kept him in the castle for a year. While there, Luther translated the New Testament into German.

Chapter 42
"Captive With and Against My Will"

Hitherto the Reformation had been centered in the person of Luther. His appearance before the Diet of Worms was doubtless the sublimest day of his life. His character appeared at that time almost spotless; and it is this which has given rise to the observation that if God, who concealed the reformer for ten months within the walls of the Wartburg, had that instant removed him forever from the eyes of the world, his end would have been as a deification. But God designs no deification for his servant; and Luther was preserved to the church, in order to teach, by his very faults, that the faith of Christians should be based on the Word of God alone. He was transported suddenly far from the stage on which the great revolution of the sixteenth century was taking place; the truth, that for four years he had so powerfully proclaimed, continued in his absence to act upon Christendom; and the work, of which he was but the feeble instrument, henceforward bore the seal not of man, but of God Himself.

Germany was moved at Luther's captivity. The most contradictory rumors were circulated in the provinces. The reformer's absence excited men's minds more than his presence could have done. In one place it was said that friends from France had placed him in safety on the other bank of the Rhine; in another, that he had fallen by the dagger of the assassin. Even in the smallest villages inquiries were made about Luther; travelers were stopped and questioned, and groups collected in the public places. At times some unknown orator would recount in a spirit-stirring narrative how the doctor had been carried off; he described the cruel horsemen tying their prisoner's hands, spurring their horses, and dragging him after them on foot until his strength was exhausted, stopping their ears to his cries, and forcing the blood from his limbs. "Luther's body," added he, "has been seen pierced through and through." As they heard this, the listeners uttered cries of sorrow. Luther's friends trembled with indignation and swore to avenge his death. Women, children, men of peace, and the aged beheld with affright the prospect of new struggles.

In no place was there such commotion as in Worms itself; resolute murmurs were heard among both people and princes. Ulrich von Hutten and Hermann Busch filled the country with their plaintive strains and songs of battle. Charles V and the nuncios were publicly accused. The nation took up the cause of the poor monk, who, by the strength of his faith, had become their leader.

At Wittenberg, his colleagues and friends, and especially Melancthon, were at first sunk in the deepest affliction. The consternation at Wittenberg was extreme—like that of an army, with gloomy and dejected looks, before the blood-stained body of their general who was leading them on to victory.

Suddenly more comforting news arrived. "Our beloved father lives," exclaimed Philipp in the joy of his soul; "take courage, and be firm." But it was not long before their dejection returned. Luther was alive, but in prison. The edict of Worms, with its terrible proscriptions, was circulated by thousands throughout the empire, and even among the mountains of the Tyrol. Would not the Reformation be crushed by the iron hand that was weighing upon it? Melancthon's gentle spirit was overwhelmed with sorrow.

But the influence of a mightier hand was felt above the hand of man; God Himself deprived the formidable edict of all its strength. The German princes, who had always sought to diminish the power of Rome in the empire, trembled at the alliance between the emperor and the pope, and feared that it would terminate in the destruction of their liberty. Accordingly, while Charles in his journey through the Low Countries greeted with an ironical smile the burning piles which flatterers and fanatics kindled on the public places with Luther's works, these very writings were read in Germany with a continually increasing eagerness, and numerous pamphlets in favor of the reform were daily inflicting some new blow on the papacy. The nuncios were distracted at seeing his edict, the fruit of so many intrigues, producing so little effect. "The ink with which Charles V signed his arrest," said they bitterly, "is scarcely dry, and yet the imperial decree is everywhere torn in pieces."

The people were becoming more and more attached to the admirable man who, heedless of the thunder of Charles and of the pope, had confessed his faith with the courage of a martyr. "He offered to retract," said they, "if he were refuted, and no one dared undertake the task. Does not this prove the truth of his doctrines?" Thus the first movement of alarm was succeeded in Wittenberg and the whole empire by a movement of enthusiasm. Even the archbishop of Mentz, witnessing this outburst of popular sympathy, dared not give the Cordeliers permission to preach against the reformer. The university, which seemed on the point of being crushed, raised its head. The new doctrines were too firmly established for them to be shaken by Luther's absence, and the halls of the academy could hardly contain the crowd of hearers.

Meantime the knight George, for by that name Luther was called in the Wartburg, lived solitary and unknown. "If you were to see me," wrote he to Melancthon, "you would take me for a soldier, and even *you* would hardly recognize me." Luther at first indulged in repose, enjoying a leisure which had not hitherto been allowed him. He wandered freely through the fortress, but could not go beyond the walls. All his wishes were attended to, and he had never been better treated. A crowd of thoughts filled his soul, but none had power to trouble him. By turns he looked down upon the forests that surrounded him and raised his eyes toward heaven. "A strange prisoner am I," exclaimed he, "captive with and against my will."

"Pray for me," wrote he to Spalatin; "your prayers are the only thing I need. I do not grieve for anything that may be said of me in the world. At last I am at rest." This letter, as well as many others of the same period, is dated from the island of Patmos. Luther compared the Wartburg to that celebrated island to which the wrath of Domitian in former times had banished the apostle John. In the midst of the dark forests of Thuringia, the reformer reposed from the violent struggles that had agitated his soul.

Luther's calmness was not of long duration. Seated in loneliness on the ramparts of the Wartburg, he remained whole days lost in deep meditation. At one time the church appeared before him, displaying all her wretchedness; at another, directing his eyes hopefully toward heaven, he could exclaim, "Wherefore hast thou made all men in vain?" (Ps. 89:47). And then giving way to despair, he cried with dejection, "Alas, there is no one in this latter day of His anger, to stand like a wall before the Lord, and save Israel."

Then recurring to his own destiny, he feared lest he should be accused of deserting the field of battle, and this supposition weighed down his soul. "I would rather," said he, "be stretched on coals of fire, than lie here half dead."

Gentler thoughts, however, brought a truce to such anxiety. Everything was not storm and tempest for Luther; from time to time his agitated mind found tranquility and comfort. Next to the certainty of God's help, one thing consoled him in his sorrows: it was the recollection of Melancthon. "If I perish," wrote he, "the gospel will lose nothing: you will succeed me as Elisha did Elijah, with a double portion of my spirit." But calling to mind Philipp's timidity, he exclaimed with energy, "Minister of the word, keep the walls and towers of Jerusalem, until you are struck down by the enemy. As yet we stand alone upon the field of battle; after me, they will aim their blows at you."

But sickness brought him down from those high places on which his courage and his faith had placed him. He had already suffered much at Worms; his disease increased in solitude. He could not endure the food at the Wartburg, which was less coarse than that of his convent; they were compelled to give him the meager diet to which he had been accustomed. He passed whole nights without sleep. Anxieties of mind were superadded to the pains of the body. "Seated by night in my chamber, I uttered groans like a woman in her travail; torn, wounded, and bleeding." Then breaking off his complaints, touched with the thought that his sufferings were a blessing from God, he exclaimed with love, "Thanks be to Thee, O Christ, that Thou wilt not leave me without the precious marks of Thy cross." But soon growing angry with himself, he cried out, "Madman and hardhearted that I am. Woe is me. I pray seldom, I seldom wrestle with the Lord, I groan not for the church of God. Instead of being fervent in spirit, my passions take fire; I live in idleness, in sleep, and indolence." Then, not knowing to what he should attribute this state, and accustomed to expect everything from the affection of his brethren, he exclaimed in the desolation of his heart, "O my friends, do you then forget to pray for me, that God is thus far from me?"

Those who were around him, as well as his friends at Wittenberg and at the elector's court, were uneasy and alarmed at this state of suffering. They feared lest they should see the life they had rescued from the flames of the pope and the sword of Charles V decline sadly and expire. Was the Wartburg destined to be Luther's tomb? "I fear," said Melancthon, "that the grief he feels for the church will cause his death. A fire has been kindled by him in Israel; if he dies, what hope will remain for us? Would to God that, at the cost of my own wretched life, I could retain in the world that soul which is its fairest ornament. O what a man!" exclaimed he, as if already standing on the side of his grave; "we never appreciated him rightly."

What Luther denominated the shameful indolence of his prison was a task that almost exceeded the strength of one man. "I am here all the day," wrote he on May 14, "in idleness and pleasures"—alluding doubtless to the better diet that was provided him at first. "I am reading the Bible in Hebrew and Greek; I am going to write a treatise in German on auricular confession; I shall continue the translation of the Psalms, and compose a volume of sermons, so soon as I have received what I want from Wittenberg. I am writing without intermission." And yet this was but a part of his labors.

As Luther's health continued feeble, he thought of leaving the place of his confinement. But how could he manage it? To appear in public would be exposing his life. The back of the mountain on which the fortress stood was crossed by numerous footways, bordered by tufts of strawberries. The heavy gate of the castle opened, and the prisoner ventured, not without fear, to gather some of the fruit. By degrees he grew bolder, and in his knight's garb began to wander through the surrounding country, attended by one of the guards of the castle, a worthy but somewhat churlish man. One day, having entered an inn, Luther threw aside his sword, which encumbered him, and hastily took up some books that lay there. His nature got the better of his prudence. His guardian trembled for fear this movement, so extraordinary in a soldier, should excite suspicions that the doctor was not really a knight. At another time the two comrades alighted at the convent of Reinhardsbrunn, where Luther had slept a few months before on his road to Worms. Suddenly one of the brothers uttered a cry of surprise. Luther was recognized. His attendant perceived it and dragged him hastily away; and already they were galloping far from the cloister before the astonished brother had recovered from his amazement.

The military life of the doctor had at intervals something about it truly theological. One day the nets were made ready; the gates of the fortress opened; the long-eared dogs rushed forth. Luther desired to taste the pleasures of the chase. The huntsmen soon grew animated; the dogs sprang forward, driving the game from the covers. In the midst of all this uproar, the knight George stood motionless; his mind was occupied with serious thoughts; the objects around him filled his heart with sorrow. "Is not this," says he, "the image of the Devil setting on his dogs; that is, the bishops, those representatives of antichrist, and urging them in pursuit of poor souls?" A young hare was taken: delighted at the prospect of liberating it, he wrapped it carefully in his cloak, and set it down in the midst of a thicket; but hardly had he taken a few steps before the dogs scented the animal and killed it. Luther, attracted by the noise, uttered a groan of sorrow and exclaimed, "O pope, and thou too, Satan, it is thus ye endeavor to destroy even those souls that have been saved from death."

Chapter 43
On Marriage and Monasticism

While the doctor of Wittenberg, thus dead to the world, was seeking relaxation in these sports in the neighborhood of the Wartburg, the work was going on as if of itself: the reform was beginning; it was no longer restricted to doctrine; it entered deeply into men's actions. Bernard Feldkirchen, pastor of Kemberg, the first under Luther's directions to attack the errors of Rome, was also the first to throw off the yoke of its institutions. He married.

The Germans are fond of social life and domestic joys; and hence, of all the papal ordinances, compulsory celibacy was that which produced the saddest consequences. This law, which had been first imposed on the heads of the clergy, had prevented the ecclesiastical fiefs from becoming hereditary. But when extended by Gregory VII to the inferior clergy, it was attended with the most deplorable results. Many priests had evaded the obligations imposed upon them by the most scandalous disorders and had drawn contempt and hatred on the whole body; while those who had submitted to Hildebrand's law were inwardly exasperated against the church, because, while conferring on its superior dignitaries so much power, wealth, and earthly enjoyment, it bound its humbler ministers, who were its most useful supporters, to a self-denial so contrary to the gospel.

"Neither popes nor councils," said Feldkirchen and another pastor named Seidler, who had followed his example, "can impose any commandment on the church that endangers body and soul. The obligation of keeping God's law compels me to violate the traditions of men." The reestablishment of marriage in the sixteenth century was a homage paid to the moral law. The ecclesiastical authority became alarmed and immediately fulminated its decrees against these two priests. Seidler, who was in the territories of Duke George, was given up to his superiors and died in prison. But the elector Frederick refused to surrender Feldkirchen to the archbishop of

Magdeburg. "His highness," said Spalatin, "declines to act the part of a constable." Feldkirchen therefore continued pastor of his flock, although a husband and a father.

The first emotion of the reformer when he heard of this was to give way to exultation: "I admire this new bridegroom of Kemberg," said he, "who fears nothing, and hastens forward in the midst of the uproar." Luther was of opinion that priests ought to marry. But this question led to another—the marriage of monks; and here Luther had to support one of those internal struggles of which his whole life was composed. Melancthon and Carlstadt, the one a layman, the other a priest, thought that the liberty of contracting the bonds of wedlock should be as free for the monks as for the priests. The monk Luther did not think so at first. One day the governor of the Wartburg having brought him Carlstadt's theses on celibacy, "Gracious God," exclaimed he, "our Wittenbergers then will give wives even to the monks." This thought surprised and confounded him; his heart was troubled. He rejected for himself the liberty that he claimed for others. "Ah," said he indignantly, "they will not force *me* at least to take a wife."

There was indeed a great difference between the two questions. The marriage of priests was not the destruction of the priesthood; on the contrary, this of itself might restore to the secular clergy the respect of the people; but the marriage of monks was the downfall of monasticism. It became a question, therefore, whether it was desirable to disband and break up that powerful army which the popes had under their orders. "Priests," wrote Luther to Melancthon, "are of divine appointment, and consequently are free as regards human commandments. But of their own free will the monks adopted celibacy; they are not therefore at liberty to withdraw from the yoke they voluntarily imposed on themselves."

The reformer was destined to advance and carry by a fresh struggle this new position of the enemy. Already had he trodden underfoot a host of Roman abuses, and even Rome herself; but monasticism still remained standing. Monasticism, that had once carried life into so many deserts, and which, passing through so many centuries, was now filling the cloisters with sloth and often with licentiousness, seemed to have embodied itself and gone to defend its rights in that castle of Thuringia, where the question of its life and death was discussed in the conscience of one man. Luther struggled with it: at one moment he was on the point of gaining the victory, at another he was nearly overcome. At length, unable longer to maintain the contest, he flung himself in prayer at the feet of Jesus Christ, exclaiming, "Teach us, deliver us, establish us by thy mercy in the liberty that belongs to us; for of a surety we are thy people."

He had not long to wait for deliverance; an important revolution was effected in the reformer's mind, and again it was the doctrine of justification by faith that gave him victory. That arm which had overthrown the indulgences, the practices of Rome, and the pope himself, also wrought the downfall of the monks in Luther's mind and throughout Christendom. Luther saw that monasticism was in violent opposition to the doctrine of salvation by grace, and that a monastic life was founded entirely on the pretended merits of man. Feeling convinced from that hour that Christ's glory was interested in this question, he heard a voice incessantly repeating in his conscience, "Monasticism must fall." "So long as the doctrine of justification by faith remains pure and undefiled in the church, no one can become a monk," said he. This conviction daily grew stronger in his heart, and about the beginning of September he sent "to the bishops and deacons of the church of Wittenberg," the following theses, which were his declaration of war against a monastic life:

"Whatsoever is not of faith is sin (Rom. 14:23).

"Whosoever maketh a vow of virginity, chastity, of service to God without faith, maketh an impious and idolatrous vow, a vow to the Devil himself.

"To make such vows is worse than the priests of Cybele or the vestals of the pagans; for the monks make their vows in the thought of being justified and saved by these vows; and what ought to be ascribed solely to the mercy of God, is thus attributed to meritorious works.

"We must utterly overthrow such convents, as being the abodes of the Devil.

"There is but one order that is holy and makes man holy, and that is Christianity, or faith.

"For convents to be useful, they should be converted into schools, where children should be brought up to man's estate;

instead of which they are houses where adult men become children, and remain so forever."

We see that Luther would still have tolerated convents as places of education, but erelong his attacks against these establishments became more violent. The immorality and shameful practices that prevailed in the cloisters recurred forcibly to his thoughts. "I am resolved," wrote he to Spalatin on November 11, "to deliver the young from the hellish fires of celibacy." He now wrote a book against monastic vows, which he dedicated to his father.

"Do you desire," said he in his dedication to the old man at Mansfeldt, "do you still desire to rescue me from a monastic life? You have the right, for you are still my father, and I am still your son. But that is no longer necessary: God has been beforehand with you and has Himself delivered me by His power. What matters it whether I wear or lay aside the tonsure and the cowl? Is it the cowl, is it the tonsure that makes the monk? 'All things are yours,' says St. Paul, 'and you are Christ's.' I do not belong to the cowl, but the cowl to me. I am a monk, and yet not a monk; I am a new creature, not of the pope, but of Jesus Christ. Christ alone and without any go-between is my bishop, my abbot, my prior, my lord, my father, and my master; and I know no other. What matters it to me if the pope should condemn me and put me to death? He cannot call me from the grave and kill me a second time. . . . The great day is drawing near in which the kingdom of abomination shall be overthrown. Would to God that it were worthwhile for the pope to put us all to death. Our blood would cry out to heaven against him, and thus his condemnation would be hastened, and his end be near."

The transformation had already been effected in Luther himself; he was no longer a monk. It was not outward circumstances, or earthly passions, or carnal precipitation, that had wrought this change. There had been a struggle: at first Luther had taken the side of monasticism; but truth also had gone down into the lists, and monasticism had fallen before it. The victories that passion gains are ephemeral; those of truth are lasting and decisive.

Chapter 44
Making God Speak German

The hour had come in which the Reformation, from being a mere theological question, was to become the life of the people; and yet the great engine by which this progress was to be effected was not yet in being. This powerful and mighty instrument, destined to hurl its thunderbolts from every side against the proud edifice of Rome, throw down its walls, cast off the enormous weight of the papacy under which the church lay stifled, and communicate an impulse to the whole human race which would not be lost until the end of time—this instrument was to go forth from the old castle of the Wartburg and enter the world on the same day that terminated the reformer's captivity.

The further the church was removed from the time when Jesus, the true light of the world, was on the earth, the greater was her need of the torch of God's Word, ordained to transmit the brightness of Jesus Christ to the men of the latter days. But this divine Word was at that time hidden from the people. Several unsuccessful attempts at translation from the Vulgate had been made in 1477, in 1490, and in 1518; they were almost unintelligible, and from their high price, beyond the reach of the people. It had even been prohibited to give the German church the Bible in the vulgar tongue. Besides which, the number of those who were able to read did not become considerable until there existed in the German language a book of lively and universal interest.

Luther was called to present his nation with the Scriptures of God. That same God who had conducted St. John to Patmos, there to write His Revelation, had confined Luther in the Wartburg, there to translate His Word. This great task, which it would have been difficult for him to have undertaken in the midst of the cares and occupations of Wittenberg, was to establish the new building on the primitive rock, and after the lapse of so many ages, lead Christians back from the subtleties of the schoolmen to the pure fountainhead of redemption and salvation.

The wants of the church spoke loudly; they called for this great work; and Luther, by his own inward experience, was to be led to perform it. In truth, he discovered in faith that repose of the soul which his agitated conscience and his monastic ideas had long induced him to seek in his own merits and holiness. The doctrine of the church, the scholastic theology, knew nothing of the consolations that proceed from faith; but the Scriptures proclaim them with great force, and there it was that he had found them. Faith in the Word of God had made him free. By it he felt emancipated from the dogmatical authority of the church, from its hierarchy and traditions, from the opinions of the schoolmen, the power of prejudice, and from every human ordinance. Those strong and numerous bonds which for centuries had enchained and stifled Christendom were snapped asunder, broken in pieces, and scattered round him; and he nobly raised his head, freed from all authority except that of the Word. This independence of man, this submission to God, which he had learned in the Holy Scriptures, he desired to impart to the church. But before he could communicate them, it was necessary to set before it the revelations of God. A powerful hand was wanted to unlock the massive gates of that arsenal of God's Word from which Luther had taken his arms and to open to the people against the day of battle those vaults and antique halls which for many ages no foot had ever trod.

Luther had already translated fragments of the Holy Scripture; the seven penitential Psalms had been his first task. John the Baptist, Christ Himself, and the Reformation had begun alike by calling men to repentance. It is the principle of every regeneration in the individual man and in the whole human race. These essays had been eagerly received; men longed to have more; and this voice of the people was considered by Luther as the voice of God Himself. He resolved to reply to the call. He was a prisoner within those lofty walls; what of that? He would devote his leisure to translating the Word of God into the language of his countrymen. Erelong this Word will be seen descending from the Wartburg with him, circulating among the people of Germany, and putting them in possession of those spiritual treasures hitherto shut up within the hearts of a few pious men. "Would that this one book," exclaimed Luther, "were in every language, in every hand, before the eyes, and in the ears and hearts of all men." "Scripture without any comment," said he again, "is the sun whence all teachers receive their light."

Such are the principles of Christianity and of the Reformation. According to these venerable words, we should not consult the Fathers to throw light upon Scripture, but Scripture to explain the Fathers. The reformers and the apostles set up the Word of God as the only light, as they exalt the sacrifice of Christ as the only righteousness. By mingling any authority of man with this perfect righteousness of Christ, we vitiate both the foundations of Christianity. These are the two fundamental heresies of Rome; and these, although doubtless in a smaller degree, some teachers were desirous of introducing into the bosom of the Reformation.

Luther opened the Greek originals of the evangelists and apostles and undertook the difficult task of making these divine teachers speak his mother-tongue. Important crisis in the history of the Reformation—from that time the Reformation was no longer in the hands of the reformer. The Bible came forward; Luther withdrew. God appeared, and man disappeared. The reformer placed *the book* in the hands of his contemporaries. Each one may now hear the voice of God for himself; as for Luther, henceforth he mingles with the crowd and takes his station in the ranks of those who come to draw from the common fountain of light and life.

In translating the Holy Scriptures, Luther found that consolation and strength of which he stood so much in need. Solitary, in ill health, and saddened by the exertions of his enemies and the extravagances of some of his followers—seeing his life wearing away in the gloom of that old castle, he had occasionally to endure terrible struggles. In those times men were inclined to carry into the visible world the conflicts that the soul sustains with its spiritual enemies. Luther's lively imagination easily embodied the emotions of his heart, and the superstition of the Middle Ages had still some hold upon his mind, so that we might say of him as it has been said of Calvin with regard to the punishment inflicted on heretics, there was yet a remnant of Roman Catholicism in him.

Satan was not, in Luther's view, simply an invisible though real being; he thought that this adversary of God appeared to men as he had appeared to Jesus Christ. Although the authenticity of many of the stories on this subject contained in *Table Talk* and elsewhere is more than doubtful, history must still record this failing in the reformer. Never was he more assailed by these gloomy ideas than in the solitude of the Wartburg. In the days of his strength he had braved the Devil in Worms, but now all the reformer's powers seemed broken and his glory tarnished. He was thrown aside; Satan was victorious in his turn, and in the anguish of his soul Luther imagined he saw his giant form standing before him, lifting his finger in threatening attitude, exulting with a bitter and hellish sneer, and gnashing his teeth in fearful rage. One day especially, it is said, as Luther was engaged on his translation of the New Testament, he fancied he beheld Satan, filled with horror at his work, tormenting him, and prowling round him like a lion about to spring upon his prey. Luther, alarmed and incensed, snatched up his inkstand and flung it at the head of his enemy. The figure disappeared, and the missile was dashed in pieces against the wall.

The printing of the New Testament was carried on with unexampled zeal. One would have said that the very workmen felt the importance of the task in which they were engaged. Three presses were employed in this labor, and ten thousand sheets, says Luther, were printed daily.

At length, on September 21, 1522, appeared the complete edition of three thousand copies, in two folio volumes, with this simple title: *The New Testament—German—Wittenberg.* It bore no name of man. Every German might henceforward procure the Word of God at a moderate price.

The new translation, written in the very tone of the holy writings, in a language yet in its youthful vigor, and which for the first time displayed its great beauties, interested, charmed, and moved the lowest as well as the highest ranks. It was a national work—the book of the people; nay, more, it was in very truth the Book of God. Even opponents could not refuse their approbation to this wonderful work, and some indiscreet friends of the reformer, impressed by the beauty of the translation, imagined they could recognize in it a second inspiration. This version served more than all Luther's writings to the spread of Christian piety. The work of the sixteenth century was thus placed on a foundation where nothing could shake it. The Bible, given to the people, recalled the mind of man, which had been wandering for ages in the tortuous labyrinth of scholasticism to the divine fountain of salvation. Accordingly the success of this work was prodigious. In a short time every copy was sold. A second edition appeared in the month of December; and in 1533, seventeen editions had been printed at Wittenberg, thirteen at Augsburg, twelve at Basel, one at Erfurt, one at Grimma, one at Leipzig, and thirteen at Strasburg. Such were the powerful levers that uplifted and transformed the church and the world.

While the first edition of the New Testament was going through the press, Luther undertook a translation of the Old. This labor, begun in 1522, was continued without interruption. He published this translation in parts as they were finished, the more speedily to gratify public impatience, and to enable the poor to procure the book.

From Scripture and faith, two sources which in reality are but one, the life of the gospel has flowed, and is still spreading over the world. These two principles combatted two fundamental errors. Faith was opposed to the Pelagian tendency of Roman Catholicism; Scripture, to the theory of tradition and the authority of Rome. Scripture led man to faith, and faith led him back to Scripture. "Man can do no meritorious work; the free grace of God, which he received by faith in Christ, alone saves him." Such was the doctrine proclaimed in Christendom to the study of Scripture. In truth, if faith in Christ is everything in Christianity, if the practices and ordinances of the church are nothing, it is not to the teaching of the church that we should adhere, but to the teaching of Christ. The bond that unites to Christ will become everything to the believer. What matters to him the outward link that connects him with an outward church enslaved by the opinions of men?

Thus, as the doctrine of the Bible had impelled Luther's contemporaries toward Jesus Christ, so in turn the love they felt to Jesus Christ impelled them to the Bible. It was not, as has been supposed in our days, from a philosophical principle, or in consequence of doubt, or from the necessity of inquiry, that they returned to Scripture; it was because they there found the Word of Him they loved. "You have preached Christ to us," said they to the reformer, "let us now hear Him Himself." And they seized the pages that were spread before them, as a letter coming from heaven.

But if the Bible was thus gladly received by those who loved Christ, it was scornfully rejected by those who preferred the traditions and observances of men. A violent persecution was waged against this work of the reformer's. At the news of Luther's publication, Rome trembled. The monk in his cell, the prince on his throne, uttered a cry of anger. Ignorant priests shuddered at the thought that every citizen, nay, every peasant would now be able to dispute with them on the precepts of our Lord. The king of England denounced the work to the elector Frederick and to Duke George of Saxony. As early as the month of November the duke had ordered his subjects to deposit every copy of Luther's New Testament in the hands of the magistrates. Bavaria, Brandenburg, Austria, and all the states devoted to Rome published similar decrees. In some places they made sacrilegious bonfires of these sacred books in the public places. Thus did Rome in the sixteenth century renew the efforts by which paganism had attempted to destroy the religion of Jesus Christ, at the moment when the dominion was escaping from the priests and their idols. But who can check the triumphant progress of the gospel? "Even after my prohibition," wrote Duke George, "many thousand copies were sold and read in my states."

God even made use of those hands to circulate His Word that were endeavoring to destroy it. The Catholic theologians, seeing that they could not prohibit the reformer's work, published a translation of the New Testament. It was Luther's version, altered here and there by the publishers. There was no hindrance to its being read. Rome as yet knew not that wherever the Word of God is established, there her power is shaken. Joachim of Brandenburg permitted all his subjects to read any translation of the Bible, in Latin or in German, provided it did not come from Wittenberg. The people of Germany, and those of Brandenburg in particular, thus made great progress in the knowledge of the truth.

The publication of the New Testament in the vulgar tongue is an important epoch in the Reformation, perhaps the most important of all. It worked an entire change in society: not only in the presbytery of the priest, in the monk's cell, and in the sanctuary of our Lord; but also in the mansions of the great, in the houses of the citizens, and in the cottages of the peasants. When the Bible began to be read in the families of Christendom, Christendom itself was changed. Then arose other habits, other manners, other conversations, and another life. With the publication of the New Testament, the Reformation left the school and the church to take possession of the hearths of the people.

Chapter 45
The Zwickau Prophets

Whenever a great religious ferment takes place in the church, some impure elements always appear with the manifestations of truth. We see the rise of one or more false reforms proceeding from man, which serve as a testimony or countersign to the real reform. Thus many false messiahs in the time of Christ testified that the real Messiah had appeared. The Reformation of the sixteenth century could not be accomplished without presenting a similar phenomenon. In the small town of Zwickau it was first manifested.

In that place there lived a few men who, agitated by the great events that were then stirring all Christendom, aspired at direct revelations from the Deity, instead of meekly desiring sanctification of heart, and who asserted that they were called to complete the Reformation so feebly sketched out by Luther. "What is the use," said they, "of clinging so closely to the Bible? The Bible; always the Bible. Can the Bible preach to us? Is it sufficient for our instruction? If God had designed to instruct us by a book, would He not have sent us a Bible from heaven? It is by the Spirit alone that we can be enlightened. God Himself speaks to us. God Himself reveals to us what we should do and what we should preach." Thus did these fanatics, like the adherents of Rome, attack the fundamental principle on which the entire Reformation is founded: the all-sufficiency of the Word of God.

A simple clothier, Nicholas Storch by name, announced that the angel Gabriel had appeared to him during the night, and that after communicating matters which he could not yet reveal, said to him, "Thou shalt sit on my throne." A former student of Wittenberg, one Mark Stubner, joined Storch, and immediately forsook his studies; for he had received direct from God, said he, the gift of interpreting the Holy Scriptures. Another weaver, Mark Thomas, added to their number; and a new adept, Thomas Numzer, a man of fanatical character, gave a regular organization to this rising sect. Storch, desirous of following Christ's example, selected from among his followers twelve apostles and seventy-two disciples. All loudly declared that apostles and prophets were at length restored to the church of God.

The new prophets, pretending to walk in the footsteps of those of old, began to proclaim their mission: "Woe, woe," said they; "a church governed by men so corrupt as the bishops cannot be the church of Christ. The impious rulers of Christendom will be overthrown. In five, six, or seven years, a universal desolation will come upon the world. The Turk will seize upon Germany; all the priests will be put to death, even those who are married. No ungodly man, no sinner will remain alive; and after the earth has been purified by blood, God will then set up a kingdom; Storch will be put in possession of the supreme authority, and commit the government of the nations to the saints. Then there will be only one faith, only one baptism. The day of the Lord is at hand, and the end of the world draweth nigh. Woe, woe, woe!" Then declaring that infant baptism was valueless, the new prophets called upon all men to come and receive from their hands the true baptism, as a sign of their introduction into the new church of God.

This language made a deep impression on the people. Many pious souls were stirred by the thought that prophets were again restored to the church, and all those who were fond of the marvelous threw themselves into the arms of the extravagants of Zwickau.

But scarcely had this delusion found followers when it met with a powerful antagonist in the Reformation. Nicholas Hausmann (of whom Luther gave this powerful testimony, "What we preach, he practices") was pastor of Zwickau. This good man did not allow himself to be misled by the pretensions of the false prophets. He checked the innovations that Storch and his followers desired to introduce, and his two deacons acted in unison with him. The fanatics, rejected by the ministers of the church, fell into another extravagance. They formed meetings in which revolutionary doctrines were professed. The people were agitated, and disturbances broke out. A priest, carrying the host, was pelted with stones; the civil authority interfered and cast the ringleaders into prison. Exasperated by this proceeding, and eager to vindicate themselves and to obtain redress, Storch, Mark Thomas, and Stubner repaired to Wittenberg.

They arrived there on December 27, 1521. Storch led the way with the gait and bearing of a trooper. Mark Thomas and Stubner followed him. The disorder then prevailing in Wittenberg was favorable to their designs. The youths of the academy and the citizens, already profoundly agitated and in a state of excitement, were a soil well fitted to receive these new prophets.

Thinking themselves sure of support, they immediately called on the professors of the university, in order to obtain their sanction. "We are sent by God to instruct the people," said they. "We have held familiar conversations with the Lord; we know what will happen; in a word, we are apostles and prophets, and appeal to Dr. Luther." This strange language astonished the professors.

"Who has commissioned you to preach?" asked Melancthon of his old pupil Stubner, whom he received into his house.

"The Lord our God."

"Have you written any books?"

"The Lord our God has forbidden me to do so."

Melancthon was agitated; he grew alarmed and astonished. "There are indeed extraordinary spirits in these men," said he; "but what spirits? . . . Luther alone can decide. On the one hand, let us beware of quenching the Spirit of God, and on the other, of being led astray by the spirit of Satan."

Storch, being of a restless disposition, soon quitted Wittenberg. Stubner remained. Animated by an eager spirit of proselytism, he went through the city speaking now to one, then to another; and many acknowledged him as a prophet from God. He addressed himself more particularly to a Swabian named Cellarius, a friend of Melancthon's, who kept a school in which he used to instruct a great number of young people, and who soon fully acknowledged the mission of the new prophets.

Melancthon now became still more perplexed and uneasy. It was not so much the visions of the Zwickau prophets that disturbed him, as their new doctrine on baptism. It seemed to him conformable with reason, and he thought that it was deserving examination; "for," said he, "we must neither admit nor reject anything lightly."

The elector himself, whom Melancthon styled "the lamp of Israel," hesitated. Prophets and apostles in the electorate of Saxony as in Jerusalem of old! "This is a great matter," said he; "and as a layman, I cannot understand it. But rather than fight against God, I would take a staff in my hand and descend from my throne."

At length he informed the professors, by his councilors, that they had sufficient trouble in hand at Wittenberg; that in all probability these pretensions of the Zwickau prophets were only a temptation of the Devil; and that the wisest course, in his opinion, would be to let the matter drop of itself; nevertheless that, under all circumstances, whenever his highness should clearly perceive God's will, he would take counsel of neither brother nor mother, and that he was ready to suffer everything in the cause of truth.

Luther in the Wartburg was apprised of the agitation prevailing in the court and at Wittenberg. Strange men had appeared, and the source whence their mission proceeded was unknown. He saw immediately that God had permitted these afflicting events to humble his servants and to excite them by trials to strive more earnestly after sanctification.

"Your electoral grace," wrote he to Frederick, "has for many years been collecting relics from every country. God has satisfied your desire, and has sent you, without cost or trouble, a whole *cross,* with nails, spears, and scourges. . . . Health and prosperity to the new relic. . . . Only let your highness fearlessly stretch out your arm, and suffer the nails to enter your flesh. . . . I always expected that Satan would send us this plague."

But at the same time nothing appeared to him more urgent than to secure for others the liberty that he claimed for himself. He had not two weights and two measures. "Beware of throwing them into prison," wrote he to Spalatin. "Let not the prince dip his hand in the blood of these new prophets."

Circumstances were becoming every day more serious in Wittenberg. Carlstadt rejected many of the doctrines of the new prophets, and particularly their sentiments on baptism; but there is a contagion in religious enthusiasm that a head like his could not easily resist. From the arrival of the man of Zwickau in Wittenberg, Carlstadt accelerated his movements in the direction of violent reforms. "We must fall upon every ungodly practice, and overthrow them all in a day," said he. He brought together all the passages of Scripture against images, and inveighed with increasing energy against the idolatry of Rome. "They fall down, they crawl before these idols," exclaimed he; "they burn tapers before them, and make them offerings. . . . Let us arise and tear them from the altars."

These words were not uttered in vain before the people. They entered the churches, carried away the images, broke them in pieces, and burned them. It would have been better to wait until their abolition had been legally proclaimed; but some thought that the caution of the chiefs would compromise the Reformation itself.

To judge by the language of these enthusiasts, there were no true Christians in Wittenberg, save those who went not to confession, who attacked the priests, and who ate meat on fast days. If any one was suspected of not rejecting all the rites of the church as an invention of the Devil, he was set down as a worshipper of Baal. "We must form a church," cried they, "composed of saints only."

The citizens of Wittenberg laid before the council certain articles, which it was forced to accept. Many of the articles were conformable to evangelical morals. They required more particularly that all houses of public amusement should be closed.

But Carlstadt soon went still farther: he began to despise learning; and the old professor was heard from his chair advising his pupils to return home, to take up the spade, to guide the plough, and quietly cultivate the earth, because man was to eat bread in the sweat of his brow. George Mohr, the master of the boys' school at Wittenberg, led away by the same fanaticism, called to the assembled citizens from the window of his schoolroom to come and take away their children. Why should they study, since Storch and Stubner had never been at the university, and yet they were prophets? A mechanic, therefore, was as good as all the doctors in the world, and perhaps better, to preach the gospel.

Thus arose doctrines in direct opposition to the Reformation, which had been prepared by the revival of letters. It was with the weapon of theological learning that Luther had attacked Rome; and the enthusiasts of Wittenberg, like the fanatical monks with whom Erasmus had contended, presumed to trample all human learning under foot. If this vandalism succeeded in holding its ground, the hopes of the world were lost; and another irruption of barbarians would extinguish the light that God had kindled in Christendom.

The results of these strange discourses soon showed themselves. Men's minds were prejudiced, agitated, diverted from the gospel; the university became disorganized; the demoralized students broke the bonds of discipline and dispersed; and the governments of Germany recalled their subjects. Thus the men who desired to reform and vivify everything were on the point of ruining all. One struggle more, exclaimed the friends of Rome, who on all sides were regaining their confidence, one last struggle, and all will be ours.

Promptly to check the excesses of these fanatics was the only means of saving the Reformation. But who could do it? Melancthon? He was too young, too weak, too much agitated himself by these strange apparitions. The elector? He was the most pacific man of his age. To build castles at Altenburg, Weimar, Lochau, and Coburg; to adorn churches with the beautiful pictures of Lucas Cranach; to improve the singing in the chapels; to advance the prosperity of his university; to promote the happiness of his subjects; to stop in the midst of the children whom he met playing in the streets, and give them little presents—such were the gentle occupations of his life. And now in his advanced age, would he contend with fanatics; would he oppose violence to violence? How could the good and pious Frederick make up his mind to this?

The disease continued to spread, and no one stood forward to check it. Luther was far from Wittenberg. Confusion and ruin had taken hold of the city. The Reformation had seen an enemy spring from its own bosom more formidable than popes and emperors. It was on the very verge of the abyss.

"Luther! Luther!" was the general and unanimous cry at Wittenberg. The citizens called for him earnestly; the professors desired his advice; the prophets themselves appealed to him. All entreated him to return.

We may imagine what was passing in the reformer's mind. "If I knew," he had once said, "that my doctrine injured one man, one single man, however lowly and obscure—which it cannot, for it is the gospel itself—I would rather die ten times than not retract it." And now a whole city, and that city Wittenberg, was falling into disorder. True, his doctrine had no share in this; but from every quarter of Germany voices were heard accusing him of it.

The news communicated to Luther of the inspiration of these new prophets, and of their sublime interviews with God, did not stagger him one moment. He knew the depth, the anguish, the humiliation of the spiritual life: at Erfurt and Wittenberg he had made trial of the power of God, which did not so easily permit him to believe that God appeared to His creatures and conversed with them. "Ask these prophets," wrote he to Melancthon, "whether they have felt those spiritual torments, those creations of God, that death and hell which accompany a real regeneration. . . . And if they speak to you only of agreeable things, of tranquil impressions, of devotion and piety, as they say, do not believe them, although they should pretend to have been transported to the third heaven. Before Christ could attain His glory, He was compelled to suffer death; and in like manner the believer must go through the bitterness of sin before he can obtain peace. Do you desire to know the time, place, and manner in which God talks with men? Listen: 'As a lion, so hath he broken all my bones: I am cast out from before his face, and my soul is abased even to the gates of hell.' . . . No; the divine Majesty, as they pretend, does not speak directly, so that men may see; for 'no man can see my face, and live.' "

But his firm conviction of the delusion under which these prophets were laboring, served but to augment Luther's grief. Had the great truth of salvation by grace so quickly lost its charms that men turned aside from it to follow fables? He began to feel that the work was not so easy as he had thought at first. He resolved, at the hazard of his life, to return to Wittenberg.

At that time he was threatened by imminent dangers. The enemies of the Reformation fancied themselves on the very eve of destroying it. George of Saxony, equally indisposed toward Rome and Wittenberg, had written, as early as October 16, 1521, to Duke John, the elector's brother, to draw him over to the side of the enemies of the Reformation. "Some," said he, "deny that the soul is immortal. Others—and these are monks—attach bells to swine, and set them to drag the relics of St. Anthony through the streets, and then throw them into the mire. All this is the fruit of Luther's teaching. Entreat your brother the elector either to punish the ungodly authors of these innovations, or at least publicly to declare his opinion of them. Our changing beard and hair remind us that we have reached the latter portion of our course and urge us to put an end to such great evils."

After this, George departed to take his seat in the imperial government at Nuremberg. He had scarcely arrived when he made every exertion to urge it to adopt measures of severity. In effect, on

January 21, this body passed an edict in which it complained bitterly that the priests said mass without being robed in their sacerdotal garments, consecrated the sacrament in German, administered it without having received the requisite confession from the communicants, placed it in the hands of laymen, and were not even careful to ascertain that those who stood forward to receive it were fasting.

Accordingly the imperial government desired the bishops to seek out and punish severely all the innovators within their respective dioceses. The latter hastened to comply with these orders.

Such was the moment selected by Luther for his reappearance on the stage. He saw the danger; he foreboded incalculable disasters. "Erelong," said he, "there will be a disturbance in the empire, carrying princes, magistrates, and bishops before it. The people have eyes: they will not, they cannot be led by force. All Germany will run blood. Let us stand up as a wall to preserve our nation in this dreadful day of God's anger."

Such were Luther's thoughts; but he beheld a still more imminent danger. At Wittenberg, the conflagration, far from dying away became fiercer every day. From the heights of the Wartburg, Luther could perceive in the horizon the frightful gleams, the signal of devastation, shooting at intervals through the air. "More serious intelligence reaches me every day," wrote he. "I shall set out: circumstances positively require me to do so."

Accordingly he rose, on March 3, with the determination of leaving the Wartburg forever. He bade adieu to its time-worn towers and gloomy forests. He passed beyond those walls where the excommunications of Leo X and the sword of Charles V were unable to reach him. He descended the mountain. The world that lay at his feet, and in the midst of which he was about to appear again, would soon perhaps call loudly for his death. But it mattered not: he went forward rejoicing; for in the name of the Lord he was returning among his fellow men.

Chapter 46
Luther Returns

Time had moved on. Luther was quitting the Wartburg for a cause very different from that for which he had entered it. He had gone thither as the assailant of the old tradition and of the ancient doctors; he left it as the defender of the doctrine of the apostles against new adversaries. He had entered it as an innovator and as an impugner of the ancient hierarchy; he left it as a conservative and champion of the faith; and with this weapon he had thrown down mighty superstitions. But if there was a time for destroying, there was also a time for building up. The Roman hierarchy might perhaps have driven the reformer to extremes; the sects which then so boldly raised their heads brought him back to the true path of moderation. The sojourn in the Wartburg divides the history of the Reformation into two periods.

Luther was riding slowly on the road to Wittenberg; it was already the second day of his journey, and Shrove Tuesday. Toward evening a terrible storm burst forth, and the roads were flooded. Two Swiss youths, who were traveling in the same direction as himself, were hastening onward to find a shelter in the city of Jena. They had studied at Basel, and the celebrity of Wittenberg attracted them to that university. Traveling on foot, fatigued, and wet through, John Kessler of St. Gall and his companion quickened their steps. The city was all in commotion with the amusements of the carnival; balls, masquerades, and noisy feasting engrossed the people of Jena; and when the two travelers arrived, they could find no room at any of the inns. At last they were directed to the *Black Bear,* outside the city gates. Dejected and harassed, they repaired thither slowly.

The landlord received them kindly. They took their seats near the open door of the public room, ashamed of the state in which the storm had placed them, and not daring to go in. At one of the tables sat a solitary man in a knight's dress, wearing a red cap on his head, and breeches over which fell the skirts of his doublet; his right hand rested on the pommel of his sword, his left grasped the hilt; and before him lay an open book, which he appeared to be reading with great attention. At the noise made by the entrance of these two young men, he raised his head, saluted them affably, and invited them to come and sit at his table; then alluding to their accent, he said, "You are Swiss, I perceive; but from what canton?"

"From St. Gall."

"If you are going to Wittenberg, you will there meet with a fellow countryman, Dr. Schurff."

Encouraged by this kind reception, they added, "Sir, could you inform us where Martin Luther is at present?"

"I know for certain," replied the knight, "that he is not at Wittenberg; but he will be there shortly. Philipp Melancthon is there. Study Greek and Hebrew, that you may clearly understand the Holy Scriptures."

"If God spare our lives," observed one of the young men, "we will not return home without having seen and heard Dr. Luther, for it is on his account that we have undertaken this long journey. We know that he desires to abolish the priesthood and the mass; and as our parents destined us to the priesthood from our infancy, we should like to know clearly on what grounds he rests his proposition."

The knight was silent for a moment, and then resumed: "Where have you been studying hitherto?"

"At Basel."

"Is Erasmus of Rotterdam still there? What is he doing?" They replied to his questions, and there was another pause. The two Swiss knew not what to think. "Is it not strange," thought they, "that this knight talks to us of Schurff, Melancthon, and Erasmus, and on the necessity of learning Greek and Hebrew."

"My dear friends," said the unknown suddenly, "what do they think of Luther in Switzerland?"

"Sir," replied Kessler, "opinions are very divided about him there as everywhere else. Some cannot extol him enough, and others condemn him as an abominable heretic."

"Ha, the priests, no doubt," said the stranger.

The knight's cordiality had put the students at their ease. They longed to know what book he was reading at the moment of their arrival. The knight had closed it and placed it by his side. At last

Kessler's companion ventured to take it up. To the great astonishment of the two young men, it was the Hebrew Psalter. The student laid it down immediately and, as if to divert attention from the liberty he had taken, said, "I would willingly give one of my fingers to know that language."

"You will attain your wish," said the stranger, "if you will only take the trouble to learn it."

A few minutes after, Kessler heard the landlord calling him: the poor Swiss youth feared something had gone wrong; but the host whispered to him, "I perceive that you have a great desire to see and hear Luther; well, it is he who is seated beside you."

Kessler took this for a joke and said, "Mr. Landlord, you want to make a fool of me."

"It is he, in very truth," replied the host; "but do not let him see that you know him."

Kessler made no answer, but returned to the room and took his seat at the table, burning to repeat to his comrade what he had just heard. But how could he manage it? At last he thought of leaning forward, as if he were looking toward the door, and then whispered into his friend's ear, "The landlord assures me that this man is Luther."

"Perhaps he said *Hutten*," replied his comrade; "you did not hear him distinctly."

"It may be so," returned Kessler; "the host said, 'It is Hutten'; the two names are pretty much alike, and I mistook one for the other."

At that moment the noise of horses was heard before the inn: two merchants, who desired a lodging, entered the room; they took off their spurs, laid down their cloaks, and one of them placed beside him on the table an unbound book, which soon attracted the knight's notice. "What book is that?" asked he.

"A commentary on some of the gospels and epistles by Dr. Luther," replied the merchant; "it is just published."

"I shall procure it shortly," said the knight.

At this moment the host came to announce that supper was ready. The two students, fearing the expense of such a meal in company with the knight Ulrich von Hutten and two wealthy merchants, took the landlord aside, and begged him to serve them with something apart. "Come along, my friends," replied the landlord of the *Black Bear;* "take your place at table beside this gentleman; I will charge you moderately."

"Come along," said the knight, "I will settle the score."

When supper was over, the merchants left the table; the two Swiss remained alone with the knight. He then rose, flung a military cloak over his shoulder, and extending his hand to the students, said to them, "When you reach Wittenberg, salute Dr. Schurff on my part."

"Most willingly," replied they; "but what name shall we give?"

"Tell him simply," added Luther, "He that is to come salutes you." With these words he quitted the room, leaving them full of admiration at his kindness and good nature.

Luther, for it was really he, continued his journey. It will be remembered that he had been laid under the ban of the empire; whoever met and recognized him might seize him. "Satan," said he, "is enraged, and all around are plotting death and hell. Nevertheless, I go forward, and throw myself in the way of the emperor and of the pope, having no protector save God in heaven. Power has been given to all men to kill me wherever they find me. But Christ is the Lord of all; if it be His will that I be put to death, so be it."

Luther reentered Wittenberg on Friday, March 7, having been five days on the way from Eisenach. Doctors, students, and citizens all broke forth in rejoicing. The elector, who was at Lockau with his court, felt great emotion. He was desirous of vindicating him before the diet. "Let him address me a letter," wrote the prince to Schurff, "explaining the motives of his return to Wittenberg, and let him say also, that he returned without my permission." Luther consented.

"I am ready to incur the displeasure of your highness and the anger of the whole world," wrote he to the prince. "Are not the Wittenbergers my sheep? Has God not entrusted them to me? And ought I not, if necessary, to expose myself to death for their sakes? Besides, I fear to see a terrible outbreak in Germany, by which God will punish our nation. Let your highness be well assured, and doubt not that the decrees of heaven are very different from those of Nuremberg." This letter was written on the very day of Luther's arrival at Wittenberg.

The following day, being the eve of the first Sunday in Lent, Luther visited Jerome Schurff. Melancthon, Jonas, Amsdorff, and Augustin Schurff, Jerome's brother, were there assembled. Luther eagerly questioned them, and they were informing him of all that had taken place, when two foreign students were announced, desiring to speak with Dr. Jerome. On entering this assembly of doctors, the two young men of St. Gall were at first abashed; but they soon recovered themselves on discovering the knight of the *Black Bear* among them. The latter immediately went up to them greeted them as old acquaintances, and smiling said, as he pointed to one of the doctors, "This is Philipp Melancthon, whom I mentioned to you." The two Swiss remained all day with the doctors of Wittenberg, in remembrance of the meeting at Jena.

One great thought absorbed the reformer's mind and checked the joy he felt at meeting his friends once more. It was a question whether that doctrine which he had derived from the Word of God, and which was ordained to exert so mighty an influence on the future development of the human race, would be stronger than the destructive principles that threatened its existence. It was a question whether it were possible to reform without destroying, and clear the way to new developments without annihilating the old. To silence fanatical men inspired by the energy of a first enthusiasm; to master an unbridled multitude, to calm it down, to lead it back to order, peace, and truth; to break the course of the impetuous torrent which threatened to overthrow the rising edifice of the Reformation, and to scatter its ruins far and wide—such was the task for which Luther had returned to Wittenberg. "We must now trample Satan underfoot and contend against the angel of darkness," said he. "If our adversaries do not retire of their own accord, Christ will know how to compel them. We who trust in the Lord of life and of death are ourselves lords of life and of death."

But at the same time the impetuous reformer refused to employ the anathemas and thunders of the Word and became a humble pastor, a gentle shepherd of souls. "It is with the Word that we must fight," said he; "by the Word must we overthrow and destroy what has been set up by violence. I will not make use of force against the superstitious and unbelieving. Let him who believeth draw nigh; let him who believeth not keep afar off; no one must be constrained. Liberty is the very essence of faith."

The next day was Sunday. The church was filled with an attentive and excited crowd. Luther went up into the pulpit; there he stood in the presence of the flock that he had once led as a docile sheep but which had broken from him like an untamed bull. His language was simple, noble, yet full of strength and gentleness: one might have supposed him to be a tender father returning to his children, inquiring into their conduct, and kindly telling them what report he had heard about them. He candidly acknowledged the progress they had made in faith, and by this means prepared and captivated their minds. He then continued in these words:

"But we need something more than faith; we need charity. If a man who bears a sword in his hand be alone it is of little consequence whether it be sheathed or not; but if he is in the midst of a crowd, he should act so as to wound nobody.

"What does a mother do to her infant? At first she gives it milk, then some very light food. If she were to begin by giving it meat and wine, what would be the consequence? . . .

"So should we act toward our brethren. My friend, have you been long enough at the breast? It is well, but permit your brother to drink as long as yourself.

"Observe the sun. He dispenses two things, light and heat. There is no king so powerful as to bend aside his rays; they come straight to us, but heat is radiated and communicated in every direction. Thus faith, like light, should always be straight and inflexible; but charity, like heat, should radiate on every side and bend to all the wants of our brethren."

Luther having thus prepared his hearers, began to press them more closely:

"The abolition of the mass, say you, is in conformity with Scripture. Agreed. But what order, what decency have you observed? It behooved you to offer up fervent prayers to the Lord and apply to the public authority; then might every man have acknowledged that the thing was of God.

"The mass is a bad thing; God is opposed to it; it ought to be abolished; and I would that throughout the whole world it were replaced by the supper of the gospel. But let no one be torn from it by force. We must leave the matter in God's hands. His Word must act, and not we. And why so? you will ask. Because I do not hold men's hearts in my hand, as the potter holds the clay. We have a right to speak: we have *not* the right to act. Let us preach; the rest belongs unto God. Were I to employ force, what should I gain? Grimace, formality, apings, human ordinances, and hypocrisy. . . .

But there would be no sincerity of heart, nor faith, nor charity. Where these three are wanting, all is wanting, and I would not give a pear stalk for such a result.

"Our first object must be to win men's hearts, and for that purpose we must preach the gospel. Today the Word will fall in one heart, tomorrow in another, and it will operate in such a manner that each one will withdraw from the mass and abandon it. God does more by His Word alone than you and I and all the world by our united strength. God lays hold upon the heart; and when the heart is taken, all is won.

"I do not say this for the restoration of the mass. Since it is down, in God's name there let it lie. But should you have gone to work as you did? Paul, arriving one day in the powerful city of Athens, found there altars raised to false gods. He went from one to the other and observed them without touching one. But he walked peaceably to the middle of the marketplace and declared to the people that all their gods were idols. His language took possession of their hearts, and the idols fell without Paul's having touched them.

"I will preach, discuss, and write; but I will constrain none, for faith is a voluntary act. See what I have done. I stood up against the pope, indulgences, and papists, but without violence or tumult. I put forward God's Word; I preached and wrote—this was all I did. And yet while I was asleep, or seated familiarly at table with Amsdorff and Melancthon, the Word that I had preached overthrew popery, so that neither prince nor emperor has done it so much harm. And yet I did nothing; the Word alone did all. If I had wished to appeal to force, the whole of Germany would perhaps have been deluged with blood. But what would have been the result? Ruin and desolation both to body and soul. I therefore kept quiet and left the Word to run through the world alone. Do you know what the Devil thinks when he sees men resort to violence to propagate the gospel through the world? Seated with folded arms behind the fire of hell, Satan says, with malignant looks and frightful grin, 'Ah, how wise these madmen are to play my game.' But when he sees the Word running and contending alone on the field of battle, then he is troubled, and his knees knock together; he shudders and faints with fear."

Luther went into the pulpit again on Tuesday, and his powerful voice resounded once more through the agitated crowd. He preached again on the five succeeding days. He took a review of the destruction of images, distinction of meats, the institution of the Lord's supper, the restoration of the cup, the abolition of confession. He showed that these points were of far less importance than the mass, and that the originators of the disorders that had taken place in Wittenberg had grossly abused their liberty. He employed by turns the language of Christian charity and bursts of holy indignation.

The crowd ceased not to fill the temple; people flocked from the neighboring towns to hear the new Elijah. Among others, Capito spent two days at Wittenberg and heard two of the doctor's sermons. Never had Luther and Cardinal Albert's chaplain been so well agreed. Melancthon, the magistrates, the professors, and all the inhabitants were delighted. Schurff, charmed at the result of so gloomy an affair, hastened to communicate it to the elector. On Friday, March 15, the day on which Luther delivered his sixth sermon, he wrote, "O what joy has Dr. Martin's return diffused among us. His words, through divine mercy, every day are bringing back our poor misguided people into the way of truth. It is clear as the sun that the Spirit of God is in him, and that by His special providence he returned to Wittenberg."

Luther had to soothe a fanaticized multitude, to tame its unbridled passions; and in this he succeeded. In his eight discourses, the reformer did not allow one offensive word to escape him against the originators of these disorders, not one unpleasant allusion. But the greater his moderation, the greater also was his strength; the more caution he used toward these deluded men, the more powerful was his vindication of offended truth. How could the people of Wittenberg resist his powerful eloquence? Men usually ascribe to timidity, fear, and compromise those speeches that advocate moderation. Here there was nothing of the sort. Luther appeared before the inhabitants of Wittenberg, braving the excommunication of the pope and the proscription of the emperor. He had returned in spite of the prohibition of the elector, who had declared his inability to defend him. Even at Worms, Luther had not shown so much courage. He confronted the most imminent dangers; and accordingly his words were not disregarded: the man who braved the scaffold had a right to exhort to submission. That man may boldly speak of obedience to God, who, to do so, defies all the persecution of man. At Luther's voice all objections vanished, the tumult subsided, seditious cries were heard no longer, and the citizens of Wittenberg returned quietly to their dwellings.

The chief prophets were not at Wittenberg when Luther returned. Nicholas Storch was wandering through the county; Mark Stubner had quitted Melancthon's hospitable roof. The old schoolmaster Cellarius alone had remained. Stubner, however, being informed that the sheep of his fold were scattered, hastily returned. Those who were still faithful to "the heavenly prophecy" gathered round their master, reported Luther's speeches to him, and asked him anxiously what they were to think and do. Stubner exhorted them to remain firm in their faith. "Let him appear," cried Cellarius, "let him grant us a conference, let him only permit us to set forth our doctrine, and then we shall see."

Luther cared little to meet such men as these; he knew them to be of violent, impatient, and haughty disposition, who could not endure even kind admonition, and who required that every one should submit at the first word, as to a supreme authority. Such are enthusiasts in every age. And yet, as they desired an interview, the doctor could not refuse it. Besides, it might be of use to the weak ones of the flock were he to unmask the imposture of the prophets.

The conference took place. Stubner opened the proceedings, explaining in what manner he desired to regenerate the church and transform the world. Luther listened to him with great calmness. "Nothing that you have advanced," replied he at last gravely, "is based upon Holy Scripture. It is all a mere fable."

At these words Cellarius could contain himself no longer; he raised his voice, gesticulated like a madman, stamped, and struck the table with his fist, and exclaimed, in a passion, that it was an insult to speak thus to a man of God. Upon this Luther observed, "St. Paul declares that the proofs of his apostleship were made known by miracles; prove yours in like manner."

"We will do so," answered the prophets.

"The God whom I worship," said Luther, "will know how to bridle your gods."

Stubner, who had preserved his tranquility, then fixed his eyes on the reformer and said to him with an air of inspiration, "Martin Luther, I will declare what is now passing in your soul. . . . Thou art beginning to believe that my doctrine is true."

Luther, after a brief pause, exclaimed, "God chastise thee, Satan."

At these words all the prophets were as if distracted. "The spirit, the spirit," cried they. Luther, adopting that cool tone of contempt and cutting and homely language so familiar to him, said, "I slap your *spirit* on the snout." Their clamors now increased; Cellarius, in particular, distinguished himself by his violence. He foamed and trembled with anger. They could not hear one another in the room where they met in conference. At length the three prophets abandoned the field and left Wittenberg the same day.

Thus had Luther accomplished the work for which he had left his retreat. He had made a stand against fanaticism and expelled from the bosom of the renovated church the enthusiasm and disorder by which it had been invaded. If with one hand the Reformation threw down the dusty decretals of Rome, with the other it rejected the assumptions of the mystics and established on the ground it had won the living and unchangeable Word of God. The character of the Reformation was thus firmly settled. It was destined to walk forever between these two extremes, equally remote from the convulsions of the fanatics and the deathlike torpor of the papacy.

A whole population excited, deluded, and unrestrained, had at once become tranquil, calm, and submissive; and the most perfect quiet again reigned in that city which a few days before had been like the troubled sea.

Perfect liberty was immediately established at Wittenberg. Luther still continued to reside in the convent and wear his monastic dress, but everyone was free to do otherwise. In communicating at the Lord's table, a general absolution was sufficient, or a particular one might be obtained. It was laid down as a principle, to reject nothing but what was opposed to a clear and formal declaration of Holy Scripture. This was not indifference; on the contrary, religion was thus restored to what constitutes its very essence; the sentiment of religion withdrew from the accessory forms in which it had well-nigh perished and transferred itself to its true basis. Thus the Reformation was saved, and its teaching enabled to continue its development in the bosom of the church in charity and truth.

Chapter 47
Luther and Henry VIII

Luther had escaped from the Wartburg and reappeared on the stage of the world; and at this news the rage of his former adversaries was revived. Luther had been three months and a half at Wittenberg when a rumor, increased by the thousand tongues of fame, brought intelligence that one of the greatest kings of Christendom had risen against him. Henry VIII, head of the house of Tudor, a prince descended from the families of York and Lancaster, and in whose person after so much bloodshed, the red and white roses were at length united, the mighty king of England, who claimed to reestablish on the continent, and especially in France, the former influence of his crown, had just written a book against the poor monk of Wittenberg. "There is much boasting about a little book by the king of England," wrote Luther to Lange on June 26, 1522.

Henry was then thirty-one years old; "he was tall, strong built and proportioned, and had an air of authority and empire." His countenance expressed the vivacity of his mind; vehement, presuming to make everything give way to the violence of his passions, and thirsting for glory, he at first concealed his faults under a certain impetuosity that is peculiar to youth, and flatterers were not wanting to encourage them. He would often visit, in company with his courtiers, the house of his chaplain, Thomas Wolsey, the son of an Ipswich butcher. Endowed with great skill, of overweening ambition, and of unbounded audacity, this man, protected by the bishop of Winchester, chancellor of the kingdom, had rapidly advanced in his master's favor. He succeeded in obtaining the first place in the king's councils, and as sole minister, all the princes of Christendom were forced to purchase his favor.

Henry lived in the midst of balls, banquets, and jousting, and madly squandered the treasures his father had slowly accumulated. Magnificent tournaments succeeded each other without interval. In these sports the king, who was distinguished above all the combatants by his manly beauty, played the chief part. If the contest appeared for a moment doubtful, the strength and address of the young monarch, or the artful policy of his opponents, gave him the victory, and the lists resounded with shouts and applause in his honor. The vanity of the youthful prince was inflated by these easy triumphs, and there was no success in the world to which he thought he might not aspire.

Catholic piety had representatives in the court of Henry VIII. John Fisher, bishop of Rochester, then nearly seventy years of age, as distinguished for learning as for the austerity of his manners, was the object of universal admiration. He had been the oldest councilor of Henry VII, and the duchess of Richmond, grandmother to Henry VIII, calling him to her bedside, had commended to his care the youth and inexperience of her grandson. The king, in the midst of his irregularities, long continued to revere the aged bishop as a father.

A man much younger than Fisher, a layman and a lawyer, had before this attracted general attention by his genius and noble character. His name was Thomas More, son of one of the judges of the King's Bench. He was poor, austere, and diligent. At the age of twenty he had endeavored to quench the passions of youth by wearing a shirt of haircloth and by self-scourging. On one occasion, being summoned by Henry VIII while he was attending mass, he replied that God's service was before the king's. Wolsey introduced him to Henry, who employed him on various embassies and showed him much kindness. He would often send for him and converse with him on astronomy, on Wolsey, and on divinity.

In truth, the king himself was not unacquainted with the Roman Catholic doctrines. It would appear that if his brother Arthur had lived, Henry was destined for the archiepiscopal see of Canterbury. Thomas Aquinas, St. Bonaventure, his mistresses—all were mixed up in the mind and life of this prince, who had masses of his own composition sung in his chapel.

As soon as Henry had heard talk of Luther, he became indignant against him; and hardly was the decree of the Diet of Worms known in England, before he ordered the pontiff's bull against the reformer's works to be put in execution. On May 12, 1521, Thomas Wolsey, who, together with the office of chancellor of England, combined those of cardinal and legate of Rome, went in solemn procession to St. Paul's. Before him walked a tall priest bearing a silver column terminated by a cross; behind him, another ecclesiastic of similar height carried the archiepiscopal crozier of York; a nobleman at his side held the cardinal's hat. Lords, prelates, ambassadors from the pope and emperor, accompanied him, followed by a long line of mules bearing chests covered with the richest and most brilliant hangings. It was this magnificent procession that was carrying to the burning pile the writings of the poor monk of Wittenberg. When they reached the cathedral, the insolent priest placed his cardinal's hat on the altar. The virtuous bishop of Rochester stationed himself at the foot of the cross, and with agitated voice preached earnestly against the heresy. After this the impious books of the heresiarch were brought together and devoutly burned in the presence of an immense crowd. Such was the first intelligence that England received of the Reformation.

Henry would not stop here. This prince, whose hand was ever upraised against his adversaries, his wives, or his favorites, wrote to the elector-palatine, "It is the Devil who, by Luther's means, has kindled this immense conflagration. If Luther will not be converted, let him and his writings be burned together."

This was not enough. Having been convinced that the progress of heresy was owing to the extreme ignorance of the German princes, Henry thought that the moment had arrived for showing his learning. The victories of his battle-axe did not permit him to doubt of those that were reserved for his pen. But another passion, vanity, ever greatest in the smallest minds, spurred the king onward. He was humiliated at having no title to oppose to that of "Catholic" and "Most Christian," borne by the kings of Spain and France, and he had long been begging a similar distinction from the court of Rome. What would be more likely to procure it than an attack upon heresy? Henry therefore threw aside the kingly purple and descended from his throne into the arena of theological discussion. He enlisted Thomas Aquinas, Peter Lombard, Alexander Hales, and Bonaventure into his service; and the world beheld the publication of the *Defense of the Seven Sacraments Against Martin Luther, by the Most Invincible King of England and France, Lord of Ireland, Henry, the Eighth of That Name.*

"I will rush in front of the church to save her," said the king of England in this treatise; "I will receive in my bosom the poisoned arrows of her assailants. The present state of things calls me to do so. Every servant of Christ, whatever be his age, sex, or rank, should rise up against the common enemy of Christendom.

"Let us put on a twofold breastplate—the heavenly breastplate, to conquer by the weapons of truth him who combats with those of error; but also an earthly breastplate, that if he shows himself obstinate in his malice, the hand of the executioner may constrain him to be silent and that once at least he may be useful to the world by the terrible example of his death."

Henry VIII was unable to hide the contempt he felt toward his feeble adversary. "This man," said the crowned theologian, "seems to be in the pangs of childbirth; after a travail without precedent, he produces nothing but wind. Remove the daring envelope of the insolent verbiage with which he clothes his absurdities, as an ape is clothed in purple, and what remains? . . . a wretched and empty sophism."

The king defends successively the mass, penance, confirmation, marriage, orders, and extreme unction; he is not sparing of abusive language toward his opponent; he calls him by turns a wolf of hell, a poisonous viper, a limb of the Devil. Even Luther's sincerity is attacked. Henry VIII crushes the mendicant monk with his royal anger, "and writes as 't were with his scepter," says a historian.

And yet it must be confessed that his work was not bad, considering the author and his age. The style is not altogether without force, but the public of the day did not confine themselves to paying it due justice. The theological treatise of the powerful king of England was received with a torrent of adulation. "The most learned work the sun ever saw," cried some. "We can only compare it," reechoed others, "to the works of Augustine. He is a Constantine, a Charlemagne." "He is more," said others; "he is a second Solomon."

These flatteries soon extended beyond the limits of England. Henry desired John Clarke, dean of Windsor, his ambassador at Rome, to present his book to the sovereign pontiff. Leo X received the envoy in full consistory. Clarke laid the royal work before him, saying, "The king my master assures you that, having now refuted Luther's errors with the pen, he is ready to combat his adherents with the sword." Leo, touched with this promise, replied that the king's book could not have been written without the aid of the Holy

Portrait of Henry VIII by Hans Holbein the Younger (Copyright © Fundacion Coleccion Thyssen-Bornemisza. Madrid)

Ghost and conferred upon Henry the title of *Defender of the Faith,* which is still borne by the sovereigns of England.

The reception which this volume met with at Rome contributed greatly to increase the number of its readers. In a few months many thousand copies were issued from different presses. "The whole Christian world," says Cochloeus, "was filled with admiration and joy."

Luther read Henry's book with a smile mingled with disdain, impatience, and indignation. The falsehood and the abuse it contained but especially the air of contempt and compassion which the king assumed, irritated the Wittenberg doctor to the highest degree. The thought that the pope had crowned this work, and that on all sides the enemies of the gospel were triumphing over the Reformation and the reformer as already overthrown and vanquished, increased his indignation. Besides, what reason had he to temporize? Was he not fighting in the cause of a King greater than all the kings of the earth? The meekness of the gospel appeared to him unseasonable. An eye for an eye, a tooth for a tooth. He went beyond all bounds. Persecuted, insulted, hunted down, wounded, the furious lion turned round, and proudly roused himself to crush his enemy.

The elector, Spalatin, Melancthon, and Bugenhagen strove in vain to pacify him. They would have prevented his replying, but nothing could stop him. "I will not be gentle toward the king of England," said he. "I know that it is vain for me to humble myself, to give way, to entreat, to try peaceful methods. At length I will show myself more terrible toward these furious beasts, who goad me every day with their horns. I will turn mine upon them. I will provoke Satan until he falls down lifeless and exhausted.

"If this heretic does not recant, says Henry VIII, the new Thomas, he must be burned alive. Such are the weapons they are now employing against me: the fury of stupid donkeys and swine of the brood of Thomas Aquinas; and then the stake. Well, then, be it so. Let these hogs advance if they dare, and let them burn me. Here I am waiting for them. After my death, though my ashes should be thrown into a thousand seas, they will rise, pursue, and swallow up this abominable herd. Living, I shall be the enemy of the papacy; burned, I shall be its destruction. Go then, swine of St. Thomas, do what seemeth good to you. You will ever find Luther like a bear upon your way and as a lion in your path. He will spring upon you whithersoever you go and will never leave you at peace, until he has broken your iron heads and ground your brazen foreheads into dust."

Luther first reproaches Henry VIII with having supported his doctrines solely by the decrees and opinions of men. "As for me," says he, "I never cease crying, The gospel, the gospel! Christ, Christ! And my adversaries continue to reply, Custom, custom; ordinances, ordinances; Fathers, Fathers. St. Paul says, 'That your faith should not stand in the wisdom of men, but in the power of God' (I Cor. 2:5). And the apostle by this thunderclap from heaven overthrows and disperses, as the wind scatters the dust, all the hobgoblins of this Henry. Frightened and confounded, these Thomists, papists, and Henrys fall prostrate before the thunder of these words."

He then refutes the king's book in detail and overturns his arguments one after the other, with a perspicuity, spirit, and knowledge of the Holy Scriptures and the history of the church, but also with an assurance, disdain, and sometimes violence that ought not to surprise us.

Having reached the end of his confutation, Luther again becomes indignant that his opponent should derive his arguments from the Fathers only: this was the basis of the whole controversy. "To all the words of the Fathers and of men, of angels and of devils," said he, "I oppose, not old customs, not the multitude of men, but the Word of eternal Majesty, the gospel, which even my adversaries are obliged to recognize. To this I hold fast, on this I repose, in this I boast, in this I exult and triumph over the papists, the Thomists, the Henrys, the sophists, and all the swine of hell. The King of heaven is with me; for this reason I fear nothing, although a thousand Augustines, a thousand Cyprians, and a thousand of these churches which Henry defends should rise up against me. It is a small matter that I should despise and revile a king of the earth, since he himself does not fear in his writings to blaspheme the King of heaven and to profane His holy name by the most impudent falsehoods."

"Papists," exclaimed he in conclusion, "will you never cease from your idle attacks? Do what you please. Nevertheless, before that gospel which I preach, down must come popes, bishops, priests, monks, princes, devils, death, sin, and all that is not Christ or in Christ."

Thus spoke the poor monk. His violence certainly cannot be excused, if we judge it by the rule to which he himself appealed—by the Word of God. It cannot even be justified by alleging either the grossness of the age—for Melancthon knew how to observe decorum in his writings—or the energy of his character; for if this energy had any influence over his language, passion also exerted more. It is better, then, that we should condemn it. And yet, that we may be just, we should observe, that in the sixteenth century this violence did not appear so strange as it would nowadays. The learned were then an estate, as well as the princes. By becoming a writer, Henry had attacked Luther. Luther replied, according to the established law in the republic of letters, that we must consider the truth of what is said and not the quality of him who says it. Let us add also that when this same king turned against the pope, the abuse which the Catholic writers and the pope himself poured upon him far exceeded all that Luther had ever said.

Great was the emotion at the king's court; Surrey, Wolsey, and the crowd of courtiers put a stop to the festivities and pageantry at Greenwich to vent their indignation in abuse and sarcasm. The venerable bishop of Rochester, who had been delighted to see the young prince, formerly confided to his care, breaking a lance in defense of the church, was deeply wounded by the attack of the monk. He replied to it immediately. His words distinctly characterize the age and the church. "Take us the foxes, the little foxes, that spoil the vines, says Christ in the Song of Songs. This teaches us," said Fisher, "that we must take the heretics before they grow big. Now Luther has become a big fox, so old, so cunning, and so sly, that he is very difficult to catch. What do I say? . . . a fox? He is a mad dog, a ravening wolf, a cruel bear; or rather, all those animals in one; for the monster includes many beasts within him."

Thomas More also descended into the arena to contend with the monk of Wittenberg. Although a layman, his zeal against the Reformation amounted to fanaticism, if it did not even urge him to shed blood. "Reverend brother, father, tippler, Luther, renegade of the order of St. Augustine, misshapen bacchanal of either faculty, unlearned doctor of theology." Such is the language addressed to the reformer by one of the most illustrious men of his age. He then proceeds to explain the manner in which Luther had composed his book against Henry VIII: "He called his companions together and desired them to go each his own way and pick up all sorts of abuse and scurrility. One frequented the public carriages and boats; another the baths and gambling-houses; a third the taverns and barbers' shops; a fourth the mills and brothels. They noted down in their tablets all the most insolent, filthy, and infamous things they heard; and bringing back all these abominations and impurities, they discharged them into that filthy kennel which is called Luther's mind. If he retracts his falsehoods and calumnies," continues More, "if he lays aside his folly and his madness, if he swallows his own filth, . . . he will find one who will seriously discuss with him. But if he proceeds as he has begun, joking, teasing, fooling, calumniating, vomiting sewers and cesspools, . . . let others do what they please; as for me, I should prefer leaving the little friar to his own fury and filth." More would have done better to have restrained his own. Luther never degraded his style to so low a degree. He made no reply.

This writing still further increased Henry's attachment to More. He would often visit him in his humble dwelling at Chelsea. After dinner, the king, leaning on his favorite's shoulder, would walk in the garden, while Mistress More and her children, concealed behind a window, could not turn away their astonished eyes. After one of these walks, More, who knew his man well, said to his wife, "If my head could win him a single castle in France, he would not hesitate to cut it off."

The king, thus defended by the bishop of Rochester and by his future chancellor, had no need to resume his pen. Confounded at finding himself treated in the face of Europe as a common writer, Henry VIII abandoned the dangerous position he had taken, and throwing away the pen of the theologian, had recourse to the more effectual means of diplomacy.

An ambassador was dispatched from the court of Greenwich with a letter for the elector and dukes of Saxony. "Luther, the real serpent fallen from heaven," wrote he, "is pouring out his floods of venom upon the earth. He is stirring up revolts in the church of Jesus Christ, abolishing laws, insulting the powers that be, inflaming the laity against the priests, and laymen and priests against the pope, subjects against their sovereigns, and desires nothing better than to see Christians fighting and destroying one another, and the enemies of our faith hailing this scene of carnage with a frightful grin.

"What is this doctrine which he calls evangelical, if it be not Wycliffe's? Now, most honored uncles, I know what your ancestors have done to destroy it. In Bohemia they hunted it down like a wild beast, and driving it into a pit, they shut it up and kept it fast. You will not allow it to escape through your negligence, lest, creeping into Saxony and becoming master of the whole of Germany, its smoking nostrils should pour forth the flames of hell, spreading that conflagration far and wide which your nation hath so often wished to extinguish in its blood.

"For this reason, most worthy princes, I feel obliged to exhort you and even to entreat you in the name of all that is most sacred, promptly to extinguish the cursed sect of Luther: put no one to death, if that can be avoided; but if this heretical obstinacy continues, then shed blood without hesitation, in order that the abominable heresy may disappear from under heaven."

The elector and his brother referred the king to the approaching council. Thus Henry VIII was far from attaining his end. "So great a name mixed up in the dispute," said Paul Sarpi, "served to render it more curious, and to conciliate general favor toward Luther, as usually happens in combats and tournaments, where the spectators have always a leaning to the weaker party and take delight in exaggerating the merit of his actions."

Chapter 48
The Peasants' War (Part 1)

A political ferment, very different from that produced by the gospel, had long been at work in the empire. The people, bowed down by civil and ecclesiastical oppression, bound in many countries to the seignorial estates, and transferred from hand to hand along with them, threatened to rise with fury and at last to break their chains. This agitation had shown itself long before the Reformation by many symptoms, and even then the religious element was blended with the political; in the sixteenth century it was impossible to separate these two principles, so closely associated in the existence of nations. In Holland, at the close of the preceding century, the peasants had revolted, placing on their banners, by way of arms, a loaf and a cheese, the two great blessings of these poor people. "The alliance of the shoes" had shown itself in the neighborhood of Speyer in 1502. In 1513 it appeared again in Brisgau, being encouraged by the priests. In 1514 Würtemberg had seen the "league of Poor Conrad," whose aim was to maintain by rebellion "the right of God." In 1515 Carinthia and Hungary had been the theater of terrible agitations. These seditions had been quenched in torrents of blood, but no relief had been accorded to the people. A political reform, therefore, was not less necessary than a religious reform. The people were entitled to this, but we must acknowledge that they were not ripe for its enjoyment.

Since the commencement of the Reformation, these popular disturbances had not been renewed; men's minds were occupied by other thoughts. Luther, whose piercing glance had discerned the condition of the people, had already, from the summit of the Wartburg, addressed them in serious exhortations calculated to restrain their agitated minds. "Rebellion," he had said, "never produces the amelioration we desire, and God condemns it. What is it to rebel, if it be not to avenge one's self? The Devil is striving to excite to revolt those who embrace the gospel, in order to cover it with opprobrium; but those who have rightly understood my doctrine do not revolt."

Everything gave cause to fear that the popular agitation could not be restrained much longer. The government that Frederick of Saxony had taken such pains to form and which possessed the confidence of the nation was dissolved. The emperor, whose energy might have been an efficient substitute for the influence of this national administration, was absent; the princes whose union had always constituted the strength of Germany were divided; and the new declarations of Charles V against Luther, by removing every hope of future harmony, deprived the reformer of part of the moral influence by which, in 1522, he had succeeded in calming the storm. The chief barriers that hitherto had confined the torrent being broken, nothing could any longer restrain its fury.

It was not the religious movement that gave birth to political agitations, but in many places it was carried away by their impetuous waves. Perhaps we should even go further, and acknowledge that the movement communicated to the people by the Reformation gave fresh strength to the discontent fermenting in the nation. The violence of Luther's writings, the intrepidity of his actions and language, the harsh truths that he spoke, not only to the pope and prelates, but also to the princes themselves, must all have contributed to inflame minds that were already in a state of excitement. Accordingly, Erasmus did not fail to tell him, "We are now reaping the fruits that you have sown." And further, the cheering truths of the gospel at last brought to light stirred all hearts and filled them with anticipation and hope. But many unregenerate souls were not prepared by repentance for the faith and liberty of Christians. They were very willing to throw off the papal yoke, but they would not take up the yoke of Christ. And hence, when princes devoted to the cause of Rome endeavored in their wrath to stifle the Reformation, real Christians patiently endured these cruel persecutions; but the multitude resisted and broke out, and seeing their desires checked in one direction, gave vent to them in another. "Why," said they, "should slavery be perpetuated in the state, while the church invites all men to a glorious liberty? Why should governments rule only by force, when the gospel preaches nothing but gentleness?"

Unhappily, at a time when the religious reform was received with equal joy both by princes and people, the political reform, on the contrary, had the most powerful part of the nation against it; and while the former had the gospel for its rule and support, the latter had soon no other principles than violence and despotism. Accordingly, while the one was confined within the bounds of truth, the other rapidly, like an impetuous torrent, overstepped all limits of justice. But to shut one's eyes against the indirect influence of the Reformation on the troubles that broke out in the empire would betoken partiality. A fire had been kindled in Germany by religious discussions, from which it was impossible to prevent a few sparks escaping which were calculated to inflame the passions of the people.

The claims of a few fanatics to divine inspiration increased the evil. While the Reformation had continually appealed from the pretended authority of the church to the real authority of the Holy Scriptures, these enthusiasts not only rejected the authority of the church, but of Scripture also: they spoke only of an inner word, of an internal revelation from God; and overlooking the natural corruption of their hearts, they gave way to all the intoxication of spiritual pride and fancied they were saints.

"To them the Holy Scriptures were but a dead letter," said Luther, "and they all began to cry, *The Spirit, the Spirit.* But most assuredly I will not follow where their spirit leads them."

The most notorious of these enthusiasts was Thomas Münzer; he was not devoid of talent, had read his Bible, was zealous, and might have done good, if he had been able to collect his agitated thoughts and find peace of heart. But as he did not know himself and was wanting in true humility, he was possessed with a desire of reforming the world, and forgot, as all enthusiasts do, that the reformation should begin with himself. Some mystical writings that he had read in his youth had given a false direction to his mind. He first appeared at Zwickau, quitted Wittenberg after Luther's return, dissatisfied with the inferior part he was playing, and became pastor of the small town of Alstadt in Thuringia. He could not long remain quiet, and accused the reformers of founding, by their adherence to the letter, a new Roman Catholicism, and of forming churches which were not pure and holy.

"Luther," said he, "has delivered men's consciences from the yoke of the pope, but he has left them in a carnal liberty, and not led them in spirit toward God."

He considered himself as called of God to remedy this great evil. The revelations of the *Spirit* were in his eyes the means by which his reform was to be effected. "He who possesses this Spirit," said he, "possesses the true faith, although he should never see the Scriptures in his life. Heathens and Turks are better fitted to receive it than many Christians who style us enthusiasts." It was Luther whom he here had in view. "To receive this Spirit, we must mortify the flesh," said he at another time, "wear tattered clothing, let the beard grow, be of a sad countenance, keep silence, retire into desert places, and supplicate God to give us a sign of His favor. Then God will come and speak with us, as formerly He spoke with Abraham, Isaac, and Jacob. If He were not to do so, He would not deserve our attention. I have received from God the commission to gather together His elect into a holy and eternal alliance."

The agitation and ferment which were at work in men's minds were but too favorable to the dissemination of these enthusiastic ideas. Man loves the marvelous and whatever flatters his pride. Münzer, having persuaded a part of his flock to adopt his views, abolished ecclesiastical singing and all other ceremonies. He maintained that obedience to princes "void of understanding" was at once to serve God and Belial. Then marching out at the head of his parishioners to a chapel in the vicinity of Alstadt, whither pilgrims from all quarters were accustomed to resort, he pulled it down. After this exploit, being compelled to leave that neighborhood, he wandered about Germany and went as far as Switzerland, carrying with him, and communicating to all who would listen to him, the plan of a general revolution. Everywhere he found men's minds prepared; he threw gunpowder on the burning coals, and the explosions forthwith took place.

Luther, who had rejected warlike enterprises, could not be led away by the tumultuous movements of the peasantry. Fortunately for social order, the gospel preserved him; for what would have happened had he carried his extensive influence into their camp? He ever firmly maintained the distinction between secular and spiritual things; he continually repeated that it was immortal souls which Christ emancipated by His Word; and if with one hand he attacked the authority of the church, with the other he upheld with equal power the authority of princes. "A Christian," said he, "should endure a hundred deaths, rather than meddle in the slightest degree with the revolt of the peasants." He wrote to the elector: "It causes me especial joy that these enthusiasts themselves boast, to all who are willing to listen to them, that they do not belong to us. The Spirit urges them on, say they; and I reply, it is an evil spirit, for he bears no other fruit than the pillage of convents and churches: the greatest highway robbers upon earth might do as much."

At the same time, Luther, who desired that others should enjoy the liberty he claimed for himself, dissuaded the prince from all measures of severity: "Let them preach what they please, and against whom they please," said he; "for it is the Word of God that must march in front of the battle and fight against them. If their spirit be the true Spirit, He will not fear our severity; if ours is the true one, He will not fear their violence. Let us leave the spirits to struggle and contend with one another. Perhaps some persons may be led astray: there is no battle without wounds; but he who fighteth faithfully shall be crowned. Nevertheless, if they desire to take up the sword, let your highness forbid it, and order them to leave the country."

The insurrection began in the Black Forest near the sources of the Danube, so frequently the theater of popular commotions. On July 19, 1524, some Thurgovian peasants rose against the abbot of Reichenau, who would not accord them an evangelical preacher. Erelong thousands were collected round the small town of Tengen to liberate an ecclesiastic who was there imprisoned. The revolt spread with inconceivable rapidity from Swabia as far as the Rhenish provinces Franconia, Thuringia, and Saxony. In the month of January 1525, all these countries were in a state of rebellion.

About the end of this month, the peasants published a declaration in twelve articles in which they claimed the liberty of choosing their own pastors, the abolition of small tithes, of slavery, and of fines on inheritance, the right to hunt, fish, and cut wood, etc. Each demand was backed by a passage from holy writ, and they said in conclusion, "If we are deceived, let Luther correct us by Scripture."

The opinions of the Wittenberg divines were consulted. Luther and Melancthon delivered theirs separately, and they both gave evidence of the difference of their characters. Melancthon, who thought every kind of disturbance a crime, overstepped the limits of his usual gentleness and could not find language strong enough to express his indignation. The peasants are criminals, against whom he invokes all laws human and divine. If friendly negotiation is unavailing, the magistrates should hunt them down, as if they were robbers and assassins. "And yet," adds he—and we require at least one feature to remind us of Melancthon—"let them take pity on the orphans when having recourse to the penalty of death."

Luther's opinion of the revolt was the same as Melancthon's, but he had a heart that beat for the miseries of the people. On this occasion he manifested a dignified impartiality and spoke the truth frankly to both parties. He first addresses the princes, and more especially the bishops:

"It is you," said he, "who are the cause of this revolt; it is your clamors against the gospel, your guilty oppressions of the poor, that have driven the people to despair. It is not the peasants, my dear lords, that rise up against you; it is God Himself who opposes your madness. The peasants are but the instruments He employs to humble you. Do not imagine you can escape the punishment He is preparing for you. Even should you have succeeded in destroying all these peasants, God is able from the very stones to raise up others to chastise your pride. If I desired revenge, I might laugh in my sleeve and look on while the peasants were carrying on their work, or even increase their fury; but may God preserve me from such thoughts. . . . My dear lords, put away your indignation, treat these poor peasants as a man of sense treats people who are drunk or insane. Quiet these commotions by mildness, lest a conflagration should arise and burn all Germany. Among those twelve articles there are certain demands which are just and equitable."

This prologue was calculated to conciliate the peasants' confidence in Luther and to make them listen patiently to the truths he had to tell them. He represented to them that the greater number of their demands were well founded, but that to revolt was to act like heathens; that the duty of a Christian is to be patient, not to fight; that if they persisted in revolting against the gospel in the name of the gospel, he should look upon them as more dangerous enemies than the pope. "The pope and the emperor," continued he, "combined against me; but the more they blustered, the more did the gospel gain ground. . . . And why was this? Because I have never drawn the sword or called for vengeance; because I never had recourse to tumult or insurrection: I relied wholly upon God, and placed everything in His almighty hands. Christians fight not with swords or arquebuses, but with sufferings and with the cross. Christ their Captain handled not the sword, . . . He was hung upon a tree."

But to no purpose did Luther employ this Christian language. The people were too much excited by the fanatical speeches of the leaders of the insurrection to listen, as of old, to the words of the reformer. "He is playing the hypocrite," said they; "he flatters the nobles. He has declared war against the pope, and yet wishes us to submit to our oppressors."

The revolt, instead of dying away, became more formidable. At Weinsberg, Count Louis of Helfenstein and the seventy men under his orders were condemned to death by the rebels. A body of peasants drew up with their pikes lowered, while others drove the count and his soldiers against this wall of steel. The wife of the wretched Helfenstein, a natural daughter of the Emperor Maximilian, holding an infant two years old in her arms, knelt before them, and with loud cries begged for her husband's life, and vainly endeavored to arrest this march of murder; a boy who had been in the count's service and had joined the rebels, capered gaily before him and played the dead march upon his fife, as if he had been leading his victims in a dance. All perished; the child was wounded in its mother's arms; and she herself thrown upon a dung-cart, and thus conveyed to Heilbrunn.

At the news of these cruelties, a cry of horror was heard from the friends of the Reformation, and Luther's feeling heart underwent a terrible conflict. On the one hand the peasants, ridiculing his advice, pretended to receive revelations from heaven, made an impious use of the threatenings of the Old Testament, proclaimed an equality of ranks and a community of goods, defended their cause with fire and sword, and indulged in barbarous atrocities. On the other hand, the enemies of the Reformation asked the reformer, with a malicious sneer, if he did not know that it was easier to kindle a fire than to extinguish it. Shocked at these excesses, alarmed at the thought that they might check the progress of the gospel, Luther hesitated no longer, no longer temporized; he inveighed against the insurgents with all the energy of his character, and perhaps overstepped the just bounds within which he should have contained himself.

"The peasants," said he, "commit three horrible sins against God and man, and thus deserve the death of body and soul. First they revolt against their magistrates to whom they have sworn fidelity; next they rob and plunder convents and castles; and lastly they veil their crimes with the cloak of the gospel. If you do not put a mad dog to death, you will perish, and all the country with you. Whoever is killed fighting for the magistrates will be a true martyr, if he has fought with a good conscience." Luther then gives a powerful description of the guilty violence of the peasants who force simple and peaceable men to join their alliance and thus drag them to the same condemnation. He then adds, "For this reason, my dear lords, help, save, deliver, have pity on these poor people. Let every one strike, pierce, and kill, who is able. . . . If thou diest, thou canst not meet a happier death; for thou diest in the service of God, and to save thy neighbor from hell."

Neither gentleness nor violence could arrest the popular torrent. The church bells were no longer rung for divine service; whenever their deep and prolonged sounds were heard in the fields, it was the tocsin, and all ran to arms. The people of the Black Forest had rallied round John Muller of Bulgenbach. With an imposing aspect, covered with a red cloak, and wearing a red cap, this leader boldly advanced from village to village followed by the peasantry. Behind him, on a wagon decorated with ribands and branches of trees, was raised the tricolor flag, black, red, and white—the signal of revolt. A herald, dressed in the same colors, read the twelve articles, and invited the people to join in the rebellion. Whoever refused was banished from the community.

Erelong this march, which at first was peaceable, became more disquieting. "We must compel the lords to submit to our alliance," exclaimed they. And to induce them to do so, they plundered the granaries, emptied the cellars, drew the seignorial fish-ponds, demolished the castles of the nobles who resisted, and burnt the convents. Opposition had inflamed the passions of those rude men; equality no longer satisfied them; they thirsted for blood and swore to put to death every man who wore a spur.

At the approach of the peasants, the cities that were unable to resist them opened their gates and joined them. In whatever place they entered, they pulled down the images and broke the crucifixes; armed women paraded the streets and threatened the monks. If they were defeated in one quarter, they assembled again in another and braved the most formidable forces. A committee of peasants was established at Heilbrunn. The counts of Lowenstein were taken prisoners, dressed in a smock-frock, and then, a white staff having been placed in their hands, they were compelled to swear to the twelve articles. "Brother George, and thou, brother Albert," said a tinker of Ohringen to the counts of Hohenlohe, who had gone to their camp, "swear to conduct yourselves as our brethren; for you also are now peasants; you are no longer lords." Equality of rank, the dream of many democrats, was established in aristocratic Germany.

Many nobles, some through fear, others from ambition, then joined the insurgents. The famous Goetz von Berlichingen, finding his vassals refused to obey him, desired to flee to the elector of Saxony; but his wife, who was lying-in, wishing to keep him near her, concealed the elector's answer. Goetz, being closely pursued, was compelled to put himself at the head of the rebel army. On May 7 the peasants entered Würzburg, where the citizens received them with acclamations. The forces of the princes and knights of Swabia and Franconia, which had assembled in this city, evacuated it, and retired in confusion to the citadel, the last bulwark of the nobility.

But the movement had already extended to other parts of Germany. Speyer, the Palatinate, Alsace, and Hess accepted the twelve articles, and the peasants threatened Bavaria, Westphalia, the Tyrol, Saxony, and Lorraine. The margrave of Baden, having rejected the articles, was compelled to flee. The coadjutor of Fulda acceded to them with a smile. The smaller towns said they had no lances with which to oppose the insurgents. Mentz, Treves, and Frankfurt obtained the liberties which they had claimed.

An immense revolution was preparing in all the empire. The ecclesiastical and secular privileges, that bore so heavily on the peasants, were to be suppressed; the possessions of the clergy were to be secularized, to indemnify the princes and provide for the wants of the empire; taxes were to be abolished, with the exception of a tribute payable every ten years; the imperial power was to subsist alone, as being recognized by the New Testament; all the other princes were to cease to reign; sixty-four free tribunals were to be established, in which men of all classes should have a seat; all ranks were to return to their primitive condition; the clergy were to be henceforward merely the pastors of the churches; princes and knights were to be simply the defenders of the weak; uniformity in weights and measures was to be introduced, and only one kind of money was to be coined throughout the empire.

Meanwhile the princes had shaken off their first lethargy, and George von Truchsess, commander in chief of the imperial army, was advancing on the side of the lake of Constance. On May 2 he defeated the peasants at Beblingen, marched on the town of Weinsberg, where the unhappy count of Helfenstein had perished, and burnt and razed it to the ground, giving orders that the ruins should be left as an eternal monument of the treason of its inhabitants. At Fürfeld he united with the elector-palatine and the elector of Treves, and all three moved toward Franconia.

The Frauenburg, the citadel of Würzburg, held out for the princes, and the main army of the peasants still lay before its walls. As soon as they heard of Truchsess's march, they resolved on an assault, and at nine o'clock at night on May 15, the trumpets sounded, the tricolor flag was unfurled, and the peasants rushed to the attack with horrible shouts. Sebastian von Rotenhen, one of the warmest partisans of the Reformation, was governor of the castle. He had put the fortress in a formidable state of defense, and having exhorted the garrison to repel the assault with courage, the soldiers, holding up three fingers, had all sworn to do so. A most terrible conflict then took place. To the vigor and despair of the insurgents, the fortress replied from its walls and towers by petards, showers of sulphur and boiling pitch, and the discharges of artillery. The peasants, thus struck by their unseen enemies, were staggered for a moment; but in a instant their fury grew more violent. The struggle was prolonged as the night advanced. The fortress, lit up by a thousand battle fires, appeared in the darkness like a towering giant, who, vomiting flames, struggled alone amidst the roar of thunder for the salvation of the empire against the ferocious valor of these furious hordes. Two hours after midnight the peasants withdrew, having failed in all their efforts.

They now tried to enter into negotiations, either with the garrison or with Truchsess, who was advancing at the head of his army. But this was going out of their path; violence and victory alone could save them. After some little hesitation, they resolved to march against the imperial forces, but the cavalry and artillery made terrible havoc in their ranks. At Königshofen, and afterwards at Engelstadt, those unfortunate creatures were totally defeated. The princes, nobles, and bishops, abusing their victory, indulged in the most unprecedented cruelties. The prisoners were hanged on the trees by the wayside. The bishop of Würzburg, who had run away, now returned, traversed his diocese accompanied by executioners, and watered it alike with the blood of the rebels and of the peaceful friends of the Word of God. Goetz von Berlichingen was sentenced to imprisonment for life. The Margrave Casimir of Anspach put out the eyes of eighty-five insurgents who had sworn that their eyes should never look upon that prince again; and he cast this troop of blinded individuals upon the world, who wandered up and down, holding each other by the hand, groping along, tottering, and begging their bread. The wretched boy who had played the dead-march on his fife at the murder of Helfenstein, was chained to a post; a fire was kindled around him and the knights looked on laughing at his horrible contortions.

Public worship was everywhere restored in its ancient forms. The most flourishing and populous districts of the empire exhibited to those who traveled through them nothing but heaps of dead bodies and smoking ruins. Fifty thousand men had perished, and the people lost nearly everywhere the little liberty they had hitherto enjoyed. Such was the horrible termination of this revolt in the south of Germany.

Chapter 49
The Peasants' War (Part 2)

But the evil was not confined to the south and west of Germany. Münzer, after having traversed a part of Switzerland, Alsace, and Swabia, had again directed his steps toward Saxony. A few citizens of Mülhausen, in Thuringia, had invited him to their city and elected him their pastor. The town council having resisted, Münzer deposed it and nominated another, consisting of his friends, with himself at their head. Full of contempt for that Christ, "sweet as honey," whom Luther preached and being resolved to employ the most energetic measures, he exclaimed, "Like Joshua, we must put all the Canaanites to the sword." He established a community of goods and pillaged the convents. "Münzer," wrote Luther to Amsdorff on April 11, 1525, "is not only pastor, but king and emperor of Mülhausen." The poor no longer worked. If any one needed corn or cloth, he went and demanded it of some rich man: if the latter refused, the poor man took it by force; if he resisted, he was hanged.

As Mülhausen was an independent city, Münzer was able to exercise his power for nearly a year without opposition. The revolt in the south of Germany led him to imagine that it was time to extend his new kingdom. He had a number of heavy guns cast in the Franciscan convent, and endeavored to raise the peasantry and miners of Mansfeldt. "How long will you sleep?" said he to them in a fanatical proclamation. "Arise, and fight the battle of the Lord. The time is come. France, Germany, and Italy are moving. On, on, on! . . . Heed not the groans of the impious ones. They will implore you like children; but be pitiless. On, on, on! . . . The fire is burning: let your sword be ever warm with blood. On, on, on! . . . Work while it is yet day." The letter was signed, "Münzer, servant of God against the wicked."

The country people, thirsting for plunder, flocked round his standard. Throughout all the districts of Mansfeldt, Stolberg, and Schwartzburg in Hesse, and the duchy of Brunswick, the peasantry rose in insurrection. The convents of Michelstein, Ilsenburg, Walkenried, Rossleben, and many others in the neighborhood of the Hartz, or in the plains of Thuringia, were devastated. At Reinhardsbrunn, which Luther had visited, the tombs of the ancient landgraves were profaned and the library destroyed.

Terror spread far and wide. Even at Wittenberg some anxiety was felt. Those doctors who had feared neither the emperor nor the pope trembled in the presence of a madman. They were always on the watch for news, and every step of the rebels was counted. "We are here in great danger," said Melancthon. "If Münzer succeeds, it is all over with us, unless Christ should rescue us. Münzer advances with a worse than Scythian cruelty, and it is impossible to repeat his dreadful threats."

The pious elector had long hesitated what he should do. Münzer had exhorted him and all the princes to be converted, because, said he, their hour was come; and he had signed these letters, "Münzer, armed with the sword of Gideon." Frederick would have desired to reclaim these misguided men by gentle measures. On April 14, when he was dangerously ill, he had written to his brother John: "We may have given these wretched people more than one cause for insurrection. Alas, the poor are oppressed in many ways by their spiritual and temporal lords." And when his attention was directed to the humiliation, the revolutions, the dangers to which he would expose himself unless he promptly stifled the rebellion, he replied, "Hitherto I have been a mighty elector, having chariots and horses in abundance; if it be God's pleasure to take them from me now, I will go on foot."

The youthful Philip, landgrave of Hesse, was the first of the princes who took up arms. His knights and soldiers swore to live and die with him. After pacifying his own states, he directed his march toward Saxony. On their side, Duke John, the elector's brother; Duke George of Saxony; and Duke Henry of Brunswick advanced and united their troops with those of Hesse. The peasants, terrified at the sight of this army, fled to a small hill, where, without any discipline, without arms, and for the most part without courage, they formed a rampart with their wagons. Münzer had not even prepared ammunition for his large guns. No succors appeared; the rebels were hemmed in by the army; they lost all confidence. The princes, taking pity on them, offered them propositions which they appeared willing to accept. Upon this, Münzer had recourse to the most powerful lever that enthusiasm can put in motion. "Today we shall behold the arm of the Lord," said he, "and all our enemies shall be destroyed." At this moment a rainbow appeared over their heads; the fanatical host, who carried a rainbow on their flags, beheld in it a sure omen of the divine protection. Münzer took advantage of it. "Fear nothing," said he to the citizens and peasants; "I will catch all their balls in my sleeve." At the same time he cruelly put to death a young gentleman, Maternus von Geholfen, an envoy from the princes, in order to deprive the insurgents of all hope of pardon.

The landgrave, having assembled his horsemen, said to them, "I well know that we princes are often in fault, for we are but men; but God commands all men to honor the powers that be. Let us save our wives and children from the fury of these murderers. The Lord will give us the victory, for He has said, 'Whosoever resisteth the power, resisteth the ordinance of God.' " Philip then gave the signal of attack. It was May 15, 1525. The army was put in motion; but the peasant host stood immovable, singing the hymn "Come, Holy Ghost" and waiting for heaven to declare in their favor. The artillery soon broke down their rude rampart, carrying dismay and death into the midst of the insurgents. Their fanaticism and courage at once forsook them; they were seized with panic and ran away in disorder. Five thousand perished in the flight.

After the battle, the princes and their victorious troops entered Frankenhausen. A soldier who had gone into a loft in the house where he was quartered, found a man in bed. "Who art thou?" asked he; "art thou one of the rebels?" Then observing a pocketbook, he took it up and found several letters addressed to Thomas Münzer. "Art thou Münzer?" demanded the trooper. The sick man answered, "No." But as the soldier uttered dreadful threats, Münzer, for it was really he, confessed who he was. "Thou art my prisoner," said the horseman.

When Münzer was taken before Duke George and the land-grave, he persevered in saying that he was right to chastise the princes, since they opposed the gospel. "Wretched man," replied they, "think of all those of whose death you have been the cause." But he answered, smiling in the midst of his anguish, "They would have it so." He took the sacrament and was beheaded at the same time with Pfeiffer, his lieutenant. Mülhausen was taken, and the peasants were loaded with chains.

A nobleman having observed among the crowd of prisoners a peasant of favorable appearance, went up and said to him, "Well, my man, which government do you like best—that of the peasants or of the princes?" The poor fellow made answer with a deep sigh, "Ah, my lord, no knife cuts so deep as the rule of peasant over his fellows."

The relics of the insurrection were quenched in blood; Duke George, in particular, acted with the greatest severity. In the states of the elector, there were neither executions nor punishment. The Word of God, preached in all its purity, had shown its power to restrain the tumultuous passions of the people.

From the very beginning, indeed, Luther had not ceased to struggle against the rebellion, which was, in his opinion, the fore-runner of the judgment day. Advice, prayers, and even irony had not been spared. At the end of the articles drawn up at Erfurt by the rebels, he had subjoined as a supplementary article, "*Item,* The following article has been omitted. Henceforward the honorable council shall have no power; it shall do nothing; it shall sit like an idol or a log of wood; the commonalty shall chew its food, and it shall govern with its hands and feet tied; henceforth the wagon shall guide the horses, the horses shall hold the reins, and we shall go on admirably, in conformity with the glorious system set forth in these articles."

Luther did not confine himself to writing. While the disturbance was still at its height, he quitted Wittenberg and went through some of the districts where the agitation was greatest. He preached, he labored to soften his hearers' hearts, and his hand, to which God had given power, turned aside, quieted, and brought back the impetuous and overflowing torrents into their natural channels.

In every quarter the doctors of the Reformation exerted a similar influence. At Halle, Brentz had revived the drooping spirits of the citizens by the promises of God's Word, and four thousand peasants had fled before six hundred citizens. At Ichterhausen, a mob of peasants having assembled with an intent to demolish several castles and put their lords to death, Frederick Myconius went out to them alone, and such was the power of his words, that they immediately abandoned their design.

Such was the part taken by the reformers and the Reformation in the midst of this revolt; they contended against it with all their might, with the sword of the Word, and boldly maintained those principles which alone, in every age, can preserve order and subjection among the nations. Accordingly, Luther asserted that if the power of sound doctrine had not checked the fury of the people, the revolt would have extended its ravages far more widely, and have overthrown both church and state. Everything leads us to believe that these melancholy prophecies would have been realized.

If the reformers thus contended against sedition, it was not without receiving grievous wounds. On the side of the princes, it was continually repeated that Luther and his doctrine were the cause of the revolt; and however absurd this idea may be, the reformer could not see it so generally entertained without experiencing the deepest grief. On the side of the people, Münzer and all the leaders of the insurrection represented him as a vile hypocrite and flatterer of the great, and these calumnies easily obtained belief. The violence with which Luther had declared against the rebels had displeased even moderate men. The friends of Rome exulted; all were against him, and he bore the heavy anger of his times. But his greatest affliction was to behold the work of heaven thus dragged in the mire and classed with the most fanatical projects. He exclaimed, "Soon, perhaps, I also shall be able to say, 'All ye shall be offended because of me this night'" (Matt. 26:31).

Yet in the midst of this deep bitterness, he preserved his faith: "He who has given me power to trample the enemy under foot," said he, "when he rose up against me like a cruel dragon or a furious lion, will not permit this enemy to crush me, now that he appears before me with the treacherous glance of the basilisk. I groan as I contemplate those calamities. Often have I asked myself whether it would not have been better to have allowed the papacy to go on quietly, rather than witness the occurrence of so many troubles and seditions in the world. But no, it is better to have snatched a few souls from the jaws of the Devil, than to have left them all between his murderous fangs."

Now terminated the revolution in Luther's mind that had begun at the period of his return from the Wartburg. The inner life no longer satisfied him: the church and her institutions now became most important in his eyes. The boldness with which he had thrown down everything was checked at the sight of still more sweeping destructions: he felt it his duty to preserve, govern, and build up; and from the midst of the bloodstained ruin with which the peasant war had covered all Germany, the edifice of the new church began slowly to arise.

These disturbances left a lasting and deep impression on men's minds. The nations had been struck with dismay. The masses, who had sought in the Reformation nothing but political reform, withdrew from it of their own accord when they saw it offered them spiritual liberty only. Luther's opposition to the peasants was his renunciation of the ephemeral favor of the people. A seeming tranquility was soon established, and the noise of enthusiasm and sedition was followed in all Germany by a silence inspired by terror.

Thus the popular passions, the cause of revolution, the interests of a radical equality, were quelled in the empire; but the Reformation did not yield. These two movements, which many have confounded with each other, were clearly marked out by the difference of their results. The insurrection was from below; the Reformation from above. A few horsemen and cannons were sufficient to put down the one; but the other never ceased to rise in strength and vigor, in spite of the reiterated assaults of the empire and the church.

Chapter 50
Luther's Marriage

In the monastery of Nimptsch, near Grimma, in Saxony, dwelt nine nuns who were diligent in reading the Word of God and who had discovered the contrast that exists between a Christian and a cloistered life. Their names were Magdalen Staupitz, Eliza Canitz, Ava Grossen, Ava and Margaret Schonfeldt, Laneta Golis, Margaret and Katherine Zeschau, and Katherine von Bora. The first impulse of these young women, after they were delivered from the superstitions of the monastery, was to write to their parents. "The salvation of our souls," said they, "will not permit us to remain any longer in a cloister." Their parents, fearing the trouble likely to arise from such a resolution, harshly rejected their prayers.

The poor nuns were dismayed. How could they leave the monastery? Their timidity was alarmed at so desperate a step. At last, the horror caused by the papal services prevailed, and they promised not to leave one another, but to repair in a body to some respectable place, with order and decency. Two worthy and pious citizens of Torgau, Leonard Koppe and Wolff Tomitzsch, offered their assistance, which they accepted as coming from God Himself and left the convent of Nimptsch without any opposition and as if the hand of the Lord had opened the doors to them. Koppe and Tomitzsch received them in their wagon; and on April 7, 1523, the nine nuns, amazed at their own boldness, stopped in great emotion before the gate of the old Augustinian convent in which Luther resided.

"This is not my doing," said Luther, as he received them; "but would to God that I could thus rescue all captive consciences and empty all the cloisters—the breach is made." Many persons offered to receive these nuns into their houses, and Katherine von Bora found welcome in the family of the burgomaster of Wittenberg.

If Luther at that time thought of preparing for any solemn event, it was to ascend the scaffold and not to approach the altar. Many months after this he still replied to those who spoke to him of marriage, "God may change my heart, if it be His pleasure; but now at least I have no thought of taking a wife: not that I do not feel any attractions in that estate; I am neither a stock nor a stone; but every day I expect the death and the punishment of a heretic."

Yet everything in the church was advancing. The habits of a monastic life, the invention of man, were giving way in every quarter to those of domestic life, appointed by God. On Sunday, October 9, 1524, Luther, having risen as usual, laid aside the frock of the Augustinian monk and put on the dress of a secular priest; he then made his appearance in the church, where this change caused a lively satisfaction. Renovated Christendom hailed with transport everything that announced that the old things were passed away.

Shortly after this, the last monk quitted the convent, but Luther remained; his footsteps alone reechoed through the long galleries; he sat silent and solitary in the refectory that had so lately resounded with the babbling of the monks. An eloquent silence, attesting the triumphs of the Word of God. The convent had ceased to exist. About the end of December 1524, Luther sent the keys of the monastery to the elector, informing him that he should see where it might please God to feed him. The elector gave the convent to the university and invited Luther to continue his residence in it. The abode of the monks was destined erelong to be the sanctuary of a Christian family.

Luther, whose heart was formed to taste the sweets of domestic life, honored and loved the marriage state; it is even probable that he had some liking for Katherine von Bora. For a long while his scruples, and the thought of the calumnies which such a step would occasion, had prevented his thinking of her and he had offered the poor Katherine first to Baumgartner of Nuremberg, and then to Dr. Glatz of Orlamund. But when he saw Baumgartner refuse to take her, and when she had declined to accept Glatz, he asked himself seriously whether he ought not to think of marrying her himself.

His aged father, who had been so grieved when he embraced a monastic life, was urging him to enter the conjugal state. But one idea above all was daily present before Luther's conscience, and with greater energy: marriage is an institution of God, celibacy an institution of man. He had a horror of everything that emanated from Rome. He would say to his friends, "I desire to retain nothing of my papistical life." Day and night he prayed and entreated the Lord to deliver him from his uncertainty. At last a single thought broke the last links that still held him captive. To all the motives of propriety and personal obedience which led him to apply to himself this declaration of God, "It is not good that the man should be alone" (Gen. 2:18), was added a motive of a higher and more powerful nature. He saw that if he was called to the marriage state as a man, he was also called to it as a reformer: this decided him.

"If this monk should marry," said his friend Schurff the lawyer, "he will make all the world and the Devil himself burst with laughter and will destroy the work that he has begun." This remark made a very different impression on Luther from what might have been supposed. To brave the world, the Devil, and his enemies, and by an action which they thought calculated to ruin the cause of the Reformation, prevent its success being in any measure ascribed to him, this was all he desired. Accordingly, boldly raising his head, he replied, "Well, then, I will do it; I will play the Devil and the world this trick; I will content my father, and marry Katherine." Luther, by his marriage, broke off still more completely from the institutions of the papacy; he confirmed the doctrine he had preached by his own example, and encouraged timid men to an entire renunciation of their errors. "I will bear witness to the gospel," said Luther, "not by my words only, but also by my works. I am determined, in the face of my enemies who already exult and raise the shout of victory, to marry a nun, that they may see and know that they have not conquered me. I do not take a wife that I may live long with her; but seeing the nations and the princes letting loose their fury against me, foreseeing that my end is near, and that after my death they will again trample my doctrine under foot, I am resolved for the edification of the weak to bear a striking testimony to what I teach here below."

On June 11, 1525, Luther went to the house of his friend and colleague Amsdorff. He desired Pomeranus, whom he styled emphatically "the pastor," to bless his union. The celebrated painter Lucas Cranach and Dr. John Apella witnessed the marriage. Melancthon was not present.

No sooner was Luther married than all Europe was disturbed. He was overwhelmed with accusation and calumnies from every quarter. "It is incest," exclaimed Henry VIII. "A monk has married

Katherine von Bora Luther, the wife of Martin Luther (German Information Center)

a vestal," said some. "Antichrist will be the offspring of such a union," said others; "for a prophecy announces that he will be born of a monk and a nun." To this Erasmus replied with a sarcastic smile, "If the prophecy is true, what thousands of antichrists do not already exist in the world."

But while Luther was thus assailed, many wise and moderate men, whom the Roman church still counted among her members, undertook his defense. "Luther," said Erasmus, "has taken a wife from the noble family of Bora, but she has no dowry." A more valuable testimony was now given in his favor. The master of Germany, Philipp Melancthon, whom this bold step had at first alarmed, said with the grave voice to which even his enemies listened with respect, "It is false and slanderous to maintain that there is anything unbecoming in Luther's marriage. I think that in marrying he must have done violence to himself. A married life is one of humility, but it is also a holy state, if there be any such in the world, and the Scriptures everywhere represent it as honorable in the eyes of God."

Luther was troubled at first when he saw such floods of anger and contempt poured out upon him; Melancthon became more earnest in friendship and kindness toward him; and it was not long before the reformer could see a mark of God's approbation in this opposition of man. "If I did not offend the world," said he, "I should have cause to fear that what I have done is displeasing to God."

Eight years had elapsed between the time when Luther had attacked the indulgences and his marriage with Katherine von Bora. It would be difficult to ascribe, as is still done, his zeal against the abuses of the church to an "impatient desire" for wedlock. He was then forty-two years old, and Katherine von Bora had already been two years in Wittenberg.

Luther was happy in this union. "The best gift of God," said he, "is a pious and amiable wife, who fears God, loves her family, and with whom a man may live in peace, and in whom he may safely confide." Some months after his marriage he informed one of his friends of Katherine's pregnancy, and a year after they came together she gave birth to a son. The sweets of domestic life soon dispersed the storms that the exasperation of his enemies had at first gathered over him. His Katie, as he styled her, manifested the tenderest affection toward him, consoled him in his dejection by repeating passages from the Bible, exonerated him from all household cares, sat near him during his leisure moments, worked his portrait in embroidery, reminded him of the friends to whom he had forgotten to write, and often amused him by the simplicity of her questions. A certain dignity appears to have marked her character, for Luther would sometimes call her *My Lord Katie*. One day he said playfully, that if he were to marry again, he would carve an obedient wife for himself out of a block of stone, for, added he, "it is impossible to find such a one in reality." His letters overflowed with tenderness for Katherine; he called her "his dear and gracious wife, his dear and amiable Katie." Luther's character became more cheerful in Katherine's society, and this happy frame of mind never deserted him afterwards, even in the midst of his greatest trials.

The almost universal corruption of the clergy had brought the priesthood into general contempt, from which the isolated virtues of a few faithful servants of God had been unable to extricate it. Domestic peace and conjugal fidelity, those surest foundations of happiness here below, were continually disturbed in town and country by the gross passions of the priests and monks. No one was secure from those attempts at destruction. They took advantage of the access allowed them into every family, and sometimes even of the confidence of the confessional, to instill a deadly poison into the souls of their penitents and to satisfy their guilty desires. The Reformation, by abolishing the celibacy of the ecclesiastics, restored the sanctity of the conjugal state. The marriage of the clergy put an end to an immense number of secret crimes. The reformers became the models of their flocks in the most intimate and important relations of life, and the people were not slow in rejoicing to see the ministers of religion once more husbands and fathers.

Chapter 51
Triumph in Death
(February 18, 1546)

Luther had throughout his life refused the aid of the secular arm, as his desire was that the truth should triumph only by the power of God. However, in 1546, in spite of his efforts, war was on the point of breaking out, and it was the will of God that His servant should be spared this painful spectacle.

The Counts of Mansfeldt, within whose territories he was born, having become involved in a quarrel with their subjects and with several lords of the neighborhood, had recourse to the mediation of the reformer. The old man—he was now sixty-three—was subject to frequent attacks of giddiness, but he never spared himself. He therefore set out, in answer to the call, and reached the territory of the Counts on January 28, accompanied by his friend the theologian Jonas, who had been with him at the Diet of Worms, and by his two sons, Martin and Paul, the former now fifteen, and the latter thirteen, years of age. He was respectfully received by the Counts of Mansfeldt, attended by a hundred and twelve horsemen. He entered that town of Eisleben in which he was born, and in which he was about to die. That same evening he was very unwell and was near fainting.

Nevertheless, he took courage and, applying himself zealously to the task, preached four times, attended twenty conferences, received the sacrament twice, and ordained two ministers. Every evening Jonas and Michael Coelius, pastor of Mansfeldt, came to wish him good night. "Doctor Jonas, and you Master Michael," he said to them, "entreat of the Lord to save His church."

Luther dined regularly with the Counts of Mansfeldt. It was evident from his conversation that the Holy Scriptures grew daily in importance in his eyes. "Cicero asserts in his letters," he said to the Counts two days before his death, "that no one can comprehend the science of government who has not occupied for twenty years an important place in the republic. And I for my part tell you that no one has understood the Holy Scriptures who has not governed the churches for a hundred years with the prophets, the apostles, and Jesus Christ." This occurred on February 16. After saying these words he wrote them down in Latin, laid them upon the table, and then retired to his room. He had no sooner reached it than he felt that his last hour was near. "When I have set my good lords at one," he said to those about him, "I will return home; I will lie down in my coffin and give my body to the worms."

The next day, February 17, his weakness increased. The Counts of Mansfeldt and the prior of Anhalt, filled with anxiety, came to see him. "Pray do not come," they said, "to the conference." He rose and walked up and down the room and exclaimed, "Here, at Eisleben, I was baptized. Will it be my lot also to die here?" A little while after he took the sacrament. Many of his friends attended him, and sorrowfully felt that soon they would see him no more. One of them said to him, "Shall we know each other in the eternal assembly of the blessed? We shall be all so changed!"

"Adam," replied Luther, "had never seen Eve, and yet when he awoke he did not say 'Who art thou?' but 'Thou art flesh of my flesh.' By what means did he know that she was taken from his flesh and not from a stone? He knew this because he was filled with the Holy Spirit. So likewise in the heavenly Paradise we shall be filled with the Holy Spirit, and we shall recognize father, mother, and friends better than Adam recognized Eve."

Having thus spoken, Luther retired into his chamber and, according to his daily custom, even in the winter time, opened his window, looked up to heaven and began to pray. "Heavenly Father," he said, "since in Thy great mercy Thou hast revealed to me the downfall of the pope, since the day of Thy glory is not far off, and since the light of Thy gospel, which is now rising over the earth is to be diffused through the whole world, keep to the end through Thy goodness the church of my dear native country; save it from falling, preserve it in the true profession of Thy Word, and let all men know that it is indeed for Thy work that Thou hast sent me." He then left the window, returned to his friends, and about ten o'clock at night retired to bed. Just as he reached the threshold of his bedroom he stood still and said, "Into thine hand I commit my spirit; thou hast redeemed me, O God of truth!"

February 18, the day of his departure, was now at hand. About one o'clock in the morning, sensible that the chill of death was creeping over him, Luther called Jonas and his faithful servant Ambrose. "Make a fire," he said to Ambrose. Then he cried out, "O Lord my God, I am in great pain! What a weight upon my chest! I shall never leave Eisleben."

Jonas said to him "Our heavenly Father will come to help you for the love of Christ which you have faithfully preached to men."

Luther then got up, took some turns up and down his room and looking up to heaven exclaimed again, "Into thine hand I commit my spirit; thou hast redeemed me, O God of truth!"

Jonas in alarm sent for the doctors, Wild and Ludwig, the Count and Countess of Mansfeldt, Drachstadt, the town clerk, and Luther's children. In great alarm they all hastened to the spot. "I am dying," said the sick man.

"No," said Jonas, "you are now in a perspiration and will soon be better."

"It is the sweat of death," said Luther, "I am nearly at my last breath." He was thoughtful for a moment and then said with faltering voice, "O my heavenly Father, the God and Father of our Lord Jesus Christ, the God of all consolation, I thank Thee that Thou hast revealed to me Thy well-beloved Son, Jesus Christ, in whom I have believed, whom I have preached, whom I have confessed, whom the pope and all the ungodly insult, blaspheme, and persecute, but whom I love and adore as my Savior. O Jesus Christ, my Savior, I commit my soul to Thee! O my heavenly Father, I must quit this body, but I believe with perfect assurance that I shall dwell eternally with Thee, and that none shall pluck me out of Thy hands."

He now remained silent for a little while; his prayer seemed to have exhausted him. But presently his countenance again grew bright, a holy joy shone in his features, and he said with fulness of faith, "God so loved the world that he gave his only begotten Son, that whosoever believeth in him should not perish, but have everlasting life." A moment afterwards he uttered, as if sure of victory, this word of David—"He that is our God is the God of salvation; and unto God the Lord belong the issues from death" (Ps. 68:20). Dr. Wild went to him and tried to induce him to take medicine, but Luther refused. "I am departing," he said, "I am about to yield up my spirit." Then returning to the saying which was for him a sort of watchword for his departure, he said three times successively without interruption, "Father! into thine hand I commit my spirit. Thou hast redeemed me, O God of truth! Thou hast redeemed me, O God of truth!"

He then closed his eyes. They touched him, moved him, called to him, but he made no answer. In vain they applied the cloths which the town clerk and his wife heated; in vain the Countess of Mansfeldt and the physicians endeavored to revive him with tonics. He remained motionless. The two physicians noted from minute to minute the approach of death. The two boys, Martin and Paul, kneeling and in tears, cried to God to spare to them their father. Ambrose lamented the master, and Coelius the friend, whom they had so much loved. The Count of Mansfeldt thought of the troubles which Luther's death might bring on the Empire. The distressed Countess sobbed and covered her eyes with her hands that she might not behold the mournful scene.

Jonas, a little apart from the rest, felt heartbroken at the thought of the terrible blow impending over the Reformation. He wished to receive from the dying Luther a last testimony. He therefore rose, went up to his friend, and, bending over him, said, "Reverend father, in your dying hour do you rest on Jesus Christ, and stedfastly rely upon the doctrine which you have preached?"

"Yes," said Luther, so that all who were present could hear him.

This was his last word.

The pallor of death overspread his countenance; his forehead, his hands, and his feet turned cold. They addressed him by his baptismal name, "Doctor Martin," but in vain; he made no response. He drew a deep breath and fell asleep in the Lord. It was between two and three o'clock in the morning. "Truly," said Jonas, to whom we are indebted for these details, "Thou lettest, Lord, Thy servant depart in peace, and Thou accomplishest for him the promise which Thou madest us, and which he himself wrote the other day in a Bible presented to one of his friends: 'Verily, verily, I say unto you, if a man keep my saying, he shall never see death.'"

Thus passed Luther into the presence of his Master, in full reliance on redemption, in calm faith in the triumph of truth. Luther was no longer here below, but Jesus Christ is with His people evermore to the end of the world, and the work which Luther had begun lives, is still advancing, and will extend to all the ends of the earth.

Editor's Afterword

Editing and abridging another man's work is a special challenge, especially when he is a well-known author in his own right. I recall picking up an edition of Winston Churchill's *Marlborough: His Life and Times* and noting with trepidation how editor Henry Steel Commager said in his introduction that he had cut Churchill's work by *half.* I wondered whether I would be reading some pale imitation of Churchill's work marred by numerous jerks and omissions resulting from the editor's knife. With a historian of Commager's stature, I probably should not have worried. The narrative flowed so smoothly and told the story of Marlborough's life so fully that I was not aware of Commager's work. I can only hope that I have done half so well.

The idea of condensing Merle d'Aubigné's work into a biography of Luther is not a new one. Previously there have been published in English at least four such Luther biographies from Merle's work, not to mention other condensations of Merle's work that focused on more than just Luther. This edition, however, is a completely new abridgment.

Cutting Merle d'Aubigné's multivolume history of the Reformation down to a single volume on Martin Luther was in some ways simpler than Commager's task with Churchill. The first and easiest step was to omit everything in Merle's work that did not deal with Martin Luther; that step alone eliminated over eighty percent. Also in the first cut went most of Merle's footnotes (which were almost always citations of the source of his quotations). A handful of more substantive footnotes were moved into the body of the text.

Next was the more difficult task of eliminating whole sections of the Luther narrative. Often I could accomplish this by omitting anecdotes that—however interesting they might be—did not carry forward the main narrative of Luther's struggle. I wanted to focus on the same theme that Merle focused on—how God led Martin

Luther to a discovery of biblical truth and how Luther courageously furthered that truth against great opposition. Therefore, descriptions of some persons or events that did not contribute directly to that theme were cut.

Third, I eliminated some repetitions. Merle would sometimes leave the narrative of Luther to discuss some other aspect of the Reformation and then, when he returned to Luther, offer a summary. In most cases, the summary's absence would not be missed and so could be deleted. Also, Merle in his faithful discussion of Luther's ideas sometimes repeated concepts or gave in several places selections from different writings of Luther that communicated the same ideas. I therefore eliminated some of the repetition without omitting any major idea of Luther's that Merle developed.

Finally, I did a closer edit on the very paragraphs and sentences of the work. Sometimes Merle's comments have become dated. For example, he spoke of the Hapsburgs as ruling Austria, which they did in his day. But after his death, the Hapsburgs fell from power at the end of World War I. I therefore updated such comments. Likewise, Merle sometimes felt it necessary to quote a major figure such as Luther and then offer his own comments on the quotation. In most cases, I found that I could allow those being quoted to speak for themselves without Merle's explanation.

Although I abridged Merle's work, I did not rewrite it. Over ninety-nine percent of the text is the words of Merle, or more specifically, those of the translation by Henry White (1812-80). Merle said of White's work, "I have revised this translation line by line, and word by word. It is the only one which I have corrected." The only exception is the last chapter, on Luther's death. It was edited and published after Merle's death and was translated by William L. R. Cates.

Most changes consist of conforming the spelling, capitalization, and punctuation to modern standards. (The original version, for example, used the spelling *Wittemberg* instead of the more common modern spelling *Wittenberg*.) Only with the greatest hesitation did I change any words of the text. Usually, such alterations involved changing a pronoun such as "he" to a person's name (e.g., "Luther") so that the reader could clearly understand to whom Merle was referring; some of the changes of this sort were necessitated by the abridging of the text and not from lack of clarity in Merle's original.

In all, word changes average probably fewer than a dozen per chapter. In addition, some phrases that Merle left in Latin or Greek have been translated. The author on occasion wrote in present tense in order to heighten the immediacy of the moment. Such a literary device is rare in historical writing today, and these instances have been changed to past tense; the verbs are the same, but the tense is different.

In short, I believe that I have preserved Merle's meaning and style, and I hope that I have helped to introduce another generation of Christians to his work.

Index of Persons

Adelmann, Bernard, 91, 151
Adolphus, bishop of Merseburg, 195, 197
Albert, archbishop of Mentz, 59, 65-67, 85-86, 95, 146, 183, 231, 234-35, 261, 266, 279, 317-18, 349, 378, 399
Aleander, Jerome, 261, 266, 275-78, 280-81, 286-89, 294-97, 299, 315, 318, 322, 324, 330-35, 341-42
Alexander VI, 36-37, 124, 309, 383
Ambrose, 214, 223, 239, 273
Amsdorff, Nicholas, 196, 306, 309, 311, 313, 315, 343-44, 374, 377, 403, 411
Anhalt, George of, 201, 220
Apella, John, 411
Aquinas, Thomas, 9, 44, 149, 204, 382-83, 386
Augustine, 13, 16-17, 22, 26, 29, 45, 50, 61, 108, 135, 163, 192, 203-4, 213-14, 222-23, 239, 273, 384, 387-88

Berlepsch, John of, 345
Berlichingen, Goetz von, 399, 401
Brentz, John (Brentius), 119-20, 406
Brunswick, Henry, 404
Bucer, Martin, 118-20, 315, 320
Bugenhagen, John, 305-6, 311, 386
Busch, Hermann, 348

Cajetan, 133, 141, 149, 153, 155-59, 161-65, 167, 169-71, 173-74, 178-79, 181, 186-87, 195, 248, 335
Calvi, 189
Calvin, John, 254, 359
Capito, 65, 318-19, 333, 378
Caraccioli, Marino, 261, 275-78
Carlstadt, Andreas, 42, 112, 168, 191-92, 194-98, 202-8, 218-19, 225, 263, 272, 354, 366-67
Cellarius, 365, 379-80
Charles V, 89, 129, 132-33, 181, 225, 227-31, 234-35, 237, 263-64, 266, 270, 275-77, 280-81, 284-88, 291-95, 297, 301, 303-5, 307, 313-15, 318-19, 321, 323-25, 328-32, 334, 339, 341-43, 345, 348-49, 351, 370, 392
Clarke, John, 384
Clement VI, 157, 163-64
Cochloeus, John, 314, 318, 333-35, 386
Coelius, Michael, 415, 418
Cotta, Conrad and Ursula, 5-6
Cranach, Lucas, 339, 368, 411
Cronberg, Harmurth, 232
Cuspianus, 323

Dressel, Michael, 54

Eck, John, 110-14, 191-99, 203-8, 211-21, 223-25, 237, 245-47, 249, 255-56, 261-66, 270, 276-77, 281
Eck, John ab, 322, 324, 337
Edemberger, Lucas, 19-20
Egranus, 112
Emser, Jerome, 60, 270

Erasmus, 36, 48, 50-51, 87, 89, 117-18, 140-41, 189, 195, 234-35, 266, 279-81, 311, 367, 372, 392, 413

Feilitsch, Philip of, 318, 345
Feldkirchen, Bernard, 353-54
Ferdinand, 228, 234, 321
Fisher, John, 382, 388
Francis I, 227, 229-30, 291, 330
Frederick, Elector of Saxony, 22, 28-29, 32, 41, 45, 53, 57-58, 79, 81-82, 89-90, 92, 95-96, 99, 103, 121, 128-35, 140-41, 143, 146-47, 151-53, 156, 161, 168, 171-82, 184, 186-88, 193-95, 223, 225, 230-32, 235, 237, 243, 256, 263, 266, 275-80, 286-89, 291-95, 302-6, 310, 314, 318, 327, 329-32, 341-42, 345, 353, 362, 365-66, 368-69, 374, 378, 386, 389-90, 392, 395-99, 404, 406, 410
Frobenius, John, 140, 187, 189
Fugger, 66, 72, 185, 246-47
Fulda, 399

Geholfen, Maternus von, 405
George of Saxony, 18, 58-61, 77, 194-95, 197, 201, 216, 219-20, 262, 265, 298-99, 303, 331, 333, 362, 369, 404-6
Glapio, John, 291-92, 324
Glatz, 410
Gregory of Nazianzum, 216
Gregory VII, 353
Greiffenklau, Richard of, 187, 229-30, 322-24, 327, 332-34, 336-37

Helfenstein, Louis of, 397, 400-401

Henry VIII, 229, 381-90, 411
Hesse, Eobanus, 310
Hesse, Philip of, 284, 303, 404-5
Hieronymus, bishop of Brandenburg, 27
Hochstraten, James, 109, 111
Holzhausen, Catherine of, 314
Hund, Burkhardt of, 345
Hungarus, John, 137
Huss, John, 58-59, 84, 100, 111, 170, 214-16, 222, 224, 274, 314, 318, 331, 333
Hutten, Ulrich von, 232, 234-35, 266, 279, 307, 319-20, 324, 348, 373

Innocent VIII, 65

Jerome, 50, 108, 212-13, 223, 273
Jerome, bishop of Ascoli, 133-34
Joachim, Elector of Brandenburg, 65, 79, 333, 362
Jodocus, 103
John of Saxony, 232, 235, 263, 294, 304, 310, 332, 341, 369, 404
Jonas, Justus, 311, 313, 315, 317, 343, 374, 415, 417-18
Julian II, 124
Julius II, 34, 124

Kessler, John, 371-73
Knipstrow, John, 99
Koppe, Leonard, 409

Lange, John, 45, 53, 92, 103, 116, 151, 196, 309-11, 381
Langer, J., 309
Leiffer, George, 52
Lendenau, Albert of, 317
Leo X, 64-66, 69, 90, 105, 108, 123-25, 127, 129-30, 132-33,

135, 141, 148, 156, 165, 171-72, 179, 181, 186, 245, 247, 250, 256-58, 260, 269, 275, 281, 291, 319, 330, 332, 343, 370, 384

Levita, Elias, 37

Link, Wenceslas, 111, 148, 155, 167, 169-70, 178, 255

Lowenstein, Albert of, 399

Luther, John, 1-5, 15-16, 26-27, 356

Luther, Katherine (von Bora), 409-14

Luther, Margaret (Lindeman), 1, 4

Luther, Martin
Birth, 1
School at Magdeburg, 3
School at Eisenach, 5-7
In the university, 9-13
Finds a copy of the Bible for the first time, 10
Enters the cloister, 12-16
Life in the cloister, 16-20
Meets Staupitz, 22
Conversion, 26-27
Travels to Wittenberg, 29
Journeys to Rome, 33-39
Becomes Doctor of the Holy Scriptures, 41-43
Letters of witness and consolation, 49-55
Preaches before Duke George, 59
Hears of Tetzel, 79
Posts Ninety-five Theses, 81-87
Responds to attacks on the Theses, 92-96
Responds to Prierio's attack, 108
Writes "Asterisks," 112-13
Travels to Heidelberg, 115-16
"Paradoxes," 116-18
Resolutions, 123-24
Writes to Leo X, 125-26
Receives the summons to Rome, 131
Meets Melancthon, 141
Journeys to Augsburg, 145-54
Meets with Serra Longa, 150-51
Talks with Cardinal Cajetan, 155-65
Leaves Augsburg, 171-74
Appeals to a general council, 179
Meets Miltitz, 182
Writings published throughout Europe, 187-89
Challenged by Eck, 192-93
The Leipzig disputation, 201-18
Disputes with Eck, 211-18
Abandons scholasticism, 221-22
Writes to Charles V, 231
Appeal to the German Nobility, 237-43
Publication of the papal bull, 245-50
The Babylonian Captivity of the Church, 251-55
Letter to the pope, 256-60
Against the Bull of Antichrist, 264-65
Responds to the bull, 269-70
Burns the bull, 270
States agreement with John Huss, 275
Diet of Worms convenes, 283-90
Attacked before Charles V by Aleander, 295-98
Summoned to Worms, 303-4
Journeys to Worms, 309-17
Appears before the diet, 319-28
Solicited to compromise, 332-38
Leaves Worms, 338
Edict against him published, 341-43
Taken captive, 344
Time at Wartburg, 347-70

Wrestles with the issues of marriage and monasticism, 354-56
Translates the Bible into German, 357-62
Responds to Zwickau prophets, 366, 368-70
Leaves Wartburg, 371
Arrives in Wittenberg, 374
Preaches against the Zwickau heresy, 375-79
Confers with Stubner and Cellarius, 379-80
Conflict with Henry VIII, 381-90
Peasants' War, 391-408
Gives up monasticism, 410
Marries Katherine von Bora, 411
Final days, 415-16
Death, 417-18
Luther, Martin (son), 413, 415, 418
Luther, Paul, 415, 418

Machiavelli, 37
Mansfeldt, Albert of, 146-47
Mansfeldt, Counts of, 415-18
Margaret, Governor of the Netherlands, 266
Mathesius, 2, 11, 89
Maximilian, 89, 129-31, 133, 170, 181-82, 227-28, 230, 275, 397
Melancthon, Philipp, 42, 47-48, 128, 137-43, 145, 154, 195-96, 206, 221, 223, 225, 236, 256, 272, 279, 288, 302, 305-6, 309-11, 348-51, 354, 365, 368-69, 372, 374-75, 377-79, 386, 388, 395-96, 404, 411, 413
Mentz, archbishop of, see Albert, archbishop of Mentz
Miltitz, Charles of, 132, 180-87, 192, 195, 231, 255-56, 262-63

Minkwitz, John, 337
Modo, bishop of Palermo, 318
Mohr, George, 367
More, Thomas, 343, 382, 388-89
Mosellanus, 201, 203
Muller, John, 398
Myconius, Frederick, 31, 74-75, 90-91, 310, 406

Nassau, 267
Nesse, William, 314
Niger, George, 117-18
Numzer, Thomas, 363

Pallavicini, 294, 317, 331, 336
Pappenheim, Ulrich of, 318-19
Paul, 22, 26, 30, 34, 38, 55, 61, 69, 108, 117, 141, 178, 186, 205, 207, 221-22, 236, 239, 241, 249, 313, 338, 356, 377, 379, 387
Paul III, 185
Peutinger, 151, 335-36
Pfeffinger, 57, 90, 115, 176, 180
Pfeiffer, 406
Pius II, 179
Podiebrad, George, 58, 298
Poliander, 196, 220
Pomerania, Barnim of, 100, 196, 201, 207, 219, 305-6
Pomeranus, 411
Pontanus (Gregory Bruck), 292-94
Prierio, Sylvester, 90, 105-9, 111, 113, 131, 193, 247
Pucci, 65

Ravenstein, 267
Regius, Urban, 110-11
Reuchlin, John, 138, 140-41
Rotenhen, Sebastian von, 400
Rovera, Cardinal Raphael, 126, 130

Sarpi, Paul, 65, 390
Schaumburg, Sylvester of, 232, 234
Scheurl, Christopher, 96, 113-14
Schurff, Jerome, 306, 309, 313, 315, 322, 343, 372, 374, 378, 411
Seidler, 353
Serra Longa, 149-55, 167, 172
Sickingen, Franz von, 232-33, 235, 315, 331
Sidonia, 58
Sigismund, 170, 318
Simmler, George, 138
Snepf, Ehrhard, 119-20
Spalatin, George, 45, 50, 57, 82, 95-96, 102, 115, 120, 132, 141, 145, 147, 168-69, 174, 176-77, 180, 182, 185-86, 194, 219, 225-26, 256, 267, 278-80, 302-3, 314-15, 329-30, 337, 340, 345, 349, 354, 356, 366, 386
Spenlein, George, 49-50, 52
Staupitz, John, 21-28, 31, 41-42, 45, 53, 57, 59, 79, 82, 116, 132, 145-46, 159-60, 162, 167-68, 170-71, 173, 184, 222, 224, 243, 255, 272
Storch, Nicholas, 363-65, 367, 379

Stubner, Mark, 363-65, 367, 379
Sturm, Gaspard, 304, 332, 338, 340
Suaven, Peter, 306, 309, 343
Surrey, 388

Tetzel, John, 64, 67-68, 71-77, 79-81, 86, 90, 92, 94-95, 97-100, 102-5, 111, 131, 182-83, 185-86, 191-92, 262, 283
Teutleben, Valentine, 231
Thomas, Mark, 363-65
Thun, Frederick of, 318, 327, 345
Tomitzsch, Wolff, 409
Trebonius, John, 7
Treves, see Greiffenklau, Richard of
Truchsess, George von, 400

Valdez, Alphonso, 343
Vettori, 332

Watzdorf, Vollrat of, 335
Wehe, Jerome, 333-36
Wild, 417
Wimpina, Conrad, 97, 99-100, 104
Wolsey, Cardinal Thomas, 381-82, 388
Wycliffe, John, 84, 216, 390